demopolis

The Right to Public Space

Edited by Barbara Hoidn

PARK BOOKS

TRANSFORMATIONS

PARADIGMS

INTERNATIONAL WORKSHOP

JUNGE AKADEMIE

Foreword

Inquiries into the space where we live, the space from which we operate, and the space that we have imbued with personal memories, desires, and wishes form the starting point to the exhibition *DEMO:POLIS*. People have always built and will continue building cities as living spaces, and those who live in them have the right to demand places where they can play, dream, and relax.

With this exhibition, the question that immediately comes to mind is, do we, as city dwellers, still have an influence on the place in which we live? Is it the way that we want it to be, and do we deem it viable and livable for the future? How could we change something if we wanted to do so? Who is responsible for public space, and who is allowed to deny it to us?

Following the recent terrorist attacks in Paris the public has become increasingly unsettled and keeps a distance. But it would be wrong to give up public space and our trust in it because of fear. On the contrary, it is necessary to defend public space as an achievement of democratic society through a culture of attentiveness, tolerance, and enlightenment.

What I find fascinating about the concept of this exhibition is that it shows not only negative, but also positive developments; and by that, I am not solely speaking of artists' interventions in catastrophic examples of public spaces, which can at least achieve an awareness for the situation in the broader public.

We are shown how a successful intervention in public space can lead to new impulses in city planning and a new quality of life for the region, its inhabitants, and visitors, as seen, for example, in Ljubljana, Athens, Guimarães, and Bordeaux, but also in areas defined by stark social and economic disparity, such as London and New York.

However, we are also confronted with the catastrophic results of gentrification and commercialization of public space. Shopping centers that act as public spaces, that barrage people with advertisements and commercialize needs. Airports, which hold passengers captive in unbearably perfumed shopping malls, but hardly fulfill their purpose—namely, offering travelers in transit a place to relax.

Urban public space has long become the playing field of private interests. It must be protected. And it won't be sufficient to offer artists public spaces to present their art. Urban extractivism prompts cities to change (for the worse), and thereby, the lives of inhabitants also change (for the worse). Old structures are destroyed to build speculative high-rise towers or establish cordoned-off, guarded residential areas.

David Harvey picks up on this topic in his 2012 book *Rebel Cities: From the Right to the City to the Urban Revolution*. He establishes that the obliteration of public space can only be explained from an economic perspective. He discloses that the planning of mega cities in China, Qatar, and the United Arab Emirates sets in motion the major mechanism that constitutes capitalism: inversion.

DEMO:POLIS, however, also looks at the way specific places might develop over the coming years. In order to encourage active participation of visitors, the results of an international workshop are presented, in the course of which four of Berlin's architectural and art schools discussed places as diverse as Anklam, Gelsenkirchen, and Berlin-Mitte.

My thanks go to the curator Wilfried Wang, a member of the Akademie der Künste [Berlin Academy of Arts], and Barbara Hoidn, his office partner, for their tireless dedication and hard work in preparing and designing both exhibition and catalog.

DEMO:POLIS—an ambitious project, which, on the basis of concrete examples, hopes to inspire and awaken an urge to take action. Along these lines, I wish all visitors and readers a likewise unsettling and enriching experience.

DEMO:POLIS— The Right to Public Space

We want to dare more democracy. We will reveal how we work and want to satisfy the critical need for information. We will give every citizen the opportunity to participate in reforming the state and society, and not only through hearings in the Bundestag, but also through our constant contact with representative groups within the population and by offering transparency about government policies. [...] we will have order in this country only to the extent that we encourage the sharing of responsibility. Such a democratic order needs extraordinary patience in listening, and it needs to exert extraordinary effort on behalf of mutual understanding.

—Federal Chancellor Willy Brandt in his Government Policy Statement, 1969

Democracy and public space are two inextricably linked concepts. A democratic society without public space is inconceivable, unviable, and implausible. In a democracy, the right to public space is equivalent to the policy makers' and politicians' obligation of transparency, the state's guarantee of unobstructed access to information for all, the individual's right to expression of opinion and participation, to active and politically mature forms of cooperation, and also the striving for a balance of individual and collective interests. However, the originally positive connotation of the term "public" as the counterpart of "private" or "not publicly accessible" has steadily eroded. When the protected status of the private realm in a democratic state is disputed, "public" can even transmute into a threatening scenario.

Ever since the existence of state-organized and -approved data theft has been uncovered, and against the backdrop of populist campaigns by financially powerful politicians, who with the support of their own media channels buy publicity or suspend democratic rights, there has emerged a justified concern that citizens have been degraded to the state of "vitreous" puppet voters under constant suspicion.

The World Wide Web's social networks and virtual global communities bring together people with apparently similar needs and desires to form selectively public groups with distinct rules, which are then, quite incidentally, relabeled as mere target groups and cashed in on. No one is safe from unauthorized intrusion in the name of the people. Data and private content is copied, gathered, and exploited.

Individuals' rights to public space and its protection as a neutral zone, as personal free space in the best sense of the word, whether on the internet or in the real world, is threatened and, clearly, must be permanently renegotiated. Democracy becomes a matter of trust between citizens and the representatives of the state.

For the exhibition and catalog *DEMO:POLIS—The Right to Public Space*, Wilfried Wang and I turn to this key sociopolitical, cultural, and architectural issue, which since the 1960s at the latest, since the pointed contributions by Alexander Mitscherlich, Hannah Arendt, and Guy Debord, but also by planners such as Kevin Lynch and Jane Jacobs, has been a main focus of postwar urban planning and planning sociology.

How do contemporary planners, architects, politicians, and artists currently assess the significance of public space for democratic development? Does the aspect of public space even play a substantial role in urban planning at all? How well-suited are the existing spaces for the social tasks and challenges that lie ahead? What kind of atmosphere does an urban society, a nation mediate through its public spaces? Who formulates demands and registers claims, who finances renovation when what is available no longer functions or must be modernized? How dominant are partial interests and who assures that balance is achieved? The power source for the perpetuation of democratic communities lies in a permanent redefinition and further development of the concept of public space, in changing protagonists testing the limits and appropriating space. From this emerges an ability to withstand authoritarian and dictatorial encroachments.

Taking inventory as well as presenting a snapshot of our time, the exhibition makes visible old patterns and new trends, and in doing so, also offers the people involved the opportunity to participate publicly, to enter the discourse.

The right to demonstrate— a visible expression of democracy

The German reunification succeeded because of relentless protests in the public space. Paradoxically, the ensuing rivalry of ideas and systems will most likely ultimately culminate in the total destruction of the central public symbolic sites in the former capital of the GDR between Alexanderplatz and the Foreign Ministry building.

Throughout the world, people carry out political upheavals, heated protests, silent demonstrations, courageous announcements of solidarity, and spontaneous rebellions at central symbolic sites. Demonstration is

Latz + Partner, redevelopment of Place Flagey, Brussels

the most fundamental form of expression of political will. In our era of modern media, global attention can be captured in real time. Only in this way can messages or notes of protest be spread throughout the world, plausibly and genuinely, even in remote places and often at substantial risk. People become involved and take on the hardships of political activism. Political fatigue is not discernible. Public space is made, directly and fundamentally.

Art interventions as a reminder of personal civil rights and liberties

Refined forms of politicization of public space arose in reaction to the historical event of German reunification. Symbols and commentary were implanted in public space. A multitude of individual, part planned, part spontaneous, clever, poetic, contemplative art projects and interventions in the urban landscape shaped Berlin in the years after the fall of the wall and became a powerful spoken and visual subtext of an increasingly illegible urban layout of the formerly divided city.

From retracing the now demolished Berlin Wall to the photographic posters at the former border crossing Check Point Charlie or Wilhelmstraße, the book-burning memorial at Bebelplatz, the "stumbling stones," the details along the waterfront promenade on those stretches of the River Spree that once constituted the border, and the discussions surrounding the competition for the Holocaust Memorial—recognizable in all this is the will to give back meaning to the sites through concrete information in the urban space and to allow the past to remain visible in the future.

The concept of art interventions in public space was definitively elevated to a new level by such sensational works as the memorial signs in the Bayerisches Viertel in Berlin Schöneberg or the work *Bus Stop* for the Holocaust Memorial competition. The subtle yet poetic achievement of Berlin artists Stih & Schnock—who are, themselves, permanently and contentiously rooted in the conceptual and visual world of Berlin—was to firmly anchor these artistic works in the places of historical events, pairing them with factual information, and thus avoiding the exalted atmosphere of many a memorial site. The invisible is made visible again. A place becomes a home, also in an uncomfortable sense. Art mingles with the people, as it were, in their everyday life.

Social artworks overcome clichés

Art interventions such as these, in turn, inspire other projects, which from the start are conceived as interactive social artworks or interventions. They often demand active participation or point out dysfunctional, paradoxical, or simply contrary conditions, as, for example, the different appropriations of space by urban gardening activists or the impromptu *diners en blanc*, for which hundreds of people gather at short notice at an agreed-upon site to dine together in the middle of the street.

But there are also the quiet projects that skirt the topics of hedonistic life in the metropolises around the world. The seemingly improvised projects by students at the School of Architecture in Talca, Chile, can be named as examples. They managed to restore to the city of Talca sites of public life, projects that are characterized by dignity and respect, first after the end of the Pinochet dictatorship and once again after the widespread destruction caused by an apocalyptic earthquake in February 2010.

Latz + Partner, Landschaftspark Duisburg-Nord, Duisburg

Public space equals trust in democracy

Current projects in Latin America, in particular, reveal the need to protect public space and the vulnerability of the collective city when safety is not guaranteed and drug cartels, violent gangs, and social grievances cause the public dimension to dwindle. When people's trust in the security of public spaces dissolves or they gradually stay away, it marks the beginning of the end of communal life and a disproportionately greater loss than merely a deserted place where they roll up the sidewalks in the evening. What better place in Germany to study the urgency of this phenomenon than in the rural regions with sparse population density where young people are forced to meet in informal places like the remaining benches of bus stops or at service stations for lack of other, more animated spaces.

A surge in privately initiated projects and programming of public spaces at macro and micro levels can be observed ever since the 1990s, at the latest, when city centers experienced a greater influx once again and major cities, in particular, have had to constantly reinvent themselves for tourism and in the competition between cities. These projects and programs also reflect the interests and needs of a population, which as a whole is becoming more international and thinking more internationally. Self-organized markets, coffee shops, food trucks, beach bars, and pocket parks are hybrid examples of this recapturing of the city as a place of residence by a generation with global experiences and playful ideas. These uses make no claim to permanence and thus don a changeable and transient shape from the outset. They represent an informal lifestyle and are, first and foremost, extroverted, inquisitive, and communicative.

Public space with no trade-off?

As a positive outcome of the most recent urban tourism and the capitalization of cities as property investments, official channels in many places have launched ambitious programs for the improvement of public space, the creation of squares, parks, and landscapes, or for an inventive repurposing of decommissioned industrial facilities. The most renowned example is certainly the High Line in Manhattan's former Meatpacking District, but also the recreational facilities initiated by the IBA (International Building Exhibition) Emscher Park on decommissioned industrial properties in the Ruhr area.

The price for these significant investments is often enough to equip the gentrified public parlors and parks with surveillance cameras and free Wi-Fi for greater security, but also to better locate individuals and an easy connection to appropriate apps, which make using the city and its commercial offers child's play. Especially in those global metropolises that have come under extreme pressure due to financial speculation, such as London, Paris, and New York, startling developments along these lines are taking place, ironically commented on by artists such as Banksy.

Nonetheless, these multi-million-dollar projects, such as Brooklyn Bridge Park in New York City, are the positive flipside of the new commercialization of the city with regularly held events and festivals in the urban space, which many residents see as an imposition. Games and entertainment for a traveling audience have become a fundamental income source for communities and have begun to oust everyday public life to other neighborhoods or zones. In Berlin, for example, central sites are basically rented out all year round. Berlin has a multitude of open space, parks, and urban axes, which are adored by the zeitgeist, and has therefore set new standards in the category of mass events, from the Love Parade to the cordial "summer fairy tale" with the public screenings of matches during the Soccer World Cup in 2006, flat marathon courses through a seemingly never-ending city center, soccer stadiums that can be adapted to many purposes, and fashion shows on former airport grounds, along with a steadfast tolerance of the beer bottles carried by partygoers in the Berlin subways and commuter rails running 24/7.

The finite resource of memorable urban spaces and thereby urban stages must be regularly expanded, as the creative scene steadily produces and needs new imagery. Residents thus also turn to other sites. Riverbanks and parks as formerly ancillary urban recreational areas are discovered and utilized for relaxation and enjoyment. New rituals arise and become solidified in the repeated use of such areas. Funding, as well as the permission for use, is hard-earned. Tempelhofer Feld is a prime example of this. That which is not used, or no longer used, will soon lie fallow again.

Democracy and form—democracy in transition

The Greek cities created at the drawing board of urban planner Hippodamus first gave the Attic democracy its form. The city layout consisted of separate egalitarian lots, which were structured by a network of streets on a rectangular grid, with special, communally maintained gathering places, such as the natural harbor and the marketplace, excluded from it. The public facilities, such as temple, stoa, stadium, and theater, were conceived as geometrically pure solitary structures and implanted in the city layout. The more public spaces a city had to show for itself, the higher it ranked in the polis network. The form of public buildings and the actions carried out by the people therein created an inextricable bond, mutually influencing one another. Public space only gained its complex meaning and form through formal rituals and communal use. The space was completed only through its usage. Exceptional sites were thus created that are still visited and marveled at today.

Democracy as client, what does that mean for public space nowadays? Who is responsible, who feels responsible, and how do comprehensive planning principles emerge? Who formulates them?

In the early years of the German Federal Republic, the commitment to democracy was translated almost naïvely into a simplistic architectural expression. According to the German architectural avant-garde's credo, structures had to be transparent, or else they weren't democratic. The structures of the Bonn Republic embody this attitude. The corresponding public space, however, was diffuse, defined rather by ambitious speech bubbles than actually to be experienced. Forums, agoras, amphitheaters, stadiums, and, most of all, pedestrian zones and urban landscapes were created.

But also emerging were, and still are, space-devouring suburban agglomerations of single-family homes, at best grouped into urban landscapes without any claim to collective public spaces. The public space, the "residential environment" on the periphery of cities is a clunky concept void of content. Strip malls attached themselves to these areas and, following the American model, became a replacement for public space in the suburbs. Those who can pay the entry fee are welcome.

The gradual appropriation of sidewalks in the city by food stands and ice cream parlors might have been timid and seasonal, but in any case, it was not officially planned or anticipated. The same applies to the gradual change of appearance and revitalization of depopulated city centers through the influx of Turkish guest workers and other European and non-European population groups. German tradition, however—shaped by seasonal events such as the Oktoberfest, wine festivals, Christmas markets, carnival, and church festivals—continues to define public life. The transition to a more international understanding became visible especially in the cities. Neighborhoods in close proximity to the railway stations led the way.

Youth culture with major open-air music events and festivals or political happenings changed and eased the relationship between state authority and subject. In the 1960s, authorities confronted the informal appropriation of spaces with increasing equanimity. The peace movement, squatters, and terrorist threats by the RAF, however, once again put a strain on the situation in the 1970s. Mistrust between citizens and state increased. But civil disobedience as a means to demand more democracy had already become an integral part of the debate. University campuses as breeding grounds of democratic will and rebellion gained greatly in importance. Social changes occurring at the universities were representative for society at large. Again, all of these

Barceloneta beach, Barcelona

changes were unplanned and thus not politically foreseen or approved. Evil to those who think that new university complexes are still built in isolated areas remote from the city center.

Arising as new public spaces were mainly streets, in line with a car-friendly restructuring of the city for an increasingly motorized population. At the same time, Italy's distinctive, intact, and lively city centers became sites of desire for Germans raised in purpose-oriented cities.

Tightly packed hotels and vacation-home complexes for mass tourism sprang up along the Italian and Spanish coastlines and on the Mediterranean islands, which once again, especially enticed tourists from Germany. The social behavior and atmosphere in the public spaces defined by vacationers have become legendary. Heinrich Klotz offered a beautiful memorial to this development in 1977 with the book of essays, *Die röhrenden Hirsche der Architektur*.[1]

The cautious redesigning of Barcelona's city center in preparation for the Olympic Games in 1992 inspired a number of cities to follow its example. With a meticulously planned program for the upgrading of public spaces, the extreme density of the Gothic city center was lowered, practically "aired out." Interventions in public space were supported throughout the entire city, giving rise to an unparalleled dense network of small squares, alleys, and streets. The interventions were often unnoticeable at first glance, as they assimilated through a selection of specific surfaces and proportions: a higher-quality surface here, a tree planted there, along with a bench, there a fountain, and first and foremost, art! Tradition and future complement one another symbiotically. Through the relocation of the harbor, which facilitated the connection of the city promenade Rambla to the Mediterranean, and the creation of a city beach in front of the former harbor district Barceloneta, the combination of the unique athletic event and regular urban renovation became a highpoint of design-based and farsighted urban development. Without the high qualitative demands of the local authorities, the reinvention of Barcelona would not have been possible. They showed visionary power and the courage to be extravagant. The planners focused, first of all, on the quality of life for the citizens of Barcelona, the success of businesses and industry, and only then on the streams of tourists.

The present catalog features important projects with similar objectives, small-scale changes with great effect, such as the designs in Ljubljana and Athens from the early twentieth-century, influential then as now, as well as long-term projects paired with high-quality, urban-design objectives, such as in Guimarães, London, and New York. The environmentally motivated projects at a regional planning scale, such as the protection goals for the Galician coast, constitute a new dimension of planning.

Public space can only be planned in a future-oriented way and with an open outcome

The urban planning directors of the two largest German cities, Regula Lüscher, for Berlin, and Jörn Walter, for Hamburg, provide information on how democratic forms of organization and the wishes of citizens influence their approach to current planning tasks.

In addition to classical citizen-led initiatives, there are meanwhile a number of tools of concrete civil participation in politics and planning that have proven their value in practice. A warranty of the seriousness and reliability of such processes over the long term has not

1 Heinrich Klotz, *Die röhrenden Hirsche der Architektur: Kitsch in der modernen Baukunst*, Lucerne: Verlag C.J. Bucher, 1977.

New street profile at Potsdamer Platz, Berlin

yet been sufficiently proven, and accordingly, there is still little experience with the length of time that citizens who are actively involved in their working lives are able to remain involved in processes that often develop over the course of several years. Also, the size of projects that can be accompanied by these means is disputed. The Montag Stiftung Urbane Räume based in Bonn has both led and evaluated several of these processes.

The municipal administration of Berlin is currently facing the major challenge of developing core urban areas: the Kulturforum, the Rathausforum between Alexanderplatz and Humboldtforum, the Spreebogen including the Bürgerforum, and Tempelhofer Feld. Quo vadis, Berlin?

During the exhibition, an interactive planning tool will be tested out, which arose from the cooperation of various European universities (ETH Zurich, University of Applied Sciences and Art Northwestern Switzerland, University of Northumbria, and the University of Bamberg) and uses cognitive awareness strategies. With the aid of this software, a planning game for the redesign of the central Alexanderplatz will be offered to exhibition visitors. The University of Bamberg's Forschungsgruppe Ergonomie, Psychologische Ästhetik, Gestaltung [research team for ergonomics, psychological aesthetics, and design] developed a special catalog of questions in order to systematically record opinions, moods, and, most importantly, conclusions through a visitor survey.

Berlin's Zuloark collective will set up an urban parliament during the exhibition, based on the Campo de Cebada in Madrid, which will meet regularly with the goal of presenting a communally developed *Declaration of Urban Rights*.

Public space supports social peace and democratic values

Based on information from the UN, sixty million people throughout the world were considered forcibly displaced by the end of 2015. Ten years ago that number was 37.5 million. That is an irrevocable fact. How will Europe, how will Germany, and how, ultimately, will cities deal with this? How will new population groups orient themselves? Are there spaces accessible to everyone, where casual encounters can occur, where people can learn about their new home, and pick up on normative patterns? Where can one make the claim of belonging?

Public space is fiercely contested. The political dimension has become an essential one.

Of course, it is also necessary to mention that public space is in no way accessible to all, access is not granted to everyone in the same way, and discrimination can take place here. Repeated racially motivated police actions in the USA draw attention to this, as do the *banlieues* in Paris, which have again and again gone up in flames over the years. Pegida demonstrations in Germany increasingly resemble mob rallies and zero in on feelings of insecurity and exclusion. Democracy is politically radicalized here. In times like these, is permission to openly carry weapons, as has now been granted in Texas, the right signal?

London opened its museums free of charge to develop the banks of the Thames as a huge, appealing public space. People could spend time here and enjoy themselves without horrendous consumption expenditures, and they were not discriminated against in terms of access to the most important educational and cultural facilities. That is just as much a contribution to social peace as, for example, the freely accessible

Copacabana in Rio de Janeiro or the annual free concert by the Rolling Stones and other megastars held on the beach there, which confirms the farsighted and versatile planning by Roberto Burle Marx and the then-young Republic of Brazil.

Without exaggerating, it can be noted that, regarding the topic of immigration, the difference between countryside and city has also become a public stress test for the willingness to welcome and encounter others. In areas where public space has already been devoured by ravenous shopping malls, insecurity prevails, together with a lack of informal and free opportunities to meet up in familiar, stable roles and neighborhoods. Social contact requires action and constant practice, rather than passive, supposedly bustling crowds in shopping centers, which can hardly be reached on foot.

The variety of measures and services offered by unpaid helpers and volunteers constitute an urgently required public space. Arising here is an entirely new caliber of public life without precedent and, in any case, no assistance or mandate from the administration.

Outlook

The exhibited results of a student workshop held at the Akademie der Künste in October 2015—under the professional guidance of Berlin university professors and in dialogue with international experts from New York City, São Paulo, and Havana—present, in the form of open questions, visions, and subjective impressions of places of various scales and centrality (Berlin, Gelsenkirchen, and Anklam).

The discussion surrounding the composition of public space and its significance for contemporary urban society has begun. Publicness has to be tolerated. It is obvious that quality and function of public spaces must be taken seriously as distinct and independent dimensions in urban planning.

As the seventy-year history of democracy in Germany proves: public spaces change in unforeseen ways and through their constant use. City planners must be alert and evaluate, as Jane Jacobs once did. Public space is a reflection of successful politics and the approval of responsible citizens. Behavioral patterns that are encountered, are copied. When there are none, a void remains. For that reason, taking a position is called for, now more than ever before. We must not forget the images of the shoes on Paris's Place de la République in November 2015—representative of the demonstrations that were called off for security reasons, due to the terror risk during the climate summit. We need more than abstract demands of politics and administration for more protective measures. We must design a future.

Projects that use and spatially realize the population's proposals and willingness to help are to be concretized as integration measures. Language acquisition and access to educational facilities and information technology are the primary instruments and next steps to generating a shared public life. Politics can easily and purposefully decide upon corresponding infrastructural projects for kindergartens, schools, and vocational schools, which can be implemented by administration. Proportionate housing contingents in new building projects can be secured for migrants. One must simply exercise a will and cease the shrill slogans.

Either Western democracies, their citizens, and the vocal proponents of Western values prove capable of sustaining Western values in public spaces and mediating them through appropriate role models and patterns of behavior, or the lights will slowly go out in "Dunkeldeutschland" and elsewhere. We are confronted with tangible, concrete problems that cannot be made taboo or put aside with a smile, but instead, must be solved pragmatically—problems which, approached without a charity attitude, will unfurl economic benefits.

Violence, racism, and right-wing hate speech against personal civil rights and liberties, and human dignity are unacceptable and counterproductive in the irreversible transformation process of becoming the immigration country Germany, Europe, world.

Some understand this sooner, some later, some never. That, too, is a part of democracy.

Shoes on the Place de la République during the Climate Change Conference 2015, Paris

On Virtual and Real Public Space

I treasure the public space of urban parks. When I'm in New York City, I like to stroll around Central Park, Frederick Law Olmsted's publicly funded gift to New York civic life. In London, I enjoy losing myself on the crooked pathways of Hampstead Heath. In San Francisco, I've always taken my kids to Golden Gate Park, William Hammond Hall's magnificent West Coast contribution to nineteenth-century urban landscape architecture. In each public space, my family and I are guaranteed both anonymity and freedom. We can go anywhere in these parks without being identified. Entry into these public spaces doesn't require membership or any kind of personal trade of information; they are free to anyone, irrespective of their ethnicity, their age, their citizenship, or their beliefs. These *public* spaces are a guarantee of *privacy*. They capture the essence of individual liberty and autonomy in the contemporary physical world.

The world's greatest cities are distinguished by these public spaces. Berlin, for example, has more than 2,500 public parks and gardens in which anyone—Berliners or visitors—can stroll. But public space in the contemporary world isn't just made up of urban gardens and parks. The streets and squares and transportation systems—the "operating system," if you like, of our twenty-first-century physical existence—are distinguished by their *publicness*. This space is, in a sense, collectively owned and is thus financed and administered by public authorities. Such public space isn't limited to the city. In the United Kingdom, for example, the public paths in the countryside, which are known as "public right-of-ways," represent a collective space in which anyone can freely walk across privately owned land.

Unfortunately, some of today's public physical space is under threat. Our collective paranoia with terrorism and crime is triggering the creeping (and creepy) surveillance of public urban space. In the United Kingdom, for example, there are more than 70,000 publicly monitored cameras, including 13,000 on the London tube (underground) system alone, filming public space, supposedly on our collective behalf. And in some of the world's largest cities, particularly in the developing world, private residential areas replete with high-tech metal gates and uniformed security guards blight the urban landscape. Meanwhile, the hostility towards large public projects in many post-industrial countries, particularly in the United States, has resulted in the replacement of Frederick Law Olmsted's nineteenth-century urban landscapes with shopping malls, airports, sports stadiums, private university campuses, and other for-profit architectural projects.

That said, however, public space still remains the dominant operating system for early twenty-first century life. Much of it we simply take for granted without even thinking twice about our interaction with this physical space. We assume that our public streets, squares, parks, and libraries can be freely and universally accessed without us having to trade anything in exchange for entry. We take for granted that we all experience an identical public space—and not something "personalized" to our income, consumer habits, or political opinions. And even in privately funded shopping malls, airports, and sports stadiums, we assume that we aren't being spied on wherever we go.

But John Perry Barlow was wrong to imagine what he called "cyberspace" as being intrinsically disconnected from physical space. You see, despite its virtual nature, the Internet has a very real history. And it's in this concrete history of digital architecture that we can trace the tragedy of virtual public space in our networked age.

In the beginning, the ideal of public space figured prominently among the pioneers of cyberspace. The fathers (and they were all men) of the Internet—American technology wonks like Vannevar Bush, J.C.R. Licklider, and Norbert Wiener—believed that they were building an alternative reality that would benefit humanity because of the *publicness* of this new kind of communal space: And for the first thirty years of its existence, the architecture of the Internet was constructed on public principles little different from those that captured the work of nineteenth-century urban landscape architects like Olmsted.

Between the late 1940s and the early 1990s, the invention and development of the Internet was funded by public agencies like the Advanced Research Project Agency (ARPA), the governmental organization that, with a million-dollar grant in 1966, funded and built ARPANET, the original computer network. The first computer-to-computer communications, enabled through the packet-sharing digital technology developed by publicly funded scientists Paul Baran and Donald Davies, took place in 1969 between computers at four public universities on the West Coast. By 1981, ARPANET had grown to include 213 mostly public institutions

Alexanderplatz, Berlin, 2015

on its network before the publicly funded National Science Foundation Network (NSFNET) replaced it as the Internet's backbone in 1985. Other mostly publicly funded digital communications networks also emerged in this period, including the French CYLCLADES, the radio-based PRNET, and the satellite network SATNET.

The next stage in the history of virtual space was the tying together of these networks as a condition for the creation of a single public realm of computer-to-computer communications. This was first achieved by two American academics at UCLA, Bob Kahn and Vint Cerf, who invented two complimentary protocols called TCP and IP that enabled communication across networks. TCP/IP were publicly owned protocols that allowed users on ARPANET, SATNET, PRNET, CYLCLADES, and all the other networks to e-mail each other. The Internet now had a postal system. And it was public property, owned by all computer users.

The public Internet reached its apotheosis in 1989 with Tim Berners-Lee's invention of the World Wide Web. A young British researcher at the European Particles Physics Laboratory (CERN) in Geneva, Berners-Lee imagined what he described as "marrying together" the technological advances already made by pioneers like Davies, Baran, Kahn, and Cerf. Berners-Lee's goal was to establish a connection between the people, the computers, and the projects at CERN. He was to create a revolutionary new thing—a virtual space which we could all equally share.

"Suppose all the information stored on computers everywhere were linked, I thought," Berners-Lee later wrote in his autobiography about the invention of the World Wide Web. "Suppose I could program my computer to create a space in which anything could be linked to anything. All the bits of information in every computer at CERN, and on the planet, would be available to me and to anyone else. There would be a single global information space." And that "single global information space," Berners-Lee might have added, was a defiantly *public* space. Up until 1991, the Internet was a publicly managed network run by the US government. Companies that sought access to NSFNET, the Net's backbone, had to sign an "Acceptable Use Policy" that limited their use to non-commercial "research and education." As somebody who fiercely embraced the idea of the Internet as a public space which allowed anyone to freely use his World Wide Web technology, Berners-Lee was particularly committed to its non-commercial development. Indeed, he regarded the attempt to charge a license fee for one of the early Web browsers "an act of treason in the academic community and the Internet community."

Unfortunately, however, what Berners-Lee viewed as "treason" became the norm on the World Wide Web. Virtual space—once the preserve of publicly spirited academics and technologists—dramatically changed in the early 1990s, when the US government shut down NSFNET and handed over the running of the Internet backbone to commercial Internet service providers (ISPs). The virtual public space had been privatized, and it triggered one of the most dramatic gold rushes in history.

The first Internet boom of the 1990s generated multi-billion-dollar, venture-capitalist-financed start-ups like Netscape, Amazon, and Yahoo. But this turned out to be nothing compared to the so-called Web 2.0 period of the last fifteen years, in which a new series of multi-billion dollar global leviathans like Google, Facebook, Twitter, YouTube, and Instagram have come to define both business and culture of our digital age.

The confusing thing is that many of these Internet companies market themselves as platforms of virtual public space. Google, for example, forever boasts about itself as the provider of free information to a world hungry for data. Facebook says that it is enabling connectivity for the more than one billion members of its community. Twitter claims that it has created a public space for the sharing of opinions. YouTube says it is the public space where anyone can broadcast and watch video, while Instagram has become the public stage on which we can show off our photographs to each other.

At first glance, it might seem as if Google's or YouTube's virtual space is as public as Frederick Law Olmsted's Central Park. After all, we can all, at will, stroll online through the Google search engine or the YouTube collection of videos. Nobody is denied entry to these services. They exist for the benefit of everyone. And they are free!

But here's the catch: What appears to be "free" in virtual reality is anything but free. Today's dominant Internet companies like Google and Facebook, with their stratospheric valuations in the hundreds of billions of dollars, are "big data" companies. Their business model is appropriating our most intimate personal data to sell to advertisers. The Internet, therefore, has become a giant panopticon in which our buying habits, our desires, our identities, and, above all, our relationships are being mined for profit. Contemporary virtual reality is a privatized *1984*, in which a snooping Big Brother has been replaced by an increasingly ubiquitous artificial algorithm that knows us better than we know ourselves.

So what appears to be virtual public space is, in fact, the reverse. On the Internet, we have all become a product, packaged up by all-powerful Silicon Valley corporations. It's as if there's a sophisticated camera and microphone on every blade of grass in what appears to be a virtual public park but is actually a prison. And those cameras and microphones are recording everything, absolutely everything, about us, destroying our privacy, transforming the world into what Mark Zuckerberg all-too-naïvely described as a "well-lit dorm room."

Real public space is universal. When we walk into a public square, street, or building, they don't change their shape or identity according to who we are. But on the Internet, virtual reality has been so privatized—what Silicon Valley euphemistically calls "personalized"—that the universal has been replaced by the infinitely particular. And so, for example, when we go shopping on Amazon, we are presented with what the algorithm assumes, given our previous purchases, we want to buy. The Internet has, in fact, become a giant mirror, a "filter bubble," in which the personal has replaced the public ethic. Virtual reality is a private reality. On the network, we are, as the MIT social scientist Sherry Turkle so memorably put it, "alone together." No wonder the most popular cultural artefact of virtual space is the "selfie"—that narcissistic manifestation of our alienation and loneliness.

This crisis of the virtual public sphere is emerging as the central problem of our contemporary age. When Tim Berners-Lee invented the World Wide Web in 1989, the Internet only had 800 networks, 150,000 registered addresses, and a few million computers. Today, there are almost two billion people on the network, with the rest of the world's four billion people about to come online. Today, billions of increasingly affordable smartphones have made the Internet central to our social, economic, and political lives. Today, we are on the brink of an age of big data, in which everything—from our cities to our cars to our homes to our clothing to our bodies—will be connected through digital technology.

The absence of virtual public space in our networked age is deeply disturbing. Many of our troubling problems—the weakening of community, the increasing subjectivity of thought, the personalization and narcissism of cultural life—are both a cause and consequence of the digital revolution. The operating system for early twenty-first-century life is, therefore, severely malfunctioning. To borrow a popular Silicon Valley term, the Internet is currently an "epic fail."

So what is to be done? Some idealistic technologists like Tim Berners-Lee still believe that his original project—an open Internet built around the ideal of public space—can be recreated through an Internet bill of rights and a return to the non-commercial principles of the digital pioneers. But we can't retreat to a pre-1989 Internet, just as we can't go back to the analogue certainties of the predigital past. History doesn't work like that—especially the history of networked technology with its perpetual Schumpeterian creative disruption.

Rather than technological, today's struggle is political. Frederick Law Olmsted's nineteenth-century urban landscape architecture was part of the political struggle against private interests to create public space in the industrial city. Today, the political struggle is against big data companies from Silicon Valley like Google and Facebook with their greed for our personal data and their blatant disregard for the public good. The political challenge is to carve out a public space in this virtual world where our individual liberty and autonomy can be respected. What we need are anti-surveillance laws that force Silicon Valley companies to reinvent their flawed business models. What we need is an operating system for the twenty-first century that recognizes the intrinsic value of public space, virtual or otherwise.

The Constitution of Public Space

At first glance, preparing an up-to-date assessment of the constitution of public space may seem an impossible undertaking.[1] Public space takes diverse shapes: from the often romanticized agora of antiquity to decorative urban squares, reconstructed based on historical designs, district centers along arterial roads, through to landscaped traffic islands, green banks along highways, parklands, or the green spaces between postwar housing blocks, originally intended for drying laundry. Public spaces face increasingly multifaceted and complex demands.

They are to be spaces of informal education and social interaction, ideally transgenerational and intercultural. At a local level, they may serve food and energy production, act as urban cold islands in the face of climate change, and provide space for endangered species and sustainable surface water drainage, while, at the same time, paying for themselves through commercial offerings or other sources of income. And, naturally, they are also still expected to fulfill all the traditional functions of public space as a place for presentation and representation, ensuring the safe and efficient movement of traffic and providing a suitable stage for the surrounding buildings and urban life in general. The definition of public space in terms of ownership and access rights is equally multifaceted. A public space is, first and foremost, a space that is in the public hand and publicly accessible—whether open-air or covered. The principal idea associated with such spaces is that the public hand provides them for the common good.

Ever more spaces in the city are publicly accessible but owned by private entities, who enjoy authority over them and are thus entitled to make their own bylaws for the use of and behavior within these spaces. Belonging in this category are elaborately designed corporate public spaces in conjunction with major office projects, which have long been common practice in London, for example in "urban quarters" such as More London, Broadgate, or Bishops Square. Also in this category are the access and circulation spaces and "piazzas" in shopping centers, which are often barely distinguishable from publicly owned public spaces—except for usually being maintained to a much higher standard. To many people, these spaces are more successful at fulfilling the functions commonly associated with public spaces: having a cup of coffee or an ice cream, meeting friends. Commercial interests are generally predominant in these public spaces, which is expressed, for example, in political demonstrations being banned, as they would detract from the shopping experience.

In the course of the paradigm shift from welfare state to neoliberal state, the public realm in general has been in decline for quite some time and, particularly—though not exclusively—in the Anglo-Saxon world, has become stigmatized. In British society, those who can afford it tend to opt out of public services, i.e. by sending their children to private rather than state schools, using private healthcare providers rather than relying on the National Health Service, and spending their leisure time in private tennis clubs instead of public parks.[2] In Germany, too, public buildings have been sold off to a large extent over the last decade—and are currently being repurchased, at great effort, by some communities. The poor state of repair of many public squares and parks reflects the lack of value attributed to this common property. In Berlin, the priority given to some publicly owned spaces over others is evident, for example, in the costly extension of the Autobahn A100 across the Spree river, which stands in stark contrast to the sluggish development of the cycle path network and the significant cuts in the maintenance budget for urban parks and green spaces.

The state and design of public spaces, but also the definition of what constitutes acceptable behavior and the approaches taken to the assignment of zones for specific uses, is always a reflection of society and, as such, the perception of how we are to conduct ourselves within urban space. Public green spaces and urban squares play an increasingly important role as an extended living room or a place of informal education—in particular for socially disadvantaged groups who don't have access to private gardens. In the face of dwindling public resources and rising user numbers, it is clear that the many and diverse demands made of public spaces can no longer be fulfilled, not just in growing cities such as Berlin. All the more important is it to consider the factors currently influencing the constitution of public space and discuss which developments should be viewed as desirable and which should be prevented.

Reurbanization instead of decay—a renaissance of public space

Reurbanization, the influx of people into more attractive cities, is an ongoing trend in many European countries.[3] Instrumental in this has been a renewed relevance of the inner city, initiated by strategic urban policies promoting an "urban renaissance." For large parts of middle-class society it is once again desirable to take up residence in the densely built nineteenth-

1 My thanks go to Jörn Gertenbach and Thomas Hauck for their useful feedback and comments.

2 Nick Cohen, "We're All in a Class Apart: Thatcher's Legacy Is an Increasingly Divided Britain. Blair Is Doing Nothing to Change That," in *The Observer*, February 15, 2004.

3 Klaus Brake and Günter Herfert (eds), *Reurbanisierung*, Wiesbaden: Springer, 2012.

Berlin Lichterfelde, ca. 2005

century neighborhoods of the inner city, rather than in single-family detached homes in the suburbs.[4] More homes are needed as a result, but so are spaces for infrastructure, retail, offices, etc. Following the sustainable planning principle of "interior development before exterior development"—i.e. brownfield before greenfield—priority is given to the development of former industrial sites, railway sidings or depots, and other land previously used for transportation infrastructure: all spaces that once shaped the image of Berlin as an "unfinished city."[5] These types of wasteland have evolved to become informal green spaces in many cities, turned into caravan communities or impromptu beach bars, used for dog walking or repurposed for sporting activities. Whether industrial wasteland sites along the Spree in Berlin, the grounds of the former Bishopsgate Goodsyard on the eastern edge of the City of London, or the surroundings of the NDSM Wharf in Amsterdam—these sites were used as experimental urban spaces for many years, which led to new innovative uses, while also providing ecological niches with considerable biodiversity. Their redevelopment, the recycling of these areas, which, in principle, makes sense from an urban planning perspective as it minimizes urban sprawl into the periphery, deprives the city of open spaces of a very unique quality, valued by many precisely because of their unplanned character.

Urban growth in the course of reurbanization also means that existing public spaces experience an intensified use. The alarming scenario of urban streets, squares, and parks becoming underused and desolate as a result of globalization, information technology, and negative growth has now given way to the detrimental effects of overuse. In London, the significance of these spaces in light of the city's considerable population growth—from 6.9 million in 1991 to 8.2 million in 2011—is being officially acknowledged. In an increasingly densely populated and ever more crowded metropolis, open spaces must be well designed to assure safe and comfortable access, and be able to deal with larger crowds. London's mayor Ken Livingstone (in office 2000–2008) pursued a strategy of turning London into one of the most pedestrian-friendly cities in the world by 2015, using well-designed public spaces to persuade people of the advantages of walking and cycling—and to prevent complete traffic gridlock in the city.[6] As a result, numerous small parks and squares were redesigned and the design guidelines for major roads reviewed.[7] With the overhaul of public spaces and squares, as well as the construction of new pedestrian connections and footbridges, the public hand thus prepared the ground, which was then to be followed by private investment. Well-designed parks and public open spaces were seen as drivers of an urban renaissance and the revitalization of inner-city neighborhoods.

The public space as a stage

One of the key aspects of the inner-city renaissance is that, in addition to functions related to access and transportation, public spaces are now once again serving as communal spaces and are turning from mere transit zones into stages for different uses and offerings. The reasons for this redefinition are manifold: on the one hand, it is rooted in the transformation of society—a higher number of single-person households, for example—and a more flexible lifestyle, which goes hand in hand with changes in leisure behavior and more time spent in the public realm. On the other hand, many towns and cities now recognize the importance

4 Harald Bodenschatz (ed.), *Renaissance der Mitte: Zentrumsumbau in London und Berlin*, Berlin: Braun, 2005.

5 Philipp Oswalt, *Berlin, Stadt ohne Form: Strategien einer anderen Stadt*, Berlin: Prestel, 2000.

6 See Mayor of London/ Transport for London, *Making London a Walkable City: The Walking Plan for London*, London: Transport for London, 2004.

7 Cordelia Polinna, *Towards a London Renaissance: Projekte und Planwerke für des städtebaulichen Paradigmenwechsels im Londoner Zentrum*, Detmold: Verlag Dorothea Rohn, 2009, pp. 109–145.

The former "death strip" along the Berlin Wall between Treptow and Neukölln, 2015

Karaoke in the Mauerpark, Berlin Prenzlauer Berg, 2012

of public spaces, which, alongside the major places of interest, form the glue that holds together a city's tourist landscape. As a result, they are now designed, equipped, and arranged accordingly. Streets, parks, and squares provide the settings for important historic buildings, leisure shopping, events such as Christmas markets or marathons, fashion weeks, or the public screening of sports events, and for anything from a leisurely stroll to a bachelor party.

In the era of easyJet and Airbnb, public space has more than ever become an important commodity, its respective qualities creating the unique selling points of a city. The Admiralbrücke in Kreuzberg at sunset or the Mauerpark have become major tourist hotspots in Berlin thanks to their special atmosphere or view. The use of public spaces as stages for city tourism and entertainment is no longer confined to the center, but continues to extend outwards into other densely developed neighborhoods—Berlin's fast-changing hipster hotspots or *Kieze*—thus turning these areas into the backdrop for a supposedly "alternative" tourism.

Significant revenue is generated for the (mainly private) tourism industry, but also for the municipality in the form of taxation. At the same time, however, the inconveniences associated with this "stage" function of public spaces are increasingly perceived as a problem: litter, noise, increasing maintenance costs, road closures, views obstructed by temporary stages, food stands, or marquees. To master these challenges, legal frameworks for new private-public control instruments, such as Business Improvement Districts, are defined that serve to generate additional funds for upkeep and maintenance, but—like in London—are also useful to install private security services or implement restrictive regulations for dealing with street merchants and musicians.[8] The financing of these measures is provided by private-public partnerships, in return for which the private parties demand more influence over matters of design and management. The structures of ownership and management of public and private open spaces are thus becoming increasingly blurred. Private entities are gaining more influence over the public realm, while the public sector is forced to play by the rules of the private sector.

The Smart City—a new dimension of control

Growing demands for security during major events, terrorist threats, as well as the prevention of real or perceived crime already have a strong impact on the usability of public spaces. Costly security requirements—such as fences to be set up around street festivals—make non-commercial community events nearly impossible. Increasing camera surveillance and the designation of crime hotspots as "danger zones," where police are authorized to stop and search even without reasonable grounds, already triggered extensive discussions about the introduction of strategic police control regimes and the role of the "surveillance state" in the 1990s and 2000s.[9]

The debate on surveillance and behavior in the public realm has now been taken to a whole new level as surveillance technologies are becoming ever more sophisticated, with increasingly inconspicuous cameras streaming images to the internet and linking data with face recognition software and social media profiles. With contact lens cameras and displays and wearable technologies, such as Google Glass, no longer confined to the realm of science fiction, the right to privacy of people who happen to be in the vicinity of such devices has to be renegotiated. When someone wearing smart

8 Ibid.

9 Klaus Ronneberger, Stephan Lanz, and Walther Jahn, *Die Stadt als Beute*, Bonn: Dietz, 1999; Richard J. Williams, *The Anxious City: English Urbanism in the Late Twentieth Century*, London/New York: Routledge, 2004.

Playground on Maybachufer, Berlin Neukölln, 2015

glasses walks across a public square and is notified by facial recognition of who is approaching and how they present themselves in their Facebook or Tinder profile, then the anonymity associated for centuries with urban life is profoundly challenged.

The spread of so-called smart technologies has also led to a shift in the definition of what is considered "normal" behavior. Social and moral norms are no longer primarily informed by the state and by major institutions such as the church, schools, or the military.[10] Instead, a popularization of surveillance technologies is taking place and, with that, a new definition of what is acceptable. We are no longer living under the control of the "evil Big Brother state": now everyone can report deviant behavior. This swarm intelligence, which can be highly useful in some situations—a website that collects information on danger spots for cyclists, for example—can also, with hardly a stretch of the imagination, turn the Internet into a pillory and significantly limit personal freedom in the public realm.

Will people still demonstrate for human rights in public if it is possible to identify instantly who, from which country, is for or against something? Or will the true public space of the future be a closed, sealed area without camera surveillance or observation by supposed "smart" technologies? Will these developments result in a retreat into the private sphere or explicitly designated "no surveillance" zones—as is already the case in Berlin's legendary Berghain club? At the club, which is famous for its sexual permissiveness, smartphone camera lenses are covered with stickers in an attempt to enforce its "no photos" policy. Another conceivable scenario, however, is that people will practice ever stricter self-discipline, as they have to assume that they will be filmed and "put online" at any time.

Questioning the car-friendly city

In the light of climate change and Germany's current *Energiewende* [energy transition], the ideal of the automotive city has become highly questionable; a rethinking of the associated urban structures seems urgently needed. Over the course of the second half of the twentieth-century, (private) vehicle traffic has radically transformed many cities. Fostered by generous postwar-era subsidies, a problematic urban planning heritage has been created: gigantic thoroughfares and interchanges, designed with the primary aim of promoting fast-flowing traffic, and sprawling low-density housing estates that dedicate large parts of their total area to parking and traffic zones—or simply leave them as "leftover" spaces.

Reorganizing these car-friendly streets and urban spaces will become an important task for planners and urban designers in the coming years. Public spaces that enable safe and comfortable pedestrian and bicycle traffic, and low-barrier, fast, and flexible transitions between walking, cycling, and public transportation can promote post-fossil-fuel mobility. Especially with a view to demographic change, a compact city with pedestrian-friendly public spaces is an opportunity to allow senior citizens a self-determined life in their own homes. Designing public spaces that make non-motorized mobility attractive and convince people that forgoing their cars is a valid choice plays a central role in moving away from cities dominated by the private motorized vehicle.

On the outskirts of the city, in particular, but also in those parts of the inner city designed to give priority to the car, a new balance in favor of pedestrians, cyclists, and public transportation could potentially release large areas for new uses. One only has to recall the aftereffects

10 Michel Foucault, *Geschichte der Gouvernementalität I: Sicherheit, Territorium, Bevölkerung. Vorlesung am Colleges de France 1977/78*, Frankfurt am Main: Suhrkamp, 2004.

Underneath the highway interchange in Berlin Neukölln, 2013

of the release of vast plots of land in the course of deindustrialization, which led to interim uses, repurposing, new parks, etc., to see the great potential of a departure from the car-friendly city. Once again, large areas will become available for new uses—for urban renewal and redensification, but also for additional public open and green spaces.

Making your city your own—participation in the public realm

More than ever before, people now want to be actively involved in shaping their urban environment. New ways of appropriating open spaces are called for, which question and go beyond the traditional concepts of public urban spaces and parks. Many people no longer want pristine and perfectly designed parks, but would rather have areas that are less highly maintained and instead offer more freedom and a wider range of uses. Community gardens and places such as the Tempelhofer Feld (the former airfield of Tempelhof Airport, which has been appropriated by the public for a variety of impromptu uses) show that public spaces whose designated purpose is only minimally formalized are gaining in relevance. Vegetable patches that can be rented seasonally to grow produce for personal consumption are booming in cities such as Berlin, as is "solidarity agriculture." Here, part of the concept is that city dwellers who subscribe to vegetable box schemes go and help out in the fields themselves a few times a year. The Preußenpark in Berlin-Wilmersdorf is regularly transformed into a Thai street market; and the undefined space underneath the highway interchange in Berlin-Neukölln is used for impromptu parties known as "Free Open Airs."

Interesting constellations arise when this call for more participation and self-governance is seen in the context of the dramatically changing role of the public sector, which, in the face of dwindling resources and the resulting loss of scope, is forced to make cuts to services that used to be taken for granted, such as park maintenance. Allowing local communities more of a say and leeway for their own initiatives can easily seem like a pragmatic solution in the effort to make cost savings. Outsourcing the maintenance and design of green spaces to civil society also fits in with the logic of neoliberal urban development strategies: Everything is being privatized, even the beautification of one's own neighborhood. Nonetheless, bottom-up-initiatives concerning the activation of public space in particular are easy to engage in, which makes them an important component in stakeholder-supported urban development.

Outlook

The trends concerning the development of public spaces that have been sketched out here cover a broad spectrum and allow for diverse scenarios for possible future approaches to the design of public urban spaces. In the face of diminishing public-sector spending and intense competition for inner-city spaces, there is clearly a need to expand the definition of what is deemed attractive public space. Leftover land, for example around traffic infrastructure, offers new opportunities. Cities such as Tokyo, which have had to deal with growing population densities for quite some time, are examples of how new urban qualities can be created through a layering of uses. The large paved area in front of Berlin's Max-Schmeling-Halle in Prenzlauer Berg or the Tempelhofer Feld demonstrate how well a public space that simply offers room for flexible use can function.

A major opportunity for reconquered, additional public spaces lies in an intensified exploration of the twentieth-century planning legacy of the automotive city with its traffic infrastructure and the associated land, its low-density housing estates with large undefined areas, and its car-friendly commercial and shopping-center developments with extensive car parks. Currently, there is little appeal for pedestrians and cyclists. Redefining these spaces must become a central task of urban planning in the coming years. In light of the growing competition for space and the increasing number of tasks that open spaces in the city have to perform, it will seem even more absurd in the future to surrender such vast swathes of public land to the sole purpose of accommodating moving and stationary vehicle traffic.

Which of the many visions regarding the future constitution of public space will become reality depends mainly on the changes in direction effected today to influence the character of open spaces: increasing or reducing public investment, increasing or reducing civic participation, vehicle traffic, orientation on economic interests, biodiversity, surveillance, use of "smart" technologies, etc. Many of these developments will lead to a questioning of the established culture of public space. For that reason, there is an urgent need to create locations and occasions to negotiate and discuss what rules should apply in the future to the use and design of public space and how responsibilities can be shared. When the freedom, anonymity, and openness of public space is threatened, it is the task of the state to protect these valuable commodities—from surveillance, commercialization, exclusion, and one-sided appropriation by individual interest groups.

The Politics of Public Space—London and New York Compared

Public space is political. The current Mayor of New York City, Bill de Blasio, a Democrat committed to wiping out inequality in his city, recently announced his plans to reverse Snøhetta's multi-million dollar pedestrianization of Times Square, commissioned by his predecessor, the right-leaning billionaire Michael Bloomberg. Expressing his disgust at the apparent invasion of New York's most emblematic public space by half-naked entertainers, De Blasio seemed serious about bringing back cars and reducing the pavements in an effort to "clean up" the city for innocent New Yorkers.

"As a human being and a parent," he exclaimed, "I don't think it's appropriate, in the middle of one of the busiest squares in New York City, that women should display themselves that way." Even though few natives of the city actually actively use this outdoor cathedral of populist entertainment flooded by millions of tourists on a daily basis, De Blasio chose his words carefully to redefine his mayoral role as that of a moral guardian. *The New York Times*' architecture critic Michael Kimmelman wryly commented: "Not for the first time, Mr. de Blasio is creating a peevish impression that, even now, he is running against his predecessor when he needs to be running the city." Public space remains a contested political item in this city.

Across the Atlantic, the idiosyncratic Mayor of London, Boris Johnson, found himself in the awkward position of unveiling a highly political piece of art on the highly visible Fourth Plinth in London's central Trafalgar Square. Commissioned by the Mayor's own cultural agency, German-American artist Hans Haacke's sculpture *Gift Horse* features an LED bow that shows a ticker of the latest London stock prices tied around the bronze skeleton of a horse. It was conceived—and is now perceived—as a symbol of the ravages of the market, placed squarely at the heart of the most public of London's public squares. A veteran art critique suggested it was a bit "like letting Trotsky loose on Buckingham Palace."

Boris Johnson had to resort to his quick-witted tongue for a response. "There will be those who say that this undeniably underfed beast," Johnson quipped, "is a symbol of the excessive pursuit of austerity and the [Conservative Government's] diet approach to life. But I say, absolutely not [...]. In those fabulous tubular structures you will see symbolised the vital infrastructure [...] that has received such fantastic investment [...] playing a part in the greatest economic recovery this city has ever seen [...] and the driving force of the UK and indeed the European economy." A not-so-veiled endorsement of the Conservative Government's policies just a few weeks before the national election in May 2015.

Earlier on in 2009, artist Antony Gormley recognized the full political potential of the Fourth Plinth in Trafalgar Square, but from a more populist perspective. For his installation *One & Other*, he invited members of the public to stand on the empty plinth. Every hour, 24 hours a day, for 100 days, 2,400 people sang, campaigned, performed, undressed, or simply stood on the plinth. To Gormley, this display in one the most symbolic places in the country gave individuals the opportunity to represent a cross-section of the visual and oral history of Britain, "allowing the 'plinthers' to represent humanity itself."

While these anecdotes do not compare with the highbrow rivalry of Bernini and Borromini and their respective papal patrons in seventeenth-century Rome, they point to the deep association that exists between political power, individual expression, and public space. In the 1980s, President Mitterand of France displayed a top-down understanding of this dynamic through the Parisian *grands projets*; while Barcelona's *petits projets*, implemented by the mayors of the post-Franco era, signaled the democratization of the Catalan city. The impact of these profoundly political acts still marks the socio-spatial urban culture of these cities today. In this regard, London and New York are relative newcomers to the public space game, reflecting a new balance of power within the city and its institutions.

Regardless of the artistic or architectural merits of Haacke's sculpture or Snøhetta's designs, it is the sites of these interventions, and their patrons, that make them so politically charged. Both Times Square in New York and Trafalgar Square in London are canonical public spaces in their own right. They are repositories of collective memory, physical manifestations of national politics and culture. It is here that citizens come together to celebrate and demonstrate. They are the viewing points for millions of visitors who come to admire the emblems of national culture—from Nelson's Column and Big Ben to the world's largest and most profitable commercial billboards displaying live results from the stock market and the latest MTV videos (that show far more skin than any street performer).

Yet, they were both—until recently—traffic junctions or roundabouts, dominated by cars, taxis, and buses. Camera-wielding tourists jostled with vehicles

Diller Scofidio + Renfro and James Corner Field Operations, High Line, New York City

to capture their own personal image of these urban icons. In the last decades, they have both been given a good scrubbing and a face-lift to reflect the aspirations of urbanity embraced by these centers of Anglo-Saxon neoliberalism. Both initiatives are a physical embodiment of the rediscovery of the power of metropolitan institutions and a reaffirmation of the significance of the office of mayor.

Bloomberg began his first term as mayor only a few months after 9/11 and gained credit for New York City's ability to bounce back. Building on the achievements of his predecessor Rudy Giuliani's tough anti-crime stance and budget-balancing abilities, Bloomberg focused on improving public services (such as schools) and developing PlaNYC—a comprehensive, environmentally driven strategy, which promotes more sustainable and resilient lifestyles, including investment in cycleways and walkable neighborhoods. Central to this strategy was a series of public space interventions across the city, which required the closure of key New York streets to traffic, including sections of Broadway at Times Square, Herald Square, and Flatiron Plaza.

The controversial but effective wholesale rezoning of nearly 40 percent of New York—with over 115 rezoning plans covering more than 10,300 blocks—has delivered a transformation of much of the Brooklyn Waterfront. Some of the most notable projects include: investments in public open space, including Michael Van Valkenburgh's Brooklyn Bridge Park; the uber-gentrifying magnet of the High Line designed by Diller Scofidio + Renfro and Field Operations (where New Yorkers walk more slowly than on the ground); and the bloated redevelopment of Hudson Yards, masterminded by KPF. Bloomberg's Planning Commissioner claims that "our ambitions are as broad and far-reaching as those of Robert Moses, but we judge ourselves by Jane Jacobs' standards." The new wave of private real-estate investment has had its critics; however, this did not stop Bloomberg. He received enough support to change New York's legal constitution to be reelected for a third term in 2009 to "finish the job." From Times Square to Williamsburg, Bloomberg's functional public-space improvements across the city are the tangible evidence of his twelve-year legacy.

Rather than reinvigorate old political institutions as in New York, London actually created a new one, which has affected the character and scale of investment in public space. In 2000, the UK's capital invented the new post of executive "mayor" to make up for years of fragmented metropolitan governance willfully imposed by Margaret Thatcher in the mid-1980s. Left-leaning Ken Livingstone, who swept to power as the city's first directly elected mayor, effectively claimed the newly pedestrianized Trafalgar Square as the symbol of a more open, inclusive London—even though it was conceived and implemented by the (national) Government Office for London. Not only is Trafalgar Square the technical centerpoint of London (from which all distances are measured), it is also the setting of festivals, rallies, and public events that regularly champion London's diversity and achievements (such as the celebrations for winning the Olympics in July 2005, followed two days later by the cruel bombings of the London transport system).

London has grown by over a million since 2001 and is set to reach ten million inhabitants by 2030. A key component of Livingstone's "London Plan" was to accommodate the city's projected population growth within its existing footprint and the Green Belt. This required building at much greater densities, on brownfield sites near public transport hubs (such as the 2012 Olympics site in East London), and providing more and better public space in new developments and existing neighborhoods. As a result of the influence of his architectural adviser Richard Rogers, Livingstone launched an ambitious—and never fully realized—campaign to create the "Mayor's 100 Public Spaces," modeled on Barcelona's achievements of the previous decade.

Following his election as mayor in 2008, the Conservative Boris Johnson has more or less followed the same development growth strategy. The one exception is that he replaced the "100 Public Spaces" with "London's Great Outdoors," a not completely dissimilar "place-based approach" which focuses more on leafy, affluent outer-London suburbs—occupied by Conservative voters—than the gritty, inner-London, hard-landscaped spaces favored by Ken Livingstone and inhabited largely by Labour sympathizers. The political and the physical in London have always been neatly aligned.

It is not by chance that the Danish public space expert Jan Gehl influenced Michael Bloomberg's decision to try out a "temporary" pedestrianization experiment in New York. In London, another academic, Professor Bill Hillier, provided the "scientific" evidence for Norman Foster to implement an idea initially muted by his old Team 4 partner Richard Rogers in the mid-1980s. Trained as an engineer, Bloomberg has always been attracted to technical, measurable solutions to urban problems. Together with his Transport Commissioner Janette Sadik-Khan he implemented a plan designed to reduce accidents and injuries, apart from enhancing the aesthetics of the city's public spaces. In Times Square alone, pedestrian injuries have dropped by 35 percent, and injuries to drivers and passengers in cars have fallen by 63 percent since 2009. And all of this he had to do with stealth.

Despite his far-reaching authority, the Mayor of New York does not control public transport (and consequently much of the public realm) in the five boroughs of the 8.5 million metropolis. The public transportation system is in the hands of the MTA—the Mass Transit Authority—which is controlled by the Governor of the State of New York, a political antagonist with a very different set of political priorities who holds the purse strings of all major investments in the city's public transport. Seen from the vantage point of the State capital Albany, New York City's needs seem distant, parochial, and expensive.

The result of this tortuous political condition is reflected in the fragmented design of the city's public spaces. The partial and temporary pedestrianization of key streets had to be sold as an "experiment" by the mayor to ensure support from the powerful Community Boards. They were rough-and-ready affairs: a few traffic cones and some painted asphalt defined the new public spaces of the city. Not the delicate design-led interventions of European or Latin-American counterparts. If they failed, they could be easily reversed. If they succeeded, they would stay. Moveable tables and chairs were the only concession to the city's Planning Commissioner Amanda Burden's more spatial sensitivities.

The lack of "total" political control explains why Congestion Charging was never approved in New York, but rapidly expedited by the Mayor of London, who, in contrast, was given full power over Transport for London (TfL), which controls the tube, buses, and regional rail with a budget of 7 billion euros. In fact, it is TfL—an agency made up of 27,000 engineers and project managers and a few designers, but chaired by the mayor—that has had the greatest impact on public space in London. TfL owns the land and holds the bulk of the public budget for such works. Through its "Better Streets" program and the inauspiciously named Roads Task Force, it has delivered over eighty projects across the city since 2009.

While the total impact of these projects has affected the look and feel of many London neighborhoods, it is fair to say that few stand out for their design or originality, reflecting the highly technical (as opposed to ideological) criteria set by the client body. One exception is the 70-million-euro Exhibition Road scheme by Dixon Jones, which has modified the public realm at the heart of London's historic Museum Quarter in Kensington with some conviction. But even here, the technical constraints imposed by the main funders (TfL) and the vested interests of the local authority (which insisted on car parking for local residents) has resulted in a well-intended but compromised solution.

The lack of design finesse has less to do with sparse funding than with the laborious and highly project-managed procurement process involved in public infrastructure projects in the UK. In fact, London has benefited from a massive investment in public transport in the last decade, including over 30 billion euros for the new high-speed CrossRail line opening in 2018, which bisects the city from east to west, and another 7 billion euros of infrastructure development in East London connected to the 2012 Olympics. In 2014, the Mayor agreed to spend over 1.2 billion euros on a network of Copenhagen-style dedicated cycleways across London, which will not only transform travel patterns, but also change the appearance of the city's open spaces. While a precise figure is not available, the public funding allocated to open spaces and landscaping in the last decade in London runs into the hundreds of millions of euros, even though a line for "public space" does not appear in the Mayor's annual budget.

But, as with everything else in London, private sector interests loom large. Reflecting the city's intrinsically pro-market disposition, many public space initiatives have been realized on the back of property developments in a period during which London has seen exceptional growth in both population and investment. Due to the arcane planning system, local authorities can get "ransom money" from developers to help fund projects of public interest. The so-called Section 106 Agreements allow developers to negotiate a financial contribution towards affordable housing, public space improvements, or other social facilities in exchange for planning permission. Some argue that this is a cynical device which allows powerful investors to get what they want, others feel that this is the only way to force the private sector into contributing to the public well-being of the city.

The results of this mediated and compromised process are, predictably, mixed. Because of the multi-headed nature of the funding, some projects have ended up as high-end bijoux projects with a strong corporate identity and do little to enhance the experience of everyday Londoners. Canary Wharf in London's Docklands or Paddington Basin in central London stand out for their ghetto-like qualities despite the undoubted stature of individual design contributions. The ongoing 3-billion-euro King's Cross development in the former railway goods yards in central North London offers perhaps the best example of privately developed public space frequented by students, office workers, and commuters—even though the level of surveillance and control through CCTV and security guards is palpable.

1 Adam Greenfield, "Perilous Asymmetries: Playing With Trust in the 'Smart City,'" August 22, 2011, http://urbanscale.org/news/2011/08/22/perilous-asymmetries-playing-with-trust-in-the-smart-city (accessed on January 14, 2016).

Foster + Partners, redevelopment of Trafalgar Square, London

In fact, London has the unenviable record of being one of the most over-surveilled cities in the world, with around one million closed-circuit video cameras. In a recent study, Adam Greenfield calculated that a Londoner can expect to traverse a camera's field of operation some 300 times a day. Despite the assurance that cameras are there for "purposes of crime prevention and public safety," they appear to be having a negligible impact on crime. "Official Metropolitan Police statistics admit," Greenfield notes, "that fewer than one in every thousand street crimes in London is resolved with the aid of CCTV footage. Conversely, the cameras' advent is demonstrably making Londoners less safe. [...] The visible presence of a camera in the streetscape makes people less likely to intervene personally in emergent situations, presumably on the theory that Someone Official is observing anything untoward, and will surely intervene."[1] In this regard, it is worth noting that the provision of free Wi-Fi in New York's Bryant Park was instrumental in ensuring its successful makeover into one of the city's most-frequented public plazas.

Designed to guarantee total security for athletes and visitors during a few weeks in the summer of 2012, the Olympic Games have provided London with the most recent, comprehensive opportunity to address one of its deepest structural imbalances. Generations of Londoners recognize the stark differences between an affluent West and deprived East. Life expectancy drops by seven years as you move eastwards from salubrious Westminster to Stratford, the East London hub of the Olympic Games. The central government, the Mayor, and the local authorities were united in their ambition to use the 10-billion-euro budget to make a lasting difference that would help kick-start the regeneration of a forgotten but well-connected former industrial area.

The armature of public space was—and remains—at the heart of the "legacy" master plan for the Olympic neighborhood developed by Kees Christiaanse, Allies & Morrison and EDAW. Centered on waterways and new parks, an infrastructure of movement is emerging that will sustain the thirty thousand inhabitants who will come to live and work in the area in the next decades. While the "public" spaces of the popular Westfield Shopping Centre attract the crowds, the sophisticated landscape designs by James Corner Field Operations and Vogt Landscape Architects already succeed in creating a sense of place for the first cohorts of local residents and visitors to the area. The master plan has established a web of connectivity to the surrounding deprived boroughs that will help mitigate the risk of creating an introverted urban ghetto, notoriously exemplified by the Canary Wharf and other London Docklands developments.

While it is too early to tell whether the public spaces of the Olympic neighborhood will feel genuinely integrated into the urban fabric, they possess the robustness and resilience to adapt to changing circumstances—one of the key ingredients of successful public space. Zaha Hadid's elegant and popular Aquatic Centre, intensively used thanks to an entrance fee of only two pounds sterling is set to become the centerpiece of an emerging Cultural Quarter, with new outposts for the Victoria and Albert Museum (designed by O'Donnell + Tuomey), Saddlers Wells Dance Theatre, and Washington, D.C.'s Smithsonian Institution. Once again, the mayor has dug into his pockets and convinced central government to pump-prime what could become a major anchor for visitors and inhabitants of this emerging "piece of city."

Snøhetta, redevelopment of Times Square, New York City

London has not solved the public space problem, but it has recognized its political importance. Boris is competing with Ken as to who will have a stronger impact on the public realm of London. Ken brought in the Congestion Charge, but Boris will be remembered for his investment in the new cycling infrastructure in the city. Ken appropriated Trafalgar Square and claimed the success of the 2012 Olympics. With the failure of his harebrained idea for a new airport on "Boris Island" (to the far east of London), the current Mayor has committed 35 million euros to what he hopes will be his lasting public space legacy—Thomas Heatherwick's Garden Bridge folly, which may never be built.

New York and London, like many other cities, continue to play chess with our public spaces. Whatever De Blasio ends up doing to Times Square, it is unlikely that he will leave as strong a physical imprint on the city as Bloomberg has done. Boris Johnson's successor will struggle to find a *grand projet* of iconic resonance. Only when political vision is aligned with political power will New York or London have an opportunity to compete with Paris, Bogota, and Barcelona in creating an urban environment that recognizes public space as both a political *and* a design issue.

Urban Design through Public Space

Cities have the capability of providing something for everybody, only because, and only when, they are created by everybody.
—Jane Jacobs

Over 70 percent of the world's population will live in cities by 2050. Making room for one million additional New Yorkers is a major challenge in a dense city bounded by water. A vibrant public realm—parks, plazas, streets, public buildings, and transportation—is essential.

Historically, the government has taken sole responsibility for planning, creating, and caring for public space. Increasingly, however, in New York City and cities across the globe, citizens and community organizations are sparking new ideas to create more and better open spaces, as well as to maintain them. Redefining public space and improving the functionality of undervalued or degraded places to serve multiple purposes is ever more critical to the ecology of a successful metropolis. This essay will cover five emerging strategies: renewing existing parks; repurposing streets, making new places; reclaiming industrial areas and infrastructure; creating privately owned public spaces; and seeding transformation with urban agriculture.

The success of these strategies benefits from public-private partnerships and changes in institutional practices. For the past twenty years, the Design Trust for Public Space has catalyzed new thinking that unlocks the potential of public space in New York City by working with government agencies, community groups, architects, landscape architects, urban designers, and artists. We jumpstarted the High Line with its feasibility study to reclaim the structure and led the way for the city's first custom-built taxi with a design competition and guidelines. The Design Trust and its Fellows deliver innovative, yet feasible solutions with our project partners. This leads to new laws or zoning resolutions and guidelines for how public space is designed, operated, and maintained. Other cities and communities have been adopting our approach, guidelines, and recommendations.

Renewing existing parks

The Design Trust's 2014 Call for Projects jury selected the *World's Park* project, proposed by NYC Parks and the Queens Museum, who sought to repurpose and connect Flushing Meadows Corona Park with its neighbors. Built for the 1939/40 and 1964/65 World's Fairs, the park was designed to be reached by automobile and then to funnel thousands of ticket holders into and around its themed exhibits. Today, seven million New Yorkers a year enter the 897-acre park primarily on foot, by bicycle, or subway, using its original circulation paths and outdated spatial organization for current needs and uses, soccer fields, stadiums, and cultural amenities.

Community organization and a Community Design School were the key components of the project. Twenty-three community advisors were selected from neighborhood groups. The Design Trust Fellows team—a design educator, designer and writer, and community organizer—prepared the curriculum for the eight weekly sessions and two public forums. Advisors learned about the park's history, solving problems with design, then proposed their own design ideas for improved access to, way-finding within, and new functions for the park.

As a result, NYC Parks and the Design Trust are exploring pilot projects, such as themed art entrances to improve access and orientation. NYC Parks has engaged several community advisors as co-facilitators in park visioning sessions. The Queens Museum will host artist residencies and activities in the park to develop other new ideas.

Repurposing streets, making new places

New York City, Chicago, Los Angeles, New Orleans, Philadelphia, San Francisco, Auckland, Mexico City, and Vancouver have converted pavement to "parklets" with trees and plantings, playgrounds, fountains, and cafés. They attract and retain residents, promote public health, contribute to cleaner air, capture storm water, boost real estate values, and draw together people from different walks of life. They are successful when they reflect the hopes and aspirations of each community.

In San Francisco, local activists Rebar Design Collective employed guerrilla tactics to initiate the idea of parklets in 2005. Commandeering one metered parking space on Mission Street at noon, they unrolled ten strips of sod, planted a bench at one end and a tree at the other end, lounging until their meter ran out at 2 PM. A year later, they partnered with the nonprofit Trust for Public Land to spread "PARKing Day" to thirteen cities. It has since become an annual experiment for 162 cities in thirty-five countries, reclaiming metered parking spaces on the third Friday in September.

Diller Scofidio + Renfro and James Corner Field Operations, High Line, New York City

The San Francisco parklets now span two parking spaces with a platform extending the sidewalk with landscaping, bicycle parking, and seating. They must be free and open to the public. Proposals are selected from the adjacent ground-floor business owners, nonprofit groups, or local improvement districts, who bear the costs of up to 25,000 dollars, pay for permits, and maintain the parklets.

To date, over fifty mini-parks have been built, with twenty-five more to come. "In a very real way, these diminutive nooks are San Francisco's most influential urban design innovation," says John King. "The best parklets combine design ambition with a genuine desire to engage the passersby." Blaine Merker of Gehl Studio noted, "they're important when they're seen as the right of citizens to shape our environment and prod cities to do better."

Design Trust for Public Space, *Taxi of Tomorrow* design competition, New York City

Reclaiming industrial areas and infrastructure

New York City's nearly seven hundred miles of elevated transportation infrastructure covers dark, noisy, and neglected spaces, an area four times the size of Central Park. The Design Trust's pivotal study that saved the High Line and its recent *Under the Elevated* project, in partnership with the NYC Department of Transportation, investigated how to reclaim these spaces and to reconnect communities.

In Chicago, Josh Deth and Ben Helphand co-founded Chicago's Friends of the Bloomingdale Trail (FBT) in 2003 to advocate for conversion of a dormant Canada Pacific Railway elevated spur and thirty-seven viaducts into a 2.7-mile-long linear park and bike trail. After their year-long process of charrettes, surveys, and public meetings, the city adopted the "Community Visioning Update" for its Request for Proposal for the

Design Trust for Public Space, NYC Parks, and the Queens Museum, *World's Park* forum, New York City

Parklet, Duane Street, New York City

Chicago Department of Transportation, Bloomingdale Trail, Chicago

Privately owned public space (POPS): Tod Williams and Billie Tsien, David Rubenstein Atrium at Lincoln Center, New York City

project. The Trust for Public Land assisted the city in acquiring access points to the trail.

The first section, Julia de Burgos Park, designed by JJR landscape architects with artist Phil Schuster, opened in summer 2010, galvanizing neighborhood support for the entire trail. In 2011, the Chicago Department of Transportation's "Bloomingdale Trail and Park Framework Plan" expanded the off-road trail network, a mayoral open-space priority. Then Chicago's planners greenlighted nearly 50 million dollars in federal funds with state and local matches for the trail, designed by Michael Van Valkenburgh Associates, which opened in 2015 at a total cost of 95 million dollars. The FBT has now applied to the Chicago Park District to be the official park advisory council.

Repurposing industrial areas and infrastructure is not a new concept, but has become ever more significant to retain urban fabric and memory of historic patrimony in growing urban centers.

Creating privately owned public space (POPS)

In New York City, the 1961 Zoning Resolution inaugurated the incentive zoning program that encouraged private developers to create plazas, small parks, atriums, and through-block arcades within or adjacent to buildings in exchange for increased density or additional floor area in high-density districts.

Hundreds of POPS exist across the globe in Berlin, Chicago, London, New York City, Los Angeles, San Francisco, Seattle, Seoul, and Toronto. Over five hundred POPS in 325 buildings are now part of NYC's urban landscape. They provide hundreds of workers, residents, and visitors with open space. However, these spaces, in their quality and upkeep, often become

I Can Change the World with My Two Hands, communal garden, Amsterdam

inhospitable, trash-strewn, windswept, or inaccessible to the public. Some private entities renovated POPS without the public in mind and without permission from NYC Planning. They removed public seating or denied right of entry under the guise of additional security. In 2007, New York City's zoning text was amended to provide design and operational standards to improve the quality of these public spaces.

One of the most successful POPS is the David Rubenstein Atrium at Lincoln Center, initiated by the NYC cultural institution and designed by architects Tod Williams and Billie Tsien. The formerly bleak arcade with an artificial rock climbing wall between Broadway and Columbus Avenue was transformed into a welcoming space with a host of amenities—free performances, Wi-Fi access, vertical gardens, a textile installation by Dutch artist Claudy Jongstra, a fountain, sixteen "oculi" skylights, information desk, box office for discount tickets, and a gourmet sandwich shop.

Civic activists' protests in Tahrir Square during the Arab Spring and the Occupy Wall Street encampment in Zuccotti Park in 2011 sparked debate about the role that public space plays in societies and cities, especially when the rights to freedom of assembly are exercised on public space that is privately owned. The occupation surfaced questions about the meaning of *public*, about who should have access, how POPS should be managed, and how they should function.

"The planning process is where the private aspirations and the public interest is ultimately reconciled (or not) and therefore is the key to ensuring that this form of public good is as 'good' and as 'public' as we would desire," Matthew Carmona, Professor of Urban Planning at The Bartlett said. "[...] Once permission is given, it is too late."

Seeding transformation with urban agriculture

Conversion of vacant lots for farming and gardening in Detroit, where there has been urban flight, as well as in rapidly urbanizing areas such as Amsterdam, Hong Kong, or New York is seeding transformation through urban agriculture. The legacy of Victory Gardens during the World Wars and community gardening movements of the 1960s and 1970s, such as the Green Guerillas, who reclaimed urban land to solve problems plaguing their neighborhoods, serves as the foundation for vital public space. In the Design Trust's Five Borough Farm project, we found benefits from local farming and community gardening extended well beyond growing food. They build community networks, provide exercise, capture storm water, and clean the air, offer leadership and job-training skills and earned income.

In Landlust, Amsterdam, local artist Natascha Hagenbeek and thirty-five other neighborhood volunteers seized the opportunity to transform a 1,200-meter former swimming pool and playground at a nearby housing block into a communal garden. At the outset, there was no program in place, and public authorities declined turning over public property to private citizens. With strong community support and advocacy to elected officials, the "I Can Change the World with My Two Hands" garden was established in 2010. It provided locally produced fresh food for over one hundred residents, optimizing public space in a cost-effective manner, by working with farmers on the outskirts of the city, and strengthening the social resilience of the neighborhood. Although there was a high percentage of seniors, plots were reserved for neighborhood youth, creating intergenerational opportunities. In 2013,

Participatory design for the Choi Yuen Ecological Village, Hong Kong

a small convenience store called "Access to Tools" opened to sell local products.

Another example of bottom-up planning through urban agriculture is Choi Yuen Ecological Village in Hong Kong's New Territories. In December 2009, two hundred villagers and thousands of supporters protested against relocating the village for the installation of a high-speed rail link from Hong Kong to Beijing. Choi Yuen, which means "vegetable garden," drew unprecedented attention to key issues—under what circumstances should rights of habitation be pushed aside in favor of development concerns? How can Hong Kong maintain a system of sustainable agriculture and a symbiotic relationship between its developing rural areas and green urban areas? Wang Weijen Architecture led a participatory design process that gave professionals greater insight into local needs and resulted in a public-private partnership for an ecological, car-free village with a large communal farm.

Community-led gardens play a transformative role in mitigating the effects of depopulation, displacement, and underemployment during times of economic downturn. The benefits must be maintained when cities start to repopulate and seek development sites. Every effort must be made to achieve a balance between the value of urban farms and community gardens and the need for new housing, transportation, and other needs for a growing population.

Conclusion

Each of these examples demonstrates that any vacant or underused space can be converted into a beneficial public space, if we test different approaches, adapt existing rules of use, care, and modification, and if people and government collaborate to devise ways to share the responsibility to design, construct, and maintain them. This process may be challenging and provoke controversy, but it will undoubtedly lead to new opportunities, new types of places, and improved economic and social well-being in our rapidly urbanizing metropolises.

Matthew Carmona, "41: Neo-Liberal Public Space (and Beyond)," Urban Design Matters (blog), The Bartlett, February 5, 2014, http://www.bartlett.ucl.ac.uk/cross-faculty-initiatives/urban-design/urban-design-matters/urban-design-matters-41-neo-liberal-space.

City & County of San Francisco Planning Department, *Privately Owned Public Space and Public Art*, http://www.sf-planning.org/index.aspx?page=3339 (accessed January 21, 2015).

Mitch Dudek, "Bloomingdale Trail Opening Set for June 6," in *Chicago Sun Times*, April 20, 2015.

Lincoln Center, *David Rubenstein Atrium at Lincoln Center Fact Sheet*, November 13, 2013, http://www.aboutlincolncenter.org/pdfs/transforming/factsheet-atrium.pdf.

John King, "How S.F.'s Parklet Movement Has Grown Across Globe," in *San Francisco Chronicle*, March 30, 2015.

Francesca Miazzo and Tris Kee (eds), *We Own the City: Enabling Community Practice in Architecture and Urban Planning*, Amsterdam: Valiz, 2014.

Making New Parks in North America—New Needs, New Challenges, New Opportunities

Since the late 1980s, my office has been continuously involved in park planning and design in the United States and Canada. While it is difficult to write about history as it is happening, it seems that a twenty-first-century parks movement is in progress in North America at the moment; and from this groundswell of park making, several lessons have emerged.

1. Parks are often commissioned by well-meaning private citizens—civic leaders with little or no experience in park making.

With the exception of existing city parks departments—which my office works with, though very rarely—most clients have the highest aspirations for their parks but often almost no experience in anything related to making a park. Take, for example, the High Line in New York City. It was helmed by Joshua David and Robert Hammond, two young men who had a vision and the political connections to spearhead in less than two decades what would represent close to 500 million dollars in investment. Or Brooklyn Bridge Park, which Joanne Witty, a community organizer, made possible.

Not a single leader of these efforts had ever had anything to do with making a park before, with understanding its cost, its political structure, the importance of consensus building among public and private interests, its physicality, or how to take care of it once it is built. So a major lesson is the mentoring of these people, helping them understand all of the complex interrelationships that come into play, in order for good intentions to turn into a great park. There has emerged a whole world of support groups and professional organizations that address these issues, including private consulting firms that specialize in park management, in park programming, in park economics.

We are also seeing more and more private equity directed toward park making. In Tulsa, Oklahoma, the George Kaiser Family Foundation gave over 200 million dollars for our office's Gathering Place for Tulsa, an eighty-five-acre park on the Arkansas River, which will be the largest privately funded project of its kind ever to be built. And this is just one of several gifts of 100 million dollars or more toward park making across the United States.

2. Today's parks are built on unconventional, challenging sites that require closely assessing unique limits and carefully fitting a vision to those limits.

Sites for urban park making in this century come in many forms, from waterfronts that modern technology and industry have recast to sites affected by rising sea levels to brownfields to seemingly useless elevated rail lines. But they are all generally fragmented and heavily affected by prior land uses. Compare these with, for example, the site for Frederick Law Olmsted and Calvert Vaux's Central Park in New York, which was so large and relatively pristine that its spatial narrative could be left to their imaginations. Fragmented twenty-first-century sites instead offer different and, in some ways, more limited challenges—and often require different spatial strategies altogether. In exchange, these limits often open the door to creative explorations into the spatial design of parks.

Brooklyn Bridge Park was one of my firm's earlier full-blown explorations of new methods of spatial design. We had to forge new kinds of connections with a waterfront and new modes of integrating fragmented spaces. The riverfront at the site is a long strip of relatively narrow land parallel to a major double-stacked highway (the Brooklyn–Queens Expressway), punctuated by a series of abandoned five-acre piers held up by wooden piles—a monotonously long river-edge condition interspersed with totally artificial platform peninsulas.

To create spatial coherence, we made the park a sort of collage. We took advantage of its long, narrow shape to build a thirty-foot-wide, combined walking-and-biking trail to link distant parts. And we turned the isolation of the piers into a virtue. Two piers are totally devoted to active sports so their noise and activities do not distract users in the rest of the park. The lightweight courts and fields of these landscapes also reduced the cost of building on the pile-supported pier decks, encouraging us to put the more traditional, soil-heavy park landscapes on land at the park's edge, where there are no limitations on weight. On Pier 3, in the middle, we designed a more introverted landscape, a central one-acre lawn space with a kind of interiority, surrounded by a landform built with structural foam. We could not have put so large a lawn on the linear uplands. Through the solitude of this pier in the river, the lawn becomes a more focused phenomenon. A rhythm of active and passive landscapes greets you as you move through the park, and this patchwork of program and character throughout the piers stems from both the park's spatial logic and the Brooklyn community's needs.

Given how climate change is elevating sea levels and how often urban parks front the sea, oceanfront parks must now deal with higher, more violent, and

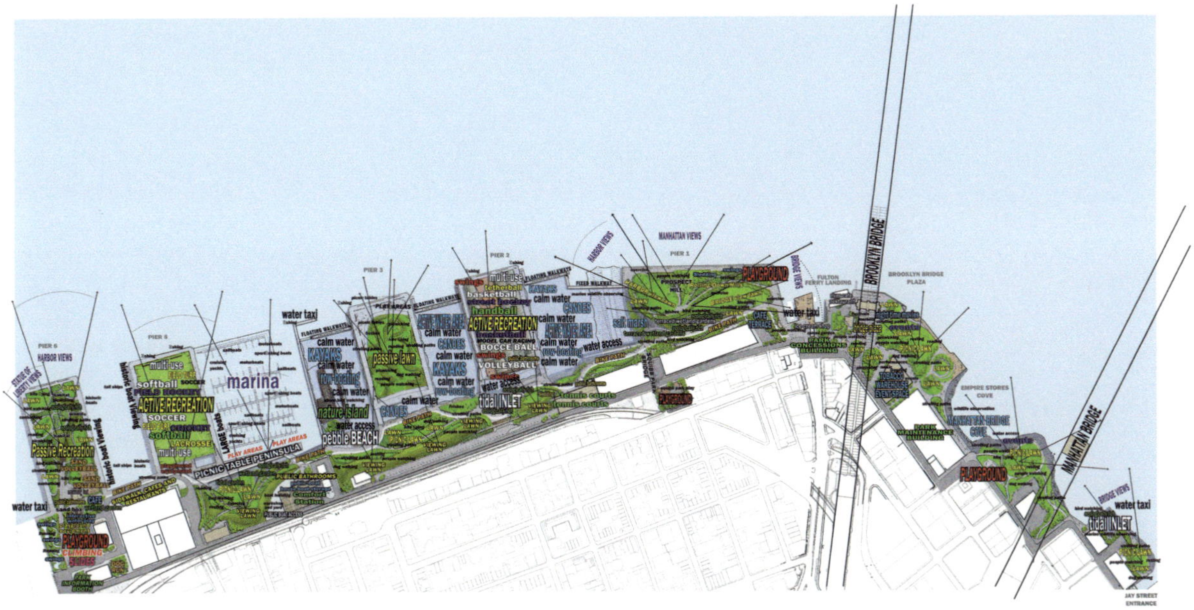

Michael Van Valkenburgh Associates, programming diagram, Brooklyn Bridge Park, New York City

more frequent flooding. Of course, riverfront parks must also deal with flooding. I was fortunate to have been compelled to confront flooding design in my first really big commission.

In 1989, MVVA was chosen to create a master plan for the eighty-five-acre Mill Race Park in Columbus, Indiana—a site that is subject to extreme annual flooding. With fees and costs paid by the Cummins Foundation, the Columbus Parks Board administered the project at the confluence of the Flatrock and Driftwood Rivers in Columbus. The site floods ferociously nearly every spring, with runoff spreading about a foot of water over the entire park. While flooding at the land margins of rivers and oceans imposes limits by requiring that all of the park elements survive the flow of water across the site, these sites can become not only viable but potentially wonderful terrains for parks. Being near water is always wonderful, and the dynamism of the flooding creates its own drama in the park.

We encountered similar issues in 1994, when we were hired to work on a narrow strip of land adjacent to downtown Pittsburgh on the Allegheny riverfront. The difference was that this site was exceptionally narrow—a ribbon of space. Carol Brown, president of the Pittsburgh Cultural Trust—a well-funded not-for-profit agency that had renovated many theaters and even created a cultural district—was advocating downtown as a place to live and believed that the river had great potential to enhance daily life there. Addressing the technical demands of a site that floods violently, and adapting to a very frugal budget, did not preclude a beautiful project. We studied trees found on sites nearby that were subject to the same flooding and used them in our design. We also covered the ground with

Michael Van Valkenburgh Associates, Mill Race Park, Columbus, Indiana

Michael Van Valkenburgh Associates, Mill Race Park, Columbus, Indiana (flood condition)

Michael Van Valkenburgh Associates, Teardrop Park, New York City

heavy stones that would hold the soil in place when the flood water covered the park. This became a major component of the stabilization of the East River edge in Brooklyn Bridge Park a decade later.

3. New urban parks must address the need for well-financed, long-term maintenance.

Allegheny River Park has suffered badly, because our clients, like all others at the time, did not put a maintenance plan in place. A few years later, maintenance became a key consideration in the development of Teardrop Park, which is still my favorite MVVA project and which set the standard for maintenance planning for our firm from then on. For the tiny two-acre park in the Battery Park City neighborhood of Manhattan, New York, the client asked that we use my boyhood region—the Catskill Mountains, two-and-a-half hours' drive north of the site—as inspiration to bring to city kids something that captured some of the wildness of a larger rural landscape. As naïve as this was, and as hard as it was to do on such a small site (in a city where Olmsted tried something similar on nine hundred acres), it was liberating. The centerpiece is an eighteen-foot-high wall of cut bluestone, patterned to suggest the layers of bluestone and their uplift through plate tectonics; ice or water can be found on the rocks year round.

The client had the brilliant foresight to include the staff of the Parks Maintenance Department for Battery Park City in the design process, knowing that as a park's design evolves, it needs to address the personnel and methods of park maintenance. The staff's criticisms of our proposals became drivers of the design, and as a result the transition from design to construction to maintenance flowed seamlessly. If only other New York parks could unfold this way.

In 1998, when we were on a team to master-plan Brooklyn Bridge Park, determining and meeting the future need for maintenance funding was also a major focus. The park resulted from a decade-long discussion about the use of its waterfront land. The story of how the park was created is one of the great stories of New York's history. It began in 1985 with Brooklyn Heights neighbors gradually organizing funding to commission a master plan. The real stroke of genius came when the professionals who developed the park's economic master plan asked Mayor Michael Bloomberg and Governor George Pataki to form a partnership and put up the capital for the park. Led by the economic-planning firm HR&A Advisors, they created a proposal that took the new housing that almost always gets built along the edges of parks and, instead of channeling its real-estate tax revenues into the general city or state tax stream, pooled the money in a fund that maintains the park in perpetuity.

Michael Van Valkenburgh Associates, Penn Park, Philadelphia

Michael Van Valkenburgh Associates, Penn Park, Philadelphia

The political kernel of HR&A's idea was that the city and the state only had to come up with the money to build the park. The Port Authority gave the land and the new tax revenue would pay for the maintenance. The property tax idea offered a new model, shrewdly redirecting the value added by the park back to the park itself.

Urban history, especially in New York, underscores the prudence of this new mode of financing. Just a few decades ago, parks in New York City were in terrible shape. Central Park tends to be seen as the favorite daughter, held up as the shining example of a park brought back from the brink. But it is important to remember that other places, like Brooklyn's Prospect Park, also neared collapse. In economic downturns, guaranteeing that streets are still plowed and garbage is still picked up often means that park maintenance funding is gutted. The potential for this kind of sudden recession can threaten the future of any large city park.

Some have argued, perhaps rightly so, that cities owe their citizens the building and upkeep of parks without requiring the parks to be self-sustaining through development. But American urban history since the late 1880s has shown that even though cities can build large, magnificent parks, these parks can be destroyed by the intensity of their use, unless their maintenance is vigilant and ongoing. And parks are extraordinarily expensive to maintain. Brooklyn Bridge Park's maintenance funding approaches 15 million dollars per year. The 400-million-dollar price tag of its design and construction, considerable in its own right, will be matched by the maintenance cost of the park in just three decades. Still, the property-tax solution is the most controversial aspect of the park.

Even if its tax revenue were not available for maintenance costs, our team felt that putting housing along the park was the right thing to do. The park is isolated from existing housing in adjacent neighborhoods by the colossal Brooklyn–Queens Expressway. My firm argued that both the park and housing would be safer and more pleasant if the proposed housing was attached at the edge below the Expressway—not floating in the park, but next to it, like the apartments that line Prospect Park and Central Park.

4. Contemporary urban parks offer a way to encourage positive social interaction and tolerance.

In 1989, Mill Race Park signaled the beginning of an era when cities again wanted their downtown residents to have places for outdoor enjoyment, with parks as important restorative escapes. (What would become the "project for public spaces" movement to intensively activate parks with people was then beginning. While this isn't a bad impulse in itself, of course, what it sometimes resulted in was the often cheesy commercialization of parks with kiosks and cafés at every turn.) Along with this push for outdoor activities came an unprecedented interest in sports, fitness, nutrition, and health among Americans, and in many parks one can observe a kind of exercise exhibitionism. In park planning, this plays itself out with great drama in the age-old debate about how much of the landscape should be assigned to active uses and how much to passive appreciation.

These days, active is winning, hands down. My firm's Penn Park at the University of Pennsylvania in Philadelphia is in a sense distinctive, since it was made primarily to expand the university's athletic facilities and only secondarily to provide parklands. But Penn Park serves as a good example of how far a park can go toward being a place of sports and activity and still have a lot else to offer. The landscape device that counterbalances the extensive, flat sports fields is a highly animated circulation spine that sweeps down to the sunken site from the surrounding elevated streets. A system of large, sculptural landforms further organizes the site and gives pedestrians views of the nearby athletic areas and the city of Philadelphia in the distance.

Brooklyn Bridge Park was planned, early on, to include a wide range of active recreational opportunities. Facilities for volleyball, basketball, soccer, handball, boccie, boating, roller-skating, and more are all woven into the park, along with several places for concerts and large gatherings. Early in the planning process, though, it became evident that some affluent Brooklyn Heights residents—many of the same people who worked so hard to make a park possible in the first place—weren't eager to have the rest of Brooklyn's residents come to the park. They thought it would be spoiled.

The rest of Brooklyn is significantly more racially and socioeconomically diverse. Fifteen years after those contentious planning meetings, Pier 2 is finished. Over half of it is devoted to full-court basketball, under a roof, lighted at night, and floating in the East River—truly one of the most amazing places in the world to play basketball. And those Brooklyn neighbors were partly right: when you build a glorious place to play ball on a summer night, kids of different ethnic backgrounds will come from neighborhoods all over Brooklyn. On the upland of Pier 5, at what we call the Picnic Peninsula, lots of picnic tables, shade umbrellas, and grills are free to use. When we designed this area, we knew it would not be for those summering in the Hamptons—or summering anywhere at all, for that matter—but its visitors would come and enjoy an unexpected community of people sharing a beautiful and functional public space.

The wealthy neighbors were fundamentally wrong to think that the park would be harmed. The diverse users attracted to Brooklyn Bridge Park have demonstrated how parks can change our feelings and loosen our stereotypes about groups of people that we do not know particularly well. Many nights this summer I have been taking a sunset stroll, and I have seen groups of five or six black young men walking with a basketball into the park, often (I know from asking) from far-flung parts of Brooklyn.

What is the significance of all this? It has to do with the imperative to overcome the racist stereotyping that has led to violence in the United States in recent years. Parks can help. Olmsted is said to have made the paths in Central Park curve so you would be forced to encounter strangers that you could not see coming. More important than anything else that this (or any) park may offer—more than views of the harbor and places to play in water in the summer heat, volleyball on a summer night, soccer in February on a lit field, a wedding on a granite prospect, or a ride on a carousel—is the fact that you do these things next to people whom you do not know, and then you see that we are all alike in at least one way: how parks make us feel good.

Michael Van Valkenburgh Associates, Brooklyn Bridge Park, basketball courts, Pier 2, New York City

Strolling through Public Space—Remarks on the City and the Public Realm in the Early Twenty-First Century

"On the Greek island of Santorini the tourists applaud the sunset every evening. Hence, we can't rule out that the sun sets at this site for aesthetic reasons."[1] This observation by Bert Theis, an artist from Luxembourg, refers to the typical "event marketing" of everyday life processes, particularly in the highly technologized societies of the early twenty-first century: everything is staged and marketed, the star cult has outdone itself, even a sunset is experienced as though it were a play. Causal responsibility goes to the completed passage from "old" industrial societies to "new" information societies over the past twenty years, during which people have personally experienced becoming anonymous and de-individualized on a daily basis.

Parallel to this, despite substantial relief through the Internet and mobile phones, the course of the day has become increasingly rapid, even reaching a tearing pace. To counteract this, urban planners and artists demand a "deceleration" of public space, since according to the American artist Vito Acconci: "Time is fast, and space is slow. Space is an attempt to place time and understand time."[2]

But where is public space and where is the site of art in this arrangement?[3] The term "Public Art" generally designates works outdoors, in outside space, which are not obliged to any museum-based or other institutional context. However, outdoors means more than simply the opposite of the white cube's indoor space: What is crucial here is the specification as so-called "public" space. One would have a hard time identifying a field in Germany's Allgäu or a beach on the North Sea as a public space; instead, they would simply be classified as "areas."[4] In contrast, "public space" always indicates a city-based, i.e. urban, structure as a user surface for human communication. On the other hand, in recent years an increasing privatization of public space can be observed: a succinct example of this is Potsdamer Platz in Berlin, where, although freely accessible by all, if necessary, even the practicing of basic civil rights such as demonstrations can be prohibited. To this extent, public space is a social and psychological state—or in an artistic sense—a space of narration that is subjected to concrete architectural, historical, and social conditions rather than a geographically or topographically specified site. In blunt terms, the *white cube* of the museum as an exhibition site for autonomous art thus faces the *dirty space* of the city as a venue for Public Art.[5]

Since the mid-1990s, the virtual field of new media—the Internet, electronic correspondence, home shopping, mobile telephoning, and mainly social media—has been added at an unprecedented speed to concretely graspable public space in the organization and realization of human activities and sensibilities, and now clearly dominates the structures of everyday life. Already in 1974, in a study financed by the Rockefeller Foundation, no less than the likes of Nam June Paik, the "pope of video art," quasi-clairvoyantly demanded a "free haven for information."[6] According to Paik, trade in cars, washing machines, televisions, etc., must be replaced in the future by trade in information, i.e., knowledge, to guarantee Western societies a perspective for the future. Now, a good forty years later, the worldwide flows of information and data highways, which Paik already identified back then as "Electronic Superhighways," are self-evident components of our everyday lives. But this virtual space of action has in no way been able to replace the traditional public space of the city—quite the opposite: precisely the new, media-induced retreat into one's own four walls—PlayStation rather than playground, Facebook rather than face-to-face in the pub—has made obvious the necessity and continuity of a city's urban structures as venues of human dialogue. To this extent, art in these public spaces has an increasingly concrete function on an equal footing alongside architectural and urban planning, which through the creation of pedestrian zones, urban furniture, and shopping streets in past decades, have led many European cities to become gray, isolated deserts. After closing hours, city centers are vacated with menacing speed and turn desolate; subway tunnels and underground pedestrian passageways become platforms for violence, the aesthetics defined by what urban planners call "secondary architecture": containers for old glass, waste paper baskets, park benches, streetlights, bicycle stands, boundary posts, etc.; urban furniture, i.e., what today carpets all Western European city centers—in particular their lifeless pedestrian zones. Here, the key significance of art in the city—to quote the French old master Daniel Buren—is to "give each of us, whether we are aware of it or not, the possibility to breathe [...] contemporary art, like philosophy is decisive for the development of humanity, for its urge for freedom."[7]

1 Bert Theis, "Einige Samples," in Florian Matzner (ed.), *Public Art: Kunst im öffentlichen Raum*, Ostfildern: Hatje Cantz, 2001, p. 112.

2 Vito Acconci, "Leaving Home: Notes on Insertions into the Public," in Matzner, *Public Art*, p. 46.

Thomas Hirschhorn, *Bataille-Monument*, 2002, Friedrich-Wöhler-Siedlung in Kassel, on the occasion of *documenta 11*

But over the past forty years these venues of—mainly also—artistic freedom have significantly changed and fundamentally shifted within urban structures: whereas the 1960s and 1970s were influenced by Minimal Art, Land Art, Concept Art, and autonomous interventions by Donald Judd and Robert Smithson or Richard Serra and Claes Oldenburg, in the early 1980s a fundamental change occurred. Under the buzzword "site-specific", it was most likely Robert Smithson who first postulated that, "the artwork is not set up at a site, the site itself is the artwork."[8] And Richard Serra also confirmed that "at least with most sculptures, the experience of the work is inseparable from the place in which the work resides. Apart from that condition, any experience of the work is a deception."[9] In this discussion, "drop sculptures" were set opposite the "site-specificity" of an artwork: the "drop sculptures" appear without any comprehensible meaningful or formal reference to their location, as if "dropped from the sky," which disqualifies such sculptures as, for example, those of Henry Moore. In contrast, one propagated the site-specificity of an artwork that had a concrete relationship to the architectural, urban, and historical context of its location and created a dialogue between "site" and "work," so that a previously meaningless site is made to "speak."

"I don't know for sure everything that is public space for me. Simply being able to pose, for just a second, a provisional, temporary question in it is a lot. In this context, also temporary answers are interesting, because a colossal notion can also come at that moment, in this second."[10] The Düsseldorf artist Bogomir Ecker thus voiced his mistrust of how artists deal with public space and its rapid change and new definition after the boom of Public Art in the 1980s. Since the mid-1990s, added to the site-specific is the—let's call it—"audience-specific," which means the artist's attempt to work with concrete social groups, to include them in the process of creation and realization. The artwork is only complete through a high share of participation, through actively participating and intervening recipients. Rather than prominent spots or squares in the city, non-sites and non-places are deliberately chosen that often previously had no urban or social function.

Indicated examples are two outstanding projects of such artistically "provoked" audience specificity: Thomas Hirschhorn realized his *Bataille-Monument* in the summer of 2002 at the *documenta 11* in Kassel. After personally living and working on site for several months, Hirschhorn created his project outside the official exhibition route in cooperation with mainly Turkish youths and under the guidance of a professional social worker. The *Bataille Monument* is thus to be understood as a provocative artistic rejection of the *documenta* as an exhibition institution, while on the other hand, precisely the non-local audience was shown a part of Kassel and a local social situation that an art connoisseur would normally not notice or want to notice. In addition, as a countermove, a sector of society for whom contemporary art is often a foreign word was actively confronted with art. A second example is the contribution by the young, Vienna-based artist Anna Witt to the *Emscherkunst.2013* exhibition in the summer of 2013. Like Thomas Hirschhorn, she quite deliberately realized her project in a social hotspot. In the Marxloh neighborhood of the German city of Duisburg in the Ruhr region, in cooperation with the local population, she realized what at first glance appeared to be an odd project entitled *Breaking New*. With a team of roaming craftsmen under the aesthetic and conceptual

3 The present text is the revised and updated version of two articles on the theme of public art in Söke Dinkla (ed.), *PubliCity: Constructing the Truth*, exhibition catalog, Nuremberg: Verlag für Moderne Kunst, 2006, pp. 18–21, and Barbara Lutz-Sterzenbach et al. (eds), *Bild und Bildung*, Munich: kopaed, 2014, pp. 497–504; see also Florian Matzner, "Einige Anmerkungen zur Öffentlichkeit in Kunst," in Ulrich Hatzfeld et al. (eds), *Kunst (be)zeichnet Stadt*, Münster: Imrode Kunst und Projektberatung, 2000, pp. 40–45; Matzner et al. (eds), *No Art=No City! Stadtutopien in der zeigenössischen Kunst*, Ostfildern: Hatje Cantz, 2003; Matzner, "Kunst im öffentlichen Raum: Geschichte und Konzepte," in Österreichischer Skulpturepark Privatstiftung (ed.), Garten der Kunst: *Österreichischer Skulp-turenpark Graz*, Ostfildern: Hatje Cantz, 2006, pp. 45–67; the catalog for the exhibition *Emscherkunst 2010* and *2013*, Florian Matzner et al. (eds), Ostfildern: Hatje Cantz, 2010 and 2013, and finally Florian Matzner (ed.), *Tatort Paderborn*, Bielefeld: Kerber, 2014.

4 Walter Grasskamp, "Kunst und Stadt," in Klaus Bußmann, Klaus König, and Florian Matzner (eds), *Skulptur.Projekte in Münster 1997*, ex. cat., Ostfildern: Hatje Cantz, 1997, pp. 11–13; see also glossary in Brigitte Franzen, Kaspar König, and Carina Plath (eds), *skulptur projekte münster 07*, ex. cat., Cologne: Walther König, 2007, pp. 323–475.

5 Stephan Huber, Florian Matzner, and Hermann Pitz, "Never Evergreen," in Stephan Huber et al. (eds), *Evergreen*, ex. cat., Munich: Akademie der Bildenden Künste, 2005, esp. p. 14.

6 Nam June Paik, "Venice III: 1975, The City of Cologne Stole My Idea, Venice IV: 1993, Bill Clinton Stole My Idea," in Klaus Bußmann and Florian Matzner (eds), *Nam June Paik: eine DATAbase*, ex. cat., Ostfildern: Cantz, 1993, pp. 109–114.

Thomas Hirschhorn, *Bataille-Monument*, 2002, Friedrich-Wöhler-Siedlung in Kassel, on the occasion of *documenta 11*

Anna Witt and Uglycute, *Breaking New*, 2013, Duisburg Marxloh, on the occasion of the exhibition *Emscherkunst.2013*

guidance of the Swedish designer group Uglycute, she had the daily bulky waste that the residents put out on the street at night "recycled" into new furniture and other functional objects and thus practically upgraded: she opposed a throw-away ideology with a strategy of sustainability, adding a touch of humor.

Artist, art, and audience enter into a new, different mutual relationship in the sense of this "audience specificity," whereby the artist becomes the moderator of a not always calculable social situation—a situation that still bears significant risk and is open-ended.

Public Art is not all that has changed fundamentally over the past twenty years—above all, so has its stage, the city itself—and vice versa: the latest studies show that many major Western European cities will shrink considerably in the coming decade. What is meanwhile obvious for Detroit in the US, Manchester and Liverpool in Great Britain, and Halle in Germany will also be important for entire regions and agglomerations such as the Ruhr region, including Essen and Duisburg where a depopulation of more than 10 percent is anticipated.[11] Added to that are modern nomadism, emigration and immigration, and the separation of work and living areas, as the classic "guest worker" of the 1960s and 1970s is replaced in future by foreign workers living in containers, who along with their families at home, do not even know exactly which metropolis they are currently in. Added to that are gated communities,which will no longer be limited to the US alone.[12] The first gated cities have meanwhile been built in Europe: more than ten years ago in Berlin, under the deceptive name *Arcadia*, "exclusive residences in valuable locations" were more or less isolated from the outside world by means of security measures, locked walls, guard services, entry restrictions, etc., much like the Novartis Campus in Basel, a "forbidden city," as the architectural historian Andreas Tönnesmann describes it.[13] Added to that are the so-called televillages, which have already been planned and realized close to Paris: neighborhoods where people not only live, but are faced with the threatening loss of all connection to reality as they sit at local computer work stations and do not even have to leave their apartments to shop, as supermarket purchases made by e-mail or SMS are, of course, delivered free, and social interactions are maintained in a conflict-neutral way, via Facebook.[14]

Concrete vacant spaces, extra areas, and non-sites will thus arise in cities, which can be understood as a chance or risk. Numerous artists have confronted these motifs in past years and—incidentally, faster and more efficiently than urban planners and social psychologists—developed alternatives, such as Marjetica Potrč from Slovenia who in her "case studies" records and develops solutions for urban and social problems in major Western cities—in doing so, the artist becomes a hi-tech nomad![15] Already years ago, Potrč stated, "I think that cities need empty buildings (calm sites), just like a person needs a place to sleep. Apart from that, vacant urban spaces are good for daydreaming."[16] The area of the former Tempelhof Airport in Berlin is a succinct example of the occupation and reutilization of a former abandoned area. In the French city of Nantes, free areas—parks as well as traffic islands—were transformed in a grand style to agriculturally cultivated grounds in which the inhabitants experience public space in an entirely new and different way, as owners, so to speak.

The motif of empty spaces, residual areas in the city that are unused and therefore extensively available for new, different functions in the future, also occupied

7 Daniel Buren, "Über die Funktion der zeitgenössischen Kunst," in Florian Matzner, "Künstlerumfrage," in Olaf Metzel, *Basisarbeit*, Munich: Akademie der Bildenden Künste, 1999, p. 178.

8 Robert Smithson, *Gesammelte Schriften*, ed. Eva Schmidt and Klaus Vöckler, Cologne: Walther König, 2000, p. 242; Andreas Sieckmann pointed out that Smithson was probably the first to introduce the term "site-specificity" in 1970 at the Earth Symposion at Cornwall University, see Sieckmann, "Timeline zur Ausstellungspolitik," in Markus Wailand and Vitus H. Weh, *Zur Sache Kunst am Bau: Ein Handbuch, Vienna: Triton*, 1998, p. 72.

9 Richard Serra, "Extended Notes from Sight Point Road," in Serra, *Recent Sculptures in Europe 1977–1985*, Bochum: Galerie m, 1985, p. 12.

10 Bogomir Ecker, qtd. in Florian Matzner, *Dokumentationskarten Petuelpark München*, Munich: Baureferat der Stadt München, 2004, n.p.

11 On shrinking cities, see Philipp Oswalt, *Schrumpfende Städte*, Ostfildern: Hatje Cantz, 2005.

Anna Witt and Uglycute, *Breaking New*, 2013, Duisburg Marxloh, on the occasion of the exhibition *Emscherkunst.2013*

the German artist Olaf Nicolai. He thereby introduced the motif of freedom, i.e., human autonomy, in *Exterritorial*, a concrete project in which he postulated, "guaranteeing an area the legal status of extraterritorial grounds, and documenting this attempt at its various phases—from legal opinion to the formation of public opinion, through to political decision making. The discussion of the possibility or impossibility of such a site shows the boundaries of a social concept of space and law and the position of the individual in and to it."[17] What Nicolai provocatively addresses and at the same time calls for, corresponds with an aspect that has been referred to several times already: along with the increasing anonymization and acceleration of the course of our everyday lives, public space and people's behavior in and with it has also attained a different quality. Whereas "before," one closed the door of the room to talk on the telephone in peace, today, pressing relationship issues that cannot be put off are taken care of on cell phones in street cars with countless witnesses. The slow industrial society of the late twentieth-century has suddenly become the fast information society of the twenty-first century, or as Bert Theis stated, a "neoliberal stress society" that succumbs to the sham of dealing more efficiently and thriftily than previous generations with the "factor of time."[18] Precisely here, contemporary art has the task of addressing the boundary, which is beginning to blur, between acceleration and deceleration. To quote Vito Acconci once again, "time is fast, and space is slow. Space is an attempt to place time and understand time; space is a need to have something to see and solid ground to stand on; space is a desire to follow the course of events and to believe in cause and effect." In this context of locating the individual in the network of space and time, the intersections between privacy and publicity, and furthermore, between virtuality and reality, seem to be losing their validity at an increasing rate. In connection with her *Urban Case Studies*, Marjetica Potrč realized: "but there is a twist there: we gladly sublimate reality, don't we? It is not reality that is there—what's there is what we believe reality to be."[19]

12 Annabel Dillig, "Wohnst Du noch oder wachst Du schon? Sicherheit als Statussymbol. Auch in Europe schotten sich immer mehr Menschen in Gated Communties ab," in *Süddeutsche Zeitung*, January 13, 2006.

13 "Von der Wiederkehr der verbotenen Stadt. Interview mit Andreas Tönnesmann," in *Süddeutsche Zeitung*, February 10, 2014.

14 Florian Matzner, "Kunst und öffentlicher Raum: ein Forderungskatalog," in Elisabeth Montag Stiftung (ed.), *Lasst uns 3 Hütten bauen: Zeitgenössische bildende Kunst und Architektur im Dialog*, Bramsche: rasch, 2005, esp. p. 101.

15 Lívia Páldi, "Die Neuverortung der Vorstellungskraft," in Matzner, *No Art=No City!*, pp. 124–129.

16 Marjetica Potrč, in Bußmann et al., *Skulptur. Projekte in Münster 1997*, p. 324. See also corresponding documentation in Susanne Witzgall, Florian Matzner, and Iris Meder (eds), *(Re) Designing Nature: Aktuelle Positionen der Naturgestaltung in Kunst und Landschaftsarchitektur*, ex. cat., Ostfildern: Hatje Cantz, 2011.

17 Olaf Nicolai, "Vorschlag für ein Projekt," in Matzner, *No Art=No City!*, p. 108 ff.

18 Theis, "Einige Samples," p. 110.

19 Marjetica Potrč, in Metzel, *Basisarbeit*, p. 187.

Art in Public Space as a Metaphor for the City

Up until the 1960s, public space was dominated by two art forms: eminent male figures in bronze or representative large sculptures in front of bank buildings. But art interventions and the opportunities that arose with the new medium of television soon after revolutionized public space as an artistic medium. New, more radical schools of thought invaded the urban environment. The idea of ownership of the public space was redefined, and artists purposely directed attention to peripheral sites like parking decks or landfills.

All of a sudden, artistic interventions that were happening in New York could also be seen in Cologne or Munich; world art became part of collective memory. Artists began to tap into these new possibilities, trying to involve parts of society that traditionally had little connection to the art world through experimental methods of art expression and communication. German public television broadcasted these new art movements like Happening or Fluxus, showed video installations and performance art, covered the *documenta* in Kassel, and even brought progressive action artist Joseph Beuys into the studio, who, squeezed in between the slots of popular comedian Loriot and sundry quiz shows, elaborated on his progressive artistic idea of the social sculpture and has since been commonly known as "the man with the hat."

Cellist and performance artist Charlotte Moorman envisioned an art that would be free and openly accessible to anyone. In 1963, she founded the Avant-Garde Festival in New York, which brought art projects to parks and public spaces with the idea to reach out to the general population of the city. Moorman defined art as dialogue and accordingly cooperated with a whole number of protagonists in the multimedia art scene of the time, among them John Cage, Yoko Ono, John Lennon, Joseph Beuys, Wolf Vostell, and Carolee Schneemann. The performances she created with Nam June Paik, *TV Bra for Living Sculpture and Chamber Music* (both 1969), in particular, were spectacular happenings for which she ordained her naked body with the new medium video in the form of TV screens. (The media scandalized these video concerts as sex orgies and labeled Moorman a "topless cellist"). These kinds of artistic cooperations and dialogues spawned entirely new democratic and interdisciplinary art forms, through which artists could now formulate their visions communally—a concept that was diametrically opposed to the then-prevalent and age-old tradition of the lone, self-obsessed male artist wolf.

Art in the public urban space—in contrast to art in the white cubes of museums and other cultural institutions—reaches a much broader audience that, in turn, might have ambivalent reactions to it. Christo and Jeanne-Claude with their bold large-scale spatial projects reference phantastical constructions in relation to landscapes and buildings, for example, when covering up the Reichstag in Berlin in 1995. Richard Serra's sculpture *Tilted Arc*, meanwhile, exhibited on the Federal Plaza in Lower Manhattan in 1981 as part of the "Art in Architecture" program, was met with little appreciation from the public. With the sculpture at the center of the square, passersby felt hindered from crossing the plaza diagonally, which led to protests and eventually, in 1989, resulted in the removal of the 37-meter-long curved steel scultpure. What we learn from this anecdote is that art, zeitgeist, and social and urban space are all part of a symbiosis and that an installation of any kind in public space has to be in tune with the psychological quality of its location. At the same time, artists cannot be expected to simply cover up social, municipal, or architectural misplanning.

As early as 2001, Thomas Levin, curator of the exhibition *control space* at the Center for Art and Media Technology (ZKM) in Karlsruhe, Germany, drew attention to the pervasive surveillance of public space by investigating the "spectrum of social control mechanisms" in history and presenting different artistic methods to render these visible and reduce them to absurdity.

Teaching at the Maryland Institute College of Art in Baltimore in 2009 (the city has one of the highest crime rates in the US and several no-go zones), Frieder Schnock and I invited a high-ranking police official to speak to the students of our seminar "Art Goes Public" and to offer a different reading of the city of Baltimore, far from architectural and historical conceptions, far from an artist's perspective. Who lives where? Which areas are dangerous? How can we tell? And what could be possible artistic means to address this? Baltimore uses surveillance cameras and blue lights to indicate difficult neighborhoods. "Blue light districts" were created with the idea to warn passersby not to linger there. Together with our students, we created the public-space project *Bleu du mal* (inspired by Baudelaire's *Fleurs du mal*) to investigate the extent to which blue light can influence social space and if there are ways to eradicate social injustice through aesthetic means, or to use art to increase orientation in deprived areas. We wanted to find out if art can be an instrument to introduce residents of these neighborhoods to the architecture and history of their city and to involve them in creative processes. What we found, however, was that artistic interventions can only ever be effective when combined with fundamental improvemens in the welfare of citizens.

For other installations our aim was to reinterpret specific public spaces through art. *Einladung* was conceived as a social experiment in the Alexanderplatz subway station of line U2 in Berlin. The station had already served as a public underground exhibition space before the fall of the Berlin Wall ("Art instead of Ads"). If only for a few moments, these kinds of places facilitate interaction between people who either have something to give or are looking for something. Thus, we transformed this transitory space into a swap meet for human needs and exhibited existing social conditions on thirty-two colorful billboards. In the exhibition catalog, Andreas Ruby writes, "step by step, from billboard to billboard, it dawns on us that this is a showcase of Berlin's support groups. People fighting problems of whose existence we might be aware, but which we never actually see out in the open. A silent part of society, a minority that is pushed into the blind spots of public perception. Now they are out in the spotlight of the big city, visible for everyone [...]. And by directly and boldly addressing the 'normal' public, the campaign makes us consider these mechanisms of exclusion and think about the part we ourselves might play in them."

On the public stage of a subway station, people are making a decision for themselves if they are willing to take responsibility; they become interpreters of their own character and assume an objective perspective. A different approach was taken by the Viennese Actionism (1968) protagonists VALIE EXPORT and Peter Weibel with their performance piece *Aus der Mappe der Hundigkeit*—during which she lead a crawling Peter Weibel through the city on a leash—or the protagonists of Tino Sehgal's roleplays, who subjects his audience to surprising, but meticulously planned situations. Both projects follow in the footsteps of the *Volkstheater* [popular theater].

Propagandistic methods that can be translated into a public or museum space enable a direct dialogue with the audience. For Eckhart Gillen's exhibition *Deutschlandbilder*, we created the work *Neues Deutschland/BILD*, presenting the struggle of East German vs. West German ideology by comparing headlines from two influential dailies, the *Neues Deutschland* and the *Bild* on a day-to-day basis from ten significant years between 1945 (end of World War II) and 1989 (fall of the Berlin Wall). We originally planned to install the ten-hour-long video as an LED wall on the façade of the Martin-Gropius-Bau in central Berlin, thus broadcasting its message far into the urban surroundings

Stih & Schnock, *Bus Stop*: Berlin–Buchenwald, 1995

like the Springer high-rise once did (and is once again doing today). The installation had to be moved inside for reasons of building heritage protection, but it still managed to fascinate multitudes of visitors for hours on end. This modern history collection mobilizes moments of collective memory, while simultaneously encouraging the audience to draw individual conclusions. Today, the video installation is part of the Zeitgeschichtliches Forum Leipzig, the very place where the democratic movement of the GDR originated.

A similar idea lies at the heart of Daniela Comani's piece *ich war's* [it was me], however, she chronicles global events of the entire twentieth-century in the style of a diary, day by day; she defines them as her personal historiography and takes responsibility for each and every event. Her work was translated into numerous languages and different media and was exhibited worldwide, both in museums as well as outside, on façades, as for example at the 2011 Art Biennale in Venice.

This type of remembrance art, in particular, became an important part of Berlin's identity after the fall of the wall. In those years, Frieder Schnock and I formulated the memorial concepts *Orte des Erinnerns* and *Bus Stop*. In the early 1990s, our familiar postwar world order was changing, East–West, North–South relations were falling apart and were being pieced together in new yet different constellations. West Berlin was suddenly open, penetrable, unprotected; East Berlin seemed freely accessible. In these moments of confusion in reunited Germany, art provided a constant, and topics of cultural politics, like the artistic confrontation of the German past, the Third Reich, and especially the Holocaust came to the fore. Public space became a democratic soapbox; (pre-Internet) media outlets like newspapers, television, or radio extensively contributed

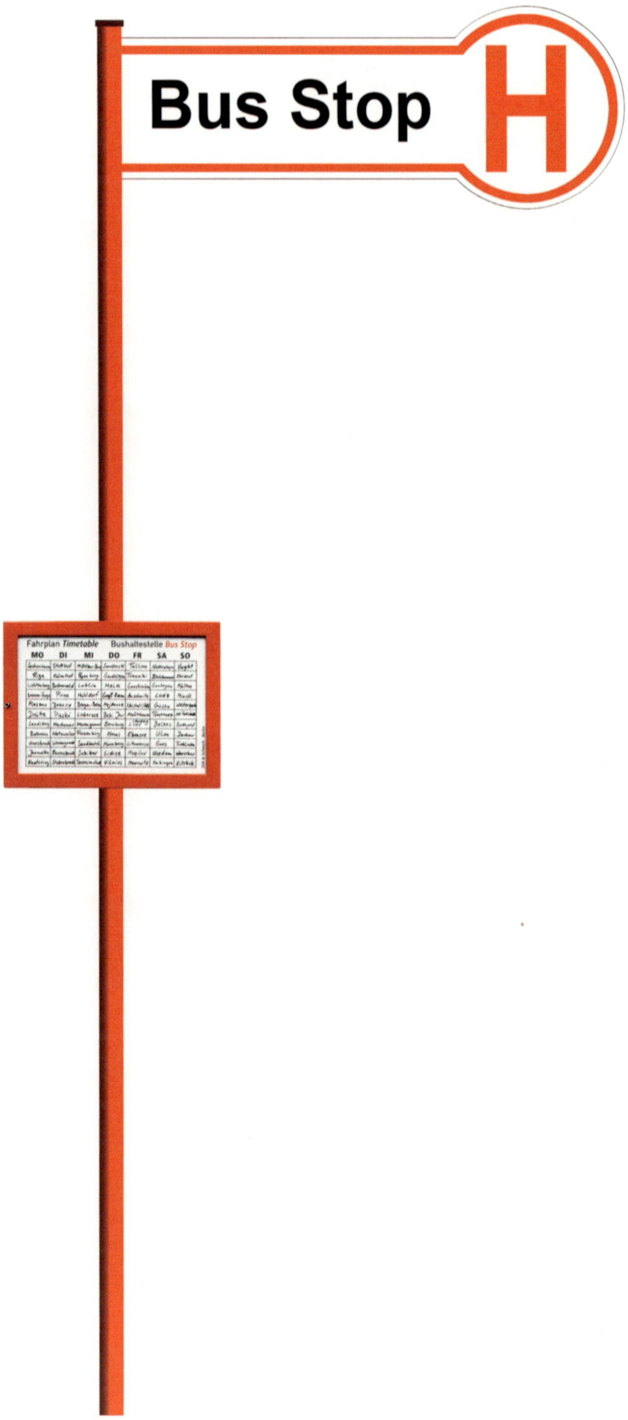

Stih & Schnock, *Bus Stop*: destinations and schedule, 1995

to the discussions and documentation. It was a time of democratic departure that once again called for new concepts of art and communication. And once more, art left the confines of the museum to conquer urban space—under the critical scrutiny of the institutions.

History was reconsidered; citizen-led campaigns sprang up which investigated and brought to light the historical traces of National Socialism in their own neighborhoods. Their objective was a new culture of visibility of the past and the creation of monuments and memorials, as for example in the "Bayerisches Viertel," part of Berlin's district of Schöneberg. Also known as "Jewish Switzerland" before 1933, the neighborhood was home to a number of intellectuals such as Hannah Arendt, Gisèle Freund, Albert Einstein, and Carl Einstein. This harmonious community was destroyed after the Nazis' rise to power, and Jewish life, Jewish culture was eradicated. Schöneberg's aim was to show that these events had not been forgotten, and thus, Berlin's Senator for Building and Housing announced an open, two-stage competition in 1991, which received submissions from ninety-six artists. The proposed designs were then presented to residents in exhibitions and round-table discussions over the course of two years. From these ninety-six submissions, a jury of art professionals finally chose Stih & Schnock's concept *Orte des Erinnerns*, which did, in fact, not in the least comply with the original demands of the competition brief, but ventured an entirely new, more radical concept of a decentralized memorial.

The original idea foresaw the erection of a memorial in the middle of the Bayerischer Platz on Grunewaldstraße in memory of the Jewish citizens who had seen their rights taken away, who had been persecuted and murdered by the Nazi regime. In our opinion, however, the square was ill-suited for an art installation; its once elegant, sober layout, redesigned in the 1950s, now appeared overblown and crowded.

At the time, the district displayed a typical West German building stock, a mix of *Gründerzeit*-style grand townhouses interspersed with the prosaic public housing projects of the postwar period, disjointed gap sites, and traces of bullet holes on dull façades. The Senate of West Berlin had resided here before the reunification; Kennedy had spoken his legendary words "Ich bin ein Berliner" here (1963), and the Shah of Iran's security squad clashed with protesters (1967); but now the streets appeared empty. The occasional dogwalker, a neighbor polishing their car—the eerie silence of complacent middle-class life. At first glance, there was no sign at all of the dramatic events that had taken place here between 1933 and 1945, something we planned to change once and for all with *Orte des Erinnerns*.

Dismissing the Bayerische Platz as a location, we wanted to situate the memorial in close proximity to the local residents, thereby giving this urban space a new face. We aimed to create an art concept that would actively work against oblivion, one that would be hard to miss, that would be explanatory, and include familiar areas of everyday life, easy to understand for children, adolescents, as well as the coming generations.

Extensive research went into the development of *Orte des Erinnerns*, a process that would become symptomatic for our collaborative work. We interviewed passersby on the streets using concealed recording devices to find out how much of these historical events was still present in people's memory. These findings were later documented in the publication *Arbeitsbuch für ein Denkmal*, which has been published as part of the memorial since it was first installed. The memory of the city, which can be found in the collections of the Berlinische Galerie and the archives of the Akademie der Künste, the Haus der Wannsee-Konferenz, the Research Center on Anti-Semitism, and the direct-democratic New Society for Visual Arts (NGBK)—they all served as sources of information.

A fundamental source for our research was Joseph Walk's book *Das Sonderrecht für die Juden im NS-Staat. Eine Sammlung der gesetzlichen Maßnahmen und Richtlinien—Inhalt und Bedeutung*, which minutely sums up the perfidious anti-Jewish laws of the Nazi regime. We chose eighty of these legislative texts and rewrote them in a shorter, more contemporary wording, developing a kind of catchline style. These revised law texts are written in present tense but bear the original dates of their issuance, thus creating a connection between past and present.

Eighty double-sided signs, a colorful image on one side, revised paragraphs of anti-Jewish legislation from the years 1933–1945 in black and white on the other, confront the passersby with the almost forgotten history of this neighborhood and accompany them throughout their day-to-day routines. The image motifs are familiar: a dog, a cat, a pearl necklace, swimming trunks, a book—objects that are tied to special memories. Barbara Straka commented on this in the *Arbeitsbuch für ein Denkmal*, "collection points for deportation were set up in the Bayerisches Viertel as in other places. The residents slowly disappeared, but their possessions stayed behind: everyday objects like watches, bicycles, radios, clothing, jewelry, and mundane household goods."

By distributing the signs all over the streets of the neighborhood, we created a kind of walk-through documentation and interlocked the memorial with the urban environment. We mounted the double-sided image-text-signs on existing structures—lamp posts—and choreographed their positioning based on location- and content-related aspects. Spread out over the whole area, the memorial becomes a metaphor for the daily hardships, the deprivation, and, ultimately, the deportation and murder of Jewish citizens during the Third Reich.

One of the images shows a typical Berlin street sign with the name Haberlandstraße on it. It honors the founder of the Bayerisches Viertel, Jewish entrepreneur Georg Haberland, and is installed in the place of his former home. The sign draws attention to the renaming of Haberlandstraße to Treuchtlinger and Nördlinger Straße, enacted during the Nazi regime and not yet revised at the time the memorial was installed in 1993. Some years later, the district administration of Schöneberg decided to rename Nördlinger Straße back to its original name Haberlandstraße; Treuchtlinger Straße was not renamed.

Three large maps are part of the memorial as well—seemingly normal maps of the city that provide orientation and indicate the locations of the eighty image-text-signs. The maps are mounted on boards in front of the city hall, on the Bayerischer Platz, and in front of the school on Münchner Straße. On closer inspection, however, these boards actually show two maps that have been superimposed: one is from 1933, the dawn of the Nazi regime, the other from 1993, when the memorial was inaugurated. This overlay highlights differences in the urban structure and blends past and present.

In order to translate a decentralized sculpture from the public space into a museum exhibition, its concept has to be transferred into a different medium. The video documentation of a walk through the Bayerisches Viertel, which is shown in the exhibition *DEMO:POLIS*, offers an impression of the statements and situations created on the streets; it was produced for an exhibition at the Jewish Museum New York in 2003. Further translations of the work, with German and English texts but different pictograms, were printed onto banners and hung in museums and libraries, for example at the ICA in Boston or the Martin Luther King Jr. Memorial Library in Washington, D.C. (a Mies van der Rohe building), thus broadening the discussion on human rights and political responsibility.

At Princeton University—where many of the exiled intellectuals from Germany held teaching positions—in the East Pyne Building, which houses the Department of German, two lightboxes show the memorial with its pictograms and law texts, illustrating its topography and content. They are not only part of the university's art program, but are also used for teaching purposes, for which they are critically examined.

The concept of creating dialogue through art and directly addressing the public was also applied for later joint projects. Shortly after our work on *Orte des Erinnerns* was completed, the competition for the *Denkmal für die ermordeten Juden Europas* [Memorial to the Murdered Jews of Europe] in Berlin was announced. For this, we created *Bus Stop*, a concept that steered the memorial away from a gigantomaniac sculpture and towards the more authentic sites of remembrance that can be found all over Europe. Once again, the idea was that of a decentralized installation—not limited to a single neighborhood this time, but stretching a whole continent. For the designated site of the national memorial, flanked by the Tiergarten, the US Embassy, and the Adlon Hotel, we foresaw a bus stop as a kind of central information point, which, however, would be connected to a network of other significant research sites worldwide—long before the underground place of information of Eisenman's memorial was in the works. Our aim was to create a work of art that would facilitate "active remembrance" through a network of places and information, encouraging discussion instead of ending it by adding a presentable copestone to this societal process.

In the newspaper *Die Woche* from July 14, 1995, Gabriele Riedle described *Bus Stop* in the following way: "Instead of a memorial, they planned to erect a bus stop on the site, from which red buses would leave for the actual concentration and extermination camps in the immediate and wider surroundings, even as far as Auschwitz or Sobibor. The buses would display the destination along with the words 'Memorial to the Murdered Jews of Europe.' That way, the memory of the Holocaust would be kept alive, but instead of linking it to this staged site in the center of the capital, it would be at the center of our own mundane everyday life in a mobile society [...]. The presence of the elongated glass terminal on the empty site, along with the red, illuminated buses that seem to become a single luminous sculpture at night, is a strong provocatory statement in itself, precisely because of its stark simplicity in the middle of Berlin's most upmarket development area. And the names of the victims are not forgotten either with Stih and Schnock: they are listed in a pavilion, where visitors can access extensive information on the organization of the NS regime, the camps, and the Holocaust in the form of maps, publications, and interactive computer systems [...]. At any rate, as Stih and Schnock say, 'the often invoked responsible citizen faces up to the issue.' This act of taking responsibility as an individual would fall short in a predominantly representative design of collective remembrance."

The plan was to install red bus stop signs all over the city in front of specific institutions, as was done for the exhibition *DEMO:POLIS* in front of the Akademie der Künste. While our concept was not realized, it was widely discussed. An Israeli television network created a two-part documentary in collaboration with the German TV station ZDF, presenting different approaches to the Holocaust Memorial. True to our idea, they labeled a red bus, filled it with students, had it drive around Berlin, past the Ministery of Foreign Affairs, along the famous street Unter den Linden, and through the Brandenburg Gate. At the same time, they asked passersby their opinion on the topic.

The artistic idea for *Bus Stop* was realized for the New Society for Visual Arts in Berlin as a social sculpture—a publication which, in the form of an up-to-date Deutsche Bahn train schedule, also documents the history of the listed destinations and the crimes that have taken place there along with the departure times. The schedule can be used to go on a tour, alone or as a group, to retrace the history of NS crimes in specific locations. Ten years later, on the occasion of the inauguration of the Holocaust Memorial, the schedule was once more republished for the IFA exhibition *Stets gern für Sie beschäftigt ...*, expanded with an English translation by the Washington University in St. Louis, and presented as a wall installation at the IFA Gallery in Berlin.

Both memorial concepts, *Orte des Erinnerns* and *Bus Stop*, applied the idea of social as well a topographical networks and the overwriting of space. This approach can also be found in other joint projects by Stih & Schnock, for example the multi-part project *Die Stadt als Text*, which was created for the opening of the Jewish Museum in Munich. A Walter Benjamin quote sets the framework: the map of Munich is shown as a figure-ground diagram and overwritten with Jewish history. Ninety-nine episodes from different moments in history create diversity; they are linked to the corresponding locations in Munich's urban space—and through the project these locations, in turn, are linked to the Jewish Museum. The map has been realized as a carpet in combination with lightboxes at the Jewish Museum and is also available as a folding map, which can be used to explore the Jewish history of the city on one's own.

This method of "artistic research" was also brought to bear for the follow-up project *Zeige Deine Sammlung—jüdische Spuren in Münchner Museen*, for which we interviewed seventeen of Munich's cultural institutions and their respective curators on some of the artworks in their collections. These "background stories" were then presented during Munich's Long Night of Museums. The youth organization Die Falken used megaphones to blare out the history of different artifacts in front of their respective institutions; they walked from museum to museum in a kind of procession which grew, attracting more and more people as the evening progressed.

We once again involved different institutions in the making of the project *Die Kunst des Sammelns – von deutscher Art und Kunst*, for which we critically examined the art collection of Friedrich Christian Flick in the context of his family's history and accompanied the collection's ceremonial reinstallment in the Hamburger Bahnhof in Berlin with actions and performances in the public space. Through their actions they all became part of the art project: the New Society for Visual Arts as responsible body and the Akademie der Künste, which hosted a panel discussion, the German magazine *Spiegel*, which prominently advertised the project in advance, public television and radio, which broadcasted information on the topic on a daily basis, and Chancellor Schröder, who berated the critics.

Two posters illustrate the principle idea of the project. One advertises "free entry for former forced laborers" and shows the Hamburger Bahnhof in the background in Germany's national colors; the other shows the F.C. Flick Zeppelin along with the headline "tax fugitives, show us your treasures." These large posters were mounted on billboards opposite the Hamburger Bahnhof during the glamorous opening ceremony as well as installed on two trucks that drove by the event location. They were ticketed for driving too slowly. In the accompanying catalog, Tom Freudenheim wrote, "museums, after all, have been housing stolen goods since time immemorial, goods that have too often been acquired through questionable means." In this case, rather than stolen goods, as such, we addressed the issue of a tactical covering-up of family history—a history that, in part thanks to our project as well as others following it, has now finally been acknowledged and reexamined.

Stolen artifacts are an issue of some urgency in our Western collections. We already focused on this topic with our work *Life~Boat* at the Peabody Essex Museum in Salem (MA), which shone a light on the role of colonialism, in particular. The seminar "Artifacts in Transition" is continuing this research with students from the Leuphana University in Lüneburg at different museums in Hamburg and Berlin. The pressing question that needs to be answered is how we can redefine museums as "containers of memory," as art is never solely a matter of aesthetics but of human dignity as well.

We developed the environment *Was brauchen wir Kunst, wir brauchen Kartoffeln* [What do we need art for, we need potatoes] for the forecourt of the Staatsgalerie Stuttgart. The name refers to a still-popular Swabian saying from the early nineteenth century, when a famine forced Wilhelm I, King of Württemberg, to forgo the acquisition of the brothers Boisserée's art collection (which can today be found in the Alte Pinakothek in Munich). The question at the heart of this project was: How important is art in times of economic austerity? Is art, in itself, maybe a kind of nourishment, a basic human need?

The ensemble consists of two potato patches framed in gold that are planted and harvested year by year; two botanical plant labels with the "ingredients" of the artwork; a red carpet that guides visitors inside the building; and cans that the museum staff uses to water the plants. A three-part LED banner above the entrance displays, in running red-green-black text, the names of artists and titles of artworks from the Staatsgalerie collection, "publicizes" the collection, and thus carries the contents of the hermetic museum space out into the traffic flow. Everything here is in flux: plants, the texts, and the people that surround them. Thereby, a dialogue between art, history, nature, and technology is created, underlining the vital importance of art for communication in a democratic society.

Making cultural discourses public in this way requires an unhampered, flowing transition between the interior of the museum and the exterior space that extends beyond the use of posters or banners on the façade. How can the inside of institutions become visible to the outside world? How can we include passersby and noninvolved parts of society in artistic dialogue? How can we attract a younger audience that is used to the much faster flow of information commonly found in the new media?

These questions have particular currency for Berlin in light of the projected new museum dedicated to twentieth-century art at the little-frequented Kulturforum. Berlin's museums, in general, are too closed to the outside, they have not yet embraced the possibilities of interventions in the exterior space. The transparency of the Neue Nationalgalerie alone allows for exhibition concepts that integrate the public space and the audience, as recently seen with Otto Piene's impressive retrospective slide-show performance, which lasted far into the night. Art could be the key to a more conscious and animated public space; it could visually interfere with the social city and thus create the basis for a new urbanity that surpasses Happening or Fluxus.

The Glasnost of Public Participation

To make planning and architecture a task for civil society is a conflicted undertaking. Shaping and designing urban spaces and structures requires spatial and artistic skill and talent—ingenuity even. Architectural and design quality comes from the input of professionals in these fields, but that is not the only factor. Any planning and design undertaking has to deliver practical uses as well—even structures that serve representative, intellectual, or sacral purposes. The client, who commissions the work and pays for it, has always had an influence on the design, has corrected, rejected, and approved it. And in those cases in which the client was not at the same time a representative of a secular or sacral power, regulations and approval requirements still ensured that these powers reserved their right to have a say in the matter. Representative democracy, through its executive organs, made extensive use of this dynamic, too, but now civil society is preparing to wrest away some of that power.

The high-profile controversy surrounding the Stuttgart 21 project has again placed the subject in the spotlight of public attention in Germany, but the questions concerning participation in planning processes—when is the right time, what is the best approach, and what influence does participation have on the results?—have been fueling the public debate for quite some time.[1] The belief that comprehensive participation can improve both the quality and acceptance of a design has clearly resulted in a great deal of success, but also at least as much disappointment. Not every conflict can be resolved through discussion, debate, and modifications of the proposal that are satisfactory for all parties involved. Sometimes conflicts of interest or creative differences mean that a compromise is out of the question, and a decision has to be made. Regardless of these ambivalent experiences, against the backdrop of major social and technological developments over the past two decades we are forced to ask if it isn't perhaps time to rethink the established participation processes in terms of transparency and opportunities for real involvement.

1 Klaus Selle, *Über Bürgerbeteiligung hinaus: Stadtentwicklung als Gemeinschaftsaufgabe? Analysen und Konzepte*, Detmold: Verlag Dorothea Rohn, 2013, pp. 119 ff.; Ulrich Hatzfeld, "18 Millionen Meinungen über Stadt: Wie wird Stadt zum öffentlichen Thema," Ulrich Hatzfeld and Franz Pesch (eds), *Stadt und Bürger*, Darmstadt: Verlag das Beispiel, 2006, p. 10. ff., Darmstadt: Verlag das Beispiel 2006, p. 10 ff.

2 Martina Löw, "Planung im öffentlichen Interesse? Eine Legitimationsfrage in Zeiten von Pluralisierung und Individualisierung," in IBA Hamburg (ed.), *Metropole 6: Zivilgesellschaft*, Berlin: Jovis, 2012, p. 30 ff.

One of the main reasons for this could be that the increasing differentiation, pluralization, and individualization of society have made it harder to define what exactly constitutes "public interest."[2] This goes hand in hand with a dwindling affiliation with the major social institutions that traditionally represented these interests, such as political parties, churches, trade unions, etc. Coupled with a higher level of education and a longer active lifetime, the existing—and apparently growing—desire to be involved is no longer primarily directed towards these institutions, but more attention is now paid to independent, issue- and theme-related initiatives and organizations. While ties to the major social institutions and political parties have not dissolved completely, they are becoming more qualified and targeted towards specific topics. The underlying belief that all aspects of one's individual interests will be taken care of sufficiently by these institutions is dwindling.

Directly associated with this are calls for more information and transparency, for local and national referendums, with which governments are complying one step at a time. This, however, leads to a necessary rebalancing of the elements of direct and representative democracy and decision-making, which is currently not at all reflected in the formal procedures for planning approval and architectural or urban design competitions. How and at what point in the planning process should a local referendum be held to avoid that planners and architects are swallowed by frustration and inefficiency? And at what level of government should decisions about which local, regional, or national process be made?—to cite just two pressing questions. But there is more: in a bid to avoid overly simplistic yes-no questions for complex planning and design processes, increasing use is made of public participation and mediation—and rightly so. However, often it is not clear how binding the agreements thus negotiated can be in the event of individual or institutional objections as part of the formal planning approval process. After all, the planning process as such remains subject to proper professional consideration within its established legal framework.

Similar problems also arise in conjunction with new possibilities for online participation. The simplified access to information and participation platforms indisputably represents a major step forward, even if the full potential of the Internet in terms of crowdsourcing and the initiation of bottom-up processes—and their integration with traditional face-to-face formats—is nowhere near fully exploited. However, while it is already evident that online participation can reach new and larger parts of the population, it still does not involve all. Socially disadvantaged and immigrant groups, for the most part, make little use of these instruments, which is a well-known shortcoming of all traditional participation processes. Thus, even in the Internet era, the issue

Supporters' manifestation for the project Stuttgart 21 on Stuttgart's Schloßplatz, 2010

of fully inclusive representation and the legitimacy of the "democratic majority" remains unresolved.

Despite these residual shortcomings and weaknesses, a great deal speaks for the theory that, in urban design and architecture as elsewhere, the need for information, transparency, open debate, and participation will continue to grow and become more important in the future. The affected professions of architecture and urban design, planning, and civil engineering can choose to either tackle this challenge proactively or take a defensive position. In reality, the latter attitude prevails—albeit seldom openly declared—upheld by failures and disappointments resulting from aesthetically inferior compromises. However, this offers little perspective in the long run and effectively relies on the increasingly rare possibility that public debate might simply ignore one's project. A proactive approach, on the other hand, faces the difficulty that questions of use, function, percentage of affordable housing, sustainability, and energy efficiency, distribution of green spaces, playgrounds, and parking spaces, costs, etc.—in other words, those aspects of a construction project that are easily understood by the general public—tend to be at the center of the debate instead of those of aesthetic beauty or formal and spatial quality. As a matter of fact, discussion of the latter is extremely rare, which has its deeper roots in different standards and evaluation criteria and a general insecurity of the public where aesthetic and design questions are concerned.

This is not surprising insofar as the "professional culture" of architects, urban designers, and to some extent also of planners and civil engineers involves the ability to perceive architecture and public spaces in terms of their form and not just their function. Their professional background and extensive training ensures that their idea of "value" is oriented much less towards function per se, but more towards the formal design concept, artistic quality, and the aesthetic and ethical principles underpinning the design. It is thus hardly surprising that the opinions of experts and laypeople tend to diverge greatly. Often it is the limited understanding of the formal aspects of architecture and design, thus restricting public debate to functional aspects, but also the differences in each individual's canon of values, depending on origin and/or education, that cause the aesthetic judgments of experts and laypeople to drift apart.[3] In order to realign these viewpoints and criteria for evaluation, greater formal competence and maturity must be fostered on one side, and a better understanding of users' needs coupled with a closer orientation around conventional and familiar aesthetics are needed on the other. Although this is associated with a multitude of difficulties and challenges, it is the only possibility for overcoming the gridlock of non-communication between experts and the public.

This periodically raises the question, not just in interactions with the public but also among professionals, of generally applicable aesthetic and design principles: can and should there be an agreement on values? Is a generally valid concept of beauty even possible? And if so, wouldn't constant change be an inherent part of its character? These and other questions cannot be sufficiently examined here, nor do they lend themselves to superficial answers. And this is not what matters in a democracy whose main characteristic is first and foremost an agreement that "there (is) no one who can determine what art is, but the nature of art means there cannot (must not) be anyone who, on behalf of the state, can decide what is valid for all," as Adolf Arndt already pointed out in 1960 in his historic

3 Dorothee Obermaier, "Gestaltungsmonopol der Produzenten von Raum und Architektur: Fachleute unter sich," lecture manuscript, Frankfurt a. M., 2007, p. 6 ff.

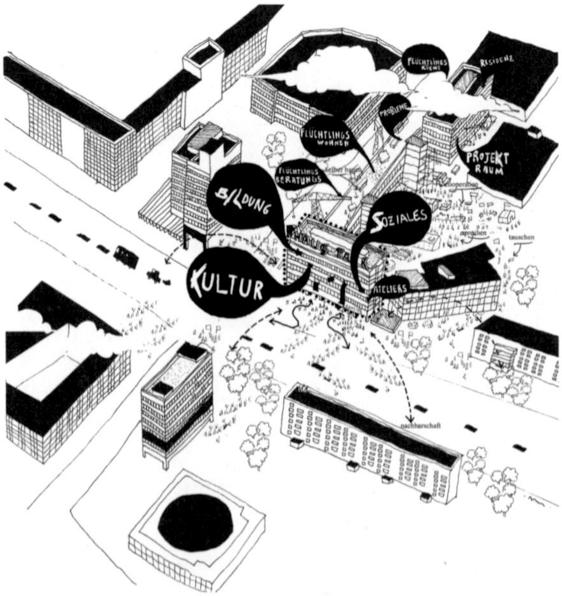

raumlabor, Workshop for House of Statistics, Berlin, 2015

talk at the Akademie der Künste.[4] What matters instead is the ability to perceive and analyze, to promote an understanding of architectural trends, their underlying motivation, their history and means of expression, along with the ability to judge the appropriateness and ethical framework of the design solutions offered.

Fostering these skills should already begin at school, as the first "Status Report on Building Culture in Germany" rightly demanded.[5] The incorporation of architectural and urban design themes into the curricula of art and geography education throughout Germany has fortunately increased in recent years, although there is still much room for improvement in terms of content, teaching materials, and teacher competence.[6] Such activities are supported by the voluntary efforts of many chambers of architects, as well as some two hundred local and national organizations and initiatives, which also promote the education of a broader public on architectural and urban design issues, using a wide variety of formats.[7] Last but not least, the Bundesstiftung Baukultur, founded in 2006, has also made an important contribution to the furthering of this cause.

Alongside the proactive communication of architectural and design knowledge, however, there is the crucial question of whether traditional planning and decision-making processes in urban design, architecture, and civil engineering can meet twenty-first-century demands for transparency, involvement, and empowerment of the general public? Looking first of all at the cornerstone of design decision-making culture, namely the procedures for urban design and architectural competitions as set out in the "Richtlinien für Planungswettbewerbe" [RPW, guidelines for design competitions], the strong emphasis on safeguarding participants' anonymity and the decidedly non-public nature of the decision-making process is striking.[8] Only the final results are to be publicized in the form of a written report. Transparency? Involvement? Participation? Fact is, they aren't factored in at all or only within extremely narrow boundaries. Thus, while citizen representatives are often involved in an advisory role or as members of the jury, and occasionally intermediary or final presentations are made to the general public—albeit independent of the actual competition jury meetings—none of this is the rule. In the future, the question will have to be answered whether the anonymity of competitions and juries, and the non-public nature of these events is still in line with the times, especially since the RPW 2013 does not rule out the use of a public jury.[9] Without doubt, there is a conflict of interests here between protecting the anonymity of competition participants and transparency in planning, which, for the benefit of the latter, can only be resolved through more openness regarding the former.

This is even more applicable to the competitive tendering processes introduced throughout Europe in an effort to ensure fair and equal conditions in the procurement of construction, maintenance, and other services. In an attempt to integrate European public procurement regulations with the equivalent German procedures, a complicated tangle of laws, regulations, and guidelines has been created, which even insiders have a hard time understanding, let alone the interested layperson. This situation could easily be left aside in the context of this essay, if it didn't also affect a number of architectural projects—with one rather serious consequence: the requirement for absolute confidentiality of all competition-related aspects of a proposal for the entire duration of the tendering process. In the case of complex procurement processes that can go on for

4 Adolf Arndt, "Demokratie als Bauherr," Ingeborg Flagge and Wolfgang J. Stock (eds), *Architektur und Demokratie*, Stuttgart: Gerd Hatje, 1992, p. 61.

5 Gerg Kähler, *Statusbericht Baukultur in Deutschland: Ausgangslage und Empfehlungen*, Berlin: Bundesministerium für Verkehr, Bau- und Wohnungswesen, 2001, p. 53.

6 Hannes Weeber, Rotraut Weeber, and Gert Kähler, *Baukultur! Zweiter Bericht zur Baukultur in Deutschland*, ed. Bundesministerium für Verkehr, Bau- und Wohnungswesen, Hamburg: Junius, 2005, p. 134 ff.

7 *Baukulturbericht 2014/2015*, ed. Bundesstiftung Baukultur, Berlin 2014, p. 26.

8 "Richtlinien für Planungswettbewerbe" (RPW 2013), *Bundesanzeiger*, February 22, 2013.

9 RPW 2013, §6(2).

years, this leads to a lack of transparency, not only for the general public, but also for political decision-makers and government agencies to a degree that is unparalleled in a democracy. There is an urgent need to put the duty of confidentiality into perspective—especially since it usually applies to major construction projects involving integrated architectural and engineering services (hospitals, exhibition centers, universities, public transport projects, etc.).

An entirely different inherent problem regarding transparency can be traced back to German federal building law, which does not provide for any public participation in the building approval process, despite the fact that when it comes to actual, concrete construction projects—in contrast to abstract development plans—the desire and opportunity for public involvement is especially great.[10] More involvement here would not only foster closer relationships with the population, but could also open up new possibilities for architects and planners to improve understanding for their aesthetic concerns among a broader public. Relevant proposals and initiatives, however, have so far fallen on deaf ears among legislators, although there are strong indications that, against the background of a growing importance of direct democracy and the public's greater expectations regarding involvement, German planning and building law, which for historical reasons is extremely compartmentalized, urgently requires a fundamental review.[11]

These are just three starting points where overcoming structural obstacles in our legal frameworks could lead to greater transparency and openness and thus also to more opportunities for public participation in aesthetic and architectural questions. What is asked of the professions is a willingness to engage in this discussion. The ambivalence of opening ourselves up to this process has been discussed in my introductory remarks; nevertheless, there is no doubt that it is overdue. It would make sense to cultivate an open mind, even if Ulrich Conrad's concerns remain justified: "I am inclined to doubt, however, whether such processes will reveal the 'wisdom of the people,' as Bertolt Brecht calls it. As far as I can see, this wisdom is not at work in any city anywhere in the world."[12]

10 Michael Krautzberger, "Planungsrecht und Bürgerbeteiligung," in IBA Hamburg (ed.), *Metropole 6*, p. 42 ff.

11 Jörn Walter, "Zivilgesellschaft und Planungskultur," in IBA Hamburg (ed.), *Metropole 6*, p. 246 ff.

12 Ulrich Conrads, "Öffentlich planen," in Flagge and Stock (eds), *Architektur und Demokratie*, p. 51.

Participation as a Strategy for Public Consultation—The Instant City

Urban planning has today—more than ever before—become the center of discussions surrounding civic participation. Public debate, however, reveals that while participation is one of society's fundamental concerns, the ideas on its concrete definition and implementation differ greatly.

Civic participation is often equated with direct democracy and unmediated citizen-led decision-making seen as its essence. Rather than actually including citizens in planning processes, however, as the term "participation" suggests, direct democracy merely delegates decision-making authority to the population. Countries that have long-standing traditions of different forms of direct democracy, like Switzerland or the US, recognize the delegation of subject-matter-related decisions to plebiscitary processes as a fundamental building block of democratic policymaking—as shown by the regularly held national referendums in Switzerland. The tradition of national referendums, however, is almost inevitably connected to a political culture in which the decision-making power of elected bodies like the government or the parliament is relegated to the background. For the German public, in contrast—whether on a national or on state level—an expansion of structures of participatory democracy beyond the discussion of isolated processes would necessitate the establishment of a new culture of participation altogether.

Participatory processes can be applied at a much earlier stage than the instruments of direct democracy. The beginnings of any planning process or political project are usually defined by an information discrepancy between citizens on the one side and the entities in charge on the other. The governing body plans to do something, and its objective is to "let the public in" on those plans. This "notification" procedure concerns more than merely factual information: What is happening on a material level? Which interventions will be necessary? What is the legal situation? Experience shows that citizens are able to easily keep up with information on a subject-matter level, but meta-information is just as important: What are the different interests and interrelations at play? What is the relative importance of this specific procedure for the political agenda, for the involved parties, or for different parts of society?

Judged from this perspective, we can say that participatory processes are more likely to be successful if communication takes place on an equal footing. Citizens need to be able to identify with the plans and developments and say, "This is my project as well. I had a hand in it, and I have contributed to improving it." The question that naturally follows is: how can such situations be created? Generally, we can assume that the chances for communication to have a fruitful outcome are highest if no binding planning decisions have been made yet.

While developing the concept for the International Building Exhibition in Berlin in 2020, planners considered different strategies to better anticipate planning processes, make them more transparent for all parties involved, facilitate participation, and encourage shared responsibility. As a result, the "Instant City" was developed. The Instant City is an urban intervention tool that takes a process-oriented approach to planning and building and offers the possibility to "try out" plans. Short-term, but highly public practical projects are used to showcase participatory structures and "city making." These projects are likewise useful to sound out the terrain, test it for different uses, and create addresses. The urbanistic potential of new residential developments, in particular, can thereby be put to the test. The Instant City can be used as an organizational instrument to make discussion processes more goal oriented, to bridge extensive planning periods, and to process and implement productive feedback.

This brief outline points to the important role such measures can play before any actual planning process has begun, but participation is by no means only effective before the start of a project. An example for a project that had already been extensively discussed before a strategy of public participation was considered is the design for the historical city center of Berlin. For more than two decades, the site between Alexanderplatz and Humboldtforum had been at the center of a heated controversy between the advocates of different (ideological) standpoints: the proponents of a redevelopment that would follow the general historical landmarks of the city's medieval layout on the one end and people supporting the idea of an open, undeveloped public space on the other. It is easy to see why any attempt to reconcile these two positions was doomed to fail. An inclusive solution halfway between the reconstruction of historic structures and the preservation of a considerable part of the open space did not succeed in bringing the two parties closer together.

The "outcome" of this planning standoff was no outcome at all, as no decision was arrived at. This

Expert workshop for Alexanderplatz with Berlin's Senate Building Director Regula Lüscher (far left), July 9, 2015

fiasco, however, provided the basis for a completely new approach. As a reaction to the unresolved debate, the senate launched a public dialogue in early 2015 under the title "Alte Mitte – Neue Liebe?" [Old Center—New Love?]. Using a multi-stage process, it invited proposals which were then discussed and assessed. Already in its earliest stages, this procedure revealed a plethora of different ideas on the future of Berlin's city center. With that, the dichotomy of the prior controversy—open space vs. development—was suddenly no longer the main focus of the debate. It also became clear, however, that this kind of participatory strategy would not be able to provide comprehensive and effective solutions for an undertaking of this complexity and magnitude. Presenting the Berlin House of Representatives with the outcomes of this dialogue for further consideration provided another impulse to acknowledge the importance of this participatory process and its respective proposals for the overall project.

What the strategies presented here have in common is that participants are able to actively contribute to a development rather than simply vote on existing proposals. The binary division of "public opinion" vs. "politics" is jettisoned in favor of multi-party debates.

Participation is commonly understood as a process in which politics consults the public, and the public, in turn, advises politics "on an equal footing." Prerequisite for successful consultation is that all protagonists have to be acknowledged in their respective roles, have their opinions heard and be taken seriously. Citizens advise representatives to arrive at practicable solutions. The term "advice" implies that the actual decision remains with the political representatives—or is negotiated independently.

Participation-oriented city planning is not a tool to eradicate conflicting opinions or disaccord on a project, and it is, most importantly, not a blanket solution to dealing with skepticism towards planning authorities and politics. Whenever citizens are invited to express their opinion, there is a risk that partial interests will be pushed to the front, the debate polarized, or provisional solutions eternalized. The actual purpose of participatory mechanisms as additional consultational bodies for politics is to awaken the public's respect for and awareness of their own living environment and to create identities, in the best sense of the word.

Knitting the Processes—The Art of Cooperation in Complex Planning Processes

One piece of advice to begin with: this text will disappoint those who argue that a lack of participation leads to the failure of major communal and state projects. Nor will it provide any confirmation to those who believe that democracy is satisfied by participation in accordance with the building code. Instead, it aims to support those who strive to knit together something new from the complexity of planning and building and the complexity of involvement and participation.

After all, the lines drawn in conjunction with projects such as Stuttgart 21, the Schauspielhaus in Cologne, and the Tempelhofer Feld in Berlin, only seem to be clear. They are constantly shifting and upon closer observation, a new intelligence becomes evident between the state and society, which we are obliged to use!

But first of all, a look behind the preconceptions and an—admittedly simplistic—typecasting of the actors:

Anti-participationists

On the side of broadly requested participation are, for example, egocentric property owners engaging in a citizens' initiative that opposes the construction of a school because it will supposedly endanger urban ecology. In truth, however, they are afraid that property values will drop or feel that the peaceful atmosphere will be undermined. Also the well-informed swarms of protesters, fueled by the good conscience of the masses, as we saw with Stuttgart 21, have their own logic. Sometimes they do actually find the better arguments or facts that have disappeared in an overwhelmed administration; sometimes they succumb to seeking attention and thus resort to shallow argumentation, which is something politics also gladly becomes entangled in. And finally, there are the engaged circles that extend a hand to the community to collectively act on matters pertaining to general welfare, organize affordable housing, or work together to run the community swimming pool. They understand that parts of the administration have been hollowed out and no longer have enough strength to devote themselves sufficiently to such themes. (www.neue-nachbarschaft.de)

The latter are, as a rule, active in middle-class cities in wealthy neighborhoods, which while not diminishing their success, reveals how through this form of engagement, an imbalance might arise between neighborhoods with an affinity for participation and those without, which is worth monitoring.

Those skeptical of participation bring in a similar argument. They claim that widespread participation merely reinforces the interests of certain individuals, thereby suppressing mainly the politically weak. Yet their actual intention in this is to defend their hard-fought authority tooth and nail. Others have concretely experienced the instability of citizen involvement and, until now, have found no suitable ways for dealing with it. Always willing to put their professional reputation at stake for citizen-based initiatives, they have not always fared well in doing so. Then those who are acutely aware that they have no chance of prevailing against a critical public quite tactically introduce some form of participation that seldom includes genuine possibilities for control. And finally, there are the astute mayors or "department heads," for example, in Arnsberg, Mannheim, Leipzig, Nuremberg, and Wolfsburg, who are truly interested in shaping new forms of democratic negotiation processes together with the business world and civil society. They know that democracy does not mean creating a majority, but that the "control of the people" demands many forms of negotiation and invention in order to remain vital.

At the same time, it is important to keep in mind that there is sometimes discord within the groups of antagonists and protagonists, for example in the case of the Tempelhofer Feld in Berlin, where an engaged civil society dared to launch a dedicated development cooperative, only to have a different citizen group vote out this brilliant project. The same applies to the dispute over the new building and demolition of the Schauspielhaus in Cologne, where opposing positions were so entrenched at the center of the city administration, each of which was mobilizing its own powers within civil society. Just looking at these processes is enough to make one despair. After all, what can we do when there are more than just two sides to an issue and everyone adds their own interests to the argument? Is a city then still governable? Can we still influence anything at all?

Participation dilemmas

Upon closer inspection, these questions lead to the discovery of several dilemmas related to participation that one will probably never entirely resolve, but which one must be aware of in well-organized processes.

The most well-known dilemma arises from the divergent time regimes of major planning projects and

The award-winning project team of the Samtweberviertel at the end of the first project forum, June 2014

public attention. The planning of a new train line requires a minimum of ten and usually twenty-five years from the first day to the last. Countless examinations and approval processes continually narrow decision-making channels. At the point when "the public" is interested in the planning, in most cases only one viable version is possible, because problems with groundwater, biotope protection, or resident protests have prevented the others.

Added to that are an administration and citizenry controlled by extremely divergent principles: on the one hand are those who have to justify every state-invested euro and spend according to European guidelines, and on the other there are those who want more flexibility, openness, and sometimes also local aspects in decision making. And this is so because even the citizenry's elected representatives—local politicians—are overwhelmed by the complexity of projects and bids presented to them.

Finally, there is the risk dilemma. While investors bear the builder's risk, and therewith the risks of realization and financing, the others have to deal with the fact that their concrete living environment could quite possibly change for the worse. In the case of doubt, the apparently harsher and usually private risk always outweighs the diffuse, more cultural and social aspect. Yet it is important to remember that private risk also involves potential private profit, but as a rule, it is the community that has to absorb a failed project.

Nonetheless, one can counter all of this and say, "but that's why we have elected political representatives." Unfortunately however, only in very few cases do they actually build bridges between the required bureaucracy and the citizenry for whom the project is actually intended.

Success is possible!

The possible success of this type of participation has become apparent in precisely those fields where citizens take on responsibility for projects. Examples are the previously mentioned, very successful *Quartierfonds Pate* [neighborhood funding sponsor], as introduced quite superbly in Bremen (the Tenever neighborhood, in particular) and Berlin. However, not only "the social", but also "the investment-based and creative" can provide occasion for involvement and participation, as can be observed in Wolfsburg with the most recent redesigning of housing developments and schools, in Mannheim with the intense participation process for the *Konversionsflächen* [conversion sites], or in Munich with the development of the *Kreativquartier*. However, the actual coup among these innovative projects was landed by the City of Leipzig. This time, not with guardhouses and interim uses, but as a result of them. A call for bids was made for the maintenance of an urban development area (Georg-Schwarz-Strasse), which was ultimately given to the local neighborhood association. It can thus use its networks and the trust it enjoys for the transformation process and expand it over the course of time. The responsibility for urban renewal thereby remains in the neighborhood, even when the area "runs over," as they say in German "officialese."

One example with which we are personally gathering experience at the moment is the development of the Alte Samtweberei in Krefeld as a social and financial impulse for neighborhood development. The goal of the project is to invest wisely in a building and thereby reinforce the social and financial substance of the community. Before the investment decision was made, the residents of the neighborhood were informed about the

Beyond institutions—how to turn the affected into stakeholders?

Samtweber quarter in Krefeld—public discussion of project

project by both the city and the foundation, and were asked if we, the foundation—Montag Stiftung Urbane Räume—were even welcome as investors and directors of the process in partnership with the city. This openness of listening to the residents' voice has afforded us continued prestige until today. What has also brought us prestige is that the committee we appointed has true decision-making powers, allowing us to gradually accustom them to the increasing responsibility they could possibly assume in the future. In this respect, we must also learn that not every responsibility is suitable for participants from civil society and thus cannot be assumed by them. Now and probably in the future, in most cases the technical and financial development of projects in particular require professional and remunerated cooperation. Exceptions shaped by young cooperatives and syndicate projects are naturally part of the rule here.

Making use in the future of what has been learned

Several of these successful processes of partaking, participation, and involvement offer substance for new (and old) rules of the game:

Confidence and trust

Partners' confidence in one another and mutual trust are necessary at the start of all forms of participation. A culture of secrecy and exclusively scattered information policies, and the lack of confidence in a partner's abilities, lead to far too much energy flowing into control mechanisms. Yet just as one cannot start a process with a general suspicion, the same applies to an endless advance of trust. Processes must therefore be designed in such a way that manageable packets are negotiated and passed, which then gradually lead to results.

Clearly outlining the decision-making path

Public administration is frequently trapped in its own guidelines. The administration's own and EU responsibilities in the areas of energy-related renovation, the awarding of contracts, and of course money all play a decisive role, especially in construction. The public sector must be offensive in clarifying what decision-making corridors even exist, which variables are changeable, and which, like rusty screws, are best not set in motion, as they would otherwise break.

Involvement combining decision-making and responsibility

Involvement only makes sense when there is a decision to be made. Decisions can be made in a measured way only when decision-makers share responsibility for the consequences. All those who support participation must be aware that this is almost impossible with regard to details for highly complex building projects; but all representatives of the public sector must be aware that it should take place wherever the opportunity exists.

Open doors before they are forced open

The error is often made of inviting only representatives to talks, especially in participation processes in community development. This representation easily leads to a situation whereby involvement in neighborhood committees is a question of power rather than one of engagement. In the worst case, decisions are made for the sake of a victory of one's particular group, which thereby positions the neighborhood's already existing religious, economic, and other subgroups against one another. Our experience is that clearly opening the door for all to participate generates precisely the opposite effect. Only those who are interested show up, and since they are the neighborhood's natural representatives, they are the best representatives. It remains without question that good moderation of such processes is incumbent upon constantly involving new people in these processes.

Transparency at almost any price

The mistrust that many citizens have of "those up there" is steadily fueled and therefore not particularly well differentiated. For example, hasty accusations are made that wheeling and dealing at TTIP or in the EU concession directives for the water supply do, indeed, show that "the" public sector cannot be trusted. Such mistrust can be countered only by maximum transparency. And even in cases when this is not possible for contractual reasons, public decision makers must reveal, without being asked, why this is so. In terms of trust, dust collects in every corner where light does not reach. And this dust then swirls up uncontrolled and incessantly alongside key projects.

Ending the optimism of promises

The major construction projects of the Federal Republic of Germany in particular are often based on the sandy soil of a political promise-based optimism: visitor numbers, investment costs, and realization periods are systematically sugarcoated so as not to endanger projects. This is an enormous problem for the credibility of the public sector. How can citizens trust in the competence of "the administration" when, as in the case of the opera in Cologne, the administration works well, but political requirements cannot be met? How should the financial disaster of the Elbphilharmonie in Hamburg and constant readjustment of the arguments strengthen trust in public plans? Precisely at a community level, politics and administration must again converge and work together on sensible, sober, and realistic project plans, which are then also realizable.

Against the mechanics of processes

And not only with major projects, but also with seemingly small projects with a high social impact, the aim is to combine the right speed with the right expectations. Moving too slowly is tiring, while too much pressure stirs fears. Somewhere in between is right for each project, but this cannot be measured by standardized benchmarks. After all, in an urban neighborhood composed of 80 percent private owners, things will naturally move more slowly than in a housing complex with only one owner. Nonetheless, funding guidelines and bank loans frequently prescribe the same deadlines for both. This generates a compulsory mechanism that must be eliminated in order to break through the interlocking decisions, making every deviation relevant to the system. In this way—especially in urban restructuring—some projects are completed although they should have been rethought or redirected halfway through.

Relinking terrains

The fact that the terrains of participation are often clearly portioned out should not be glossed over. In situations where supposed ambiguous and social matters take place, joining in is part of the success. Where major investment measures take place, citizens are not entrusted with precisely this involvement. There must be an end to the constant subdivision between "the nice ones and the fat ones": those who spin in the cycle of their consternation without getting to the point, and those who hawk statements such as, "at the end of the day, we have to build." After all, for whom are we building "at the end of the day"? For people in our cities, who want to lead a good life in them, a life which—and we must not lose sight of this—is determined by the turning of much larger wheels, for example, educational, EU, and financial policies, which urban renewal policies and urban planning cannot change.

Acknowledgment: For this text, a great deal of inspiration came from practical experience in Cologne Kalk Nord, the Krefelder Samtweberviertel and discussions with colleagues, especially the participants at the Schader Foundation summer camp. Our thanks go to them, our text attaché Ulrich Borsdorf, and many others, for consistently good conversations and generous inspiration!

Public Space—
A Question of Structures

When we think of "public space," images of the masterpieces of the world's urban architecture might spring to mind—Italian piazzas, French boulevards, English parks, or Oriental topographies—building on our age-old knowledge of the ways in which societies settle. We cannot deny the term a certain "exaltedness."

However, it seems that sometimes it is only a short step from exalted to ridiculous, as can be witnessed on the south flank of Pariser Platz in Berlin. The middle is taken up by Frank Gehry's commanding bank building, flanked by the Akademie der Künste on the one side and the US Embassy on the other. Each of these buildings has its own individual form and architectural anatomy, but Berlin's building authority demanded that an identical eaves height be applied to the whole façade of the square—as if by pure accident or force majeure three individual buildings happened to be erected in place of a single coherent edifice spanning the whole length of the square. Looking at the realized façades, one can practically hear the screeching of the planing machine into which the model makers fed the board that was to define the height of all buildings for the city model. And indeed, "Berlin board" is a commonly used term for the strikingly homogenous height of *Gründerzeit* buildings in the inner city of Berlin. At a second glance, however, this uniformity reveals deviations—some hardly visible, some more pronounced: the rigidity of the ensemble is softened by its vivid details.

The original, highly animated silhouette of the Pariser Platz fell victim to bombs and artillery. The forced eaves height of the 1990s could thus be seen as a consequence of the Second World War—rebuilding as collateral damage of a bomb war, so to speak.

What we see here is a confusion of categories. If, as is commonly done, the building height had been prescribed in terms of structural criteria, based on the number of floors, for example, or the relation between building height and expanse of the exterior space, the three designs could have reacted to these guidelines within the logical framework of their own architectural approach. Instead, the buildings have been stringently subjected to a geometric form defined in centimeters. Already more than a hundred years ago, Camillo Sitte mocked the "blind trust" in the blessings of officially sanctioned design principles.[1]

First comes the public space

This seemingly insignificant observation at Pariser Platz points to more fundamental questions surrounding the idea of public space. These, however, primarily concern its structure, rather than its architectonic form.

The system by which a city is developed/made accessible constitutes its oldest and most important infrastructure. Being much more than the open space left between buildings, it is already laid out before any kind of construction can even begin. The interactions that define life in a community take place primarily in the public space, which is why its infrastructure is the largest, and typically oldest, social as well as cultural institution of any urban society. Before any social, political, or cultural life can take shape in a city, be it in the form of buildings or of organizational elements, the public space defines possible planning options and locations. It precedes the built environment and will survive it; it weathers the wars that ravage the urban structures, but also in times of peace outlives countless generations of ever-new construction and reconstruction. While new developments change the defined height of buildings or of whole neighborhoods over time, they have relatively little impact on the function of the public space.

Public space has been a fundamental building block for the existence of urban societies since time immemorial. Adapting an observation by Georg Simmel to that effect, it is "not a spatial fact with sociological consequences; it is a sociological fact in spatial form."[2]

Accessibility and usability

Two equally important requirements for any public space are its accessibility and its usability, but with the growth and densification of urban agglomerations, these two increasingly come into conflict. Improved accessibility is closely linked to an increase in traffic. The more an agglomeration expands, the more through traffic ensues on streets and squares. Traffic, however—not only motorized, but also pedestrian—restricts the usability of a space, the possibility to spend time in it. At the same time, public spaces intended for people to spend time in only have limited usability for traffic purposes. The dichotomy of accessibility and usability is as much functional as it is cultural. French anthropologist Marc Augé described this opposition in terms of "places" (*lieux*) versus "non-places" (*non-lieux*).[3] He distinguishes between, simply put, spaces that serve as locations for people to spend time in and to interact for

1 Camillo Sitte, *City Planning According to Artistic Principles*, New York: Random House, 1965.

2 Translated from Georg Simmel, "Soziologie des Raumes," in Heinz-Jürgen Dahme and Otthein Rammstedt (eds), *Schriften zur Soziologie: Eine Auswahl*, Frankfurt am Main: Suhrkamp, 1983, pp. 221–242.

Pedestrians at the Shibuya crossing, Tokyo, Japan

different purposes (places), and transitory spaces that are not destinations in themselves but have to be passed to "go from A to B." Typical non-places are thoroughfares that are not flanked by buildings as well as railroads or airports. To compensate for the dominance of their purely transitory function, airport planners more and more often rely on full-day shopping and entertainment complexes to attract a clientele whose interests are oftentimes completely detached from the actual purpose of an airport. An example for the combination of place and non-place is the boulevard with its interior lanes for through traffic "from A to B" and its outer lanes that service the continuous line of small-scale addresses and destinations along the road.

The double meaning of the German term *Aufenthalt*, which can express the act of spending time somewhere but can also indicate a delay, combines the two actions of moving through and spending time in a place. Applied to a train or flight schedule, it signifies a disturbance in the usual flow; when staying in one place, however, *Aufenthalt* is the very purpose of this place.

A space to be shared by everyone

Reading Hannah Arendt, the concept appears relatively simple: according to her, there are two aspects of the public space that are closely connected but not identical. First, we have the public space, which belongs to the general public, as opposed to the private space, which belongs to one particular individual or group. Second, what happens in the public space happens for the world to see—which is why anything that is not intended for the public's eyes needs its own separate space that is not publicly accessible, whereas a public space is needed for those things that are meant to be seen and heard by everyone.[4] And to effectively achieve this goal, said space has to be accessible to everyone. Yet, creating the necessary conditions for a communal space to be accessible to the general population is hardly a trivial task.

"To live together in the world," according to Hannah Arendt, "means essentially that a world of things is between those who have it in common, as a table is located between those who sit around it, the world, like every in-between, relates and separates men at the same time." Without said table, "two persons sitting opposite each other were no longer separated but also would be entirely unrelated to each other by anything tangible."[5]

A relentless battle is fought in the virtual as well as the physical public space of the city to determine who is in charge where, with individuals laying claim to their participatory rights. The players are in constant motion, new ones are joining, while others disappear from the scene. From the micro-space of the body to large-scale contexts, people apply a multitude of strategies to further their own area of control. Local residents have their own methods of laying claim to the space; they make their presence known through high buildings, tables and chairs on the sidewalks, through color, light effects, or advertisements. Yet, passersby can play in this competition as well: by generating noise or playing loud music they can increase their share in the acoustic space, with perfume, their share in the olfactory space, and with graffiti their visual reach. Moving very fast or very slow, or with a rolling, space-consuming gait, an individual can limit other people's mobility, or repel them with an unpleasant odor or through littering. A person can strip a space of its public character, for example by destroying park benches, or make it unsafe for others, be it through walking seemingly or actually dangerous dogs, through drug dealing, or violence.

3 Marc Augé, *Non-Lieux: Introduction à une anthropolologie de la surmodernité*, Paris: Éditions du Seuil, 1992.

4 Hannah Arendt, *Vita activa oder Vom tätigen Leben*, second German edition, Munich: Piper, 1981, p. 52.

5 Ibid.

Hotel Adlon at Pariser Platz, Berlin, 1909

Pariser Platz with the Hotel Adlon, Akademie der Künste, and bank building by Frank Gehry, Berlin, 2005

Criteria for the public character of a space

The question of what makes an urban space a communal one—i.e., a space that is suitable for public use—can be answered by means of a few criteria.[6] The first and most comprehensive criterion, accessibility (**1**), entails other criteria like integration (**2**), permeability (**3**), orientation (**4**), and safety (**5**). These not only apply when describing or analyzing given situations, but also influence the requirements for future city planning and development.

6 See also Bernhard Schneider, "Die Stadt als System öffentlicher Räume," in Martin Wentz, Magistrat der Stadt Frankfurt am Main (ed.), *Die kompakte Stadt* (Die Zukunft des Städtischen, Frankfurter Beiträge Series), Frankfurt am Main: Campus, 2000. Commissioned by the Senate Department for Urban Design and Environment Berlin, the concept was developed by the team "Urban Master Plan Public Space" (Undine Gieske, Edvard Jahn, Urs Kohlbrenner, Bernhard Schneider, Heinrich Suhr, Joachim Wolf, Peter Wolf).

1 / Accessibility

The public character of a place or an area of the city depends first and foremost on its unrestricted accessibility to the public at all times, for everyone, and for any purpose. Indications that a space is not intended for public use and requires special permission or authorization are usually not limited to signposts. It only takes a narrowing of the streets in a foreign city for visitors to instinctively start greeting locals, thus offering an indication of their affiliation and permission to enter this residential cosmos—a sign that the public character of said area, meaning its unrestricted accessibility, is no longer a given, and one can assume that the locals are in charge here.

Unrestricted accessibility also means that a public space cannot be exclusively assigned one specific use. To meet the requirements of its various, often simultaneous uses, its design and structure have to remain sufficiently unspecific.

2 / Integration

Accessibility and integration of urban spaces are codependent criteria. The accessibility of a space depends on its integration into the network of its urban surroundings. If a space is accessible via multiple points and from different directions, it meets the accessibility requirement better than a space that can only be entered via one or two points. A multifarious, complex infrastructural web offers alternative routes and ensures the accessibility of parts of a space, even if other entry points are temporarily blocked or a user has missed a connection. A spatial network that is limited to only a few connection points is more prone to malfunction, and thus its general accessibility decreases.

3 / Permeability

How accessible a space is also depends on its permeability, and the latter increases along with its integration into a network. Permeability defines a user's ability to move freely within a system of urban spaces. Examples for limited permeability are fences or planted medians that divide the two sides of a road for safety reasons and thus turn it into a non-place according to Marc Augé's definition. Permeability is closely linked to accessibility and orientation. Being forced to take detours because of a lack of permeability is generally detrimental to a person's sense of orientation.

4 / Orientation

Being able to easily orient oneself is key to understanding a foreign city and using it autonomously. The normal state of being of big city life, even for its own residents, is that of a foreigner. Orientation is more than a person's own ability to read a city—it is a characteristic of spatial structures. Only a space that can be mastered by anyone is a space that belongs to everyone. Orientation, thus, is also a prerequisite for accessibility. Orientation is derived from a structure of the public space that can be read and understood by anyone, including foreigners. Anyone must be able to master it, meaning being able to find their way without the help of locals. While topographical as well as architectural markers, prominent buildings, monuments, landscape elements (ramparts, rivers, etc.) play an important part in this, the layout of the street grid is key. In this respect, orientation is also connected to the integration and permeability of a system: the way in which a city's network is laid out defines the users' ability to orient themselves in it.

5 / Safety

Another central component of the unrestricted accessibility of a public space is a sufficient degree of—objective as well as subjectively perceived—safety. Orientation is key to feeling safe; disorientation leads to insecurity. Every other crime movie that is set in a big city illustrates how dangerous places that lack sufficient permeability and integration can be: the deserted blind alley as a visual representation of our "no-way-out" angst.

However, safety also depends on the way a public space is used. A place can become periodically unsafe, during certain times of the year or day for example, if it falls into the hands of specific groups—whether it be for criminal or party purposes is of secondary importance. Its public character diminishes if people stay away because of possible safety concerns. They no longer regard the space as publicly accessible. Differing ideas of "urbanity" can also easily turn into safety issues. If worst comes to worst, it might even take police enforcement or other types of security personnel to ensure the public character of a place.

The structure is what matters

The basic characteristics that turn urban spaces into public ones primarily concern questions of structure; design is usually secondary. The appearance and layout of a place might change entirely over the course of decades or centuries, but its public character continues to be defined by the same criteria: its accessibility, its integration into the surrounding network, the permeability of the system it is part of, the orientation this system provides, and, finally, the safety of its users that results from all these factors. In this light, even the height of the eaves on Pariser Platz is inconsequential.

View from a private space into a typical public space: following fixed rules, the public space is subdivided into many overlapping zones with more or less visible border lines, which are sometimes only accessible for a fee

Poetics of Space

I am Chilean. I was born in Santiago de Chile during the dictatorship and spent my entire childhood in the capital, so my first personal impressions and notions of public space are invariably tied to the Pinochet era.[1] During the dictatorship, people were expected to show a sense of homogeneity and prudence in their public behavior. For someone of my age, at that time, this homogeneity was strongly expressed, and felt, by the uniforms we had to wear (or to suffer from) when attending school. These were all made from fabrics that did not allow for extensive movement and tore easily when playing in them. Every Chilean child, no matter which latitude they lived in, had to wear this uniform. And public spaces suffered the same fate. Rigid designs, without any playful features, only allowing their users to "behave" in the way they should. The powers in Santiago dictated how the country should be, what it should look like, and how it was to behave.

During the last decade, when I was living in Talca and practicing as an architect and professor, increasingly getting to know the Maule region through the eyes of the Escuela de Arquitectura de la Universidad de Talca,[2] we went to great lengths to regain the public sphere and its spaces that had been lost. We tried to recover the public's esteem for these places, acknowledging both the value of specific locations and the universal quality contained in them that citizens had been deprived of.

These places, once remote, are now becoming as universally accessible as any other public space in a free world. Anyone can take a photo there, use them as backgrounds for "selfies," and thus disseminate them across the globe by posting on Facebook and other social media, hoping for as many "likes" as possible. And thus, public space becomes democratic and globalized. Only fifteen years before, this seemed like an impossible feat in this region, where the only valid opinion was one that came from the "center" (Santiago, New York, or London).[3]

Talca regarded itself as provincial, placed little trust in its own assets, and instead only valued what came from the outside. This went so far that until the earthquake of February 27, 2010, the lobby of the Plaza Hotel in Talca features three clocks: one keeping Talca's time, one London time, and the third Paris time.[4] This was very odd, since the hotel rarely hosted guests from abroad. The clocks were an allusion to the bon mot "Talca, Paris y Londres," originating from a bad transcription of the phrase "Talca parece Londres" (Talca is like London), once uttered by a British tourist, who, upon seeing the fog in the city, compared the two cities to each other. This inherent inferiority complex of always looking to the bigger metropolises instead of relying on local knowledge also resulted in an absence of any typical local expression in the design of public spaces.

During the early years of the Architectural School, the professors frequently heard students use the term *ganarse* (to gain something for yourself or make it your own) to explain their projects. We initially had an urge to correct this use of local language. What was this all about? To gain for yourself? You can stay somewhere, be somewhere, but how can you gain a place or make a place your own?

During the following years, however, we understood that the word *ganarse* has a territorial connotation, being used by the region's inhabitants to explain the process in which someone will colonize or seize a piece of land. It is still an applicable word as it accurately describes certain conditions. For instance, during the mushroom harvest, which takes place in the pine woods near Constitución in Maule's coastal region, the workers will *ganarse* their foraging area by exploring and rapidly demarking it with colored sticks so no other group will be allowed to forage here—thus "gaining" the space. (This happens because they don't own the land. It is privately owned, and they are only allowed to use it for mushroom collecting.)

That is exactly what we have been teaching our students over the last ten years. And since the year 2004 this idea also shines through in the students' thesis projects that consist of actual, realized works. We make public spaces "our own." We're giving them a new meaning, value, and, most importantly, we create the grounds for a wide range of activities as well as public rest areas that would not have been allowed to exist in the past. They formerly did not possess any dignity nor, for that matter, were they considered public spaces at all in the eyes of the users as well as the people in power. Through our activities, we managed to win people's trust in the communities where we realized our projects. And we have made these places "our own," by, for example, transforming a landfill or waste land into a valuable space for public use.

Following the credo that it is easier to ask for forgiveness than to ask for permission, we gave ourselves permission to take action and thus also "gained" the opportunity to test the possibilities of these spaces, try out what they could look like. We are in the middle of a story whose ending is not written yet, a long process, in

1 The Pinochet dictatorship in Chile lasted from 1973 to 1989.

2 The Architectural School of Talca was founded in 1998 and the first classes were taught in 1999. It was the first architectural school in Chile between Santiago and Concepción.

3 Even though Santiago is only 250 kilometers away, we are one of the regions that are more distant from Santiago, due to our lack of an airport.

4 The local Plaza Hotel has a very different quality standard than its counterpart in New York of the same name.

Juan Gajardo, theater, 2009

which the given matter, the territory and its inhabitants, dictate the framework that needs to be translated in to the language of the space and into a concrete work. To illustrate these ideas and some of the more than three hundred built works and thesis projects that the architectural school has implemented in the region, I will be introducing a few exemplary case studies in the following, showing different approaches to the questions of how to use and inhabit the public space, and how to democratize it in a regional context.

Juan Gajardo, theater, 2009

Bringing culture to remote areas (or how to create a cultural landscape from a void)

Many of the rural areas situated far away from Talca can only rarely participate in the big cultural events taking place in the country. On the one hand, they seldom possess the necessary venues or spaces, but they also often lack the political will to bring culture to these remote places.[5]

In order to change this, Juan Gajardo began looking for a theme and a place and met a theater group from Talca who used a valley in the mountains near the coast as their rehearsal space. The flora of this area consists mainly of small shrubs, the ground is yellow and dry, and natural erosion has created a large crevice in the ground.

A large amphitheater for open-air performances was planned and built, using only natural materials that were found on-site: the large crevice, singed tree trunks left over from a forest fire that same year, and rocks found in the vicinity. The project relied on a local workforce, and the terrain was inspected carefully to minimize interventions in the natural surroundings as much as possible but at the same time gain a maximum of usable space.

5 Projects by theater groups that were specifically aimed at these regions and submitted to a national fonds for art initiatives were rejected again and again, the reasoning being that it was "too dangerous for the groups to travel there." This proves that the people in charge had little interest in developing the cultural landscape of these areas.

Felipe Saravia Arias, soccer field, Linares, 2014

Felipe Saravia Arias, soccer field, Linares, 2014

Today people from all over the region come and attend performances by dance, music, and theater groups who can show their art here. And given the uniqueness of the place, it also attracts different groups from the region, like alternative medicine practitioners, for example.

Gaining public space from unused terrain and materials (or how to create a communal space for soccer)

Soccer fields and stadiums are valued highly and have a long-standing tradition in Chilean culture, but at the same time, their history is tinged with blood. *Fútbol*, or soccer, is the most popular sport in Chile; its fandom spans generations and creates both friendships (between the fans of one team) as well as rivalry (between different teams). These dynamic processes can be witnessed on soccer fields in the cities as well as in the country and between people of all ages.

In 1973, the Estádio Nacional in Santiago, which had been a symbol for the nation's favorite sport since its inauguration in 1962, was turned into a concentration camp, a place of torture and death. After the military coup, political enemies of the Pinochet junta were imprisoned and tortured here. A place of fair competition and triumph was transformed into a place of pain. To remember this part of history, designer Sebastián Errázuriz planted a tree in the middle of the playing field inside the stadium in 2006.

There are many places in the Maule region where football is played, but few are considered meeting places or communal spaces. Felipe Saravia sees them as places where memories are collected, memories of triumphs and defeats. By simply marking out a space in the terrain of the city, a playing field was created. The

Carolina Alejandra Molina Guzmán, pilgrimage path, Talca, 2014

border of this field is defined by trees, dead trees that have been dug up along large thoroughfares in the city of Linares and then stored in a municipal shed. These dead tree trunks still contain memories of the city as well as its inhabitants, who accepted them as their silent fellow citizens. This place with its striking border of trees on the one hand welcomes passersby, offering them a space to linger, on the other hand constitutes a worthy backdrop for the awarding of medals after a sports competition. One is instantly reminded of an atrium, an oval that "embraces" the players, and a runway or podium, upon which the winners can accept their prizes. But it also allows for more mundane uses, for eating and drinking, making it a suitable venue for the community to meet and to celebrate.

All these activities, the possibilities to play football, to convene, and to celebrate have developed from the project, and thus the community has made this place their own.

Creating public space on a barren pilgrim trail

The many pilgrims who ascend to the Madonna on top of the hill on Catholic feast days walk up this dusty barren trail. Unexpectedly, this path turns into a communal space for the pilgrims. And, if only for a moment, the eyes are no longer glued to the ground, lest one might trip over a stone, but raised up to take in the wide, open view over the landscape that opens up in front of them.

A path traditionally walked in silence is transformed into a place, where one can encounter not only oneself, but also others, greeting them with a look through the rocks or trees. Wooden planks on the path subtly encourage this exchange, conveying an impression of stability and merging with the shade the place offers. It is a place that welcomes the tired pilgrim and presents him with a view over the landscape. It is not a destination, but a place one encounters. An encounter that cannot be planned in advance but simply happens.

The built structure pays attention to and integrates the existing stone, the masonry, the foliage, and, most importantly, the path. A location is created from the act of resting. The built scenery is only completed by its visitors and at the same time brings them together, thus highlighting the presence of both. These types of places possess a fragile materiality, but a deep meaning, because they turn the declaration of the realization of a work in the public space into something that is possible and valid—in the middle of a dusty barren path.

Public Space in Our Minds

Exhibitions are meant to inform, educate, and stimulate further thinking, while also inviting different ways of thinking. Rather than attempting to conceive all possible answers and alternative scenarios, an exhibition should motivate visitors to form their own opinions and draw individual conclusions. The diversity of these thoughts can be understood as what emerges from an exhibition: along the lines of a higher and more complex, extremely individualized understanding. The problem is simply that this emergent understanding is hardly graspable and the individually formed understandings are fleeting: they may change the thinking of individuals, but the organizers of an exhibition do not receive any direct, or at least no systematic knowledge of them.

By continuously embedding the exhibition in a scientific context, *DEMO:POLIS* attempts to strategically minimize such loss of information. This is achieved by involving the Chair for General Psychology and Methodology at the University of Bamberg (Head: Prof. Dr. Claus-Christian Carbon) in the preparations right from the start. Using touchpads (Apple iPads), the opinions, moods, and especially conclusions drawn by visitors during the exhibition will be systematically gathered on site. The main goal thereby is to investigate how the city of the future, or rather public space, is envisioned and how it will change in comparison to today. At the same time, the intention is to analyze how such surveys can more self-confidently introduce the public to themes related to design, as well as the possible interplay between the survey and an increased awareness of the various addressed themes.

In order to design a questionnaire that is sufficiently rich in content and thus scientifically useful, while at the same time maintaining a realistic framework for its implementation, we made use of a minimum number of questions that are relevant for further analysis. Additionally, questions that require longer answers will be recorded using a Dictaphone. On the one hand, this greatly facilitates input, while on the other, it allows interviewees to act as spontaneously as possible—and also helps to effectively dismantle unnecessary technological barriers.

The survey, which was specially developed for *DEMO:POLIS* and programmed using a web-based tool (which also enables questioning away from the space after the exhibition, for example in the form of a smartphone or PC questionnaire at home or on the go), is structured as follows:

- **I** / Brief demographic profile
- **II** / Survey A: quantitative questionnaire with closed questions
- **III** / Survey B: qualitative questionnaire with open questions

Part I reduces the usual questioning to a minimum as the analyses will not examine any special demographically related issues; therefore, only the age and gender of the interviewees will be asked, and additionally, since it is relevant to the evaluation of the further questions, their current place of residence.

Part II poses quantitatively analyzable questions about the exhibition itself, whereby intuitive symbols and simple scales will be employed to make it as easy as possible to respond and minimize misunderstandings with regard to the scaling and valence (quality rating) of the answers. The questionnaire includes questions on expectations with regard to the exhibition, if and to what extent the exhibition generated new insight, and how informative the exhibition was felt to be. It will also ask whether the specific components of the exhibition (a. text elements, b. visual material, c. animations) were clearly designed, and finally, whether the exhibition changed the interviewee's view of the future of cities, and if so, whether in a positive or negative way. This final question on the prognosis of future development leads directly to the final part of the survey.

In Part III open questions are posed, whereby so-called audio recordings are employed to improve usability: spontaneous associations and conclusions on the city of the future and the development of public space will be gathered with the help of a functionality corresponding with that of a digital Dictaphone, which can be easily stopped and started. The concept of the audio recording is also useful in creating an appropriate framework for the survey, to allow those surveyed to answer as spontaneously and comprehensively as possible. Of vital interest will be the opinion of those surveyed regarding how their places of residence will change in the future, whereby they should talk specifically about hopes, fears, and dynamic developments. They are also asked about their wishes in terms of an ideal development of where they live, and what the anticipated dynamic consequences of that might look like. A further question will specifically address public space—how the interviewees define it, what possibilities public space creates, and to whom public space "belongs." Finally, those surveyed are able to send messages in the form of comments, feedback, and critique addressed to the exhibition creators. Entirely in line with active and repeated involvement with what one has just experienced, the survey can potentially foster additional critical reflection as well as in-depth and therefore enduring elaboration on the exhibition contents. The answers expressed verbally in Part III will then be manually transcribed at the University of Bamberg and subsequently evaluated by recording and statistically processing the individual statements within a categorization system.

The accompanying psychological research project is intended to point out and evaluate strengths and weaknesses of the exhibition, register what content the participants received positively or negatively, and what fascinated or inspired them to further contemplation. Additionally, transfer effects will be examined: the extent to which the visit to the exhibition led to insight into the development of one's own city. These conclusions will be summarized and used as a base for deriving key trends. In the end, the analyses will be processed in a generally understandable form in a report and made available to the exhibition creators in the form of graphics and text.

Participant answering a questionnaire on architectural perception

Jürgen Bortz and Nicola Döring, *Forschungsmethoden und Evaluation für Sozialwissenschaftler*, Berlin: Springer, 2006.

Claus-Christian Carbon, "Innovation in Design and Aesthetics. How Attributes of Innovation Influence Attractiveness in the Long Run," in *Perception*, 34, no. 8, supplement (2005), p. 8.

Claus-Christian Carbon, "Cognitive Continental Drift: How Attitudes Change the Overall Pattern of Cognitive Distances," in *Environment and Planning A*, 42, no. 3 (2010), pp. 715–728.

Claus-Christian Carbon, "Cognitive Mechanisms for Explaining Dynamics of Aesthetic Appreciation," in *i-Perception*, 2, no. 7 (2011), pp. 708–719.

Claus-Christian Carbon, "Predicting Preferences for Innovative Design: The 'Repeated Evaluation Technique' (RET)," in *GfK Marketing Intelligence Review*, 7, no. 2 (2015), pp. 34–39.

Donald A. Norman, *Emotional Design. Why We Love (or Hate) Everyday Things*, New York: Basic Books, 2004.

Romedi Passini, *Wayfinding in Architecture*, New York: Van Nostrand Reinhold, 1984.

Peter G. Richter (ed.), *Architekturpsychologie*, Lengerich, Germany: Papst Science Publishers, 2004.

Enabling DEMO:POLIS

We are, respectively, an architect, a cognitive scientist and a computer scientist and we have spent a large proportion of our contrasting, yet synergistic careers using and sometimes even creating numerous tools and methods intended to support the design process of public urban spaces. So first we thought it important to categorically state that we fervently and earnestly believe the public should have a say in the way that public space is defined, used and designed. A second belief that we hold is that we currently live in a time of profound transition where the relationships of power and knowledge transaction (particularly with respect to the definition, use and design of public spaces) are shifting.

As with any process that is still ongoing, it can be hard to stand back and comment upon it, let alone make predictions about where it is going, but this is what we will attempt in the course of the following few pages of text: this commentary will be based on what we already know from our respective positions as "experts" and what we, personally, would like to see happening in the near future. We will start by describing what we believe are the important topics to which current scientific knowledge and technology can contribute and we will give a brief summary of what tools are currently available for the design and evaluation of public space. We will then go on to clarify what kinds of things can already be measured by these tools and finally we will describe the differing roles of the so-called "experts" versus the "public" with respect to the use of these tools and how these roles, as well as communication between them, might be currently changing.

The kinds of tools/systems/processes that currently exist for understanding the definition, use and design of public spaces can be usefully placed into three distinct categories, which we will deal with in turn. These categories are: "Experimental" (behavioral, cognitive, and psychological), "Analytic" (spatial and visual) and "Evaluative" (typically, post-occupancy evaluations); we will start by looking at the "Experimental" methods.

Two primary aspects characterize the experimental tools. For the most part they tend to be administered or overseen by an "expert" (often a psychologist—behavioral, environment, experimental—or cognitive scientist) and are "performed" upon a member of the public or "participant" (formerly known as a "subject" but this term has fallen out of fashion in recent years). For the most part, "experimental" tools are about putting a "participant" into a public space or situational context, asking them to perform a specific task (often emulating behaviors that would naturally take place in that context) and then measuring some aspect of their performance in, typically, a quantitative rather than qualitative way (although qualitative judgments can find their way into this). The kinds of methods that are typically employed are:

- Range of behavioral experiments, i.e., wayfinding
- Eye-tracking and visual attention experiments
- Real-world observations/questionnaires
- Virtual reality simulations/"pre-occupancy" evaluations
- Task analyses and thinking-aloud protocols
- Card sorting tasks
- Cognitive walkthroughs (expert assessment)
- Personas (from HCI: a user archetype that can serve as a guide in the design process, usually synthesized from "field activities" such as those listed above)
- Video recording or tracking with GPS
- Pointing, sketch maps

For the most part, the emphasis is on objectively understanding the participant's performance or response to the experimental situation devised by the expert, rather than objectively analyzing the space/environment/design. Of course, the argument is that the space or context is a variable in the participant's performance, and that the spatial design can be understood vicariously via the participant's response to it (especially as it would be expected that the same participant would perform differently in different contexts) and for this reason, the environment itself does not become the focus of testing (this is reserved for our second category: the analytic). The kinds of things that such methods are able to measure are:

- Spatial learning
- Orientation/navigation behavior and individual navigational strategies
- Expectations (schemata) and affordances
- Attitude/aesthetic appraisal
- Wellbeing
- Locations of visual fixations and patterns of visual scanning
- Efficacy of signage

In terms of roles, this is definitely a set of methods that tend to lend themselves to having an "expert" in conjunction with a "non-expert" or "participant."

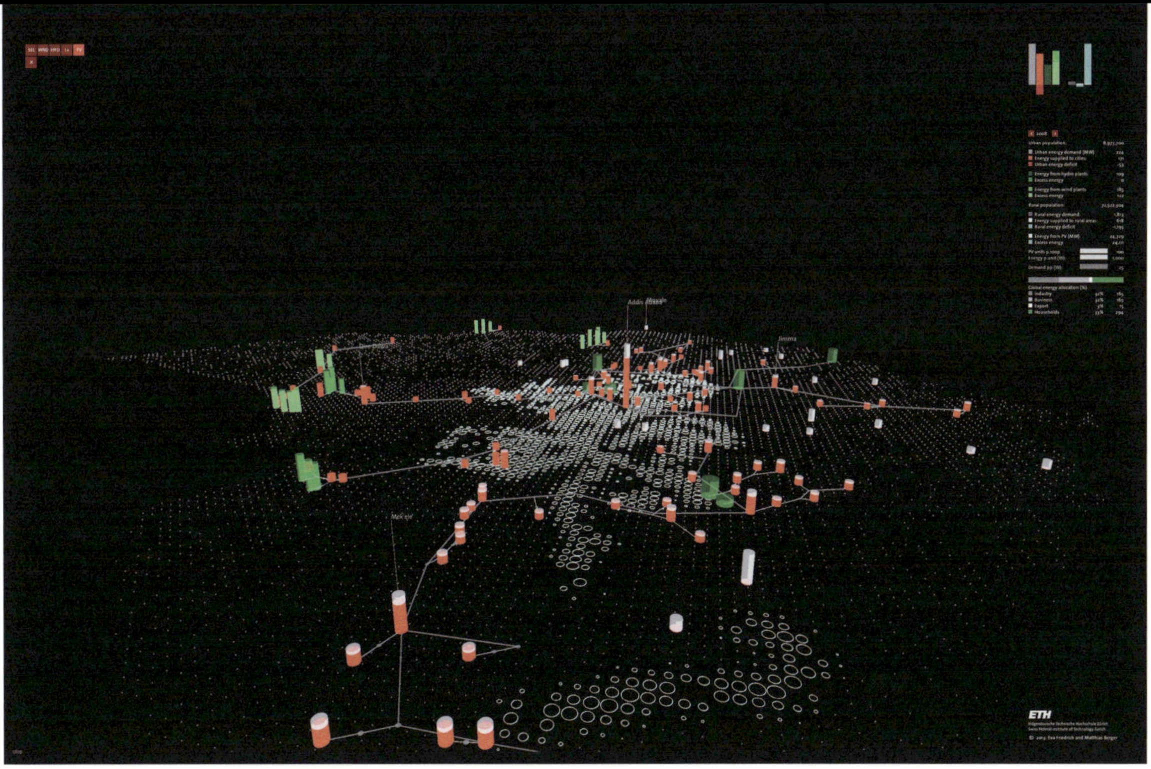

The Addis2050 energy tool, which allows exploration of future sustainable energy scenarios in Ethiopia (Image: Eva Friedrich, Matthias Berger, Stefan Müller Arisona—Future Cities Laboratory, ETH Zurich)

Typically the "expert" will be in charge, will run the "experiments" (hence creating a high bar to access), and the member of the public will participate or be "experimented" upon, rather than being the experimenter. These methods are characterized as being very "top-down," highly structured and following prescribed norms (not least of which are concerned with institutional ethics-approval processes). The scope for public participation exists but, for the most part, in a very passive, rather than active manner.

The second category of tools/systems/processes that currently exist for understanding public spaces are what we term the "Analytic." Unlike the "Experimental" methods described above, the focus of these tends to be on the design of the public space as an *artifact* rather than the public's response to it. Various software packages available for:

- Axial line (line of sight) analysis
- Convex space analysis
- Isovist (visibility field analysis) and visibility graph analysis (VGA)
- Justified graph analysis
- Graph-based analyses, also useful for social network analysis
- Agent-based simulation

There is a good page on Wikipedia that lists most of the currently available space-syntax software packages. Many programs perform more than one type of analysis: some are stand-alone and some are integrated into other CAD or GIS software.

In the recent past, many of these tools would have been used by experts who had training in both the tools themselves and the theories underpinning them.

Tools	**Expert's Role**	**Public's Role**
Experimental (behavioral, cognitive, and psychological)	Typically the expert will run the "experiments" (high bar to access)	Typically the public will participate—i.e., be "experimented" upon, rather than being the experimenter
Analytic (spatial & visual)	Formerly would have been performed only by an expert	Increasingly, tools are becoming free, accessible, open source, and useable by non-experts (lowering of bar to access)
Evaluative (POE)	In the past were very "top-down" and structured and led only by experts	Move to becoming more bottom-up, grassroots led, and led by the public, not experts, especially via social media

The software would have been hard to find, often even knowing what software to look for was hard, as it was the underlying knowledge, rather than the tools, that was promoted or publicized (the software being a mysterious "black box" seldom referred to). Access to the software became an effective gatekeeper to the knowledge/expertise. However, in the last decade there has been a radical shift with respect to the use of specialist analytic software. This process probably began with OpenStreetMap (OSM), which was created by Steve Coast in the UK in 2004 as a crowdsourced response to the expensive and inaccessible proprietary map data held in the UK. Since then there has been a growth in the amount of software that has become freely available and/or open source. A lot of software that was once regarded as "academic" software has been made available to the public—and this process will continue with not only the software, but also data being made available via recent "open source" data movement. The argument is that if academic research has been funded by national research councils, then that money has originally come from the individual taxpayer and as such, any resulting publications/data/software originating from such taxpayer-funded research should be made available to the general public. As a result a lot of "academic" software and accompanying datasets have been made available. Thus the entry bar to accessing such analytic software has been lowered considerably. In many respects, anyone with the time to learn to use these analytic tools and the disposition to understand their resultant analysis can act as an expert.

The kinds of things that can be measured with such tools are:

- Relative levels of predicted occupancy/density
- Predicted levels of pedestrian (or vehicular) flow: "footfall"
- "Desire lines" and preferential routes
- "Step depth" of key locations from entrances
- Intelligibility: a measure of how confusing a building/neighborhood is (and how likely people are to get lost!)
- Spatial configurational properties: integrated (accessible and lively) spaces/segregated (secluded) spaces
- Measures of spatial efficiency, such as axial ringiness, ratios of transition spaces to occupied spaces
- Experiential properties, spaciousness, isovist analyses

The final category of analysis is what we term here the "Evaluative." These are tools and methods typically concerned with eliciting people's qualitative responses to spaces, and where the people participating in this process are typically everyday or, at least, frequent users of that space or building. Many of these tools can come under the generic term "post-occupancy evaluation" and mostly draw upon social science methods such as interviews, focus groups, questionnaires/surveys, and manual observations (often conducted as walk-throughs), etc.

There are numerous definitions of post-occupancy evaluation that are remarkably consistent in their characterizations, suggesting that post-occupancy evaluation, or POE, covers a broad range of techniques to objectively study the performance of designed spaces with respect to their users. Since the origins of POE in the late 1960s, professionals and academics from a number of fields (i.e., architecture, urban planning, psychology, anthropology, sociology, behavioral, or human geography), often in collaboration with each other, have typically been the "experts" managing such evaluations. The kinds of things that these evaluations—of spaces in use—tend to measure are:

- Levels of occupancy/density
- Temporal habits
- Attitude/aesthetic appraisal
- Wellbeing

However, this is an area that has recently seen a major shift in power between the "experts" and the "public," via the use of social media. We recently conducted a study into the use of social media for post-occupancy evaluation and, in particular, looked at the use of review websites by members of the public, for posting their comments and reviews online about a specific designed space/place (in our study we focused on a well-known public building in North America). What was particularly interesting about this study was that unlike the highly-structured and formalized post-occupancy evaluation tools that have evolved in content, scope and complexity since they were introduced in the 1960s, these social-media reviews were simple, unstructured, unsolicited and bottom-up. It appears that people are just as willing to review a public building or an urban square/plaza, as they are to review a restaurant, hotel or plumber. Of all the tools/systems/processes for evaluating the quality of an environment, this is one that initially has the potential to be firmly wrenched from the hands of the "experts" and reclaimed by the public. In this way, anyone who wants to participate in the process of engaging with public/urban design is able to do so.

Looking towards the future, how might the active engagement of the public in public space planning/evaluation and design be encouraged? Firstly, what becomes apparent from looking at a number of so-called "review websites" is that many of the most highly used sites have a corresponding smartphone app.

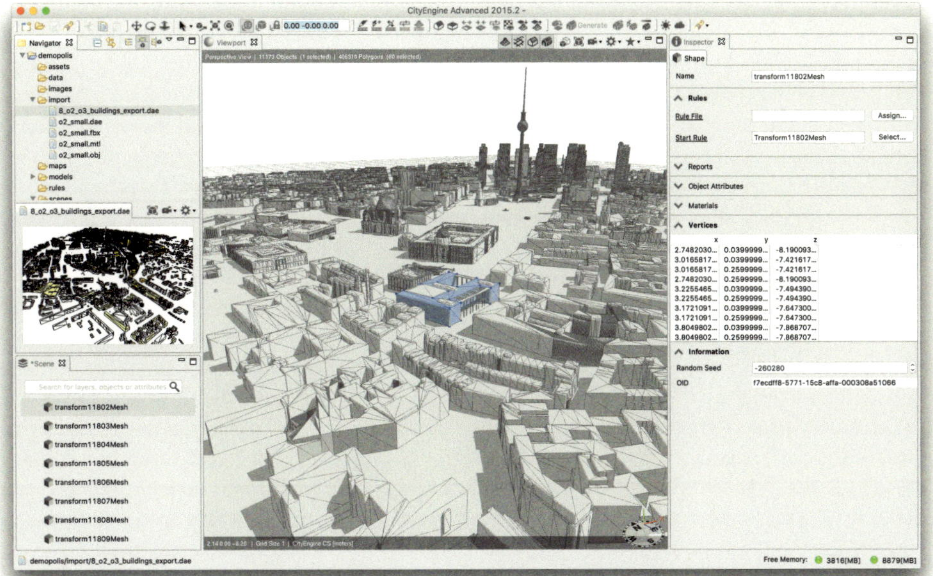

CityEngine scenario of the central Berlin Rathausforum and Alexanderplatz area, based on the 3-D planning model provided by the Senatsverwaltung für Stadtentwicklung und Umwelt Berlin, www.stadtentwicklung.berlin.de/planen/stadtmodelle/de/digitale_innenstadt/3d/index.shtml

Thus our first recommendation for any social media post-occupancy evaluation method is that it should be smartphone enabled. When using a smartphone, building users can review or comment on an urban space immediately (i.e., while still situated within the square as well as taking and posting photographs of aspects of the environment under discussion). A second suggestion is that any app should facilitate what is known as "push alerts," essentially brief notifications that appear momentarily on your phone, which in this case would prompt you to review the space (but is smart enough not to keep repeating the notification if you have already reviewed it). We also suggest that the process of providing feedback is as brief and painless as possible (see, for example, the website www.fixmystreet.com to "report, view, or discuss local problems [...] like graffiti, fly tipping, broken paving slabs, or street lighting").

Another online service, which has started to implement such a review facility, is UserVoice.com, a San Francisco-based company founded in 2008. This service designs and hosts feedback sites (both web- and mobile-based) designed specifically to elicit feedback. They have primarily been used to elicit feedback about websites, products and services and yet a number of cities have already used the service to gather feedback from their citizens about planning and governance problems and issues, for example Vancouver, Oregon, and Santa Barbara, California. Such a bottom-up approach has the advantage of being able to rapidly and automatically prioritize the key problems or suggestions raised by citizens and to encourage the exchange of ideas between community members in a more informal and immediate manner than, for example, in a traditional town hall meeting. It is also useful because it can generate issues of which the planners/designers might hitherto not have been aware. However, there are also a number of disadvantages with such a bottom-up approach: It is easy to get lost in the details as people can report on items that are essentially irrelevant; there is a potential for the feedback forum to be hijacked by a vocal minority with an issue to promote; people will often misreport issues because they lack the appropriate vocabulary or concepts; and finally, a bottom-up structure produces results that are hard to summate in the same manner as POE questionnaire responses can be analyzed, but the ranking or prioritization of issues immediately "falls out" of the emergent process.

But one issue with community-based feedback elicitation tools is that they are very text reliant. Despite the fact that they have the ability to raise some interesting issues, the predominant mode of exchange is that of the written word and this might alienate some members of the public, while also being inherently limiting. As mentioned above, general review websites, such as Yelp, do have the ability for commentators to upload photographs, so, for example, when discussing the good view of the Fernsehturm afforded by Alexanderplatz, a reviewer was able to upload an image of this view to illustrate the point. But if you are reliant on being able to upload photographs of what currently exists, what happens when you wish to discuss something that does not (yet) exist? How might these visions be uploaded, reviewed and discussed?

Architects and urban planners have always used visualizations of design proposals to communicate their ideas with members of the public. For the most part these visualizations are one-way (they are the result of designers/"experts" communicating with the public and not the other way around) and they have in the past been criticized for their static nature, that they only show what the designer wishes to show, from the specific locations chosen by them, with only the information that they wish to impart. What if it were possible to have a system in which members of the public could view a design scheme from any location they wished, see the full impact of the scheme and then, using the same software, propose their own design modifications or solutions, graphically rather than textually? This is the starting point of our vision for enabling *DEMO:POLIS*.

Imagine a system that has all the immediacy and accessibility of a review site like Yelp, which would be able to encourage even the most technophobic of citizens to express their views and opinions on a site/scheme/space due to its ease of use. Then imagine if one were able to seamlessly integrate a 3-D virtual model, using software such as CityEngine (its use in the exhibition offers a first glimpse of how such technology might enable public participation), permitting members of the public to view the model from any position and walk through the space, both as it is now and/or in multiple alternative futures. A further development is that a member of the public should even be able to tweak the model, lowering roof heights, adding trees, pedestrianizing streets, etc. Earlier on we talked about "lowering the bar" to using analytic tools, so that the "experts" do not act as gatekeepers to the software or proposals. Using CityEngine, a member of the public can play at being an "expert" and explore options for themselves. And finally, to close the loop, people should be able to share their solutions and invite comments/further refinements upon them in a manner very similar to the feedback process elicited via the UserVoice software, but with the addition of the 3-D graphic visualizations, resulting in a potential new synthesis of virtual reality programs and public participation for the design of public space/cities.

So finally, if such a system were to be made widely available, what else might be necessary to enable or encourage healthy public participation? The key thing is that this is already a very new way to think about citizen engagement and the co-creation of design solutions. Although concepts to do with participatory design have been around for decades, as we mentioned at the very beginning, everything is changing very rapidly at the moment and part of the change is about placing the user at the heart of design. So if we could get such a participatory system in use, there is every chance that it would fall onto fertile ground with citizens who are more than ready to embrace their new role. However, we believe that it would also require some education and public consciousness raising for people to be aware that such a system was available. Finally, once a critical level of awareness has been reached, our goal of using technology to help enable the interested public to participate in a meaningful way in the design of public space might finally be realized.

TRANSFORMATIONS

Public Space of the Public,
for the Public, and
by the Public.

Who owns Public Space?
Public Space belongs to the Public. Everyone has a right to use it.

Why Public Space?
Public Space is the continuous spatial fabric in which everyone has the right to move freely—unimpededly and anonymously—at all times to gain access to a community of people, to facilities, and the surroundings.

Public Space is a medium for communication. The right to free speech is exercised first and foremost in Public Space. Free speech, however, is only possible if the person wanting to speak freely can do so without surveillance, repression, or fear of retribution. People using Public Space or assembling in public space must be able to do so in complete anonymity.

Who creates Public Space?
Public Space is created by public consent. It represents the Public. It has been designed, constructed, maintained, and altered by representatives and delegates of the Public. Public Space appropriately fulfills the symbolic aspirations of the Public.

In the future, Public Space will be shaped by the Public: ***DEMO:POLIS***.
—WW

Alexanderplatz from 1900, 1950, 2000 to 2050

Public space is often associated with squares, particularly those squares located in the center of picturesque historic towns. However, public space is more than that: it includes the entire, continuously connected space that is openly accessible. This also includes the undefined area between social housing blocks, empty lots, and the interiors of publicly owned railway stations and airports. The first part of the exhibition looks at two typical elements of urban public space—the square and the street—and how they have been transformed over the last decades.

Alexanderplatz was once a cattle market on the northeastern edge of the town of Berlin. Then came the train, the tram, the S-Bahn and the U-Bahn, the office buildings, department stores, and cafés—and the market was forced out. This was followed by the destruction of the square through wartime bombing and its reconstruction in the socialist style of East Germany. In recent years, temples to consumerism have sprung up around it—the old square is changing, again and again.

No other capital city in the world has a square of this size that is still unfinished. This seems to be Berlin's destiny: to be a city in constant becoming, never complete. What did Alexanderplatz look like in 1900, in 1950, and in 2000? What brought about these changes? What will it look like in 2050? The present master plan for Alexanderplatz put forth by the architect Hans Kollhoff foresees a number of skyscrapers. Here, we document competition designs from 2014 by Kleihues+Kleihues and Barkow Leibinger for one of the skyscrapers to come. —WW

Demonstration in Alexanderplatz, 1989

Alexanderplatz

Alexanderplatz is the epitome of a city that is constantly in the process of evolving and is unlikely ever to be completed. Unlike its western counterpoint, Pariser Platz with the Brandenburg Gate (named after Prussia's victory over Napoleon in 1814), the renaming of the former Ochsenplatz into Alexanderplatz was a homage paid in 1805 to Prussia's staunch ally, Tsar Alexander I (1777–1825).

Earliest historical records show that the space now occupied by Alexanderplatz had been a market. It stood at the junction between regional trade routes that are still visible today in the major streets leading to the square. This web-like spatial logic continues uninterrupted to this day, thus reinforcing the integrative power of the public space. Some of Berlin's earliest department stores were situated there (Warenhaus Tietz, 1904), replacing outdoor with indoor markets.

As Berlin grew in population and size, new transport systems were developed and consistently located at this node: railway, underground, bus, tram, and car transport have each laid claim to space at this interchange to the extent that today, mass and individual mobility makes the strongest visual impression.

After the German Democratic Republic (GDR) was founded, the space was elevated into the new role of a symbolic urban node: at this junction the monumental east–west Stalinallee was resolved with the new north–south axis of the cleared open space—the Marx-Engels-Forum—emerging from the newly reorganized Museum Island. To mark this junction and the new central area of the socialist capital, the East German authorities erected the Fernsehturm [Television Tower].

All this is now up for grabs. These areas are all currently being reconsidered for redevelopment and the public can test out its own ideas using the interactive 3-D urban space program installed in the exhibition. —WW

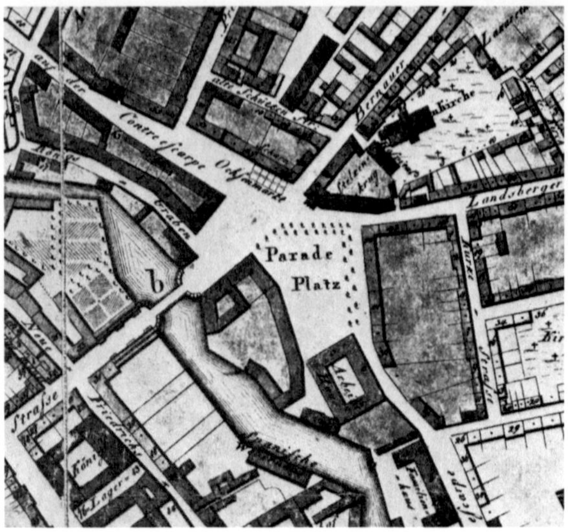

Detail of a map showing Alexanderplatz (Paradeplatz) from 1804

View of Alexanderplatz looking west, 1905

Alexanderplatz, Berlin, 1940

View of Alexanderplatz looking south, 1934

Alexanderplatz, Berlin, 1953

View of Alexanderplatz looking north, 1972

Alexanderplatz, Berlin, 1989

View of Alexanderplatz from a high-rise, corner of Hans-Beimler-Straße, 1991

View of Alexanderplatz from Fernsehturm, Berlin, 2009

Kleihues + Kleihues: High-Rise Alexanderplatz

LOCATION Berlin, Germany
ARCHITECT Kleihues + Kleihues
CLIENT Hines Germany
YEAR First phase: 2013; second phase: 2014
TYPE Mixed-use high-rise
DESIGN TEAM N/A
AREA 48,000 m² (gross floor area)

Berlin's Alexanderplatz is a place distinguished by the juxtaposition of diverse urban planning and architectural concepts: the bright, stone-clad buildings by Peter Behrens characterize the space just as much as the edifices of postwar modernism, with their abstraction and transformation of pure geometric forms. The design for this high-rise development reflects the unique and distinctive features of the surrounding buildings and reinterprets them in the form of a new building typology. As a residential tower on the Alexanderplatz, the building references the modernist structures in the area with its cubic form. The most challenging aspect of the design was developing a building that could mesh well with and react appropriately to its context, despite its prominent height and the meaning ascribed to it by its central location: a building, in other words, that—while conceived as a tower and thus inherently solitary—also has the ability to create an ensemble.

The appearance of the building when seen from afar is dominated by the clear silhouette of the tower against the sky. The appearance when seen up close, on the other hand, is defined by the building's multilayered façade treatment. The tower and its plinth are treated as independent elements and clearly separated through an indentation in the volume; at the same time, however, the two elements together form a harmonious whole. The building's geometrical character as a multifaceted prism is an expression of an architectural approach that is both rational and modern.

The interpretation of the façade as a combination of serial elements, its formal development in nuances reminiscent of sculpture, its subtly rotating volumes, and its return to classical materials both at the base and the upper areas—all of this allows the building to mediate between different periods. In contrast to the simple, sculptural structure of the building, the façade takes on a complex, multilayered, and three-dimensional character that is derived from the shape of the site. While the façade of the plinth element is smooth, the surface gradually increases in complexity and plasticity towards the top. The different functions housed in the building are easily readable on the façade: the smoothness of the plinth element reflects the serial organization of the hotel area within, while the individually articulated segments on the upper levels hint at the private apartments that are hidden behind them. Apartments on alternating floors are equipped with individual balconies, which offer grand vistas over the city in two directions while also preventing neighbors from looking into each other's apartments, resulting in a high level of intimacy. While the façade, as represented in the floor plan, appears to be based on a simple constructive principle, its physical manifestation features a fascinating play of light and shadow thanks to its various overhangs and setbacks, thus articulating a unique identity within the urban context. —KLEIHUES + KLEIHUES

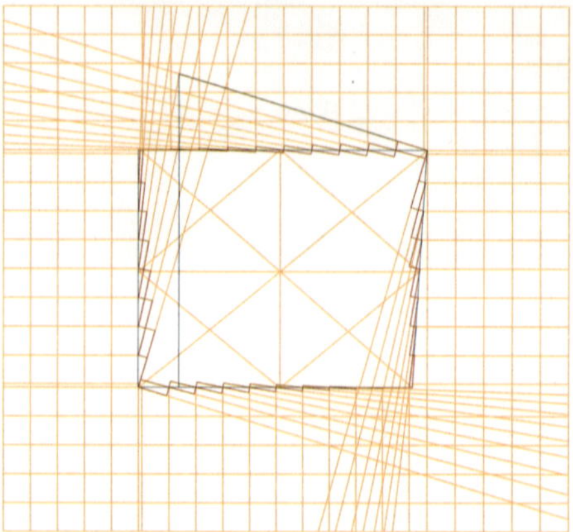

Concept diagram

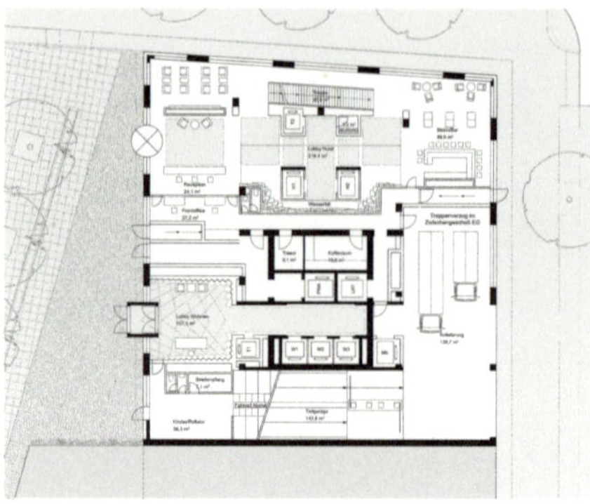

Ground floor plan

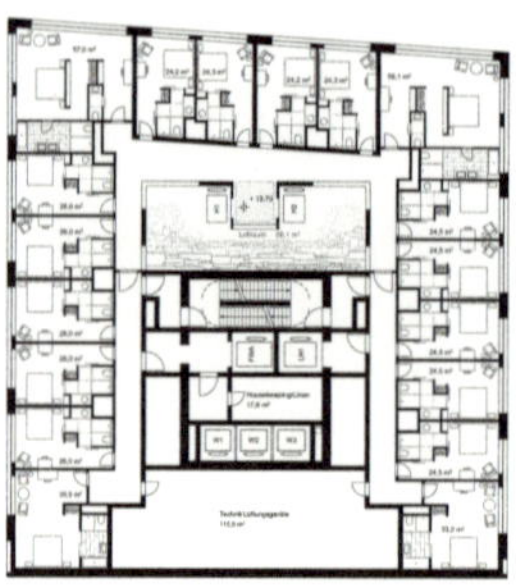

Hotel floor plan 3rd–7th floors

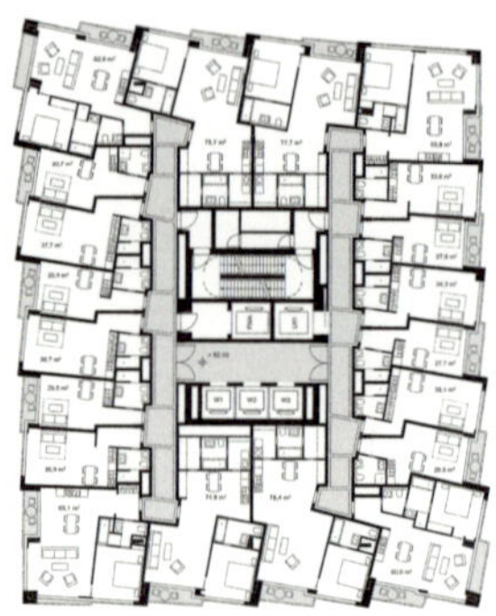

Residential floor plan 14th floor

Detail perspective with view over Berlin

Southeast elevation

Perspective view from Karl-Marx-Allee

Barkow Leibinger: High-Rise Alexanderplatz

LOCATION Berlin, Germany
ARCHITECT Barkow Leibinger
CLIENT Hines Germany
YEAR First phase: 2013; second phase: 2014
TYPE Mixed-use high-rise
DESIGN TEAM Michael Ahlers, Sebastian Awick, Martina Bauer, Sonia Cohan, Thomas Day, Nadja Jeske, Daria Khapalova, Jonathan Kleinhample, Elizaveta Mosina, Ulrich von Türckheim, Blake Villwock, Tobias Wenz, Jens Weßel
AREA ca. 50,000 m^2 (gross floor area)

For us, Alexanderplatz is not the historical Berlin of Alfred Döblin or the old empire: It is no place for sentimentality, but rather a site of modernity. It will never be a pretty, harmonious, homogeneous ensemble, nor will it be a *Stadtkrone* as Bruno Taut envisioned it, a prestigious centerpiece for the city. Instead, it will always be a lively, multilayered plaza, full of ruptures and subject to constant change. To reflect this, our aim was to design a symbolic, unmistakable building, a new, powerful freestanding structure with a figure that could also react to the square in as distinctive a way as possible. The design is self-contained, yet open to dialogue. It engages with the city's tradition of forward-looking, expressionist buildings as a starting point, building upon it to create something that is clearly new, contemporary, and appropriate to its time, while also acting as an urban, architectural mediator between the different architectural languages of Peter Behrens's New Objectivity, DDR Modernism, and the contemporary glass cube of the Saturn building.

The tower is composed of large, staggered volumes, stacked on top of each other so as to coil back upon themselves. These volumes pick up on the various heights of the neighboring buildings and orient the high-rise development, which houses both apartment and hotel functions, towards important reference points in the neighborhood in a gentle rotation. The tower thus turns towards Karl-Marx-Allee, the plaza, and the Fernsehturm in succession. The apartments feature loggias that are sheltered from the wind, and which, taken altogether, serve to break up the large volume of the building into smaller units. Thanks to their angled shape and their room-high windows, the loggias offer the residents wide vistas of the city.

With its glassy, versatile, and dynamic façade—at times transparent, at times reflective—the building makes a clear statement: It connects the urban and the private, makes visible the theme of "dwelling" in the context of Alexanderplatz, and becomes a screen for both projections and reflections of urban life exactly where Berlin is at its most metropolitan. —BARKOW LEIBINGER

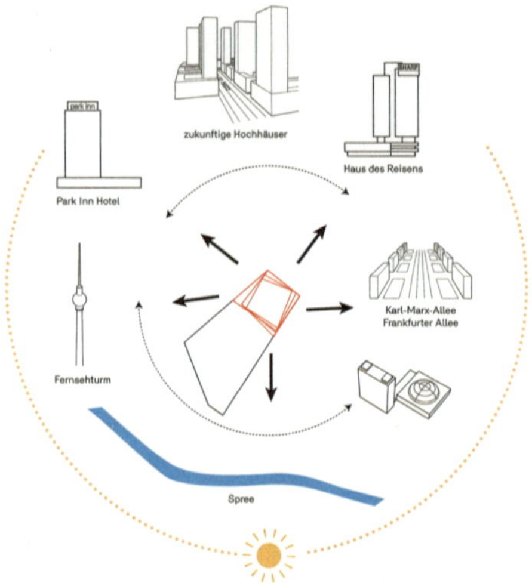

Plan, ground floor

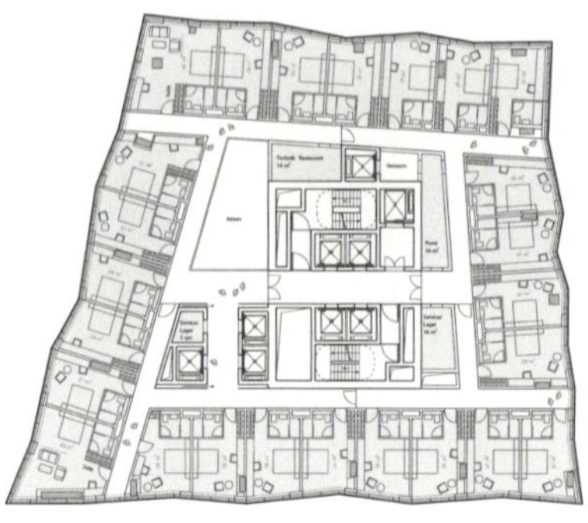
Plan, 9th–12th floors, hotel

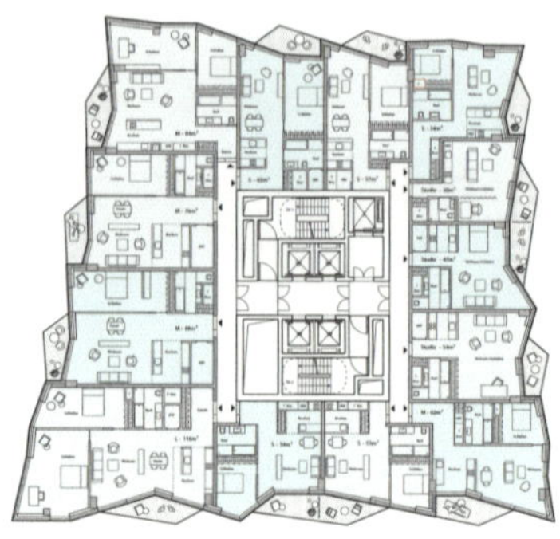
Plan, 14th–23rd floors, residential

Perspective of Alexanderplatz

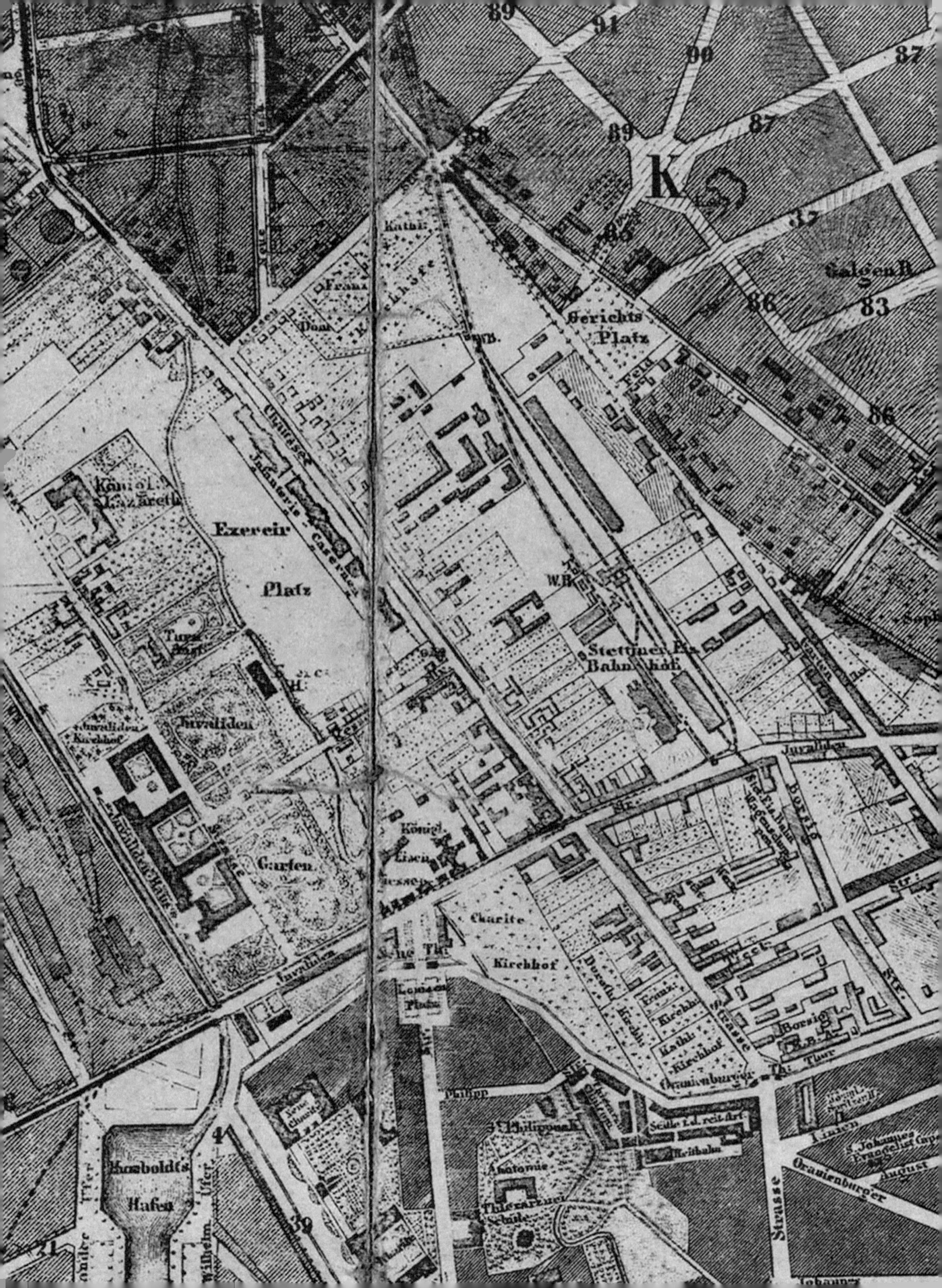

89
91
90
87
88
89
87
K
85
86
83
86
Gerichts
Platz
Exercir
Platz
Chaussee
Infanterie
Caserne
Invaliden
Garten
Charite
Kirchhof
Stettiner
Borsig
Oranienburger
Strasse
Anatomie
Hafen

Ackerstraße from 1900, 1950, 2000 to 2050

Demographic and political changes have a direct impact on the quality of public space. In a typical Berlin street, the Ackerstraße, the number and quality of shops, bars, and services have changed along with the demographic of the people living there.

In 1900, a higher number of people, young and old, lived in each apartment than in 2000. Spending capacity per capita has dropped: as a result, the types of shops in the area have changed, together with the industrialization of agriculture, centralized distribution systems, and aggressive marketing.

On top of this, Ackerstraße directly experienced the effects of the division of Berlin. The Berlin Wall ran right across the middle of the street; the northern part belonged to West Berlin, the southern part to East Berlin. Even after reunification, the scars of the wall remained visible, but now another process has taken its toll: Gentrification.

What will Ackerstraße look like in 2050? Who will live and work there? Who can afford to live and work there? Will it be purely upper middle class? Will the residents have children? And if not, what happens to the schools? Will more and more tourists come there, staying in Airbnb apartments? Who will still own a car? Anyone? What happens to the parking spaces? Can they be used for proper bicycle lanes? Or urban farming? Will this street only have offices in the future? —ww

Ferdinand Boehm, *Plan von Berlin und Umgegend bis Charlottenburg*, 1862

Ackerstraße

Ackerstraße, a nearly 1,500 meter-long thoroughfare that ties together the neighborhoods of Mitte and Wedding, is a typical Berlin street with an extraordinary history. Originally laid out starting in 1751 as part of a worker's colony northwest of the city walls, the street retained its semi-rural character and single-story development until the mid-nineteenth century, when rapid industrialization encouraged swift urban development in the north of Berlin.

A visitor to Ackerstraße in 1900 would have seen a densely built working class neighborhood with a mixture of housing, industry, and commercial functions. The street was dominated by tenement buildings called *Mietskasernen* (rental barracks), almost always five stories high and featuring one or more courtyards closed in by side and rear buildings. These were notorious for overcrowded and unsanitary living conditions: in the infamous *Meyers Hof*, a *Mietskaserne* with a record five courtyards, over two thousand people were crammed into three hundred apartments. The street, however, was lively: given the small size of apartments and the very little green space in the neighborhood, residents appropriated tenement courtyards and the street as spaces for their everyday lives.

After the establishment of the German Democratic Republic (GDR) in 1949, Ackerstraße became a street straddling two nations: all parts north of Bernauer Straße belonged to West Germany, while everything south of the street belonged to East Germany. With the construction of the Berlin Wall in 1961, a process that was already in motion with the political division of Berlin was made visually and tangibly real: Ackerstraße, once a centrally-located, lively place, became urban periphery.

In 2000, eleven years after German reunification, the street reflected the lingering effects of this division. At the former West German end, a government-led urban renewal program in the 1970s had, with the best of intentions, emptied, demolished, and rebuilt entire areas of the neighborhood as monofunctional housing blocks—thus displacing communities and severing old neighborhood ties. Since then, the northern Ackerstraße fell into an extended hibernation, its abundant open spaces not designed to serve the neighborhood's aging and economically disadvantaged population. On the other hand, the formerly East German part of Ackerstraße saw its pre-war housing stock largely intact due to a government policy that, lacking the funds for extensive urban renewal measures, instead took the approach of minimally maintaining old buildings. After reunification, this cleared the way for a new development: gentrification. From 1994 onwards, a government-initiated retrofit program has managed to transform the southern Ackerstraße into a popular location where, in the summer, the sidewalks are populated by visitors dining alfresco and enjoying the view over the street's delicately renovated nineteenth-century façades. Of course, this did not come about without a corresponding increase in rents.

Ackerstraße encapsulates many of the phenomena that have influenced urban development in Berlin: rapid industrialization and development, the division into east and west, and now, the two poles of urban stagnation and gentrification. Ackerstraße today is, in effect, two streets, running through two different worlds. What is needed to weave the two parts together again? With the help of a public questionnaire, visitors to the exhibition are invited to envision Ackerstraße in the year 2050. —YS

Where two nations once met: the corner of Ackerstraße and Bernauer Straße from above, 2016

Public life behind the street façade: a harvest festival in Meyers Hof (Ackerstraße 132/133), 1929

Ackerstraße before the war: a Sunday walk on the southern end of the street, 1929

Ackerstraße, 1910

Divided nation, divided street: looking south down Ackerstraße over the Berlin Wall

Ackerstraße, 1956 (showing outline of Berlin Wall)

Lingering traces of division: the southern Ackerstraße with its restored pre-war buildings (left), and the northern Ackerstraße with its modernist housing blocks (top right, bottom right)

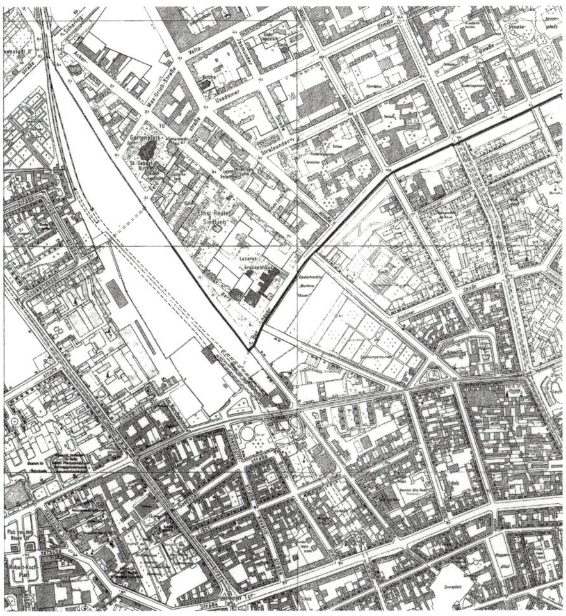

Ackerstraße, 2001 (showing outline of Berlin Wall)

Transforming Cities

Berlin's public spaces have changed in recent years, sometimes beyond recognition. In Berlin, Michael Ruetz has taken photographs from the same point year after year. The result is a breathtaking time-lapse sequence.

Each city has its own character. Michael Najjar demonstrates this cognitive phenomenon as he allows the photographs he has taken from the tops of skyscrapers around the world to fade in and out: our memories of places are stimulated by layer after layer of pixels as the profile of each city's distinct physiognomy emerges.

Public space exists even in the most modest, peripheral of contexts. Nuno Cera has taken videos of untenable housing areas in Istanbul, endless suburbs in Mexico, and soulless developments in Shanghai. They demonstrate the disdain and lack of care and respect that such leftover public spaces express vis-à-vis their population. —WW

Michael Najjar, netropolis | new york

TIMESCAPE

The research project THE TEXTURE OF TIME was launched in 1966 and has seen its most intense activity in the period since 1987. By the time the project is completed in 2016, it will have spanned over fifty years of observation.

The titles the TEXTURE OF TIME and TIMESCAPE were conceived in an ad hoc manner. Neither the *Oxford English Dictionary* nor the *Random House Unabridged Dictionary* contains an entry for the word "TIMESCAPE."

The first shot was taken on April 11, 1966. It was of the Gendarmenmarkt, which at the time was called Platz der Akademie. It was completely overgrown by yellow grass and was considered the most beautiful ruined landscape in Berlin. In fact it was a typical example of Berlin's transformation back into a landscape, a consequence of the genocidal bombing war waged by the Allies in the Second World War. The Platz der Akademie had become a habitat for rare plants, as observed by Bruce von Voorst from NEWSWEEK.

The concentrated work on THE TEXTURE OF TIME began in 1987–1989 with photographs of a slagheap from a potassium mine near Hildesheim, an urban landscape in Peine, and a CITYSCAPE in Melbourne, Australia. A basic principle of the work was to make use of locations that were easy to find again and whose existence was guaranteed in the long term, in addition to a fixed line of sight.

The long-term points of observation used in the project were distributed in an area in Europe that is roughly defined by Brielle (Netherlands) in the west, Bensersiel (Lower Saxony) in the north, Bautzen (Saxony) in the east, and the Brenner Pass (Austria) in the south—with Berlin at the center. Altogether, they include more than six hundred points; coincidentally, all of the names start with B. 360 such points were installed in Berlin alone, with around a hundred in Berlin-Mitte. The observation could not continue uninterrupted everywhere, since many observation points fell victim to new construction and other measures. One of the biggest problems, especially in central Berlin, was bureaucratic obstruction by overbearing authorities.

One may be tempted to see the observation period represented in the Berlin series (which shows the immense upheaval in the city that has taken place since the collapse of East Germany) as an inverse analogy to the bombing war. I have thus often regretted not having been able to start this project between 1939 and 1945... and then continuing it during the subsequent reconstruction years. The period of work essentially corresponds to a period that Hermann Rudolf has described in his must-read book *Berlin. Wiedergeburt einer Stadt* [Berlin: Rebirth of a City].

It was both my intention and a fortuitous coincidence—a combination of fate and intuition—that Berlin, with a singularly rapid transformation that is representative not just of Europe, became the core of this observation project.

The perspective and mode of observation are, as a matter of principle, kept as neutral as possible and are marked by an equanimous acceptance of events. The images show situations "as they are" and not "as they should be," regardless of whether they are ugly, beautiful, or whatever else. Viewers from Berlin today already have an image of what the present looks like; for them, these images will not be as startling and informative as they will doubtless be for those who see them five decades later.

TIMESCAPE 352.3, 24.06.1995, 17:09

TIMESCAPE 352.5, 01.02.1996, 12:02

TIMESCAPE 352.9, 14.12.1999, 11:10

TIMESCAPE 352.19, 01.05.2006, 11:42

The choice of observation points within these urban landscapes is based on the thesis that the condition and development of a society—that is, what we generally call "time"—can be read in the edifices it creates. In Berlin, one could read the transition from a socialist to a capitalist-democratic society, as well as the convergence of the city's neighborhoods. This can be most clearly seen at the pressure points recorded by this project.

A very good example is the metamorphosis of the Marx-Engels-Platz into the Schloßplatz. The real focus of the TIMESCAPE series that was taken at this site is not the demolition of the Palast der Republik or the reconstruction of the City Palace, but rather what the transformation of the site makes palpable: a shift in the system and its ways of thought. The former Palace of the Republic was meant to be the antithesis of a palace, signifying a move away from feudalism. It is still unclear what the reconstruction of the City Palace signifies.

A number of personal reasons caused me to begin this work, one of which was an awareness of the relentless process of aging. A faint premonition of massive upheaval in the late 1980s added to this. Both of these compelled me to start concentrating on a large, unified life work.

The entire work is intended for readers and viewers in the remote future—not least for my daughter, Anna Amalia, who will be the same age as I am today in half a century's time.

The project, which is now approaching completion, is primarily a representation of the invisible, of time. Out of a period of work that is unusually long, especially when compared to the ephemerality of contemporary photography, series of images have emerged that are in the final analysis nothing other than time-lapse films. They make time visible. The objects shown in juxtaposition in these images are, ultimately, neither the motifs nor the subject matter of the project. Certainly, what is depicted here are rural and urban landscapes, people and groups of people, as well as repeating, characteristic scenarios from daily life. Yet their ostinato is time itself.

Further essays on this project, as well as treatments of questions relating to the issue of time, can be found in almost all of my books dedicated to the theme of time.

A comprehensive presentation of the project is not planned until the years after 2018. However, some important segments of the project have already been published in the form of books and exhibitions: the exhibition SICHTBARE ZEIT (1995) in the German Historical Museum; EYE ON TIME (2007), also in the German Historical Museum; FACING TIME (2013), a portrayal of the transformation of a group of people, presented in the form of three exhibitions and a limited-edition book; and also EYE ON INFINITY and EYE ON LIGHT/DIE ABSOLUTE LANDSCHAFT, which portray the never-ending metamorphosis of a rural area in the form of two separate exhibitions and books.

My wish is that fifty years after the completion of this project (that is, around the year 2066), a few of the photographic subjects shown here, whether they be urban landscapes, situations, or people, could become objects of observation again as a continuation of their respective TIMESCAPE series.

TIMESCAPE 162.2, 28.11.1993, 11:45

TIMESCAPE 162.3, 30.06.1995, 10:01

TIMESCAPE 162.8, 06.07.1998, 12:53

TIMESCAPE 162.11, 25.04.2004, 10:43

The TEXTURE OF TIME/SICHTBARE ZEIT has not received any external financial support to date. Sympathy from public institutions has been virtually nonexistent. With its estimated duration of almost three decades, the project was a bet on the future from the very beginning. It was understandable that public support for such a shot in the dark could not be expected, as the author himself could not realistically guarantee that the project would be completed after twenty-five years. Partly for this reason, it made sense to invest the time and effort it would have taken to acquire external funds and secure grants, instead spending it on the work itself. The project is thus completely financed by my own funds.

My utmost thanks are due to three experienced and thoughtful assistants who were involved in an important part of the work: Astrid Köppe, Vincent Mosch, and Kathleen Blume. Particular thanks also go to Christoph Stölzl, who showed interest in the project from very early on, recognized its importance, and presented an early stage of the work in the exhibition SICHTBARE ZEIT in the German Historical Museum in 1995. Additional thanks go to Barbara Straka, Dieter Vorsteher and Monika Flacke, as well as Valentin Rothmaler.

—MICHAEL RUETZ

MICHAEL NAJJAR

netropolis

The work series *netropolis* (2003–2006) is an exploration of the way global cities will develop in the future. Of similar magnitude to the impact of the Industrial Revolution in the late nineteenth century, today's computer networks and the information society based on them are the key elements transforming the face of our urban living spaces.

The complexity of a megacity should be considered as the material embodiment of information density. Telematic space endows the urban environment with a new form of structure, intermingling with it and giving birth to a completely unprecedented form of interactive urban space.

The panoramic view transforms the reality of urban spatial structure into landscape. The digital fusion of panoramic views taken from different angles transforms the landscape into a woven fabric of relationships that is abstract and multilayered, yet still underpinned by a geographic reference point. Viewing the city from a distance inverses the perceptual order of objects viewed in close-up. The view from afar is oriented around what is clearly visible from a distance and provides a context for objects that appear too close when viewed in close-up, thus retaining their strangeness. In virtual space, however, distance and proximity lie on the same level. The different perspectives and relationship strands need first to be combined and interwoven before they can give rise to a completely unprecedented and imaginary form of urbanity—the telematic *netropolis*.

The *netropolis* series of works portrays the megacities of Berlin, Beijing, Dubai, Hong Kong, London, Los Angeles, Mexico City, New York, Paris, São Paulo, Shanghai, and Tokyo.

—MICHAEL NAJJAR

netropolis | berlin

netropolis | london

netropolis | shanghai

netropolis | são paulo

NUNO CERA

Futureland

The Lisbon-based video artist Nuno Cera is interested in urban surroundings, shared public spaces, and nondescript spaces around the globe. In his project *Futureland*, which was initiated in 2008, he examines the legacy of urban growth, town planning, and architecture of the twentieth-century, while keeping a close eye on current developments in city landscapes today. The project is his take on the recent astonishing growth of cities and its impact on their inhabitants and their environment. He selected different rapidly growing megacities on four continents: Istanbul, Berlin, Cairo, Dubai, Los Angeles, Mexico City, Shanghai, Hong Kong, Tokyo, Jakarta, and Mumbai. His artistic approach is not about trying to document or analyze growth in the sense of putting the process into a chronological, systematic, or comparative order. Instead, his project is a collection of subjective impressions and atmospheres, leaving it up to the viewer to judge or draw conclusions to these complex processes and the reasons behind them, as well as the consequences one can expect.

Within his artistic pilgrimage as a global experience of transformation, he collects manifold impressions of public space worldwide, which is shifting and changing at an immense speed and scale. While the perspective of the artist remains relatively neutral, the viewer starts to see how astonishing this all is after lining up all the pieces beside each other.

From informal settlements in greater Istanbul to a food joint in Los Angeles, from the fashion district in Hong Kong to the transportation veins of Dubai, from Berlin's legendary Alexanderplatz to rooftops in Cairo, *Futureland* is a capsule of information, time, and space. —JULIA ALBANI AND NUNO CERA

Tokyo, 2015

Tokyo, 2015

Mumbai, 2010

Shanghai, 2009

Dubai, 2009

Cairo, 2010

Shanghai, 2009

Jakarta, 2010

PARADIGMS

Many interest groups vie for the use of Public Space: private and public transport; pedestrians and cyclists; commerce through marketing events and advertising; sport and fashion events; demonstrators and politicians; developers and neighborhood initiatives; artists and designers. Some only have their own interest in mind; others try to be voices for the greater good. Public Space has become a battle zone of partial interest groups.

When the inner city is closed down for a marathon, when a car manufacturer is granted use of the most important thoroughfare in the city for a whole week to erect flimsy tents for a fashion show, when an international football organization can put up a pavilion in the middle of the city's most prominent square, is that acceptable? —WW

TAKE AND BAKE PIZZA
NATIONAL ACTION NETWORK
NAN

Fights for Rights

Impending changes on a local and global scale and disclosures of the illegal behavior of those in power bring about different reactions from people. The threatened closure of a hospital or library, excessive police force, the potential privatization of the legal system through international trade agreements, and the revelation of illegal secret service surveillance can be causes for which smaller or larger groups of people are willing to take to the streets.

Demonstrations are now organized more effectively via the Internet, as the Arab Spring, the events on Istanbul's Taksim Square, and Kiev's Maidan Square have shown. But also the unprecedented show of millions of people in Paris and across the globe following the massacre of the caricaturists at *Charlie Hebdo* and the murder of innocent people on November 14, 2015 have reestablished the importance of public space as the real and symbolic medium of enlightened freedom.

Public space has once again become a testing ground for the self-perception of a form of civilization that has as its cornerstones freedom from fear, freedom of expression, and the freedom to demonstrate for or against an issue in anonymity.

Today, the vast, general, law-abiding public is trapped between the need to identify potential wrongdoers at the earliest possible stage and the right to individual anonymity in both public space and the Internet. The central tenet of an enlightened legal system that an individual is innocent until he or she is proven guilty has been undermined by wholesale surveillance on the Internet. At the same time, transnational social media networks have been used by bottom-up organizers of demonstrations.

The fight for rights will become more intense, more urgent and more widespread; and that on its own is a positive indication that people are still willing to show their true colors, given that we have entered a period of unpredictable terrorist attacks. Today, the struggle for rights has become a true act of civil courage. —WW

Protests following the death of Michael Brown, 2014

Tunisian Revolution, 2010

Demonstration against the Tunisian government, Tunis, January 2011

Starting in mid-December 2010, the Tunisian Revolution (also known in various sources as the Jasmine Revolution or the Sidi Bouzid Revolt, after the city in which the first protests took place) was a sustained period of non-violent civic resistance by the citizens of Tunisia against the autocratic government of President Zine El Abidine Ben Ali. The movement was sparked by the death of Mohammed Bouazizi, a street vendor in the city of Sidi Bouzid who set himself on fire protesting against the confiscation of his wares and the humiliating treatment he faced at the hands of a police officer. Protests in Sidi Bouzid criticizing the treatment of Bouazizi quickly spread across the country, apparently serving as a release valve for long-standing frustrations over poverty, unemployment, and political repression. Protests intensified after the government began a violent crackdown on the movement, finally leading to the President's ousting in January 2011 and the installation of a new government based on democratic elections. The Tunisian Revolution is regarded as the beginning of a string of protests, riots, and revolts across the Arab world in the early 2010s, popularly called the "Arab Spring."

Both contemporary and retrospective analyses of the Tunisian protests have focused on the central role that Internet-based communication systems, and particularly social media, played in organizing the protests. In the context of a government-enforced media blackout within Tunisia on reports about the unrest, services such as Facebook and Twitter were crucial in drawing international attention to the protests and—more importantly—building coalitions between like-minded activists across the country to help the movement grow beyond the local level. The Tunisian Revolution therefore provides a potent example of how the emergence of a new, virtual public sphere on the Internet has transformed social configurations in traditional, physical space. —YS

Occupy Wall Street, 2011

Meeting on the first day of Occupy Wall Street, Zuccotti Park, New York City, September 17, 2011

On September 17, 2011, over one thousand people congregated in Zuccotti Park, a 3,100-square-meter open space in Lower Manhattan, New York. They set up tents, organized meetings, and started performing speeches. Occupy Wall Street, as the movement called itself, was a loosely organized group that sought to protest against abuses in the financial sector, wealth inequality, and capitalism in general by "occupying" the space within a stone's throw from the New York Stock Exchange.

The movement quickly took off, attracting celebrities, politicians, and thousands of activists and curious onlookers; very soon, movements in cities across the United States and the world were taking over public spaces under the Occupy name. Characteristic for the movement was its strictly non-hierarchical nature, which emphasized decision making through direct consensus and discussion. Distinctive, too, was how the movement manifested itself simultaneously in physical space (the encampment) as well as in virtual space (online forums, live tweets of assemblies in the square, etc.). The encampment, in particular, became a central feature of the movement, taking on the characteristics of a small municipality with its own alternative infrastructure for food distribution, sanitation, medical care, and media. Yet the encampment at Zuccotti Park was far more than a simple logistical headquarters; over time, it took on a symbolic dimension as well.

In the absence of visible leaders or a clear set of symbols, the image of the occupied Zuccotti Park—antisymbolic in its anonymity—functioned as a stand-in for the movement as a whole. Perhaps this is also why the movement never really recovered after Zuccotti Park was forcibly evacuated on November 15, 2011.

The movement, which attracted a whole spectrum of people with widely differing backgrounds and interests, was often criticized for what was perceived to be a chaotic organization and a lack of concrete demands. Yet, perhaps it is beside the point to evaluate the movement in terms of its fulfillment of concrete political goals. Rather, Occupy Wall Street is above all notable as a return to the spatial tactics of protest that had seemingly been on the decline since the 1980s, when major encampments such as the "Republik Freies Wendland" [Republic of Free Wendland] against the planned construction of a nuclear waste dump in Gorleben, Germany, were making headlines. Like these older movements, Occupy Wall Street succeeded in creating, if only for a few months, an agora in the truest sense: a "space of appearance" where citizens could come together and make their concerns known, a space of diverse populations and still more diverse positions, irreducible, in its democratic cacophony, to one single narrative. —YS

Gezi Park / Taksim Square Protest, 2013

Protestors gathering in Gezi Park, Istanbul, June 1, 2013

Taksim Gezi Park is a small park in central Istanbul, Turkey, located next to the important traffic node of Taksim Square. In the early summer of 2013, the park was at the center of one of the largest anti-government protests in the history of modern Turkey. The unrest was triggered by plans to raze the park—one of the last remaining green spaces in the center of the city—and replace it with a shopping mall modeled after an Ottoman-era military barracks that had once stood at the site. After police forcibly removed a group that had been occupying the park, the aim of the protests broadened from disapproval of the park's demolition to a general critique of the Turkish government under the increasingly autocratic Prime Minister Recep Tayyip Erdoğan (President since 2014). On June 1, 2013, after numerous violent skirmishes with thousands of protesters who had gathered at Taksim Square, the police decided to withdraw. For the next ten days, Taksim Square was transformed into an autonomous zone featuring various encampments with a parallel infrastructure including food, sanitation, entertainment, and media. While the movement had died down by the end of the summer, the protests were considered a significant vote of no confidence for the decade-long Erdoğan regime, shaking Turkey's reputation as a stable democracy.

A notable factor in the success of the Taksim Square protest was its decentralized organization and its refusal to define its criticism of the government within one ideological framework. This allowed it to attract a broad variety of usually antagonistic groups, including secular nationalists, Islamists, communists, environmentalists, LGBT activists, and even football hooligans. Perhaps a key aspect was the fact that the protest movement was anchored in public space—a site that, by its very nature, could not exclude anyone from literally setting up camp to air their own frustrations. —YS

Demonstrations against Internet Surveillance, 2013

Protest in support of Edward Snowden, Berlin, November 18, 2013

Starting in June 2013, a number of leaked documents from the USA's National Security Agency (NSA) brought to light the full scope of mass surveillance by the United States government and its allies. Among the allegations were the surveillance of telephone and Internet records for millions of people worldwide, many obtained by secret court order from major telecommunications companies. The documents were leaked by Edward Snowden, a former contract worker for the NSA.

The revelations were followed almost immediately by a public backlash against what many perceived was an egregious breach of privacy by government institutions. Protests took place in both physical and digital forums: rallies in the United States, the United Kingdom, Germany, and various other countries attracted thousand of protesters, while an international day of action in February 2014 named "The Day We Fight Back" called for emails to congress members and for websites to engage in civil disobedience by adding banners protesting against the NSA.

While the public demonstrations may be the most visible implication of the Snowden leaks with respect to public space, perhaps more significant is how the unveiling of the mass surveillance programs made it clear to what extent the traditional categories of public and private are breaking down in an increasingly digitalized world. All of a sudden, citizens found their private messages and data scanned by the government in the name of "public interest"; the personal, it became clear, was very much the political. The demonstrations were an attempt to bring these two spheres back into their place: the perhaps paradoxical act of going public to demand privacy, demonstrating that a "right to public space" can only exist in tandem with a "right to privacy" that forms its counterpart. —YS

Protests Following the Death of Michael Brown, 2014

Protestors form a human chain during a demonstration against police brutality, Ferguson, Missouri

On August 9, 2014, Michael Brown, an unarmed black teenager, was fatally shot by Darren Wilson, a white police officer, in Ferguson, Missouri (USA), a suburb of St. Louis. Occurring amidst a string of high-profile deaths of unarmed black men at the hands of American law enforcement officials (see, for example, the death by chokehold of Eric Garner in July 2014, or the shooting of Tamir Rice in November 2014), the shooting sparked widespread protests in Ferguson and beyond, especially after a grand jury decided in November 2014 not to indict Wilson.

While motivated in part by anger over the individual case, the protests above all called attention to systematic issues plaguing the United States, including disadvantage and poverty in black communities, the gradual militarization of law enforcement, and the disproportionately higher rate at which young black males are killed at the hands of others. Under the banner of #BlackLivesMatter, the Ferguson protests have evolved into a multifaceted, large-scale protest movement that has brought people out into public space on a scale not seen in the United States since the Occupy Wall Street protests in 2011.

Michael Brown was shot and killed in the street by a public law enforcement official. His death, then, serves as a reminder that the ability to be present in public space is asymmetrically distributed—for some, public space can just as much represent danger as it does freedom. Indeed, the images from Ferguson of a militarized police force pointing automatic rifles at protesters serve to illustrate the constant threat of violence that undergirds public space, a violence that could, at any point, be turned against you. Are the protests in Ferguson a first step in reclaiming a public space that is truly, equally open to all? —YS

Je suis Charlie, Republican Marches, 2015

Protestors on the Place de la République during the republican march, Paris

"Je suis Charlie" was a statement of solidarity designed by the French art director Joachim Roncin in the aftermath of the *Charlie Hebdo* shootings on January 7, 2015, in which twelve people related to the French satirical weekly *Charlie Hebdo* were killed by two gunmen in the paper's Paris headquarters. The perpetrators, who were later identified as acting in the name of the Islamist terror group Al-Qaida in Yemen, declared their act as revenge for what they saw as *Charlie Hebdo*'s blasphemous depictions of Muhammad. In this context, the statement "Je suis Charlie" [I am Charlie] became a slogan that signified not just condemnation of the killings, but also advocacy for the principle of free speech in general. The phrase, facilitated in its distribution through a Twitter hashtag (#jesuischarlie) and a freely downloadable logo, spread like wildfire through both the Internet and traditional media channels.

The global, digital phenomenon of "Je suis Charlie" found its spatial manifestation in the so-called "marches républicaines" [republican marches] across France on January 10 and 11, 2015. These mass rallies were meant as a demonstration of resilience in the face of the violence as well as an affirmation of French republican values, and resulted in one of the greatest turnouts for a political rally in French history: in Paris alone, the march attracted nearly two million individuals and forty world leaders. The images of crowds young and old, of all ethnicities and confessions, filling Paris's stately boulevards (which, lest we forget, were designed exactly to *prevent* mass demonstrations) on that cold winter afternoon seemed to affirm the renewed importance of politicized public space. —YS

Art Actions

For centuries, public spaces have been used as sites for impressive statues celebrating notable individuals. Yet following Andy Warhol's revolutionary prophecy that everyone will have their "fifteen minutes of world fame," artistic interventions in public spaces have questioned the right to select art, in other words the curatorship rights of the few over the many. Today, artists no longer seek permission for their works to be seen in public—they simply realize them, which represents the ultimate expression of freedom.

Graffiti and street art are among these forms of artistic communication. These symbolically encrypted demarcations of subcultural groups and bottom-up social criticism, often easily displayed in neglected infrastructural domains such as railway cuttings and inner-city motorway landscapes, are like conventional gallery art in the sense that they have themselves become subject to normative appropriation by the rich and powerful. Birgit Hein's photographic records of advertising campaigns in New York City subway stations show the subversion of commerce through bottom-up wit and ridicule. Elfi Mikesch's videos of Berlin's street art provide a candid insight into intense works, often in unlikely locations, some of which have gained the status of urban icons.

The installations by Stih & Schnock are subtle interventions in public consciousness. Using almost childlike icons in the form of street graphics and combining these with the notorious discriminatory laws of the Nazi regime, the collected signs for *Places of Memory* (1993) in Berlin's Bayrisches Viertel have retained their silent accusatory effect ever since their original installation. Even more subtle, but alas unrealized in situ, was Stih & Schnock's competition entry for the Memorial to the Murdered Jews of Europe. Instead of creating an abstract sea of concrete blocks, Stih & Schnock proposed a bus stop that would take interested individuals to the original sites of the Holocaust. For the exhibition *DEMO:POLIS*, the bus stop is erected temporarily on the grounds of the Akademie der Künste.

New paths in selecting and displaying art have been developed with the *Fourth Plinth* initiative in London's Trafalgar Square. Having remained unoccupied for over 150 years, the plinth has become the site of temporary installations determined by competition since the turn of the millennium and is currently occupied by Hans Haacke's *Gift Horse*. As an allusion to the originally intended equestrian sculpture of William IV, Haacke's *Gift Horse* is a shocking skeleton: wrapped around one leg is a ribbon commonly used to wrap around presents, displaying the electronic ticker tape of the stock exchange—a symbol of neoliberal ideology's victory over real values of liberty.

If Haacke and Stih & Schnock's works are curated forms of cultural criticism through art, then the recent Brooklyn Bridge action by Wermke/Leinkauf has created numerous collateral effects. Originally intended to honor the bridge's German-American engineer John A. Roebling, the spectacular clandestine exchange of two enormous Stars and Stripes flags with two identically sized, white versions of the American national symbol revealed the nervousness of the local media. The artists' intention of raising awareness for Roebling's achievement was overpowered by the sense of violation that was felt among those responsible for public order. Contemporary art action has become a litmus test of the public's sense of acceptable norms. Its ability to cast these norms in sharp relief at best renders new boundaries of tolerances and society's self-understanding, while at worst revealing the collective's sense of paranoia. —ww

"The Stetson" from the series *American Graffiti*, Birgit and Wilhelm Hein

American Graffiti

LOCATION New York City, USA
ARTISTS Birgit and Wilhelm Hein
YEAR 1981–1982
TYPE Slide series
COMMISSIONER N/A
FINANCED BY City of Cologne
OTHER CONTRIBUTORS N/A
COSTS N/A

American Graffiti is composed of various slide series which were taken in the New York Subway system from Chinatown, through Harlem, and up to 180th Street between the fall of 1981 and the summer of 1982. It presents anonymous inscriptions and drawings on advertisement boards. These are not mere scribblings, but rather purposeful statements that are triggered by specific aspects of the defaced posters. Far from all ads were defaced at the time. There were only about ten advertisements which were able to incite the aggression of observers and drive them to these uniform statements.

Mommie Dearest
Advertisement for the film of the same name, based on the autobiography of Christina Crawford, an adopted daughter of the actress Joan Crawford. The film depicts Christina's abuse at the hands of her adoptive mother, who most notably beat her with a wire hanger while under the influence of alcohol. These wire hangers are a recurring motif in the graffiti; they were also deployed by theater audiences during screenings of the film.

All-American Fat
Advertisement for a large roast chicken called "oven stuffer roaster." "All-American Fat" is a common expression in the USA. It describes the greedy, insatiable, and apathetic American who sees it as his right to consume a disproportionally large amount of resources without thinking about the environment or the needy.

The Stetson
An advertisement for Marlboro. The white Stetson is known as a classic cowboy hat. In the cigarette ad, the hat is worn by the "Marlboro Man," who is meant to personify the freedom and adventure of the Wild West. The "white" cowboy, representative of a closed masculine society, is here interpreted in homoerotic and facist terms.

Rocky III
An advertisement for the third installation in the *Rocky* film series, released in 1982 with Sylvester Stallone as both director and lead actor. The boxing drama about an aging Rocky, a hardened fighter who triumphs one last time over his opponent, is ridiculed as a Hollywood farce. The real Rocky is a *faggot*, a homo who needs a beating. —BIRGIT AND WILHELM HEIN

Birgit Hein

"All-American Fat"

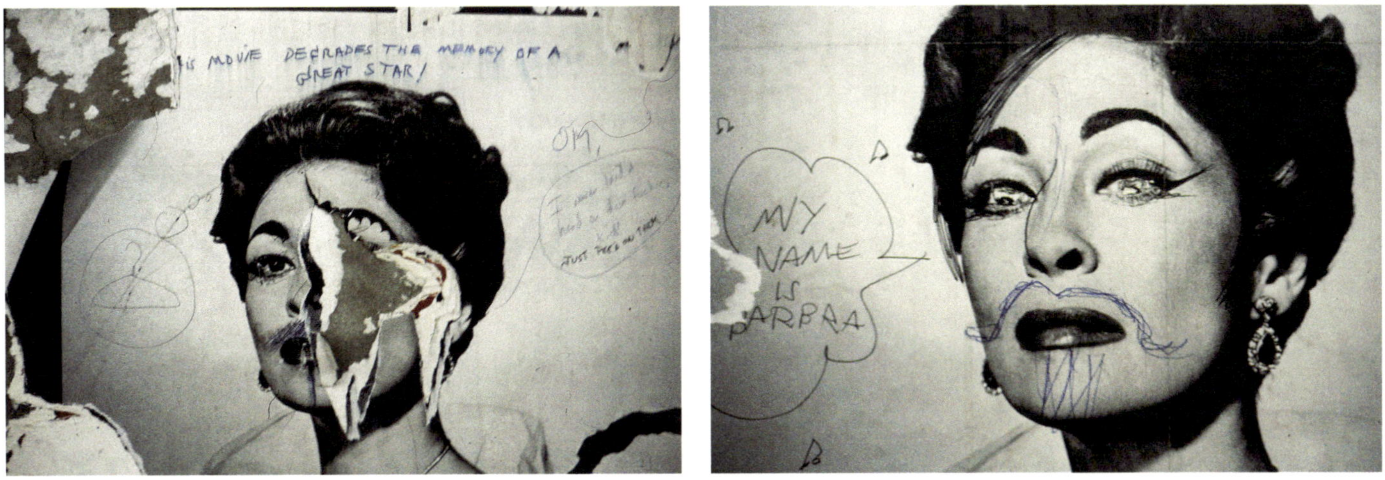

"Mommie Dearest"

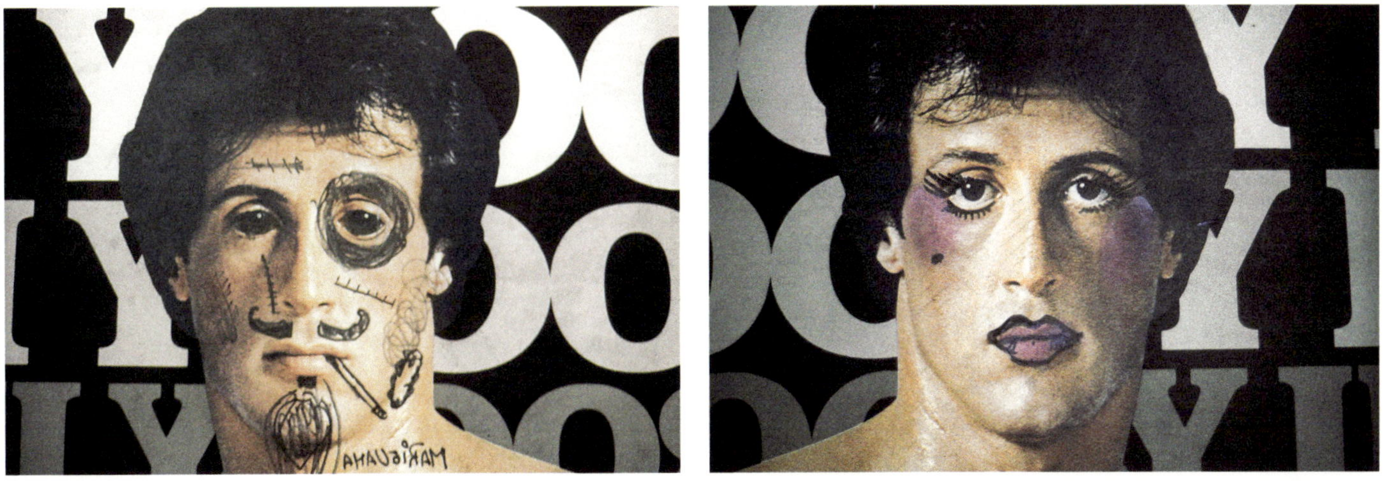
"Rocky III"

Places of Remembrance

LOCATION Bayerisches Viertel, Berlin, Germany
ARTIST Stih & Schnock
YEAR 1993–present
TYPE Site-specific artwork
COMMISSIONER Senate of Berlin
FINANCED BY Senate of Berlin
OTHER CONTRIBUTORS N/A
COST N/A

Places of Remembrance, located in the Bayerisches Viertel of Berlin's Schöneberg district, is a social sculpture that overwrites an entire neighborhood. It is a memorial that visualizes the "exclusion, disenfranchisement, displacement, deportation, and murder of Berlin's Jews between the years 1933 and 1945," and extends across the entire neighborhood in the form of various stops. It is the first decentralized monument of its kind, and was chosen after years of public discussion out of a public, two-tier competition hosted by the State of Berlin. It was inaugurated on June 11, 1993.

The memorial is composed of three map boards, eighty double-sided signs, and a publication in the form of a workbook, which explains the development of the project and has been in continuous print since its first publication. The texts and images confront passers-by with the almost-forgotten history of the Bayerisches Viertel, a place that was once called "Jewish Switzerland" and was home to Albert Einstein, Hannah Arendt, Gisèle Freund, and Carl Einstein, among others. In its diffusion across the entire neighborhood, the memorial metaphorizes the daily deprivation and disenfranchisement—all the way to deportation and murder—faced by Jews during the Nazi regime.

The primary work comprises eighty panels, printed on one side with an illustration and on the other with modified text reproducing anti-Semitic laws and ordinances from 1933 to 1945. The texts have been deliberately reworded and converted into a briefer, more contemporary idiom, so that they are still understandable today—as well as immediately readable for someone driving by. They are kept in the present tense, yet are labeled with the original dates of the decrees. In this way, they bring history and its substance to the present. The illustration side of the signs feature various pictogrammic representations of daily life and objects of remembrance, screen printed on aluminum. The colorful images contrast with the black-and-white text and, on the whole, resonate with one another in a variety of distinctive ways. With their simplified representations reminiscent of spelling books or comic strips, they serve in particular as an introduction for children and adolescents to the topic.

The eighty signs with dimensions of 50 × 70 cm have been mounted on lampposts at a height of three meters. This amounts to a reinterpretation of public infrastructures and subtly integrates the signs into the daily life of the neighborhood's residents. The signs approximate the visual character of the surrounding streets and can be discovered individually by people taking walks around the neighborhood.

The three large-scale map boards provide orientation and information: They stand in front of the Schöneberg Town Hall, at Bayerischer Platz in the center of the neighborhood, and in front of a school in Münchener Straße, imitating the design of public information panels. These boards feature two superimposed maps of the Bayerisches Viertel , one in black from 1933 and one in red from 1993, the year the work was created. The collage documents changes in the urban landscape and plots the locations of the eighty signs, which are installed throughout the neighborhood following a specific choreography based on the location and the subject of the signs.
—RENATA STIH AND FRIEDER SCHNOCK

Stih & Schnock, Memorial *Places of Remembrance*, map, 1993

With this decentrally arranged and internally networked opus, comprising moments of aesthetic surprise that both deliver a hefty charge of memory and encourage communication, the artists create an antithesis to traditional monuments and their ritualized appropriations. They thereby contribute to the identity of the neighborhood, calling for the incremental repeal of the private appropriation/suppression of history and the recreation of a public sphere that had been destroyed by the National Socialists.
—Barbara Straka, Berlin, 1993

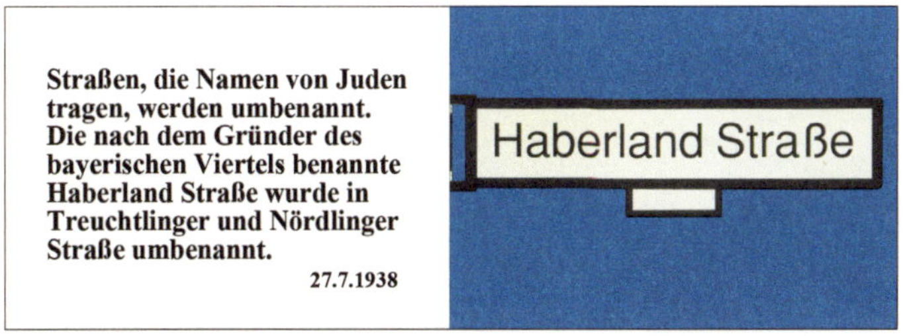

"Streets named after Jews are to be renamed. Haberland Straße—after the developer of the Quarter—was renamed Treuchtlinger and Nördlinger Straße. / July 27, 1938"

"Jews may not use the public beach at the Wannsee. / August 22, 1933"

"At Bayerischer Platz, Jews may sit only on yellow marked park benches. / Eye witness reports, 1939"

"Anti-Semitic signs in Berlin are being temporarily removed for the 1936 Olympic Games."

ELFI MIKESCH

Graffiti Over Under

LOCATION Berlin, Germany
ARTIST Elfi Mikesch
YEAR 2014–2015
TYPE Photo-film
COMMISSIONER Self-initiated
FINANCED BY N/A
OTHER CONTRIBUTORS ANONYM, Burnoutboys, Caroline Pepe, CECO, CIUS, Czarnobyl, El Bocho, EL MAC, D7606, Haevi Styles, Jeff Soto, just, just love it, mango, maxx, Michael Mráz, mocca, 1 UP, Pin Sel, The Ghettoblaster, Wurstbande, zinkete, and many more (artists, *Over Under*); Andreas Wolter (Music, *Over Under*); PHLEGM (Artist, *Parkhaus*); Amir Teymuri (Music, *Parkhaus*)
COSTS N/A

The globally active graffiti scene and its counterpart, street art, scatter symbols in the urban landscape and thereby shape it. Their manifold images, letters, and codes confront us with a fundamental and existential human need: to experience and display oneself directly in public space. To defend oneself. Virulently, too—as resistance against conformism, the technocratic expansion of market logics, and the purely function-oriented administration of the city. Graffiti is an IRREPRESSIBLE HANDWRITING that strives to assert itself in social space. It seeks expression and identity. Every city has, without doubt, its own "collective ornament" that oscillates in the space between legality and illegality. Youth and the city: the call for free space is not to be ignored. "They live the city and in the city; they think, the city belongs to them, as well."[1]

The photo-film *Over Under* (03:00 min) showcases graffiti as a self-narrating assemblage and visualizes a spectrum of concentrated vitality. Disobedience. Humor is at play. Urge, music, self-assertion. Juvenile mischief. Belonging. Transgression. Danger. In *Over Under*, we follow *tags* and *pieces*, those rebellious signs, on the surfaces preferred for graffiti—fire partitions, abandoned lots, and parking places—where they glow in iridescent collectives that seem to be communicating something. Graffiti and street art love the street, love communication.

The photo-film *Parkhaus* (08:17 min) presents street art by PHLEGM. Street art is, together with graffiti, a visual counterpoint to the norm. Using radical and critical motifs, street art agitates against the "graying and homogenization" of urban space.

These photo-films focus on another way of perceiving the city. They are a plea for more attention to be paid to social dynamics, to youth.

The Berlin Wall was once home to the longest street art and graffiti collection in the world. —ELFI MIKESCH

1 Quote from "BÖ-9," a project by pad e.V. (an alternative youth arts organization working against violence and drug addiction among youths).

PHLEGM, designed for URBAN NATION's *One Wall Project*

Czarnobyl

1 UP, mocca, and others

Areal PLATOON KUNSTHALLE, Berlin

Areal PLATOON KUNSTHALLE, Berlin

White American Flags

LOCATION New York City, USA
ARTIST Wermke/Leinkauf
YEAR 2014
TYPE Intervention in public space
COMMISSIONER N/A
FINANCED BY N/A
OTHER CONTRIBUTORS The General Public
COST Abstention from traveling to the USA for the moment

Wermke/Leinkauf, *White American Flags*, 2014

The ancient Greek polis understood its public space to be a *meson*, an "empty center," in which public affairs were discussed. Politics and art are similar in that they both share this center. On the public stage, the existential entanglement of both spheres is made visible.

With their intervention *White American Flags*, Matthias Wermke and Mischa Leinkauf used the night of July 21–22, 2014 to hoist two hand-sewn white flags above the towers of the Brooklyn Bridge in New York, replacing the American flags that usually fly there. The initially peaceful mood the next morning took a quick turn as the first helicopters arrived and a police investigation began. Against the background of the security apparatus that has been installed in New York since the terrorist attacks of September 11, 2001, the peaceful and poetic artistic gesture suddenly became a threat. For three weeks, the city discussed and puzzled over the act before the two artists admitted to their involvement in *The New York Times*. As is the case with all work that leaves the bubble of cultural institutions and takes place in public space, the discourse and controversy was perhaps something that one could have expected, but certainly not planned. The different reactions—some moved, others bewildered, yet others outraged—became a part of the work itself. In this sense, the Brooklyn Bridge under the *White American Flags* was not just a structure upon which decades of city history had left its mark; it surpassed that, becoming as a sort of public square in the city. As a meeting and discursive space for the media and the Internet, the bridge became, once again, an unoccupied, public space—the "empty center" of the city.

In New York, this "empty center" had largely disappeared from the traumatized post-9/11 urban fabric. Faced with the threatening possibility of another attack, the promise of security was bought at the price of limited freedom and increased surveillance. With their intervention, however, Wermke/Leinkauf revealed a loophole in this security apparatus, at the same time opening up a space for discourse and artistic practice that aims to win people over with charm. The image of the bridge under two white American flags raises the question of whether it is really worth giving up both public space and private freedom for a deceptive sense of security offered by New York's government. Through their intervention, Wermke/Leinkauf demonstrate that there is no such thing as absolute control, no such thing as absolute security. They remind us that the importance of artistic freedom, so championed by the leaders of our major cities, also requires social and political struggle.

In focusing on the discourse around security, art, and public space at the Akademie der Künste, Wermke/Leinkauf engage with just one aspect of *White American Flags*. The exhibition will feature a video of the Brooklyn Bridge with its white flags, artifacts from the contradictory debate surrounding the act, and video excerpts from the media coverage of the event, also dealt with in the short film *Symbolic Threats* (Leinkauf/Henke/Wermke, 2015). These objects illustrate the simultaneity of charm and threat, and investigate how one single event and its imagery can be ascribed widely different meanings. They show *White American Flags* as a public projection screen. —LUTZ HENKE (ABRIDGED)

Wermke/Leinkauf, *White American Flags*, 2014

Brooklyn Bridge with Stars and Stripes Flag

Viele Männer sind in einem Mann

A film by Michael Muschner with Reinhild Hoffmann, dancer und choreographer of the piece *The Horatian* (after Heiner Müller, featuring narration by Müller himself, recorded for the first performance of the piece in 1988). A theatrical intervention in the public space of the Soviet War Memorial in Berlin-Treptow. A TIGERFILM production.

LOCATION Soviet War Memorial, Berlin, Germany
ARTISTS Reinhild Hoffmann (choreography and dance) and Michael Muschner (production, script, and direction)
YEAR 2016
TYPE Film
COMMISSIONER N/A
FINANCED BY N/A
OTHER CONTRIBUTORS Christoph Valentien (camera), Sergej Range (editing), Soundtrax (sound)
COST N/A

"The stage is the Soviet War Memorial in Treptow, East Berlin, a memorial for fallen soldiers of the Red Army. The grounds have an area of 10 hectares; joggers, cyclists, and busloads of tourists populate the place daily. The art of dance had yet to wander into this space. Until now, when the French choreographer Boris Charmatz came up with the idea to create an open-air installation here for the 'Foreign Affairs' festival in Berlin. At his behest, '20 Dancers for the XX Century' bring the monument to life with scenographic snippets that come together in a fragmentary mosaic of the history of twentieth-century dance" (Dorion Weickmann, *Süddeutsche Zeitung*, July 1, 2014).

When Boris Charmatz asked me whether I would like to participate as one of the twenty dancers in his project *20 Dancers for the XX Century*, and then showed me the site, which he had consciously selected out of many options in Berlin, my first thought was of my solo performance in 1988, when I interpreted Heiner Müller's text *The Horatian* (narrated for me by Müller himself) from the sister's perspective.

This text, which portrays the fatal way in which fanaticism can be whipped up in times of war, to a point where empathy is completely lost—this text seemed to me like a monument in words, which needed to be made audible here, borne by a shortened version of my solo program.

For his film *Viele Männer sind in einem Mann* [Many Men Are in One Man], Michael Muschner related this performance to text from another part of the war memorial, thus opening up a space of interpretation that stretches into the contemporary politics of war and expropriation. —REINHILD HOFFMANN

Reinhild Hoffmann and Michael Muschner, still from *Viele Männer sind in einem Mann*, Reinhild Hoffmann in front of the Soviet War Memorial, Berlin Treptow, 2014

Reinhild Hoffmann and Michael Muschner, still from *Viele Männer sind in einem Mann*, Reinhild Hoffmann in front of the Soviet War Memorial, Berlin Treptow, 2014

Gift Horse

LOCATION Fourth Plinth, Trafalgar Square, London, England
ARTIST Hans Haacke
YEAR 2015–2016
TYPE Sculpture
COMMISSIONER Greater London Authority
FINANCED BY National Lottery, Arts Council of Great Britain
OTHER CONTRIBUTORS N/A
COST €400,000

The Fourth Plinth on the northwest corner of Trafalgar Square was meant to support an equestrian statue of William IV (1765–1837). It is said that, due to a lack of funds, he was never able to join his older brother, George IV (1762–1830), who was known for his "dissolute way of life" and whose horseback effigy occupies the plinth on the northeast corner of the square.

Both kings are younger contemporaries of George Stubbs (1724–1806), the English painter of horses and other animals, and whose paintings are represented in the collections of the Tate Gallery and the National Gallery at Trafalgar Square. In 1766, Stubbs published his study *The Anatomy of the Horse*, thirty etchings, all accompanied by very detailed explanations of the skeleton, muscles, and other parts of a horse's anatomy.

A digitally altered version (with adjusted orientation, limbs, neck, and head) of the first skeleton plate of Stubbs's *Anatomy of the Horse* serves to illustrate my proposal for the empty plinth.

A three-dimensional skeleton of a strutting horse occupies the plinth, facing the square, with the National Gallery in the background. Its size matches that of the horse bearing George IV.

A bow is tied around a frontal thighbone of the skeleton, as if for a gift. Both sides of the "ribbon" are capable of displaying electronic messages. They transmit the live FTSE 100 ticker of the London Stock Exchange. At times when no trading occurs, after hours, on weekends and holidays, the ticker of the most recent day's LSE activity is repeated. —HANS HAACKE

The Fourth Plinth, Trafalgar Square, London

Hans Haacke, *Gift Horse*, 2014; installation on Fourth Plinth, Trafalgar Square, London, 2015

Hans Haacke *Gift Horse*, model for Fourth Plinth, 2013

Decentralized Music / Mapping the City

LOCATION Akademie der Künste, Hanseatenweg Campus, Berlin, Germany
ARTISTS Neele Hülcker, Matthias Kaul, Christina Kubisch, Maximilian Marcoll, François Sarhan, Niklas Seidl (composers); hand werk, MAM. Manufaktur für aktuelle Musik, LUX:NM (ensembles)
YEAR 2016
TYPE Music (concerts, installations, musical-performative interventions, electrical walks)
COMMISSIONER The Music Section of the Akademie der Künste
FINANCED BY The Music Section of the Akademie der Künste
OTHER CONTRIBUTORS Stefan Streich (curator), Manos Tsangaris (Director Music Section), Evelyn Hansen, Petra Krebs
COST €40,000

In many European cities today, visitors to central public areas are showered by a constant flow of music in various genres. Anywhere in the subway system in Rome, for example, one is bound to encounter a constant stream of pop music. What is the purpose of this? To entertain guests? No—it is a means to prevent live music in public spaces. Street musicians are being driven away. These performers are the last remaining creators of public live music today, in most cases just for tips. The shows last perhaps thirty minutes, then the temporary stage is dismantled again. In Cologne, the city's Office for Public Order gives out licenses for performances that are not allowed to last longer than twenty minutes.

Having participated in the exhibition *Culture:City* with *Music in the Cloud*, a project centered on the everyday consumption of music and sound, the Music Section of the Akademie der Künste will now focus on the widely distributed forms of musical practice in public space for the exhibition *DEMO:POLIS*, using discursive and artistic means.

Street music suffuses cities with a network of decentralized performances, whose ethnic, stylistic, and social roots could not be more varied. That is our motivation for picking up on, expanding, and transforming this model within the context of *DEMO:POLIS*. *Decentralized Music/Mapping the City* takes the guerilla-like strategies of street performers (mobility, spontaneous appearance, performance, disappearance) and fills them, critically, with new content. This will all take place in and around the exhibition spaces of the Akademie der Künste's Hanseatenweg campus. Small mobile units and audio performance "ambulances" can be deployed in public settings, be it within the exhibition spaces themselves, in the foyer, or outside the building.

Anonymous street musician, Berlin U-Bahn station, 2015

Anonymous street musician, Berlin U-Bahn station, 2015

In doing so, we will employ not only conventional methods such as standard acoustic instruments, voices, etc., but also mobile electronic instruments and laptops in the form of a new street orchestra. A series of roaming musical elements are made to circulate around *DEMO:POLIS*, which serve to intervene in the situation as a whole. This is not intended as a disruption or even a wholesale destruction of present conditions, but rather as an acupunctural practice that stimulates specific nerve points in the system. For instance, a series of short, acoustic irritations will be played next to the café, adding to the conversations and conversation lulls of the guests.

This all serves to draw the map of our artificial model city. Where, how, and why is sound produced *as sound* and not just as a consequence of a function—like traffic noise, for example? This form of sound production is often considered a disturbance, more so than traffic noise. It could be because the performances are not up to the lofty, conservative standards of the originals ("... it's not as good as Bob Dylan or Ann-Sophie Mutter"), or because people feel burdened by requests for donations—that is, payment. Many passersby already carry their own soundtracks around with them, thanks to headphones. In these cases, the public performances of street musicians are little more than unwanted blotches on the urban landscape. The performative practice of street musicians is one of the last instances in urban public space where real contact points are produced, points that are generated neither by the simple movement of individuals through space, nor by activities solely meant to acquire new customers.

This is what interests us: enrichment or harassment from musical and performative claims and practices, as well as the network of smaller, mutually independent performances, which are only brought together in virtual space, so as to transform the often forbidding and purely functional user interface of the inner city into a model for internal intervention and artificial migration.

Decentralized Music/Mapping the City produces a virtual, uninterrupted stream of concerts within the constant hum of the city.
— MANOS TSANGARIS

ELESCOPE

Scenography vs. Substantive Designs

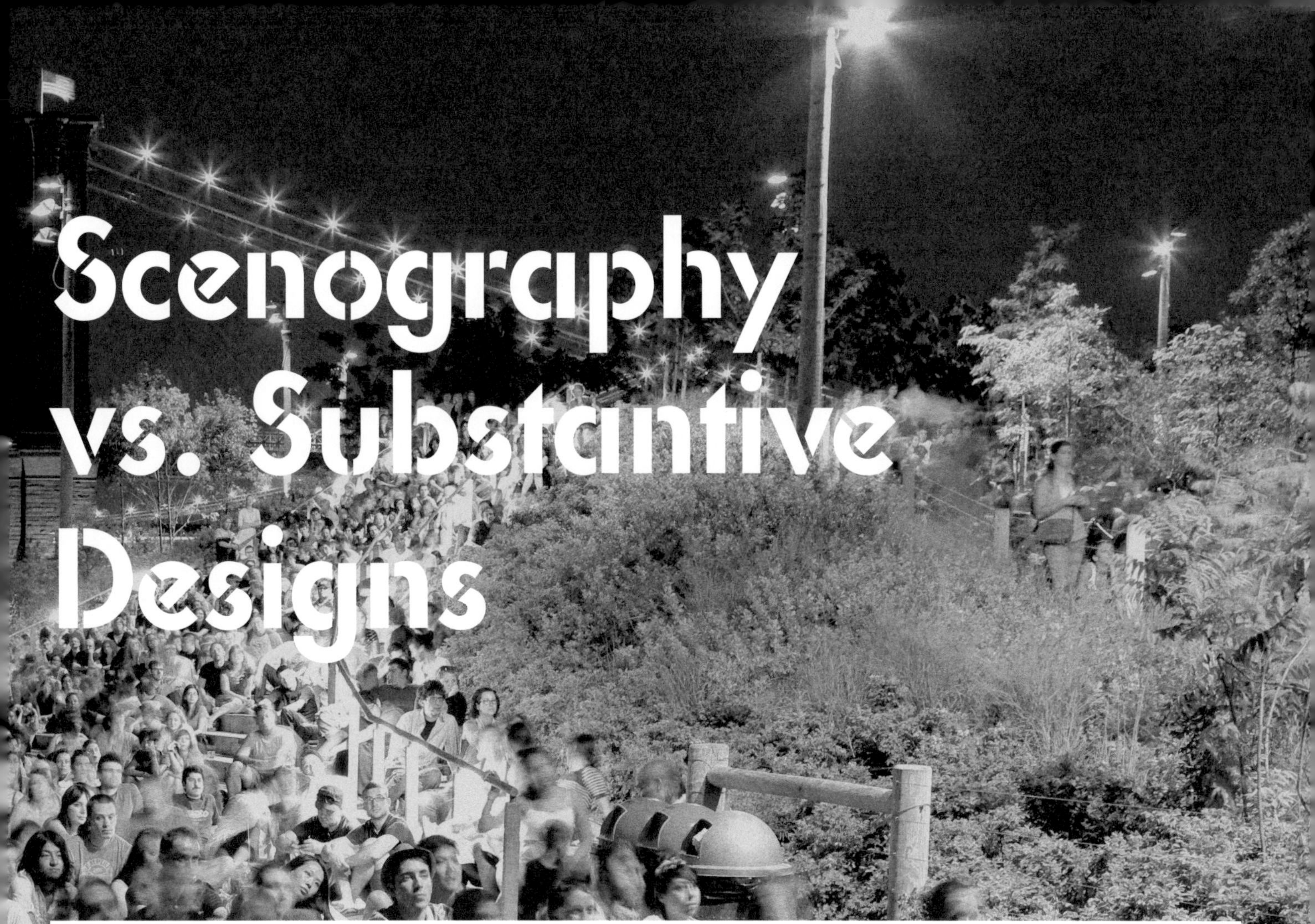

In some societies, the double destruction experienced first during the Second World War and during the so-called period of modernist reconstruction has left a deep desire for the resurrection of pre-war surfaces, as if these were able to overcome the causes that led to the catastrophic destruction. Grigory Potemkin, a Russian military leader and lover of Catherine the Great (1729–1796), devised portable village façades that were temporarily erected along the embankments of the River Dnieper to suggest that life was returning to a war-torn region. The same principle is being pursued by a number of projects, particularly in Germany. In Brunswick, for example, the façade of the former palace now fronts a shopping center. The buildings surrounding the reconstructed Frauenkirche in Dresden are in the best tradition of Potemkin. And soon, three sides of the former Hohenzollern palace will envelop a conference center and a museum on Berlin's Museum Island.

In contrast to such scenographic treatment of urban design and architecture, the selection of projects in this section demonstrates how historical substance can be properly respected, maintained, and indeed continued. Two early cases—the center of Ljubljana along the Ljubljanica River and the paths to the Athenian Acropolis—provide evidence of the sensitivity, intelligence, and inventiveness of designers when confronted by challenging tasks.

The theme of the maintenance and transformation of the historical fabric was at the forefront with respect to the UNESCO World Heritage Site of Guimarães, the first capital of Portugal. Over two decades, the buildings, streets, and squares of the inner city were carefully renovated and in some cases transformed with great empathy for the historical atmosphere.

An appreciation for the appropriateness of a place as it is led the French architects Lacaton & Vassal to recommend to the commissioning Mayor of Bordeaux not to change anything on the Place Léon Aucoc, except to request more frequent cleaning and maintenance; this attitude is also an example of "substantive design."

Two cases of reducing the presence of vehicular traffic are presented—the UNESCO World Heritage Site of Wismar and London's Trafalgar Square—to demonstrate not only the enhanced urban or architectural qualities that result, but also the improvement of the overall quality of life. Space only becomes public when territory that was once used exclusively by vehicles is reclaimed for ordinary pedestrians.

With the Brooklyn Bridge Park—a five-mile-long stretch of former harbor facilities in New York—and the Regulating Plan for the Coast of Galicia, two cases are presented to demonstrate that embankments, landscape, topography, and nature are, despite their massive scale, among the most fragile of resources. Transforming the run-down harbor into a series of public sports facilities and parks has established a paradigm for the rest of the Hudson River. The case of the coast of Galicia shows that the devastation of the excessive development along Spain's Mediterranean coast could be avoided on the Atlantic coast by a careful balance between preservation and sensitive development. —WW

Granite Prospect on Pier 1, Brooklyn Bridge Park, New York City

River Landscape along the Ljubljanica

DESIGN Jože Plečnik
YEAR 1931–1945 (Cobbler's Bridge: 1931–1932; Triple Bridge: 1931–1932; Market Hall: 1940–1942; Lock: 1939–1945)
TYPE Urban landscape
CLIENT City of Ljubljana
OTHER CONTRIBUTORS Ciril Tavčar, Janez Valentinčič (Triple Bridge); Gizela Šuklje (Market Hall); Vlasto Kopač, Božo Pengov (Lock)
COST N/A
AREA ca. 12 hectares

The Slovenian capital of Ljubljana has lived for centuries with its river, the water of which has brought both fortune and—especially in times of flooding—misfortune to the city. Before the First World War, work commenced on excavating the lateral canals on the other side of the castle hill; the streambed in the city center nearly dried out as a result, leaving the bridge fundaments in danger. It was not until the economic crisis at the beginning of the 1930s that the government sought to remediate this unfortunate situation in a scheme to counter unemployment. The director of the city building department, Matko Prelovšek, tasked the architect Jože Plečnik with the artistic direction of the project. Plečnik, who had long dreamed of beautifying his hometown, wasted no time in designing several bridges along with a sluice that was meant to keep the water level constant. He thereby attempted to correct what had happened before his time, during the Austro-Hungarian monarchy.

In particular, the excavation and concrete reinforcement of the riverbanks had caused the River Ljubljanica to lose the contact with the city that it once had, turning it into little more than a sewage canal. Following the example of the Vienna River, Plečnik initially thought to cover the entire river with concrete and shape it into a new boulevard. He later abandoned this idea, however, and designed the bridges in the form of public spaces for encounters above the water. On both sides of the existing main bridge, which dates back to the nineteenth century, he added two pedestrian bridges that combine with the poplar trees to create a triumphal arc reaching into the center of the old city. Designed according to Venetian examples, Plečnik intended these bridges to suggest the proximity of Italy and the Mediterranean Sea. Unfortunately the so-called Butcher's Bridge, which was to be covered by a Palladian roof, remained unrealized: it was supposed to constitute the centerpiece of the new market halls (also designed by Plečnik) and thereby complete their urban significance. The lock at the end of Plečnik's riverscape is a synthesis of Egyptian, Greek, and Etruscan elements, and also serves to signify the fundamental role played by water in everyday life in antiquity. The upper, unregulated stretch of the river was transformed into a romantic promenade with the help of weeping willows and steps leading down to the river.
—DAMJAN PRELOVŠEK

Jože Plečnik, sketch of the Triple Bridge, 1959, 34.2 × 16.4 cm, Plečnik's Collection, Museum and Galleries of Ljubljana

Jože Plečnik, view of the Cobbler's Bridge, 2015

Jože Plečnik, view of the Cobbler's Bridge, 2015

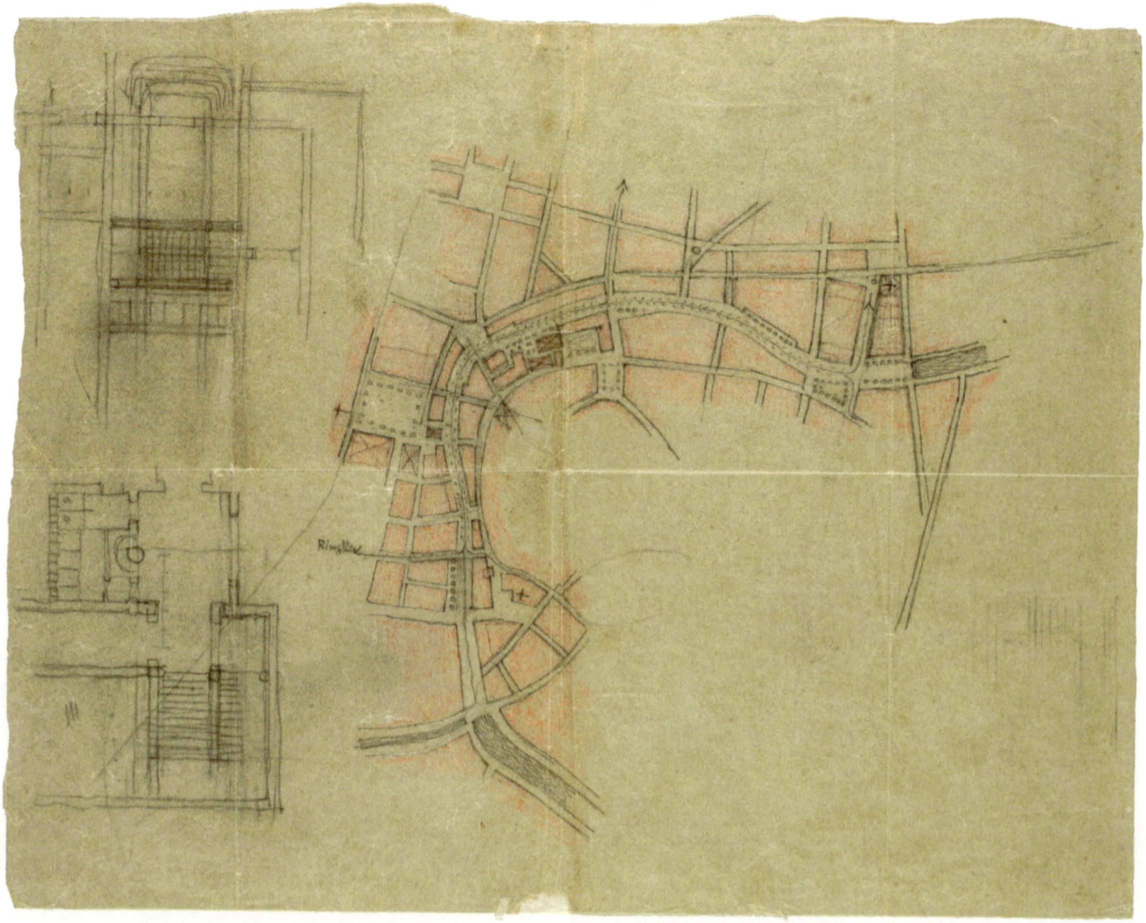

Jože Plečnik, sketch of the river landscape along the Ljubljanica, with Vienna as a reference, 1920s, 32.6 × 21.5 cm, Plečnik's Collection, Museum and Galleries of Ljubljana

Jože Plečnik, views of the Triple Bridge

Jože Plečnik, riverfront promenade

Jože Plečnik, riverfront promenade, detail views

Jože Plečnik, detail drawing of the Central Market, 1940, 72.5 × 52.8 cm,
Plečnik's Collection, Museum and Galleries of Ljubljana

Jože Plečnik, Market Hall during construction, 1941

Jože Plečnik, Market Hall

Jože Plečnik, arcades lining the Main Market in Ljubljana

Jože Plečnik, Market Hall viewed from the river

Path to the Acropolis

DESIGN Dimitris Pikionis
YEAR 1954–1957
TYPE Urban landscape
CLIENT City of Athens
OTHER CONTRIBUTORS N/A
COST 1.25 million drachmas (second phase, 1958)
AREA ca. 13 hectares

Dimitris Pikionis, access road

Dimitris Pikionis's magnum opus, the landscaping of the areas surrounding and leading to the Acropolis, is without common precedent. The design of a network of pathways and small-scale structures that transform and complement the topography constitutes a major intervention in the center of Athens, made possible through a sensitive "reading" of the city's history and its environment.

Between its inception in 1951 and its completion in 1957, Pikionis was involved daily on site together with his collaborators in designing and building this major work, which could be considered a contemporary equivalent of the ancient Panathenaic processional route. The scope of the project was to provide access for the thousands of visitors to the Acropolis of Athens and the Philopappou Hill, including the renovated chapel of St. Dimitrios Loumbardiaris. This manifold project comprises urban elements, streets, traffic nodes, parking areas, stone and paved footpaths, retaining walls, fences, seating areas, and plantation with local flora, and stretches over two hills.

Both the breadth and complexity of the project, as well as Pikionis's on-site design and construction, resulted in an unconventional piece of work that is closer to today's earthworks and land art. Pikionis works with the earth, transforming the ground so that the traveler fully experiences the topography on the ascent to the Acropolis, thereby achieving an organic unity of man and location. His painstaking involvement testifies to the fact that the process of making is as important as the work itself. He collected an enormous assortment of fragments and pieces, handpicking old and new, in order to build a veritable three-dimensional collage—as much a painting made of concrete, stone, marble, and clay, which he was able to crystallize into a coherent whole that is appropriate to the scale and meaning of this important location.

Traditional building techniques and vernacular motifs, ancient Greek fragments and Byzantine relics all coexist with Japanese detailing (e.g., wooden structures of the chapel) and modern art (Paul Klee is often cited as a relevant reference) in this eclectic bricolage. While the measures were meticulously laid by stone masons and crafted by carpenters under Pikionis's close instruction and supervision, the architect also allowed them enough leeway to make things as best as they could, according to their own professional experience.

Dimitris Pikionis, Philopappou belvedere, detail of pavement and marble bench

Dimitris Pikionis, Philopappou belvedere, detail of pavement

Dimitris Pikionis, Acropolis—Philopappou, section of the Philopappou belvedere with marble benches and the monument, 1954–1957, pencil on rice paper, 65 × 27 cm, Benaki Museum Athens

The converging and diverging stone and concrete pathways appear like shimmering streams as light falls on them from different angles, making them at times shiny then dull, smooth then rough. The seeming irregularity crystallizes here and there into regularity—but only for a moment, guiding the traveler further on. The fragmentary nature of this work, as if carved out of the rock itself, miraculously appears as a unified entity.

The wandering tourist retraces the ancient land and inhabits it anew. Pikionis's intention was to guide and comfort this modern-day pilgrim, the traveler. As an avid walker himself, he knew that to make such walks one also needs to pause, look, and reflect. The architect walks and looks ahead of the traveler, anticipating his "peripatos," his walk. The paths are not mere paving, but guide our footsteps and wisely provide for rest intervals in small groves, under a tree shade, where a rock seat formation has been made, and where views open out. On a larger scale, Pikionis organizes spaces from vantage points that correspond to Doxiadis's system of sightlines for spatial planning in Ancient Greece, to achieve a more harmonious order that is closer in spirit to the monuments. On a smaller scale, as one walks up, and as the fatigue increases, one necessarily looks downwards, so the paths and patterns become denser to entertain the eye, and support us in our ascent. Next to the earth, the sky, the mountains, and the distant buildings partake in this symphony, making the excursion a union of the "earth, the temple, and the gods" (Vincent Scully).

Pikionis's work stems from his passionate love of the region of Athens, through his walks and drawings (such as his *Attiká* series), in which he mixes images of mythical elements with the landscape and contours of the surrounding hills and mountains, with the intention to edify the intellect, stimulate memory, and arouse the senses, to manifest the "spirit of our time." His routes to the Acropolis and the Philopappou Hill relate directly to the journeys he traversed, in order to address what he believed constituted the essence of contemporary living and to capture "the common and the essential" of the genius loci.

—ELIAS CONSTANTOPOULOS

Dimitris Pikionis, detail of pavement and vegetation

Dimitris Pikionis, Acropolis—Philopappou, pavement patterns of the path to the Acropolis, 1954–1957, photocopy with additional notes, pencil, colored pencil on paper, 57 × 69.5 cm, Benaki Museum Athens

Dimitris Pikionis, detail views of pavement

Dimitris Pikionis, Acropolis—Philopappou, plan of gradual rise going up from the parking space of the Acropolis, 1954–1957, pencil on rice paper, 40.5 × 53.5 cm, Benaki Museum Athens

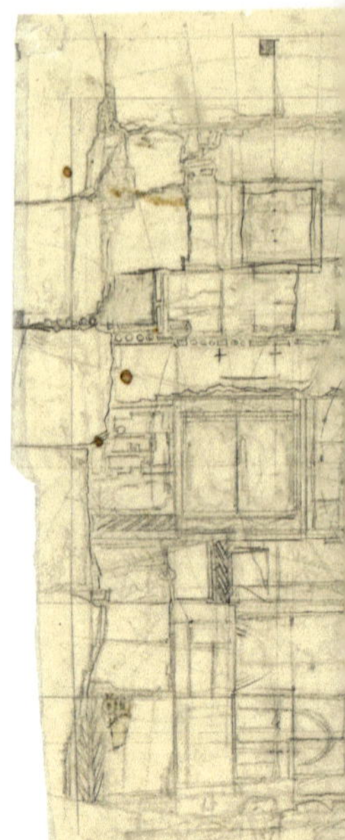

Dimitris Pikionis, Church of Agios Dimitrios Loumbardiaris, ground floor plan of resting area, 1954–1957, pencil on rice paper, 31.5 × 89.5 cm, Benaki Museum Athens

Dimitris Pikionis, detail view of the pavement pattern

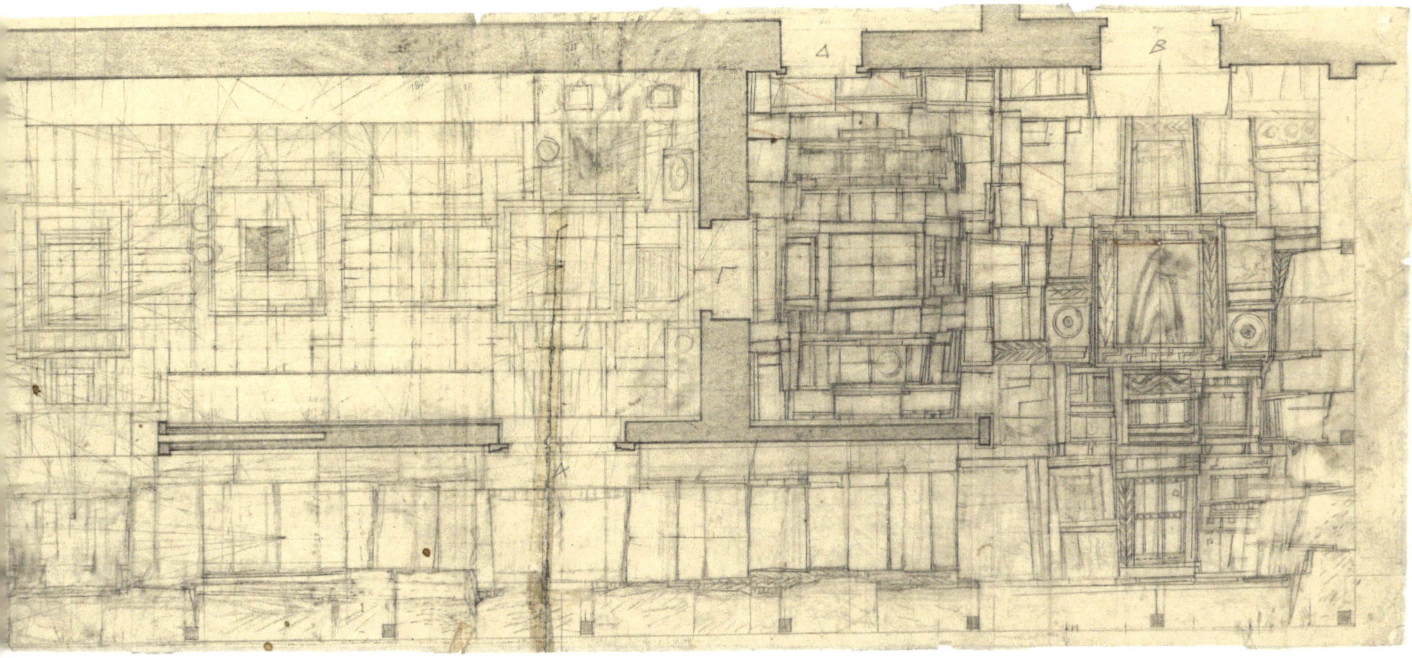

City Center

DESIGN Fernando Távora and GTL (Gabinete Técnico Local)
YEAR 1985–1992
TYPE Urban renewal
CLIENT Câmara Municipal de Guimarães
OTHER CONTRIBUTORS N/A
COST 2 million escudos
AREA 1.3 hectares

Guimarães is a historical city in the north of Portugal, better known for being the country's birthplace. When entering through the city's prominent walls or wandering through its narrow streets with vibrant façades, one cannot miss the city's unique identity.

But in the late 1970s, Guimarães was a degraded city, and the old center a symbol of poor living conditions, with narrow streets, dilapidated buildings and few open spaces.

Today, however, its urban identity can be fully enjoyed thanks to the sharp sense of self-awareness and foresight of the residents of Guimarães.

They led a pioneering quest for urban renewal by recognizing the importance of the preservation of urban ensembles and its identity before these were well-established concepts.

The municipality acted decisively by introducing the *gabinete técnico local* (GTL), or local technical office, in 1981 with Fernando Távora as a partner: the degraded areas were to be rehabilitated through minimal interventions, while the municipality would attract people to the old center through strategically relocating public infrastructures with a larger regional range. The GTL realized that the center could only maintain its identity by retaining its inhabitants. As such, it eschewed rehabilitating single building units, instead preferring to intervene in selected public areas in the bet that this would bring future private investment to the single units while avoiding rental inflation.

Four squares were renovated between 1985 and 1992. These were chosen for being representative of the city's diverse and rich past. All of these interventions show the lessons learned from Távora: to respect regional expression, determined by different local conditions, materials, and tastes that can be found through exhaustively studying each place's history—and then adapting it to contemporary needs.

The GTL's contributions to the city were reaffirmed when Guimarães was declared a UNESCO World Heritage Site in 2001. Since then, the city has continued applying the same rehabilitation strategies to an ever-growing part of the city, in an ongoing process that is far from finished. —CL

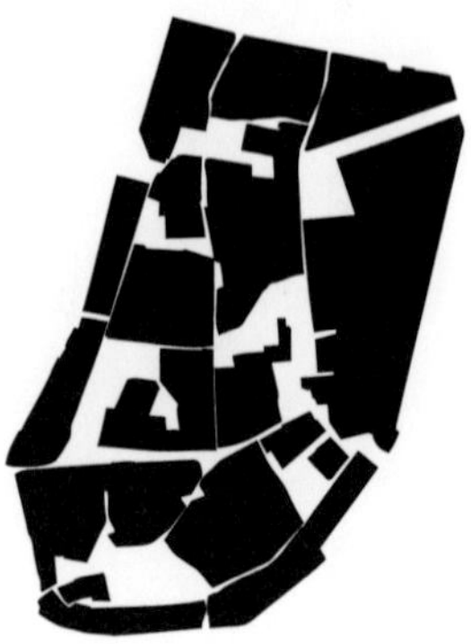

Historic center,
block structure

Historic center,
public space

Historic center,
Fernando Távora project area

Fernando Távora, Praça de S. Tiago, Guimarães, 2015

Fernando Távora, street view of the city center, Guimãraes, 2015

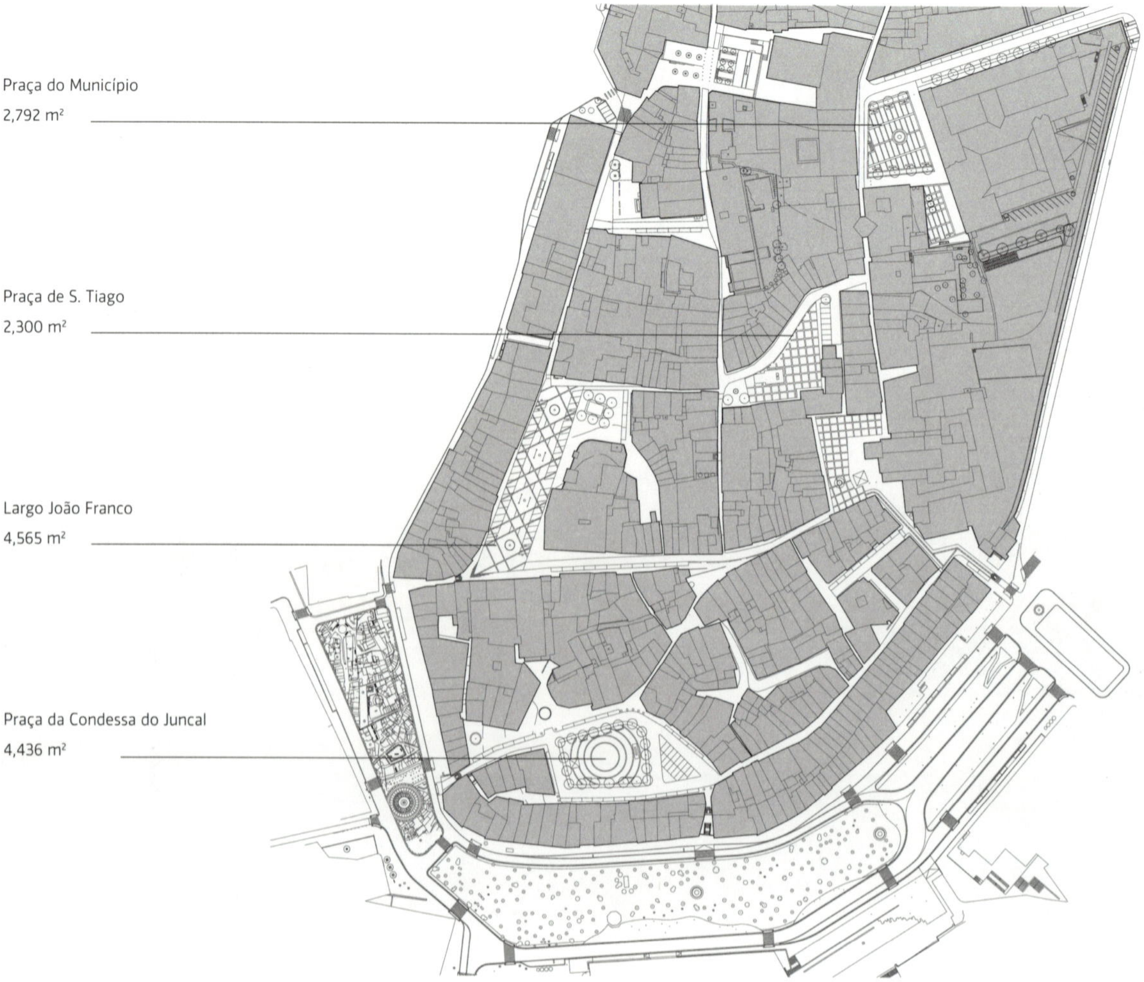

Map of city center, Guimarães

Fernando Távora, Largo João Franco, aerial view, Guimarães, 2012

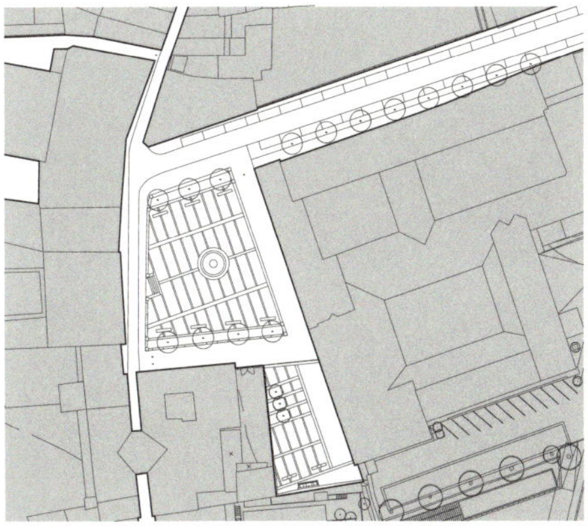

Praça do Município 2,792 m^2

Fernando Távora, Praça do Município, fountain, Guimarães, 2015

Fernando Távora, Praça de S. Tiago 2,300 m^2

Fernando Távora, Praça de S. Tiago, Guimarães, 2015

Fernando Távora, Largo João Franco 4,565 m^2

Fernando Távora, Largo João Franco, Guimarães, 2015

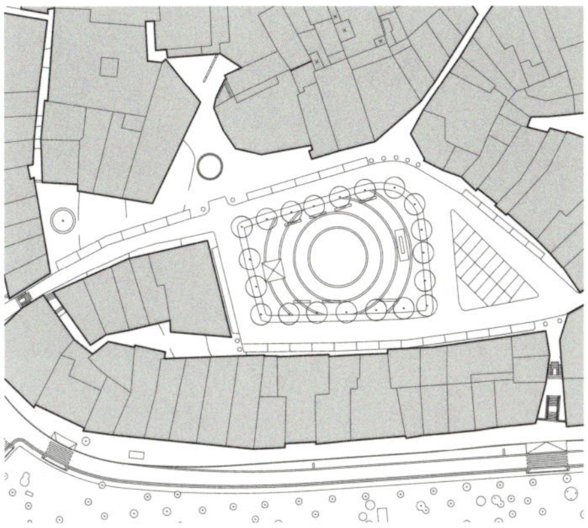

Fernando Távora, Praça da Condessa do Juncal 4,436 m^2

Fernando Távora, Praça da Condessa do Juncal, Guimarães, 2012

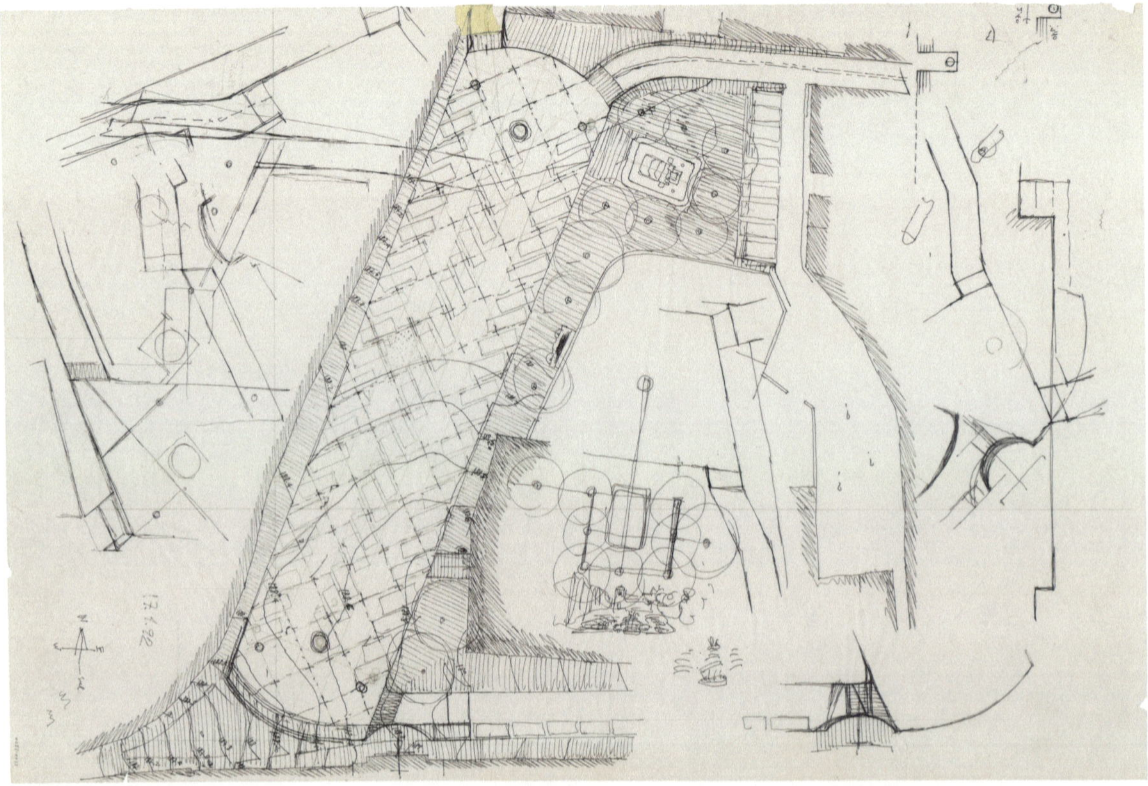

Fernando Távora, restoration of the Largo João Franco, study plan, Jan. 17, 1992, china ink on tracing paper, 75 x 49.5 cm, Fundação Marques da Silva, Porto

Largo da Misericórdia, now Largo João Franco, 1910s

Largo João Franco, 1984

Fernando Távora, Largo João Franco, 2009

Fernando Távora, Largo João Franco, stair detail, 2014

Fernando Távora, Largo João Franco, fountain, 2014

Fernando Távora, restoration of the Largo João Franco, Guimarães, fountain sketch, graphite on tracing paper, 25 × 37.5 cm, Fundação Marques da Silva, Porto

Largo do Toural and Alameda de São Dâmaso

DESIGN Maria Manuel Oliveira and Centro de Estudos da Escola de Arquitectura da Universidade do Minho
YEAR 2009–2012
TYPE Urban renewal
CLIENT Câmara Municipal de Guimarães
COST €6.4 million
AREA 3.9 hectares

The intervention area is adjacent to the medieval city center of Guimarães, Portugal, whose public spaces were renovated over the last decades of the twentieth-century under the supervision of Fernando Távora. The area incorporates different urban contexts as well as a rich architectural heritage and is still today a place that manifests the city's identity. The new designs for the Alameda de São Dâmaso, the Largo do Toural, and the Rua de Santo António sought to argue their contemporary condition as public spaces—favoring day-to-day use over seasonal use, memory under construction over tradition, reinterpretation of heritage over museology—while also acknowledging their roots in the *longue durée* of the site.

The redevelopment of the Rua de Santo António was primarily meant to facilitate pedestrian circulation and prevent the decay of the street's physical state. The Largo do Toural, on the other hand, was redesigned as an open and continuous space, allowing a new perspective on the long, plain eighteenth-century façade and the frontispiece of the Church of São Pedro. While the return of the sixteenth-century fountain to its original position was a reference to the site's past, the contemporary approach to the use of the urban space was emphasized by a public art intervention. This included an arboretum and a long iron banister, two elements meant to encourage people to stop and linger in the square, and the redesign of the quartz and basalt pavement.

The transformation of the Alameda de São Dâmaso into a grove aimed to increase its accessibility and permeability. This was achieved by dismantling its axial structure and taking a rather informal and naturalized approach in designing the ground surface. Whether as a place to walk, rest, play, or roam, the grove is meant to be a modern public "walkscape" where openness and versatility underpin a fragment of urban nature. A fourth intervention, not shown here, created a new churchyard that increased the visibility and presence of the nearby Convento de São Francisco.

By enhancing the structural qualities of the existing areas and significantly expanding the pedestrian surface, the design encourages an everyday use of these spaces without compromising their capacity to host special events or recreational activities. Thus, the project aimed to achieve a sort of flexible spatial complementarity, in which the presence of memory and contemporary ambience come together to create an intensely vital agora.
—MARIA MANUEL OLIVEIRA

Largo do Toural, aerial before intervention, 2010

Maria Manuel Oliveira, Largo do Toural, aerial after intervention

Maria Manuel Oliveira, Largo do Toural, detail of the pavement representing the historic city plan

Maria Manuel Oliveira, Largo do Toural, ground-level view

Maria Manuel Oliveira, Largo do Toural, night view

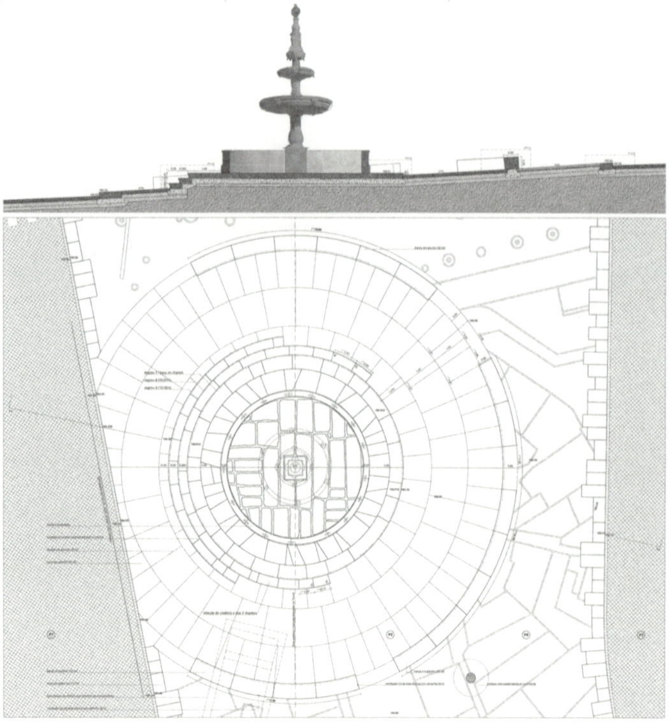

Maria Manuel Oliveira, Largo do Toural, pavement and detail surrounding the fountain

Maria Manuel Oliveira, Largo do Toural, view of the fountain

Maria Manuel Oliveira, Alameda de São Dâmaso, axonometry of the different layers

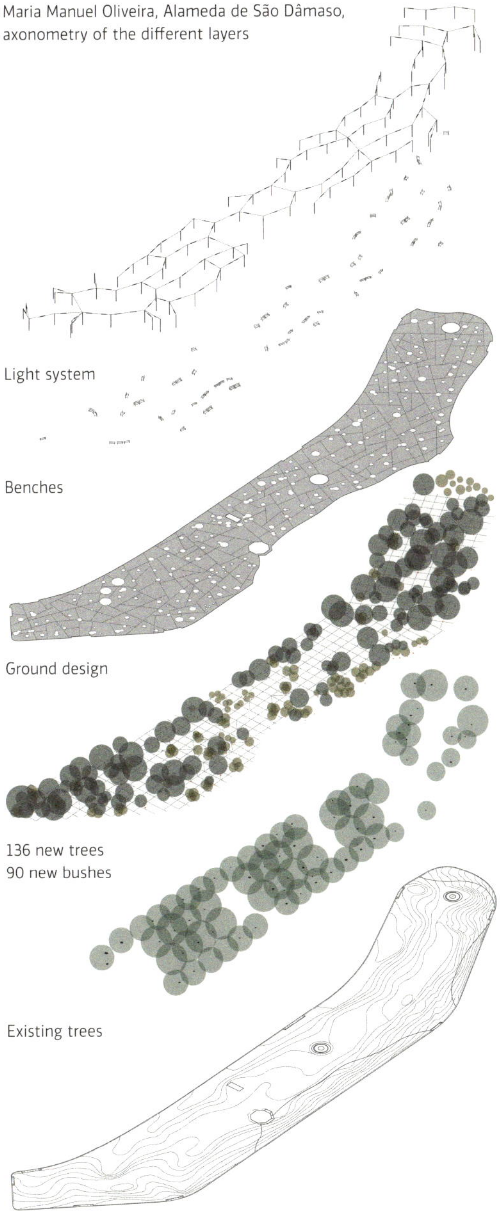

Maria Manuel Oliveira, Alameda de São Dâmaso, view from above

Maria Manuel Oliveira, Largo do Toural, view during the day

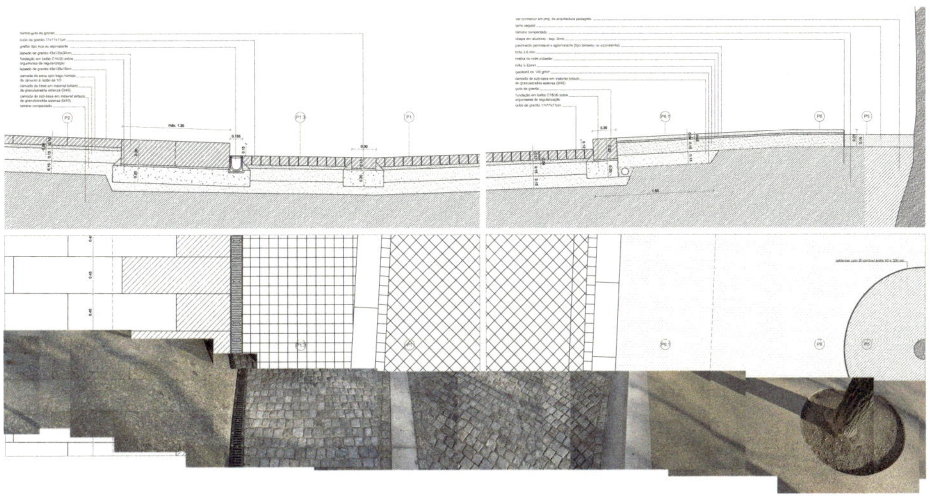

Maria Manuel Oliveira, pavement details

Place Léon Aucoc

DESIGN Lacaton & Vassal Architects
YEAR 1996
TYPE Urban renewal
CLIENT City of Bordeaux
OTHER CONTRIBUTORS N/A
COST €36,000
AREA 3,000 m²

This project fits within the framework of an "embellishment" plan for many town squares initiated by the Bordeaux City Council in 1996. We were asked to remodel one of these squares—the Place Léon Aucoc, located in a residential area near the Saint-Jean Station.

When we visited the site for the first time, we found that the square was already beautiful: it is a triangular shaped square, surrounded by trees, with benches and a space to play *pétanque.* Surrounding it, there are simple, but well-designed façades. We spent some time watching what happened there and talked to some of the local inhabitants.

The Place Léon Aucoc resembles a small town square in terms of its location, users, and architecture. The architecture is simple and structured. It is a fine example of plot subdivision and social housing.

The central gravel space is perfectly delineated by its granite edge and paved roads. It features a softer surface than any pavement or stone, on which activities such as different ball games or *pétanque* are possible, with a permeable soil for which tree grates are not required. This place is beautiful because it is genuine. It has the beauty of simplicity, of something that is both necessary and adequate. Its meaning is clear. People seem to feel at home there.

This square is fragile. It is a delicate place with a particular balance. The few drawbacks that were observed do not justify great changes. In this place harmony prevails—a tranquility shaped over many years.

Then we asked ourselves about a development project on this square with a view to its embellishment. But this place was already beautiful. There is no trace of deterioration. There is no urgent need for interventions.

What does the idea of "embellishment" boil down to? Does it involve replacing one surface material with another? A wooden bench with a more up-to-date design in stone? Or one lamp standard with another, more fashionable one? Embellishment has no place here since the quality of the space comes from its authenticity and its lack of sophistication. Quality, charm, the existing life. The square is already beautiful.

We still had to give concrete answers. As a project, we proposed doing nothing apart from some simple and rapid maintenance work (replacing the gravel, cleaning the square more often, treating the lime trees, etc.) to improve the usage of the square and satisfy the local inhabitants. —LACATON & VASSAL ARCHITECTS

Lacaton & Vassal, square after the intervention, 1997

Lacaton & Vassal, square vegetation

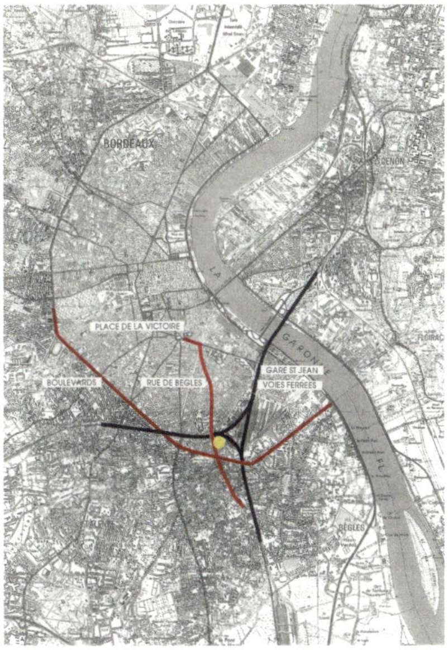

Map of Bordeaux with railway tracks

Detailed map of neighborhood

Site plan of Place Léon Aucoc

Lacaton & Vassal, asphalt pavement

Lacaton & Vassal, paved sidewalk

Lacaton & Vassal, compacted gravel

Lacaton & Vassal, view from the corner of Rue Léon Aucoc and Rue Emile Pereire

Lacaton & Vassal, views of Place Léon Aucoc after intervention

LONDON, ENGLAND

Trafalgar Square Redevelopment

DESIGN Foster + Partners and WS Atkins
YEAR 1996–2003
TYPE Traffic management
CLIENT Transport for London, Greater London Authority
OTHER CONTRIBUTORS N/A
COST €32 million
AREA 48 hectares

The transformation of Trafalgar Square represents the first phase of the practice's Central London masterplan—the culmination of many years' work to improve the urban environment in the heart of the capital. It is the result of a careful balancing act between the needs of traffic and pedestrians, the ceremonial and the everyday, the old and the new.

Trafalgar Square was laid out in the 1840s by Charles Barry. Dominated by Nelson's Column, it is lined by fine buildings, including the church of St Martin-in-the-Fields and South Africa House to the east, Canada House to the west, and the National Gallery to the north. Yet, despite its grandeur, by the mid-1990s, the square had become choked by traffic, the central area visited only by those willing to risk life and limb. There was an obvious need and support for change. Proposals were developed after consultations involving 180 separate institutions and thousands of individuals. The most significant move was the closure of the north side of the square to traffic and the creation of a broad new terrace, which forms an appropriate setting for the National Gallery and links it via a flight of steps to the body of the square. Below the terrace, a new café with outdoor seating provides a much-needed visitor amenity.

Detailed improvements to the square and the adjacent streets include new seating, improved lighting, traffic signage, and a paving strategy that utilises visual and textural contrasts. The contemporary interventions continue the boldness of Barry's original design, using traditional materials—York stone, granite, and bronze—in addition to salvaged granite bollards and slabs, which originally formed part of the north terrace retaining wall. Every aspect of the redesign improves universal access, including two new platform lifts and disabled lavatories. The cumulative effect has been to transform the life of the square. A once hostile urban environment has been restored as a truly civic space.

—FOSTER + PARTNERS

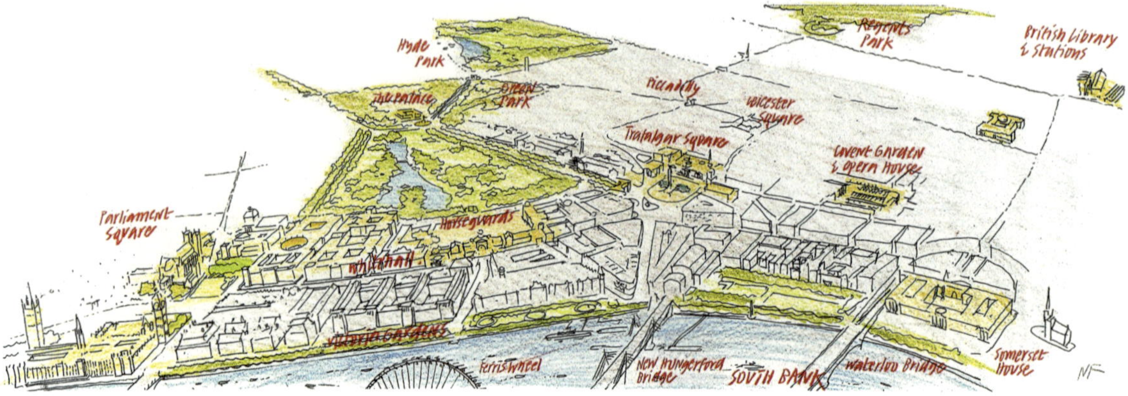

Lord Norman Foster, sketch of London's important public spaces, ca. 1996

Foster + Partners and WS Atkins, Trafalgar Square after redevelopment of the north side, 2003

Trafalgar Square, north side before redevelopment, 1996

Trafalgar Square, north side after redevelopment, 2003

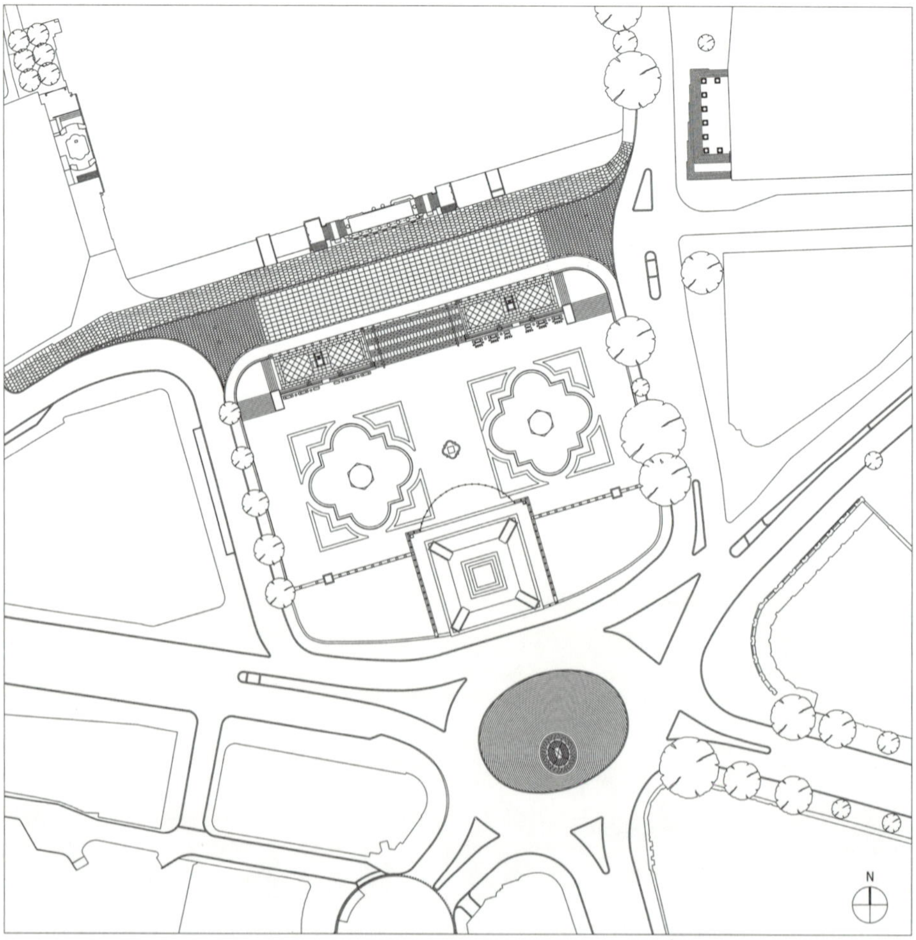

Foster + Partners and WS Atkins, plan of redevelopment of Trafalgar Square, 1996

Foster + Partners, Trafalgar Square before

Foster + Partners, Trafalgar Square after

Foster + Partners, view of Trafalgar Square from the north, 2003

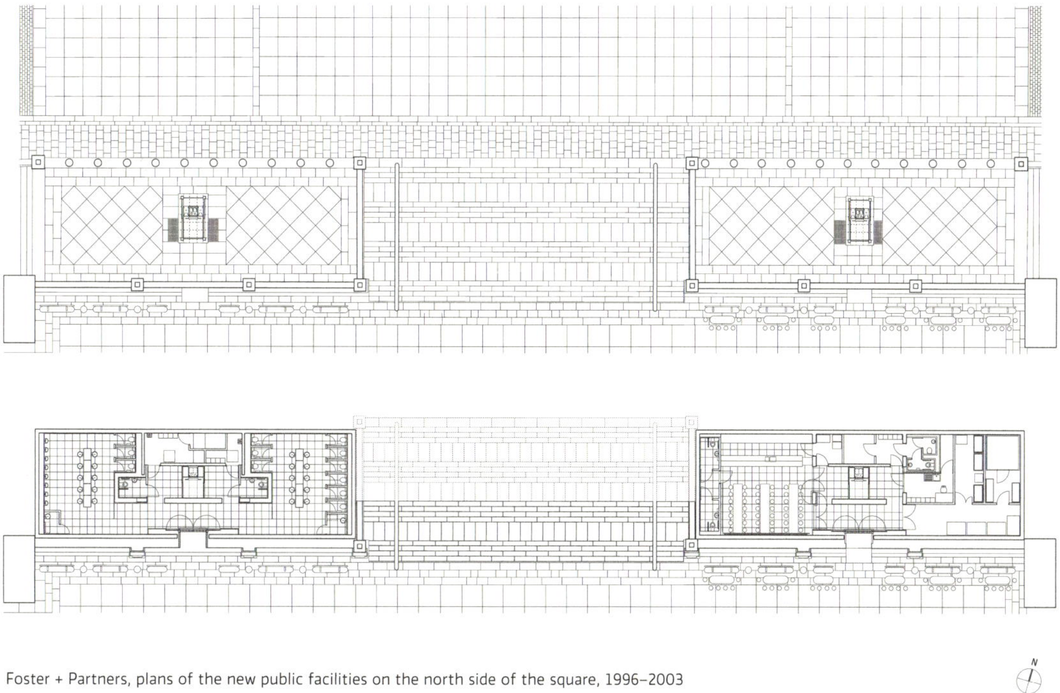

Foster + Partners, plans of the new public facilities on the north side of the square, 1996–2003

Lord Norman Foster, concept sketch for the redevelopment of Trafalgar Square, 2004

Foster + Partners, detail of stairs on north side of Trafalgar Square, 2003

Foster + Partners, detail of stairs on north side of Trafalgar Square, 2003

Foster + Partners, section through new restaurant, 1996–2003

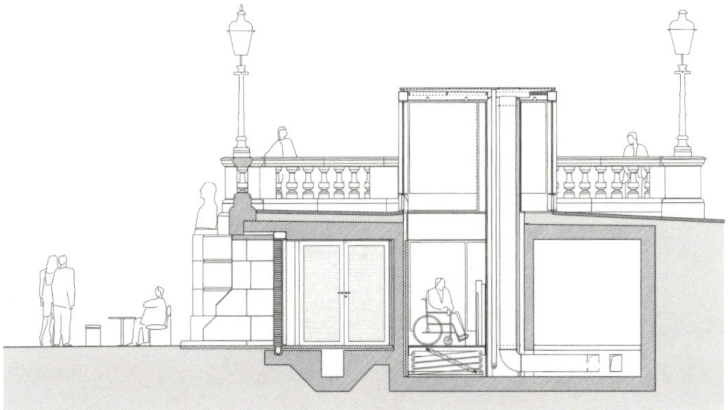

Foster + Partners, section through new public restrooms with elevator, 1996–2003

Parking Concept for the Historic Center

DESIGN Building Authority of the Hanseatic City of Wismar
YEAR 2002–2009
TYPE Traffic management
CLIENT Hanseatic City of Wismar
OTHER CONTRIBUTORS N/A
COST N/A
AREA 88 hectares (Wismar historic center)

In the historic center of Wismar, a UNESCO World Heritage Site, almost 90 percent of the buildings and 70 percent of the streets and squares have been renovated since 1990. These interventions, which were carried out by both the city government and private owners, were made possible by the drafting of an urban planning framework for Wismar's historic center, the city's acceptance into the urban development promotion program of both the federal and state governments, and the continuation of both through the general management plan for the historic center, which was produced together with the city of Stralsund in 2000 to coincide with the two cities' listings as World Heritage Sites.

Our long-term goals for this process included the preservation and improvement of the historic center as a place for living, reflecting the area's traditional residential character (the population of the historic center in 1995 was 5,000, having risen to 8,000 in 2015); and the preservation and further development of the historical center as a location for commerce and positive-impact businesses, as well as various cultural, social, and administrative facilities.

Based on these goals, we developed a core concept to reduce traffic in the historic center to an acceptable level, taking into consideration both urban planning requirements and the needs of local residents. This concept is aimed at gradually removing long-term parkers from the center, reducing traffic caused by drivers searching for parking spots, and substantially reducing noise pollution in areas with a predominantly residential character.

The plan was applied in multiple stages. First, sidewalks and the areas in front of buildings were repaved. Then, the number of parking spots in the inner city was gradually reduced from 110 to 70, and finally to 30, which is still the current number. On the market square, the introduction of parking fees was followed by a repavement of the diagonal paths that cross the square.

The result is an inner-city square that can be used in a variety of different ways, including farmers' markets that take place three times a week, diverse cultural events, and appealing dining options. These uses bring people and their activities to the foreground, relegating cars to a secondary role—where they belong.
—NORBERT HUSCHNER

Wismar Market Square, 1985

Wismar Market Square, March 2012

Wismar city center, 2012

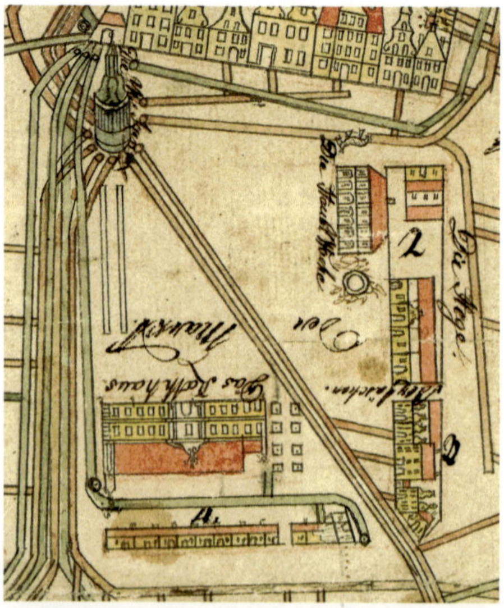

Wismar Market Square, colorized plan of water pipes, anonymous, after 1715

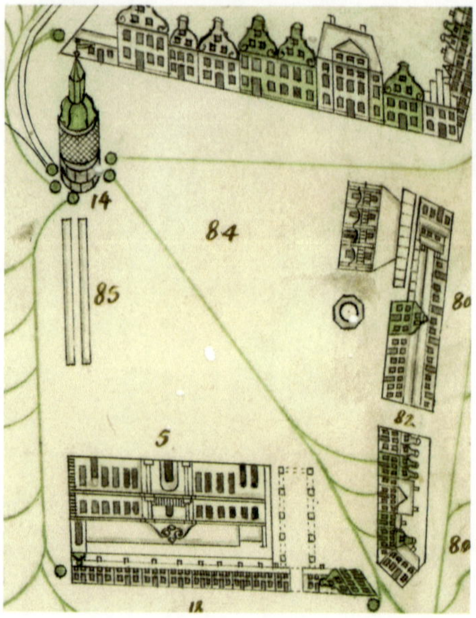

Wismar Market Square, plan of water pipes, Zacharias Voigt, ca. 1710

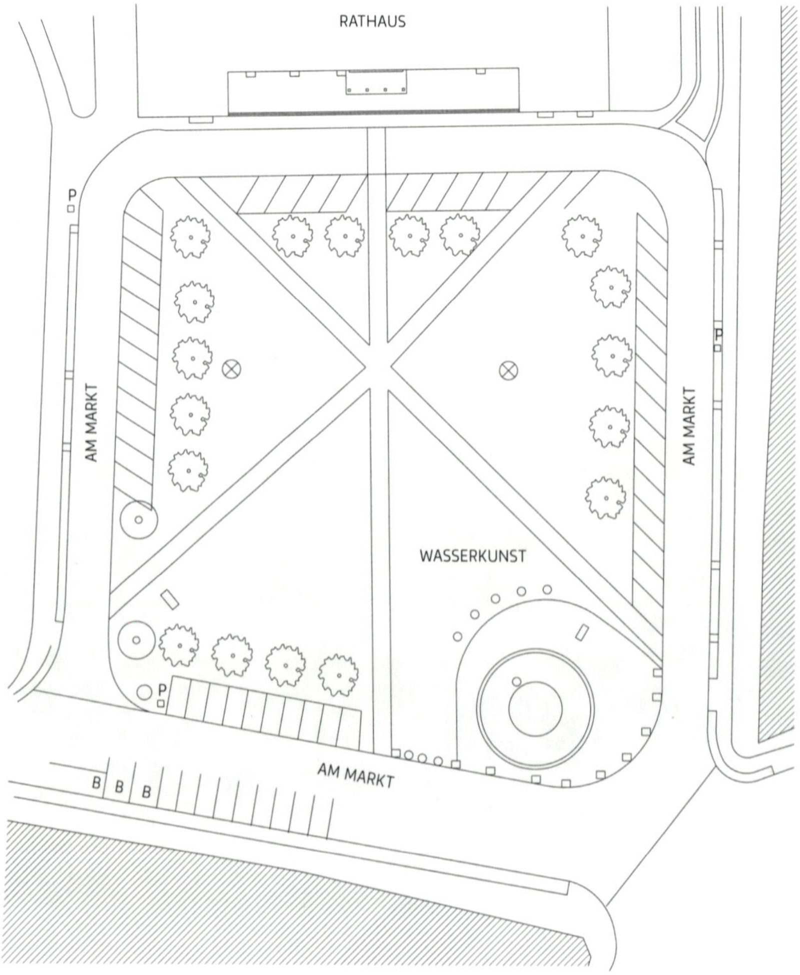

New parking spaces

Plants

Bollards

Granite pylons

Wismar Market Square, aerial view of car-free zone, 2012

Wismar, view from Krämerstraße looking south, car-free zone, 2012

Wismar, view from Lübsche Straße, car-free zone, 2012

Regulation Plan for the Coast of Galicia

DESIGN Miriam García García and Manuel Borobio Sanchiz
YEAR 2007–2011
TYPE Regulation plan
CLIENT Xunta de Galicia
OTHER CONTRIBUTORS N/A
COST N/A
AREA 215,400 hectares

The last decade has seen the Galician coast undergo rapid, uncontrolled development that has threatened to damage not only the aesthetic unity of the coast, but also its integrity as an ecological-anthropological system. The Regulation Plan for the Coast of Galicia (POL) aims to counteract this development by establishing principles and general guidelines for the integral management of the coast. Applying the criteria of durability and sustainability to urban models of land use, the plan focuses on the conservation, protection and enhancement of the importance of coastal areas. It also considers the dynamic processes implicit in the sociological evolution of the area.

One of the plan's distinctive characteristics is its use of landscape analysis and description as a method for developing a new way to read and map the site. The model proposes a structure that builds on various complementary and coexisting elements of the territory, homing in on the peculiarities of each environment in order to enable the dynamic management of the territory. The natural features of the coast are therefore interpreted as a "green infrastructure" requiring its own planning framework. Man-made features in the territory, on the other hand, are collected into the concept of a "brown infrastructure," a definition flexible enough to encompass all activities—on various scales and durations—that constitute the material and immaterial cultural heritage of the area.

Most significantly, the POL reinterprets landscape as a tool for a multiscalar approach, in which information becomes a formative component and therefore a key element for reflection and motivation in regional planning. This enables decision-making through a participatory and dynamic perspective.
—MIRIAM GARCÍA GARCÍA AND MANUEL BOROBIO SANCHIZ (ABRIDGED)

Miriam García García and Manuel Borobio Sanchiz, Regulation Plan for the Coast of Galicia, four maps used in topographic analysis

Map with measurement points for offshore visibility analysis

Map with 500-meter-wide strip of land along coast highlighted

Base map for topographic analysis

Map representing visible area from 500 meters offshore

Plancha Island, Galician Coast

Rodas Beach, Illas Atlánticas de Galicia National Park, Galician Coast

Tower of Hercules, A Coruña, Galician Coast

Cape Fisterra, Fisterra, Galician Coast

Ancoradoiro, Muros, Galician Coast

Cape Prioriño, Ferros, Galician Coast

Lighthouse at Punta Roncadoira, Xove, Galician Coast

Sisargas Islands, Malpica de Bergantiños, Galician Coast

Estuary in Ortigueria, Galician Coast

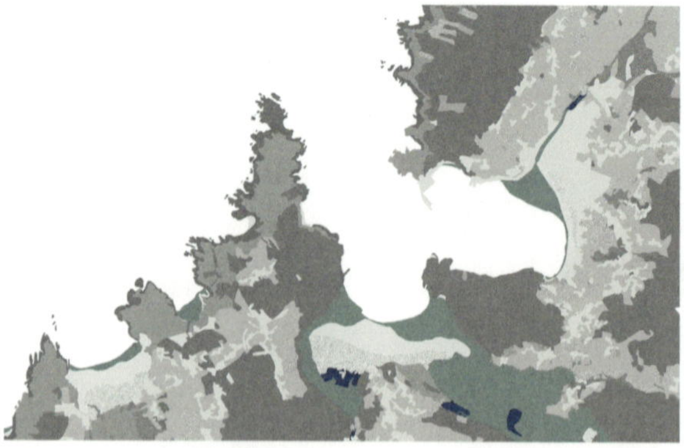

Miriam García García and Manuel Borobio Sanchiz, Regulation Plan for the Coast of Galicia, "natural dynamics: foreshore"

Carnota Beach, Galician Coast

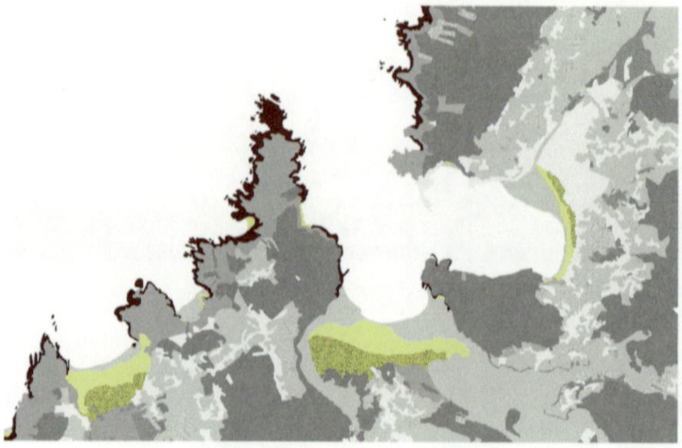

Miriam García García and Manuel Borobio Sanchiz, Regulation Plan for the Coast of Galicia, "natural dynamics: geoforms"

Forest, Galician Coast

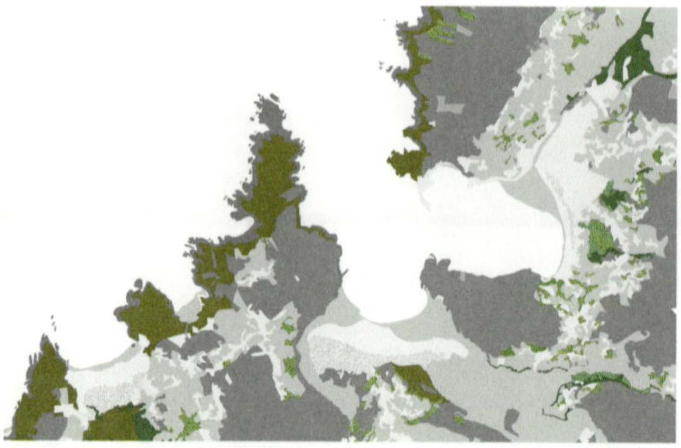

Miriam García García and Manuel Borobio Sanchiz, Regulation Plan for the Coast of Galicia, "natural dynamics: biota"

Rinlo village, Ribadeo, Galician Coast

Miriam García García and Manuel Borobio Sanchiz, Regulation Plan for the Coast of Galicia, "anthropic dynamic: cultural system, foundational and peripheral systems"

Punta Insuiña, Cambados, Galician Coast

Miriam García García and Manuel Borobio Sanchiz, Regulation Plan for the Coast of Galicia, "anthropic dynamic: agroforestry system, cultivation, and forestal exploitation"

Cereixo Harbor, Muxía, Galician Coast

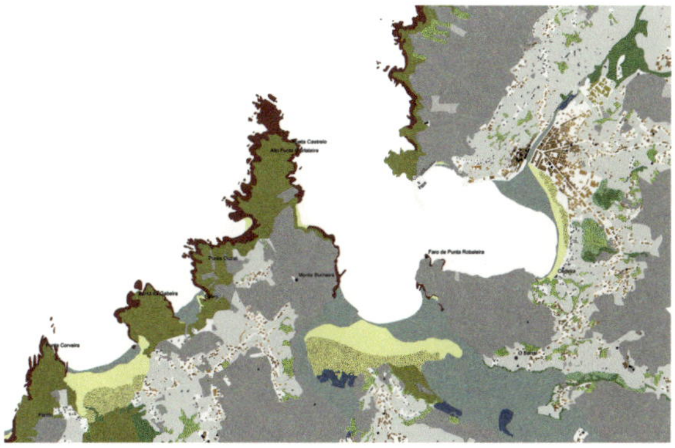

Miriam García García and Manuel Borobio Sanchiz, Regulation Plan for the Coast of Galicia, "heritage values: cultural and natural"

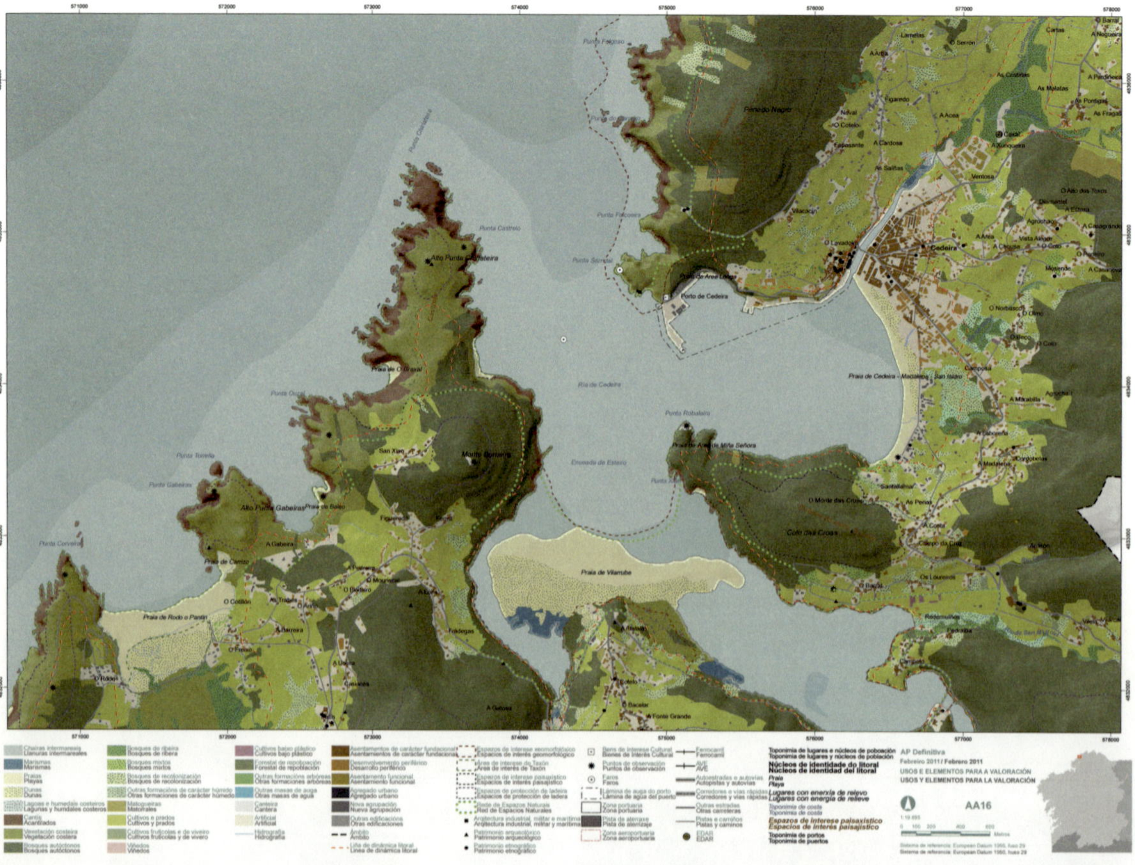

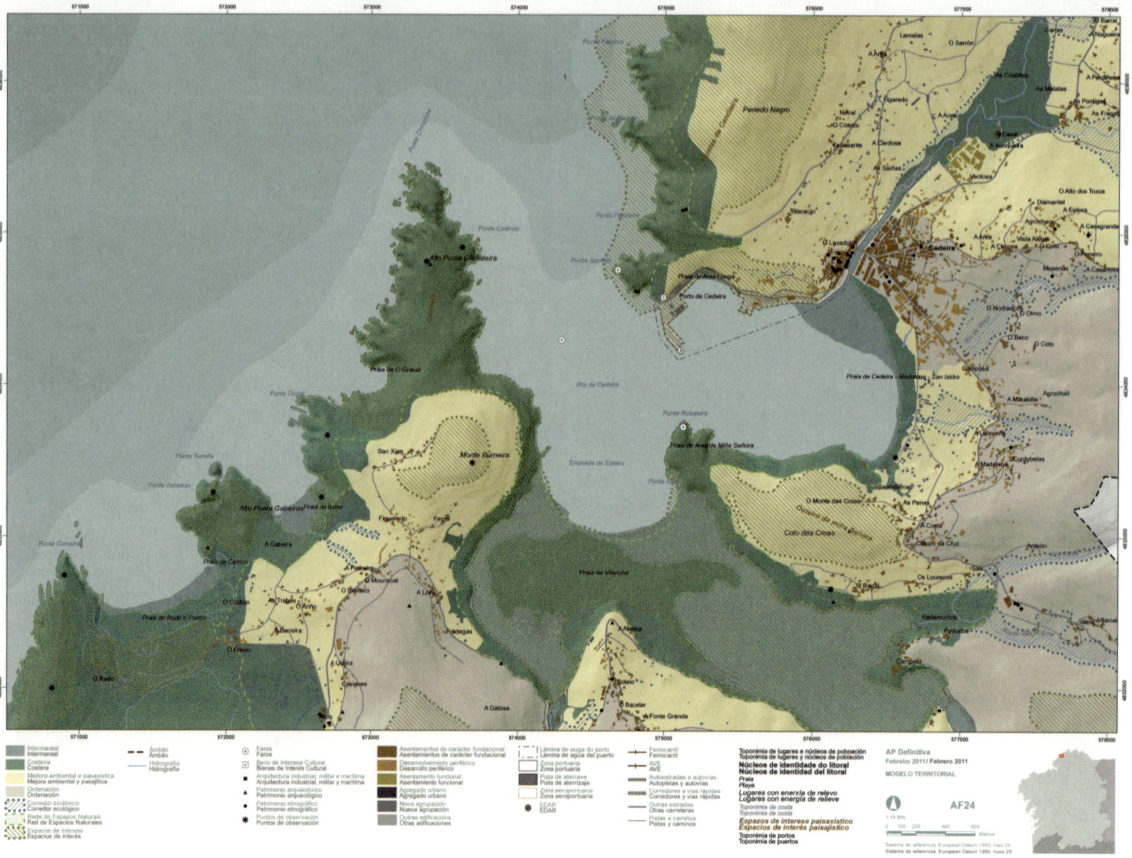

Miriam García García and Manuel Borobio Sanchiz, Galician Coast Management Plan, maps of uses and elements for assessment, 2011

Mar de Fóra Beach, Fisterra, Galicia

Brooklyn Bridge Park

DESIGN Michael Van Valkenburgh Associates, Inc.
DURATION 2008–2020 (projected)
TYPE Park
CLIENT New York City and New York State, forming the Brooklyn Bridge Park Development Corporation (BBPDC)
OTHER CONTRIBUTORS N/A
COST $350 million
AREA 85 acres (34 hectares)

The Brooklyn Bridge Park site is long and narrow, extending 1.3 miles along the shore of the East River from Jay Street to Atlantic Avenue. The majority of the site was a defunct bulk cargo shipping and storage complex, built by the Port Authority of New York and New Jersey in the 1950s, but rendered obsolete by the rise of container shipping. Out of operation since 1983 and cut off from the surrounding residential neighborhood by the Brooklyn–Queens Expressway, the complex included six piers and several upland warehouse buildings. The north end of the site is the area under and between Brooklyn and Manhattan Bridges, and was an underutilized landscape surrounded by light industrial and loft complexes.

Brooklyn Bridge Park transforms this stretch of post-industrial waterfront into a thriving 85-acre civic landscape. The park mediates a system of new and refurbished connections between the city and the river, becoming a vital urban threshold that provides space for a wide variety of activities and programming, all with spectacular views of the Manhattan skyline. Careful attention to the site's rich history and its extraordinary built and natural features ensures that this radical transformation creates an urban destination that is dynamic and engaging for generations to come.

In a city where open spaces are few and far between, Brooklyn Bridge Park exemplifies the ability of landscape architecture to recreate and adapt previously inaccessible environments for public use. The park takes a site originally designed for industrial exchange by super-human freighters and, without wiping it clean of its identity, brings it back to the human scale. With its wandering paths and surprising gardens that open into larger gathering spaces, its beaches, docks, and sports fields that serve as venues for momentary urban escape, the park as a whole facilitates social interaction that would otherwise be impossible within the constrained city limits.
—MICHAEL VAN VALKENBURGH ASSOCIATES

MVVA, Brooklyn Bridge Park, sketch of Marsh Boardwalk, ca. 2007

MVVA, Brooklyn Bridge Park, view of Brooklyn Bridge and new Squibb Park, 2010

Brooklyn waterfront before

Brooklyn waterfront after

MVVA, Brooklyn Bridge Park, kayak launch, 2010

MVVA, Booklyn Bridge Park, detailed aerial view of Picnic Peninsula, 2010

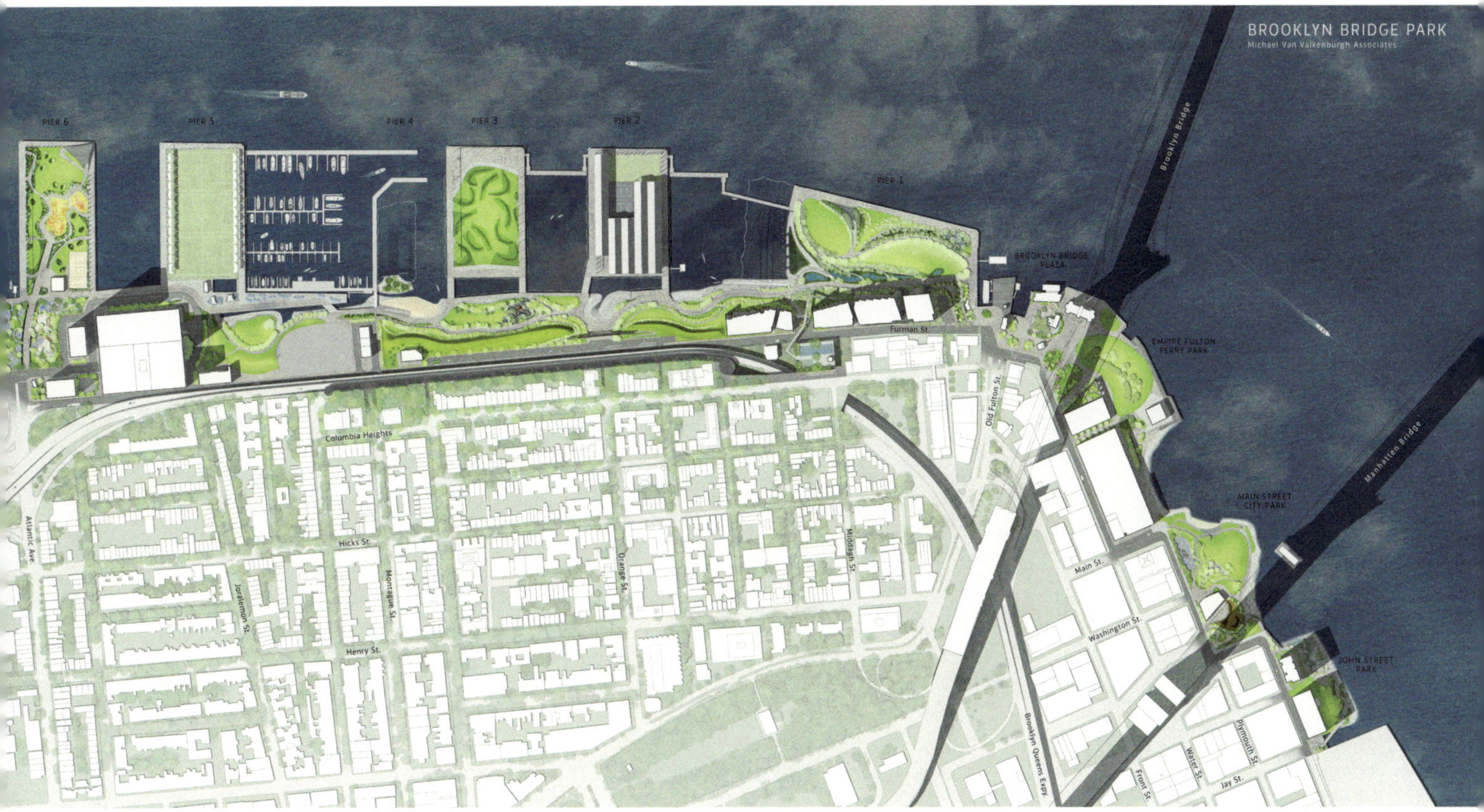

MVVA, Brooklyn Bridge Park, plan, 2008

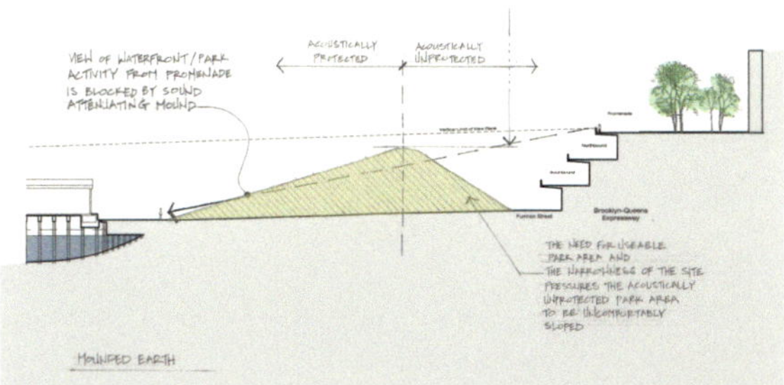

MVVA, Brooklyn Bridge Park, transformation and tunneling of Interstate 278, Section, 2008

Pedestrian Promenade Columbia Heights above Interstate 278

MVVA, Brooklyn Bridge Park, Wetland Terrace, 2010

MVVA Brooklyn Bridge Park, Pier 6 beach volleyball courts, 2012

MVVA, Brooklyn Bridge Park, Pier 6 playground, 2012

Pier 2 before

Pier 2 after

MVVA, Brooklyn Bridge Park, Pier 4 beach, 2012

MVVA, Brooklyn Bridge Park, Pier 1 Granite Prospect, 2010

Neoliberalization vs. Democratization

Public space is a medium of communication between people. Infrastructural nodes with a high density of passersby are often used by commercial and public institutions to communicate their "messages," otherwise known as advertisements. Paper posters, while still with us, have long been supplanted by mega-posters the size of buildings, neon and LED signs, projections, etc. Everywhere we turn, on train platforms, building sites, streets, and squares, we are being flooded with information or coerced by advertisements into desiring something. They are the tip of the commercial iceberg.

More obtrusive still is the temporary occupation of public space with pavilions by corporate sponsors to "celebrate" fashion week, European or world soccer championships, and so on. Other sports events, such as marathons, appear not to have any alternative routes but through inner cities. Commercial interests thus invade public space.

On the other hand, there are spaces in private ownership that appear to be part of the public space: shopping malls. Their uninterrupted connection with true public space and their interior architecture both seek to dissolve the threshold between private and public to entice the public to stroll around and encourage impulse buying.

The public's manipulability, however, is most effectively captured by commercial interests in public facilities such as railway stations and airports. At Heathrow and Madrid airports, passengers are not shown any gate information until half an hour before departure. At the same time, they are advised to arrive two hours before their flight. Spending time in the lounge is invariably coupled with the more or less reluctant spending of money: here the passengers' time is successfully turned into the airport's money.

Over the past century, commercial interests have succeeded in expanding their reach into the public realm. Helped by neoliberal ideology and a servile public administration, corporate interests have in recent decades succeeded in buying public land and public buildings everywhere around the world.

To counter this sellout, there have been thousands of grass-roots initiatives in defense of public interests. They include some notable successes in redemocratizing space that belongs to the public, such as the reclamation of the beachfront in San Juan, Puerto Rico, and the securing of public access to the Tempelhofer Feld in Berlin. —WW

Incomplete retail center Sports Park Stožice, Ljubljana

La Ventana al Mar

DESIGN Andrés Mignucci
YEAR 2000–2002 (planning), 2002–2004 (construction)
TYPE Public space
CLIENT Commonwealth of Puerto Rico, Puerto Rico Tourism Company
OTHER CONTRIBUTORS Luis Bonet, William Collazo, Marcelo López Dinardi, Maribel Ortiz, Rosa Pellerano, Gabriel Piovanetti, Luis Rafael Robles, Irvine Torres (design team); Caribe Tecno SE (contractor); Zapata & Zapata (structural engineering); EBP Design Group (civil engineering); Andrés Sánchez Carrión (electrical engineering); Wet Design (fountain design); Pedro Juan Rivera (arboriculture); Ángel Botello (sculpture)
COST $4.5 million
AREA 1.8 hectares

The character of the city of San Juan, Puerto Rico, is, to a great extent, defined by the relationship between land and water, city and ocean. Since the turn of the twentieth-century, private real estate developments have claimed the city's waterfront edge. Public perception of the oceanfront as a collective public amenity has been all but lost behind a massive urban wall that stretches along miles of waterfront. At the core of the Condado neighborhood's hotel district, a large-scale public space intervention, La Ventana al Mar, reclaims the water's edge for public use, reconnects the city and the ocean, and has served as an effective instrument of physical and economic revitalization for the area.

The government-owned land parcel was originally occupied by a large, dysfunctional convention center built in the 1970s, flanked by two landmark hotels—the "Condado Vanderbilt" (Warren & Wetmore Architects, 1919), and the "La Concha" Hotel (Toro Ferrer Architects, 1958), one of the jewels of Puerto Rico's tropical modernism. By the late 1990s, the convention center and the two hotels had closed and the government parcels were earmarked for redevelopment. This stirred a heated public debate between developers proposing the construction of a new, "all-inclusive," Mediterranean-style resort hotel on the three sites (thus perpetuating the urban wall), and advocates for the rehabilitation of the hotels and the construction of a new public space that would open the city to the ocean. Through civic involvement combined with advocacy by the College of Architects and the Municipality of San Juan, the proponents of the public space and the preservation of the La Concha and Vanderbilt hotels prevailed.

La Ventana al Mar, "a window to the sea," is the built resolution of this conflict. Here the metaphor of the "closed wall" is replaced by the metaphor of the "open window." Utilizing design strategies that operate both on the larger collective scale of the landscape and the city as well as on the intimate scale of the individual user, the project reflects the power of urban design and public space to positively transform deteriorated environments through the creation of habitable places of openness and inclusion.
—ANDRÉS MIGNUCCI

Aerial view before

Aerial view after

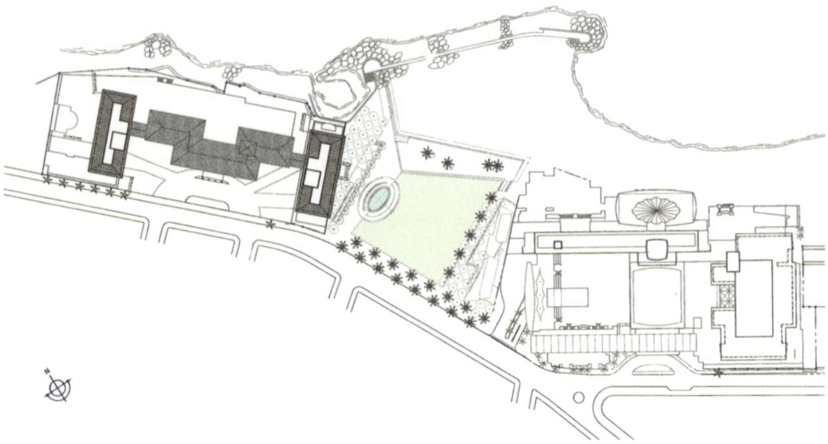
Andrés Mignucci, La Ventana al Mar, site plan with context

Andrés Mignucci, La Ventana al Mar, aerial view, 2005

Andrés Mignucci, La Ventana al Mar, promenade, 2005

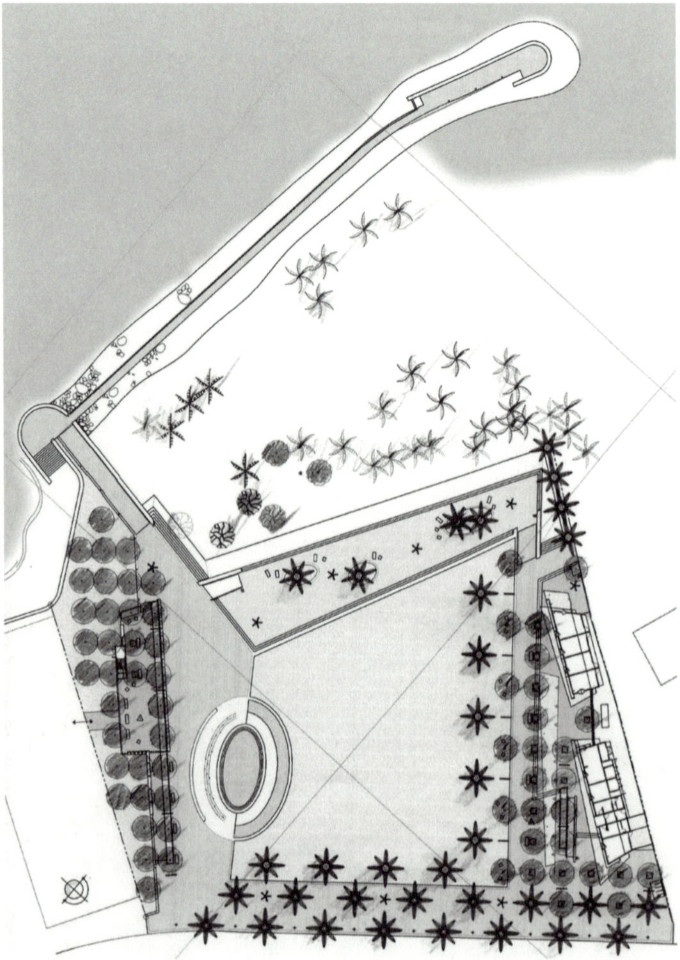

Andrés Mignucci, La Ventana al Mar, site plan, 2004

Andrés Mignucci, La Ventana al Mar, children playing

Andrés Mignucci, La Ventana al Mar, pavilion

Andrés Mignucci, La Ventana al Mar, sculpture (Ángel Botello, *Niña con Túcan*, 1983)

Andrés Mignucci, La Ventana al Mar, detailed aerial view, 2005

Andrés Mignucci, La Ventana al Mar, jazz concert

Sports Park Stožice

ARCHITECT SADAR + VUGA
LANDSCAPE ARCHITECT Studio AKKA
YEAR 1997–present
TYPE Complex with soccer stadium, multipurpose arena, retail center, and park
CLIENT City of Ljubljana, Grep d.o.o.
OTHER CONTRIBUTORS KSS London (consultation, sports architecture); Atelier One, ELEA iC, Gradis (engineering); Jelen & Zaveršnik, Lenassi (mechanical engineering); Elprojekt, Genera, UTRIS (electrical engineering); EKOsystem (fire protection engineering); LUZ (traffic and spatial planning)
COST €120 million
AREA 18 hectares

The Sports Park Stožice is a project to repurpose a former gravel pit in Ljubljana, Slovenia. It remains, to date, unfinished. In the following, the project plan from 2010 is juxtaposed with an evaluation of the project's present state in 2015.

Project text from 2010

The Sports Park Stožice is a hybrid of four projects: a 16,000-seat soccer stadium and a 12,000-seat multipurpose arena, both of which are connected by a large underground retail center with a public sports park located on top. The park creates a new public "floor," which is level with the surrounding landscape, but situated twelve meters above the ground of the former gravel pit that constitutes its site. Through its connection with the existing urban pedestrian circulation system—such as the popular Memorial Path to the south—the sports park becomes a new element in the network of green spaces in Ljubljana, thus serving the city as a whole.

The sports facilities include an outdoor basketball court, soccer field, skateboarding park, children's playground, cycling and running tracks, and large undetermined green areas reserved for sports or leisure activities. Several pavilions in the park serve to define its landscape. These accommodate sports-related facilities, such as changing rooms and gyms, as well as bars and restaurants, and serve as entry points to the retail center and the underground parking space. The 250,000-square-meter leisure-park platform on the roof of the retail center is comprised of specific micro-environments, which can accommodate the crowds before major sporting events while still offering visitors a pleasurable and comfortable space to linger or to visit independently from events in the hall or stadium. Located underneath the sports park is the large retail area. Its main urban space is an open atrium that also connects to the park above. This large sunken plaza is protected from the wind and provides intimacy for specific events, while also being wide enough to offer views of the surrounding mountains. The shops are lit by skylights oriented towards the north, which distribute diffused light and frame the views from the retail center out to the park and the sports facilities. The retail center generates activity in the park even when no events are taking place in the stadium or the multipurpose arena.

The Sports Park Stožice combines a multitude of programs within a small area, creating a complex space that caters to many different visitors at the same time. It is therefore crucial that it also provide security, effective orientation, and uncomplicated circulation. Bringing the different amenities together helps avoid the usual problem created by large, isolated sports facilities—that of becoming a grey zone within the city, only animated when events are scheduled.

SADAR + VUGA, Sports Park Stožice, concept sketch, 1997

SADAR + VUGA, Sports Park Stožice, aerial view, 2013

SADAR + VUGA, Sports Park Stožice, detail of landscaping around multipurpose arena, 2013

SADAR + VUGA, Sports Park Stožice, view of landscaping around soccer stadium, 2013

Competition 1st Prize	December 1997	1997
Master Plan	May–June 2007	2007
Master Plan Approval	March 2008	2008
Design Start	May 2008	
Construction Start	September 2008	
Change of Retail Center Operator	June 2009	2009
		2010
Opening Day (Phase 1) soccer stadium and multipurpose arena	December 2010	2011
		2015
Current State		

Five years after the opening of the soccer stadium and multipurpose arena, more than half of the sports park and the entire retail center remain unfinished. The hybrid character of the complex and its everyday life paint a different picture from how it was planned and designed—different, but not without its own qualities. The large, open, and generic spaces of the retail center attract informal sport and leisure activities that can hardly find room anywhere else in the city. What at first seems to be a failure of the unfinished project may be considered its great potential.

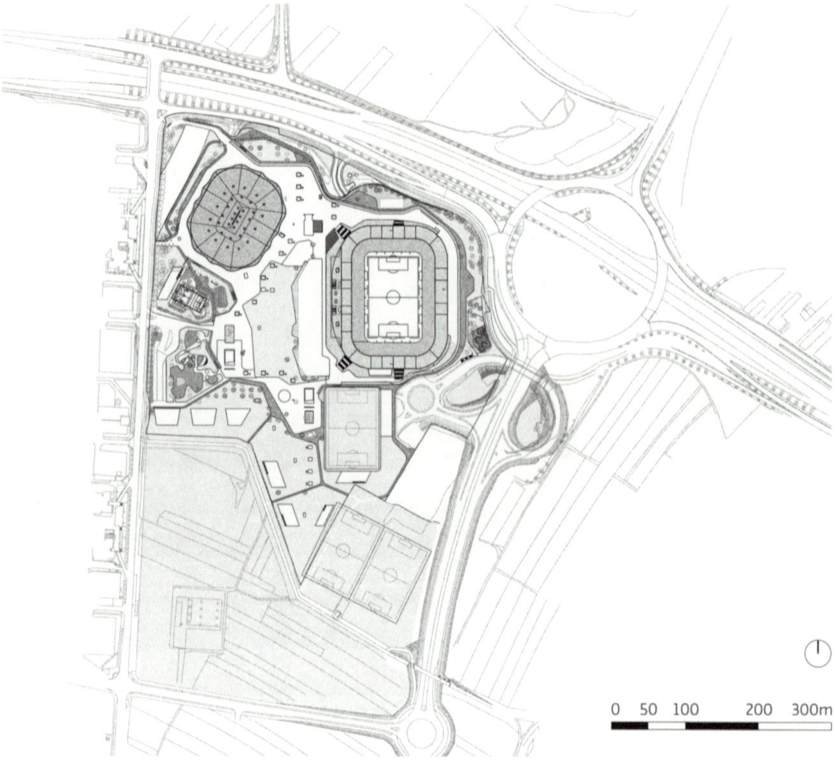

SADAR + VUGA, Sports Park Stožice, incomplete retail center, 2015

SADAR + VUGA, Sports Park Stožice, incomplete retail center, 2015

Project text from 2015

At the end of October 2015, the authors of the Sports Park design initiated and conducted an international student workshop under the name "Sports Park Stožice: Possible Futures." Students of architecture and landscape architecture from Ljubljana joined students of architecture from Münster, Germany, in researching the unfinished and abandoned construction site and testing different scenarios for its future development. The results are twofold: Firstly, different spatial zones and environments within the 80,000-square meter surface of the projected retail center were identified along with the minimum of interventions required to ensure safety in particular zones, thereby allowing them to be opened up for public use. Secondly, six proposals for different usages and programs in the identified zones were made, including an open bazaar, communal allotments located above a mushroom farm, a workshop for prototyping "smart" technologies, a campsite, and a performance space for the Academy of Performing Arts. The unfinished concrete structure inspires appropriation for urban sports activities like parkour and urban yoga.

The workshop's results aim to trigger a discussion between the city, private developers, and the public, and unveil the possibilities that this large open space offers—with the possibility of a (smaller) retail center not ruled out. —BOŠTJAN VUGA

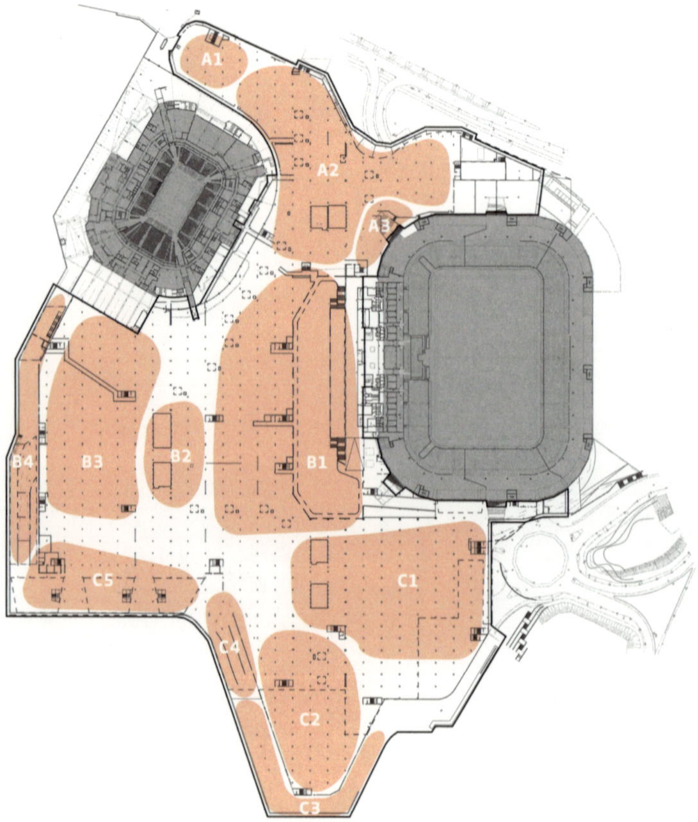

"Sports Park Stožice: Possible Futures," zoning plan of different proposals, 2015

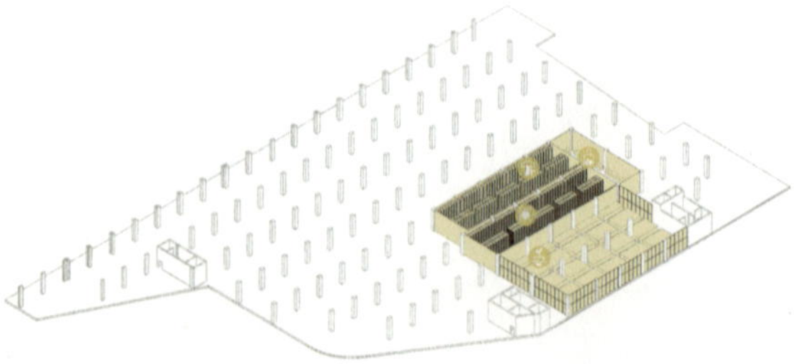

Jan Bockholt, Ronja Engelhardt, "Possible Futures," C1 urban farming

Martin T. Schulte, Stefan Pips, "Possible Futures," B3 work ateliers, 2015

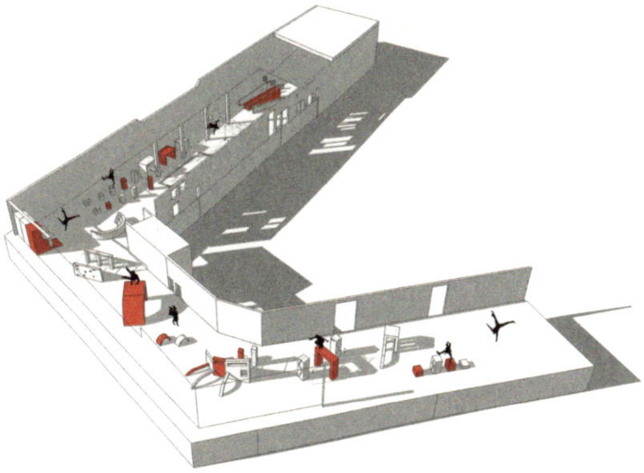

Karolina Jagła, Tomasz Madej, Maciej Oczkowski, "Possible Futures," C3 sport and recreation, 2015

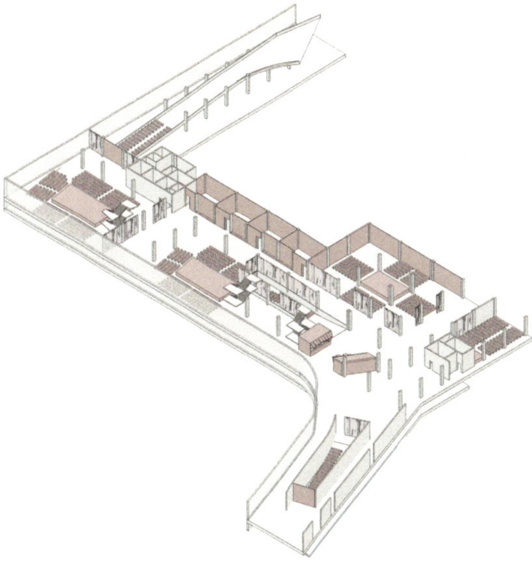

Katharina Balke, Lea Keil, "Possible Futures," C4 & C5 education and art, 2015

MADRID, SPAIN

El Campo de Cebada

ARCHITECT El Campo de Cebada
YEAR 2011–present
TYPE Collective project
CLIENT Self-initiated
OTHER CONTRIBUTORS N/A
COST N/A
AREA 2,300 m²

El Campo de Cebada (ECDC) is a collective project that reutilizes a site in central Madrid which was formerly occupied by the public swimming pool of the La Latina neighborhood. Active since 2009, it takes the form of a public forum that brings together various (sometimes even antagonistic) stakeholders in the city, with the expressed goal of innovative urban solutions by bridging the traditional communicative gap between citizens from the neighborhood and local authorities. This point distinguishes ECDC from other self-managed spaces that present themselves as autonomous from any governmental involvement whatsoever, and underlines the group's view that local administration, with all of its public tools and expertise, must cooperate with citizens to develop the city of the twenty-first century.

ECDC is a public urban infrastructure that asserts its presence in both physical and virtual space. On the one hand, the group's physical facilities in Madrid are host to a variety of activities, including urban gardening, sporting events, concerts, and artistic interventions. On the other hand, the group also maintains a constant web presence through email, a website, and social media channels. Meetings and assemblies are open to everyone, the management of resources in the space is published and transparent to all interested, and the various artistic and architectural proposals that are presented at the space are registered, uploaded, and made available for editing and appropriating by third parties. Information and knowledge is thus decentralized, establishing a network between those who are physically there in the space and those who cannot be—and those who are interested in implementing the models developed in Madrid in their own contexts. The result is an experiment in "open-source" urbanism: a tool for developing urban discourse and policy that relies on the free distribution of content and its continuous, ad hoc improvement through the collective wisdom of the crowd. Instead of an increasingly overregulated urban model in which nothing bad (or good) can happen anymore, ECDC embraces a "family-like" way of managing the city with all the failures and conflicts that come with it: a collective effort with people you like and those you don't like, the bad things and the good.

Ultimately, the project aims to implement a new paradigm for urban policy in which the citizen is no longer a passive subject of decisions taken by distant authorities, but rather an active agent in the decision-making process. To this end, ECDC works to experiment with physical and digital worlds, creating an analogous space where, just like in the digital world, there is no finite beginning or end, but rather a continuous updating.
—EL CAMPO DE CEBADA (ABRIDGED)

Postcard from Madrid showing the Plaza de la Cebada (site of El Campo de Cebada today), Louis Meunier and Nicolas Bonnart, ca. 1665, Biblioteca Nacional de España, Madrid

Postcard from Madrid showing the Plaza de la Cebada, Castañeira, Álvarez y Levenfeld, 1915, Biblioteca Nacional de España, Madrid

El Campo de Cebada, Madrid, 2015

El Campo de Cebada, event in multipurpose space, 2011. "Event urbanism: constructing the city as an infrastructure of artistic and cultural processes"

View of the site before 2007

Demolition of the public swimming pool next to the Mercado de la Cebada, 2007

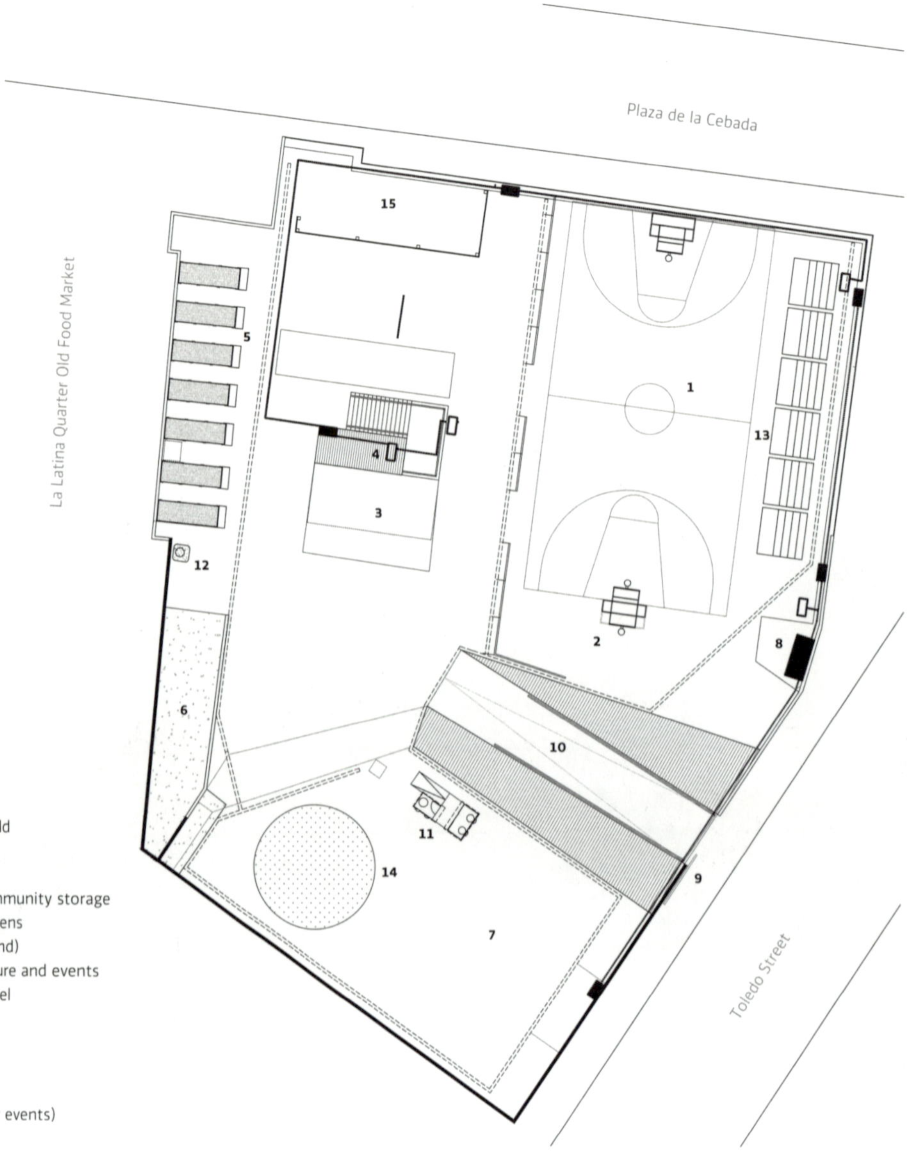

1 Basketball court/soccer field
2 Miniature basketball court
3 Resting/shadowed area
4 Elevated container for community storage
5 Green area and urban gardens
6 Aromatic garden (year round)
7 Multipurpose area for culture and events
8 Electricity distribution panel
9 Entrance
10 Access ramp
11 Restrooms
13 Moveable bleachers
14 Geodesic dome (for indoor events)
15 Outdoor storage area

El Campo de Cebada, general plan, 2011

El Campo de Cebada, panoramic view of cleared space, ca. 2008

El Campo de Cebada, aerial view, ca. 2011. "Necessity of inhabiting controversy: El Campo de Cebada is born from a process of conflict"

El Campo de Cebada, constructing the site, 2011

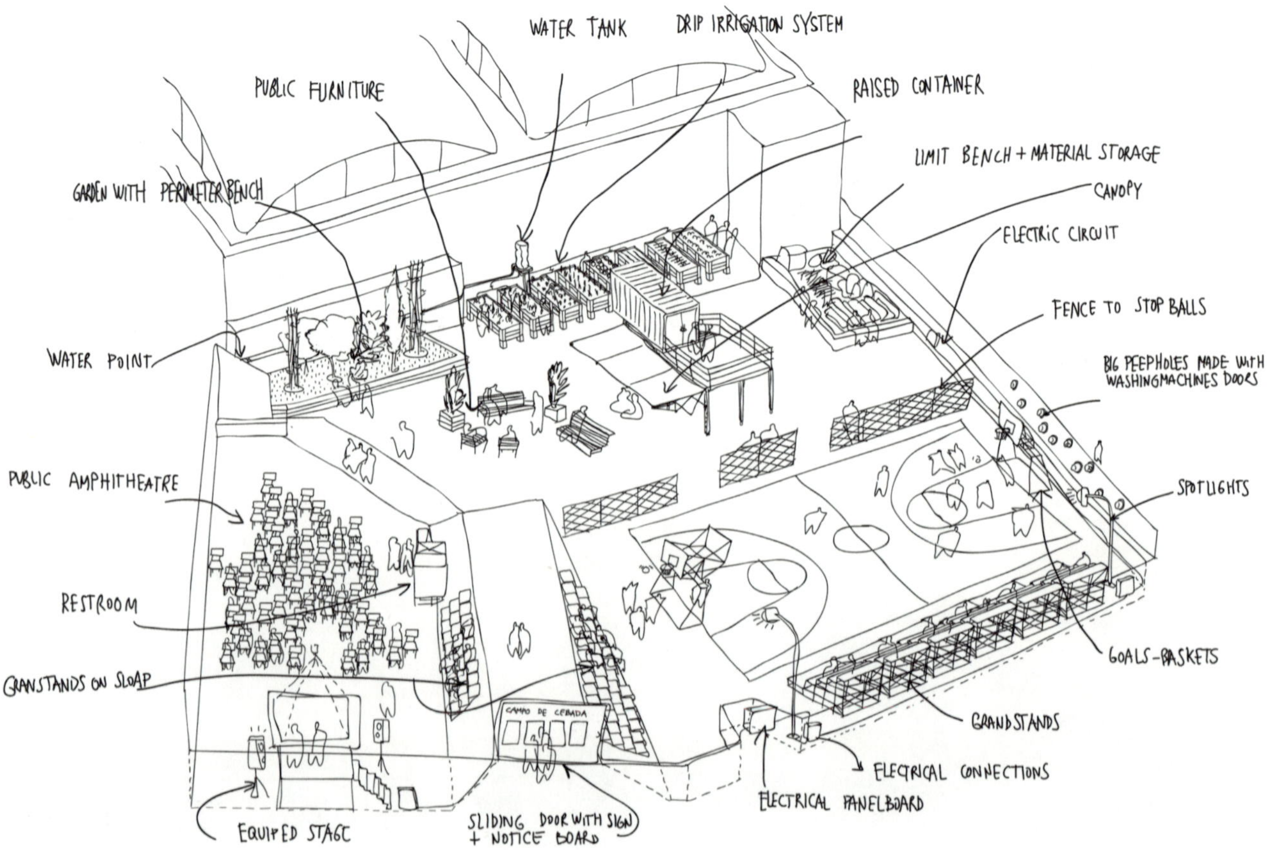

El Campo de Cebada, bird's-eye perspective drawing.
"Multilayered city: hybrid and simultaneous usage for a continuously updated city"

El Campo de Cebada, citizens' assembly. "Loudspeaker: space to build networks in internal and external contexts, where citizens can amplify their voice"

El Campo de Cebada, container for community storage.
"Public space as political space, even if you are not aware of it"

El Campo de Cebada, view through a peephole towards the basketball court. "Transparency and open data: communicating and making explicit what is going on and how it happens"

El Campo de Cebada, planting on the square. "Citizen as curator: nature and public space generate new roles"

Taller de Obras

DESIGN Blanca Zúñiga (professor) and architecture students
CLIENT Self-initiated thesis project
TYPE Interventions in public space
YEAR [1] 2012; [2] 2014; [3] 2015
AREA [1] 2,000 m²; [2] 100 m²; [3] 280 m²
COST [1] $400; [2] $800; [3] $400

Since 2004, the students of the Escuela de Arquitectura de la Universidad de Talca have been exploring the surrounding region to look for possible design interventions in public space. Their goal is to investigate new situations or find new design approaches to benefit the public sphere. In Talca as in the country as a whole, there is much to improve in this respect.

The students conduct their experiments both in nature and in the smaller towns and villages. The groups for all projects consist of around twenty-five students (from the second to fifth year of study) and one professor. They are given a budget of 400 US dollars and a timeframe of three weeks.

The selection of material presented here (images and videos) shows the results of these studies and interventions from the years 2012, 2014, and 2015. Blanca Zúñiga was in charge of supervising these projects.

Indeterminacy: building without building intervention, Carlos Trupp, Talca, Chile, 2012

1 / Indeterminacy: building without building intervention

The chosen object of study was a dusty place, a no-man's-land, undeveloped for unknown legal reasons, in the traditionally conflict-ridden neighborhood of Carlos Trupp. Public squares are lacking; there are only narrow streets or undetermined spaces in between the buildings. We took on an urban void and came to the conclusion that an exchange of ground, which possessed a maximum of indeterminacy, would have a positive impact on this space. The group decided to build without actually planning a building intervention, thus creating, with minimal means, a place to play and a meeting place for the inhabitants of the neighborhood.

Students: Yordana Andaur, Claudia Aviles, Hugo Bravo, Laura Carrasco, Felipe Figueroa, Solange Gaete, Carolina Guerra, Nathalie Hyde, Ma Jesus Molina, Yuvitza Mora, Carolina Olave, Paz Orellana, Carolina Orellana, Juan Carlos Orellana, Yorka Parra, Karen Ramirez, Jose Miguel Rivera, Carolina Valenzuela, Katherine Valenzuela, Jose Valladares, Belen Verdugo, Angela Zúñiga

House on the Move—La Novia de Maule, Putú, Chile, 2014

2 / House on the Move—La Novia de Maule

We created a house from translucent fabric and set it up in places whose beauty on the one hand and extreme use on the other stand in a tense relationship to one another. With the house, we wanted to explore concepts of scale in geographically or scenically significant locations and to investigate the impact that this installation would have on the specific locations.

Students: Barbara Acevedo, Mariela Barrios, Salvatore Bullara, Jose Bustamante, Loreto Castro, Francisca Ceron, Salvo Cucinella, Benjamin Fernandez, Valeria Fuentes, Solange Gaete, Soledad Gonzalez, Daniela Guajardo, Nathalie Guerrero, Claudio Lavin, Maria Letizia Mangiameli, Lidicet Mellado, Loreto Mellado, Patricio Navarro, Muriel Oyarzun, Sindy Palomera, Karen Ramirez, Nicole Roudergue, Federica Terruso, Eleonora Treppiedi, Estephania Valenzuela, Francisca Villalobos, Katherine Zabalaga, Angela Zúñiga

The Nest—El Nido, Talca, Chile, 2015

3 / The Nest—El Nido

Villa Francia, a neighborhood on the outermost fringe of Talca, is a heavily fragmented place due to historical processes of plot subdivision. In everyday life, this has led to a prevalent fear of "the others," as the different parts of the place do not see themselves as a coherent whole. The starting point for this project was an investigation of material: we used rather low-quality wood, as it is commonly used for houses in this part of the city. We situated the "Nest" in a strategic place where a shaded area and a meeting place for the neighborhood were to be created. The work aims to create a space in which the inhabitants can meet on an equal footing under a shady roof and with an interest in the future development of their neighborhood.

—

Students: Barbara Acevedo, Nicolas Ahumada, Arnaldo Alegria, Dario Bueno, Javier Caceres, Javier Castro, Antonio Chaparro, Felipe Contardo, Carlos Cruz, Carolina Dorador, Francisca Fuentes, Matias Jauregui, Eduardo Mardones, Felipe Miranda, Francisca Morales, Muriel Oyarzún, Felipe Padilla, Bruno Riquelme, Cecilia Silva, Carlos Toledo, Francisca Villalobos, Carolina Vivar, Katherine Zabalaga

Universal Declaration of Urban Rights / Urban Parliaments

ARCHITECT Zuloark
YEAR 2013–present
TYPE Urban infrastructure
CLIENT Various public and private institutions
OTHER CONTRIBUTORS N/A
COST €2,000–10,000
AREA 5–20 m²

More than half of the world's population is already living in urban areas, and the numbers continue to grow at a rapid rate. This situation raises questions about "urban conditions" and the great need to include citizens in the public agenda to initiate dialogue and debate for future generations.

The Universal Declaration of Urban Rights was not intended as a manifesto or a solution (as the Athens Charter was), but rather as a dynamic manual for common construction, an active thinking tool that enables the qualitative management of information about the city, and a way to understand what it means to be a citizen.

An Urban Parliament is an infrastructure for communication and knowledge that materializes one of the main goals of the Declaration of Urban Rights: debate on the city in a place where all members are equal.

This project was born as a response to such questions and seeks to be an urban infrastructure by facilitating dialogue, not just one-way conversations. The infrastructure aims to distill priorities based on consensus while focusing on the important urban and social issues of today.

To mark the Declaration of Urban Rights project's presentation at the *DEMO:POLIS* exhibition, a series of parliamentary sessions will be held at the Berlin Urban Parliament. Entry is free of charge. Once a week, the public is invited to join debates on contemporary urban issues involving representatives of city initiatives, city planners, architects, sociologists, philosophers, and others. The common aim will be to establish a Berlin Declaration of Urban Rights Open Charter. —ZULOARK AND JULIA FÖRSTER

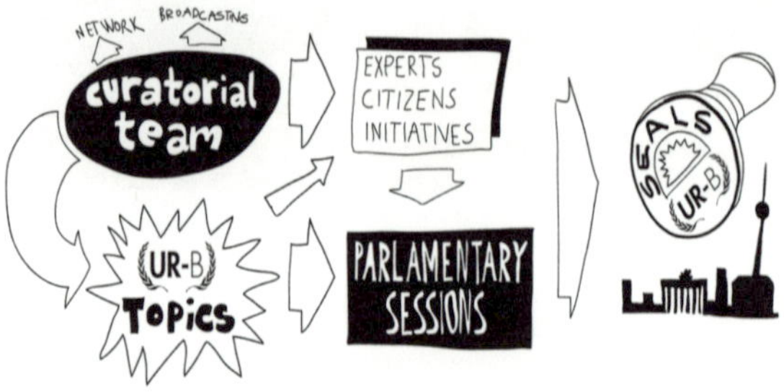

Zuloark, flowchart of the Urban Rights process for developing citizen-granted "urban quality seals" for Berlin

Zuloark, constructing the Lisbon Urban Parliament with architects, students, and volunteers, 2013

Zuloark, Lisbon Urban Parliament, MEDS Lisbon, 2013

Zuloark, parliamentary session in the Lisbon Urban Parliament, Lisbon Architecture Triennale, 2013

Zuloark, Lisbon Urban Parliament, Lisbon Architecture Triennale, 2013

Granby Park

ARCHITECT Seán Harrington Architects (pallet theater); A2 Architects (theater master plan and classroom space)
YEAR 2013
TYPE Community park including classroom space, thirty artist installations, café, children's play area, 300-person amphitheater, graffiti wall, and boules pitch, surrounded by planting and furniture
CLIENT UpStart Collaborative Ltd.
OTHER CONTRIBUTORS 400 volunteers, 1,100 supporters, and architectural designers working pro bono
COST €0 (built using donated and upcycled materials)
AREA ca. 3,000 m²

Granby Park was a temporary park built on a vacant site in Dublin's north inner city. It was open for one month—September 2013—and played host to a multitude of exhibitions, installations, events, and community activities. The park was made from upcycled, recycled, donated, and found materials and was a collaboration between some of the city's most talented artists, event coordinators, architects, performers, and creatives. Granby Park demonstrated not only an alternative model to the way that we use vacant sites, but also an innovative platform for citizens, local government, local community, business, creative professionals, and artists to work together. The city council played a valuable role in providing the site and negotiating legal and bureaucratic hurdles.

Granby Park was built on a large vacant site where a thriving inner-city community once existed. Like much of the north inner city, the Dominick Street area has had its own social problems and struggles to cope with crime and antisocial behavior.

The site was originally designated for an urban regeneration project due in 2008, to include affordable housing for families in the area. However, with the economic downturn and austerity measures, these plans were placed on hold indefinitely.

The Granby Park initiative was designed and coordinated by a young arts collective that aims to inspire creativity throughout Ireland. They wanted to demonstrate new ways of thinking and approaching the spaces in our communities. The team created the vision, concept, program, and brief. They also designed and coordinated the organization, consultation process, and production of Granby Park. The park was built by volunteers, including teenagers from loyalist parts of Northern Ireland. As a result of the project, a "new" Dubfast Ulster/Dublin Covenant was drawn up by the young people, and a partnership between youth groups was established on formal levels so that cross-border projects can be facilitated in the future.

We believe that by building a shared inner-city public park alongside the community and youth of Dominick Street, the Granby Park project contributed to a different vision of our community and our city, and at the same time developed a sense of civic responsibility towards vacant and abandoned spaces in the city.
—SEÁN HARRINGTON

Granby Park, aerial view of vacant site after demolition of social housing

Granby Park, site of demolished social housing shortly before construction of the park

A2 Architects, Granby Park, view from park entrance through polytunnel, 2013

Granby Park, spray-painted sign

A2 Architects, Granby Park, view from classroom area under roof of polytunnel towards pallet theater, 2013

Seán Harrington Architects and A2 Architects, panoramic view of Granby Park, 2013

Seán Harrington Architects and A2 Architects, Granby Park, master plan, 2013

1	Park entrance
2	Bicycle parking
3	Artwork
4	Polytunnel classroom area
5	Children's playground
6	Trade school
7	Boules pitch
8	Café
9	Grafitti wall
10	Pallet theater
11	Park exit

Seán Harrington Architects, Granby Park, pallet theater, 2013

Seán Harrington Architects, Granby Park, planting in pallet theater, 2013

Seán Harrington Architects, Granby Park, pallet theater, 2013

Seán Harrington Architects, Granby Park, theater during construction, 2013

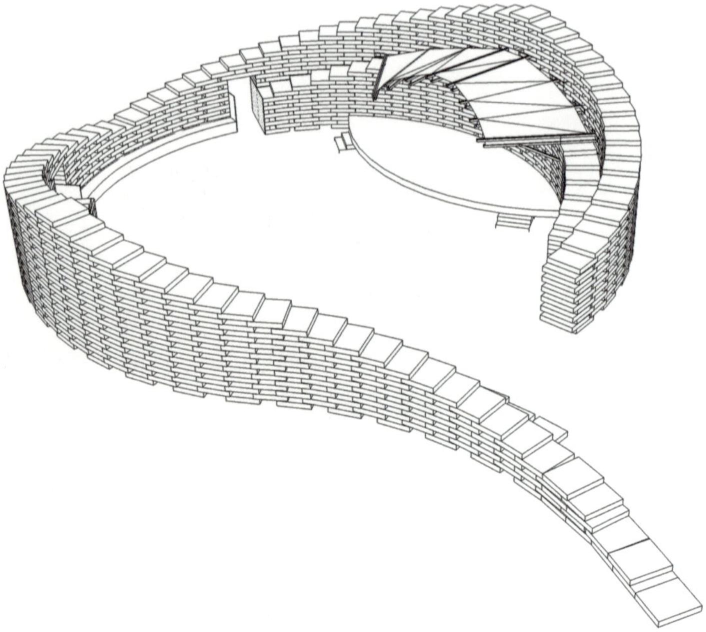

Seán Harrington Architects, overall view of the pallet theater, 2013

A2 Architects, view of classroom area under roof of polytunnel, 2013

A2 Architects, Granby Park, night view of polytunnel with lamp installation, 2013

100% Tempelhofer Feld

ARCHITECT None
YEAR 2011–present
TYPE Citizen-led development
CLIENT Self-initiated
OTHER CONTRIBUTORS N/A
COST €40,000 for the two-year campaign (2012–2014)
AREA ca. 380 hectares (Tempelhofer Feld)

Demokratische Initiative 100% Tempelhofer Feld, poster for referendum, 2014

Opened in 1923, Tempelhof Airport in Berlin used to be one of three international airports in the city. It achieved symbolic status during the Berlin Blockade of June 1948–May 1949, when the Allies airlifted necessary supplies to the airport to bypass the Soviet blockade of land routes going into West Berlin. The airport was closed in 2008 due to concerns over its urban location as well as increasing passenger numbers: suddenly, 380 hectares (940 acres) of open land became available in the middle of the city. Lacking specific solutions for how to convert the site, leading city officials opened the grounds to the public in 2010 with minimal changes. What was meant as a temporary solution, however, gradually took on the features of something more permanent as the airport grounds became one of Berlin's most beloved parks. Alongside the generous, empty green spaces, one of the main attractions is the original airport tarmac, which is popular among cyclists, roller skaters, and kiteboarders alike. The secret of the park's success seems to lie in its anti-programmatic character: (almost) every activity is allowed, and decisions on how to appropriate the space are left open to individual users.

The future of the site remains the subject of much dispute. Naturally, the prospect of a vast and well-connected lot in the middle of the city was of much interest to both local politicians and real-estate developers. In 2013, these interests crystallized in a master plan submitted by Berlin's Senate Department for Urban Development, which suggested converting the edge of the former airport grounds into a mixed-use development including housing, industry, sports, and recreational facilities, as well as a new central library. In opposition to these and similar plans, a group called the "Demokratische Initiative 100% Tempelhofer Feld e.V." has been campaigning since 2011 for the full preservation of the field as an "open landscape in the middle of the city." The group is driven by skepticism against official promises to include affordable housing in the development, concerns about the local ecosystem, and worries that the historical character of the site could be lost. In 2012, the group set into motion a general referendum to create a law that would require preserving the site in its present state. The debate over the former Tempelhof Airport was not just about the future of this particular site, however; instead, it was a struggle concerning the future of the city itself and how the constant need for new housing in Berlin ought to be balanced against the desire to preserve the city's open spaces.

The campaign featured a number of cunning strategies, such as self-made and distributed clipboards and signature lists; a mobile "bicycle table" in the form of a board that could be carried on a cyclist's back and converted into a table by laying it across the bicycle; and a campaign newspaper, which parodied the style and tone of the German tabloid *Bild*. Thanks to these and similar strategies, the group was able to collect enough signatures to clear the way for a referendum. On May 25, 2014, the day of the referendum, the group's proposal passed the necessary quorum of 25 percent of eligible votes with flying colors. Garnering 64 percent of all votes cast, the prohibition on further construction on the Tempelhofer Feld passed into law—against the majority opinion in Berlin's house of representatives. The citizens of Berlin thus claimed their right to have a say in urban development with a voice that was loud and clear. —YS

View of Tempelhofer Feld towards former airport building, 2015

Aerial view of Tempelhofer Feld, 2015

Tempelhofer Feld, various activities, 2015

Tempelhofer Feld, former radar tower, 2015

Gerhart-Hauptmann-Platz

ARCHITECT Guido Hager
YEAR 2015–present
TYPE Citizen-led development
CLIENT Fasanenplatz Citizens' Initiative
OTHER CONTRIBUTORS Andreas Pernstich, Andreas Kotlan, Monika Schenk
COST N/A
AREA 3.1 hectares

In a triangular inner-city green space in Berlin's Wilmersdorf district, bordering on Gerhart-Hauptmann-Park to the south and Fasanenplatz to the west, is a collection of four cultural institutions that have come together haphazardly over the years: the Festival Theater of the Federal Government by Fritz Bornemann (1963), previously the Freie Volksbühne (West Berlin);[1] the Music Department of the Berlin University of the Arts, housed in the former Joachimsthal School (1880); the cabaret Bar jeder Vernunft in a former Dutch *spiegeltent* (Danse Paleis of 1912); and the children's daycare center of the Catholic St. Ludwig parish, accommodated in the old faculty house of the Joachimsthal School on Fasanenplatz.

This unique assembly of different cultural institutions and its green spaces—a rare amenity in this neighborhood—should not only be protected, but also, at last, be structured in a way that reorients all of its parts to create a public space for people to meet each other.

During the neoliberal austerity era of the 1990s, the Freie Volksbühne suddenly lost its subsidies. As a private institution, the theater was forced to sell both its building and property to make up for these losses. The subsequent owner, a developer from Hamburg, attempted to construct a variety of projects over a period of fifteen years (such as plans for a high-rise development on the site of the public Gerhart-Hauptmann-Park in 2005 and plans for apartment buildings in 2009 and 2012, in part on public property). While these efforts were initially met with broad support among politicians in the local district, they ultimately failed due to opposition from both the Fasanenplatz Citizens' Initiative and voters in the district. In 2014, the federal government made partial use of its right of preemption to acquire the theater itself, but without the rest of the site. The Hamburg developer then assigned the site to a Berlin developer, who proposed a design to replace the neglected parking garage that would, however, also result in an unacceptable densification of the existing space.

Around the same time, and after thorough examination of possible and impossible options, the Fasanenplatz Citizens' Initiative worked together with landscape architect Guido Hager to develop a proposal that represents an optimal design from the point of view of the users and residents of the neighborhood. A range of options was considered, including comprehensive reuse as well as the partial and complete demolition of the car park.

Guido Hager and the users (the Berlin University of the Arts, the Festival Theater, and the Fasanenplatz Citizens' Initiative) agreed on the creation of a square between the large cultural institutions: the future Gerhart-Hauptmann-Platz, which could become a site for a variety of cultural events. Besides additional restaurants and cafés, the existing playground and soccer field, as well as the lawn with its mature trees, are to be preserved or enlarged.

With the rearrangement of the cultural quarter around a new square, the interior is finally linked up with its surroundings: Meinekestraße and Kurfürstendamm to the north, Bundesallee and the Spichernstraße subway station to the east, and Fasanenplatz and Ludwigkirchstraße to the west. An open, bright, and protected square could be created here for music students, residents, festival guests, adolescents, and children—in other words: for the public.
—WW

1 Among the names of people active at the Freie Volksbühne are Erwin Piscator (performance of Heinar Kipphardt's *In the Matter of Robert J. Oppenheimer*, 1964), Peter Zadek, Claus Peymann, Luc Bondy, Klaus Michael Grüber, Hans Neuenfels et al.

View of Gerhart-Hauptmann-Platz, Berlin, 2016

View of Festival Theater, Schaperstraße, Berlin, 2014

Public green spaces in Berlin's Wilmersdorf district

Front gardens and medians

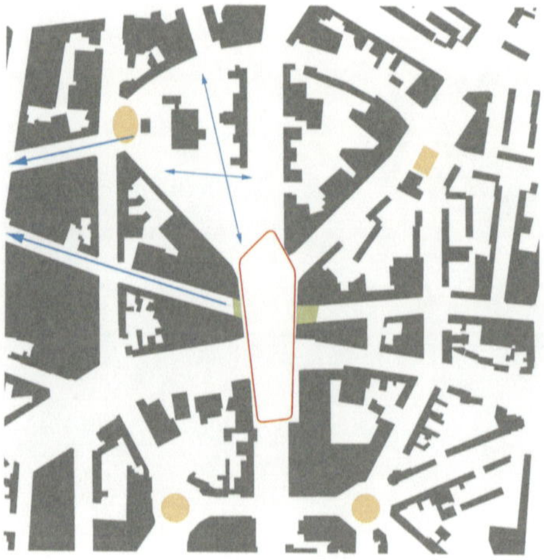

Urban composition

Fasanenplatz Citizens' Initiative, leaf collection, fall 2013

Bärbel Scherhag and volunteer, 2013

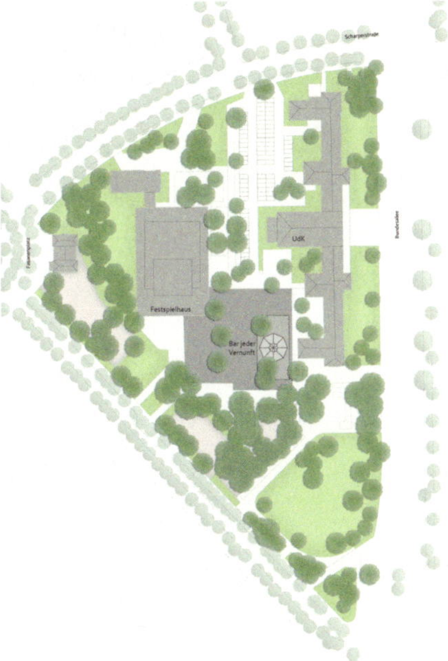

Existing buildings and vegetation

Guido Hager, master plan for a new square: Gerhart-Hauptmann-Platz

Tree planting ceremony with Thomas Oberender, Director of the Festival Theater, and Marc Schulte, Counselor for Building, Council of Charlottenburg-Wilmersdorf

Común-Unidad

ARCHITECT Rozana Montiel | Estudio de Arquitectura, Alin V. Wallach
YEAR 2015
TYPE Public space rehabilitation
CLIENT Instituto del Fondo Nacional de la Vivienda para los Trabajadores (INFONAVIT)
OTHER CONTRIBUTORS Cecilia Brañas, Luis Galán, Diana Léon, Valery Michalon
COST N/A
AREA N/A

Común-Unidad is a public space rehabilitation project for the Unidad Habitacional San Pablo Xalpa in Azcapotzalco, Mexico City. The unit used to be divided into sectors by walls, fences, and barriers built by its inhabitants over time, which did not allow the community to benefit from the available public spaces. The goal was to transform a "divided apartment unit" into a "neighborhood common-unit" by designing with, and not just for, the community through implementing several measures. The project's strategy was to work with the barriers created by its inhabitants: to permeate them, democratize them, and grant them new meaning in order to create *unity* within the unit. Before, the inhabitants of the unit's different sections would often install temporary coverings such as tarps in public areas for gatherings and parties, thus managing to extend their private area. By working with them we managed to reclaim the idea of covering certain spaces for use as recreational and socializing areas. Roofed modules were installed and equipped for different activities (blackboards, climbing walls, handrails, and nets), which is far better than covering with tarps. The recovered public space became an extension of each apartment. The strategy turned out to be efficient: people got together to contribute to the redesign of their unit, and the change in public perception that resulted was such that the neighbors themselves requested the fences be removed. The space spoke for itself and the unit's inhabitants decided to eliminate all barriers and benefit from exterior spaces, thus filling them with public and common life.
—ROZANA MONTIEL

Unidad Habitacional San Pablo Xalpa, before transformation, 2014

Rozana Montiel, Común-Unidad, Unidad Habitacional San Pablo Xalpa, after transformation, 2015

Rozana Montiel, Común-Unidad, Unidad Habitacional San Pablo Xalpa, after transformation, 2015

Rozana Montiel, Común-Unidad, Unidad Habitacional San Pablo Xalpa, section perspective, 2015

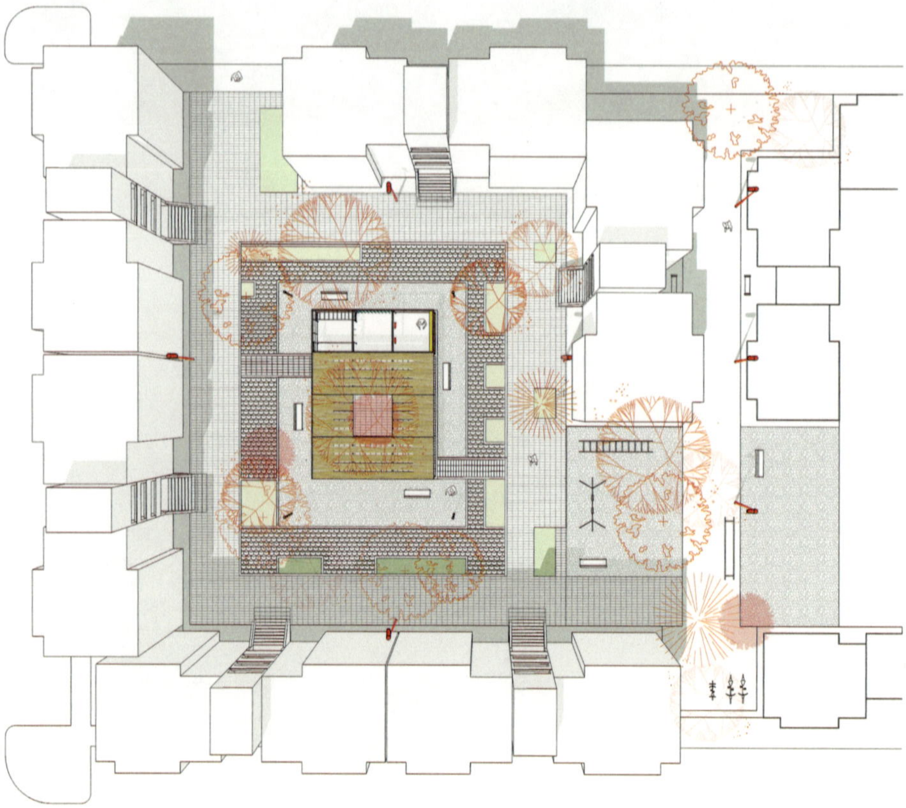

Rozana Montiel, Común-Unidad, Unidad Habitacional San Pablo Xalpa, aerial perspective, 2015

Rozana Montiel, Común-Unidad, Unidad Habitacional San Pablo Xalpa, pavilion as playground, 2015

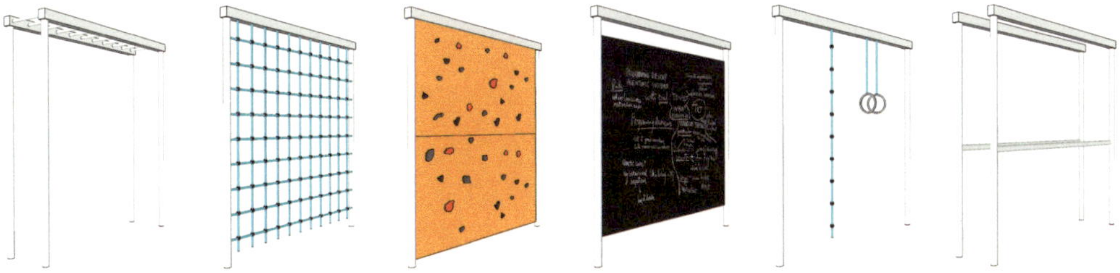

Rozana Montiel, Común-Unidad, module variations

Rozana Montiel, Común-Unidad, Unidad Habitacional San Pablo Xalpa, library, 2015

Panoramas

The following selection of sites provides a broad spectrum of public spaces:

- from traditional squares and streets in historical towns to entire landscapes;
- from the subtle design of the pedestrian paths leading to the Acropolis to the congenial insertion of bridges, embankments and other public infrastructures along the River Ljubljanica;
- from the small, unspectacular, and entirely normal neighborhood around Place Léon Aucoc in Bordeaux to the comprehensive remodeling of Brooklyn's harbor front into a series of parks and sports facilities;
- from the reclamation of public space as a result of displacing vehicular traffic in Wismar and London to the assertion of public use on Berlin's Tempelhofer Feld.

These examples celebrate the breadth and wealth of different design approaches. At the same time, they remind us of the collective achievements of generations of people who have cared and fought for them, and who continue to be committed in their struggle to maintain these and other public spaces for posterity. —WW

Galicia

Guimarães

Anklam

Alexanderplatz, Berlin

Tempelhof, Berlin

Bordeaux

Wismar

London

Brooklyn Bridge Park, New York City

Gelsenkirchen

Athens

VISIONS

The exhibition *DEMO:POLIS* is an invitation to the public to shape the city of the future. The third section of the exhibition is a laboratory for all those who want to engage: school children, students, artists, professionals, and the interested public.

The members of the *Junge Akademie* [Young Academy] display their work here, documenting their interpretation of public space. The academy's educational program—Kunstwelten—shares the virtual reality design platform with members of the public: here, anyone can engage in the design of public space and the urban fabric by determining a variety of parameters.

Finally, the exhibition presents the results of the international workshop held in October 2015 involving experts from Havana, New York, São Paulo, and Berlin with students, teachers, urban designers, landscape architects, and architects from four Berlin and Potsdam universities, who worked intensively on three archetypal cities in Germany: Anklam in Mecklenburg-Western Pomerania, Gelsenkirchen in North Rhine-Westphalia and Berlin.

A society without its own visions is a society without future.

The tools to express these visions and the means to communicate them to each other already exist, so what are we waiting for? —WW

International Workshop

In October 2015, teams from four universities in Berlin and Potsdam participated in a week-long workshop at the Akademie der Künste, where central thematic aspects of the forthcoming *DEMO:POLIS* exhibition were discussed and prepared.

Taking the cities of Anklam (13,000 residents), Gelsenkirchen (260,000 residents), and Berlin (3.5 million residents) as examples, three places—and thereby three different scales and realities—became the objects of study.

Also participating in the workshop were the architects Cristiane Muniz, Fernando Viégas, and Álvaro Puntoni from São Paulo (11.9 million residents); Susan Chin, executive director of the Design Trust for Public Space, and the landscape architect Susannah Drake from New York City (8.5 million residents); and the urban planner and architect Julio César Pérez Hernández as well as the artist and landscape architect Reinaldo de la C. Uriarte Mosquera from Havana (2.1 million residents). In daily seminars, these guests presented their own perspectives on the issue and the distinctive characteristics of their hometowns. —BH

Final review, October 9, 2015

Urban versus Rural in Cuba

The Malecón Promenade, Havana

Caesar Studio | Architects & Planners, Future proposal for expanded public space by the sea in Havana

Public space is the result of human exchange, the space that belongs to everybody and is experienced and perceived by everyone as common. It is the space where citizens can feel at ease to either stroll, talk, perform, or act.

Public space needs to be understood from a historical perspective to grasp its origins, since from the age of the world's earliest civilizations it has provided a sense of place and identity. Its spatial and cultural evolution can be better traced through Greece and Rome—the Greek *polis* and the Roman *civitas*—where the public realm was the result of a conscious combination of artistic and scientific principles applied to planning, a core often associated with an open space shaped by a group of interconnected civic structures. Both the Greek *agora* and the Roman *forum* represented the notion of a center, a key concept to understand human life and its relationship with a place that nourished the idea of public space in European cities, where public activities took place on streets and squares. Spanish colonists brought this model to the American continent after 1492, where the Spaniards found a square-like ceremonial open space for performing rites and games.

Public squares were the major urban design feature of the Spanish settlements in America. Together with the grid, they bear the hallmark of classical heritage—the Roman *castrum* particularly—that was enforced by the 1573 Law of Indies as they represented the place where power was concentrated.

In Havana, the capital of Cuba, a system of public squares marked its polycentric character and has shaped city life since colonial times. Different squares carried different functions until Havana underwent major urban transformation in the late eighteenth century and throughout the nineteenth century, which turned Plaza de Armas into the city's first civic center and expanded it beyond its walls. This expansion included the laying out of public promenades that gave the city a harmonious balance between public spaces and buildings.

In the nineteenth century, Havana's prosperity allowed colonial urbanism to be overtaken in terms of urban expansion: the layout of El Vedado and the walls introduced a new concept for open space that adapted better to the climate and contemporary needs.

In 1901, the city was re-oriented toward the landscape with the development of an iconic seaside promenade that remains the citizens' favorite public space.

Although land speculation and a lack of comprehensive planning control led to urban sprawl under the influence of the United States during the first half of the twentieth-century, Havana avoided the global urban renewal and overdevelopment that took place during the second half of the century. Even today, it retains its urban fabric and public spaces.

A masterplan for the future redevelopment of Havana was drafted to provide a long-term holistic vision that allows the city to preserve its urban and architectural heritage while also creating new urban and economic opportunities. Among the key underlying concepts is an increase in public space, the kind of public space that should be produced for future generations, anchored in the city's history and traditions, its people's idiosyncrasy and its current needs.

Public space, however, is perceived differently in rural territories where the population density is lower and its physical attributes smaller. Nevertheless, they are the favorite gathering spaces for different groups during both night and day, places where nature and social participation converge. This is the case in Pinar del Río, the westernmost province of Cuba, which is characterized by spectacular scenery. Here, public space enjoys heritage protection and affords a sense of cultural identity thanks to local planning and a group of projects aimed at healing the cities and towns, maintaining their order, and restoring the urban image and natural landscape.

Pinar del Río

These projects are based on an understanding of the cities' anatomy and physiology—their form and function—that allows a network of green public spaces to act as mediators between nature and society from a regional to a municipal scale.

Sustainable design operates on the level of the territory's landscape. *Artcity* is a comprehensive project for the city of Pinar del Río that elaborates on the links between landscape architecture and art. Its goals are to bring the peripheral vegetation and the most rural ambiences to the city center, as well as to bring art from the center of the city to the periphery.

The project encompasses the renovation of central city parks and the rehabilitation of murals and sculptures as part of a series of environmental projects that work with local vegetation as the heritage's essential resource. Another example is *Pinar*, a cultural landscape project that combines tradition and ecology in search of identity, emphasizing the notion of architecture and vegetation as allies in search of cultural identity.

Viñales

The projects also aim to increase understanding regarding the populations for whom they are intended and their function, since the global city demands a global public space, spaces of inclusion where different languages, ethnicities and species converge; spaces of respect, solidarity, and tolerance that call for a mixing of world cultures with local interests; places of identity that distinguish us and explain who and how we are, achieved by a system that activates its pedestrian, environmental and aesthetic connections with the final aim of a combination of ecology, culture, and society.

Several other projects include the Pinar del Río Botanical Garden, which aims to conserve the diversity of native flora and communicate its value, and the Viñales project. Viñales is a small town built in the vernacular style located half an hour's drive from Pinar del Río. Its distinct valley has been a UNESCO World Heritage Site since 1999 because of its particular hills and its organic agrarian traditions.

The Viñales project comprises a visitor center and a restaurant named El Palenque, which is camouflaged within the local vegetation. Its underground entryway leads to a green public space that is conceived as a square, where the most important feature is the natural vegetation that also characterizes the local *mogotes*, or breast-like hills. Wall murals allude to African religions, making the place a wonderful synthesis of nature and culture.

—JULIO CÉSAR PÉREZ HERNÁNDEZ AND REINALDO DE LA C. URIARTE MOSQUERA

Living in New York City

Over the last decade, New York City has built majestic new parks from post-industrial sites along waterfronts or converted landfills; transformed streets for pedestrian safety and occupation; and reshaped elevated structures as public space, resulting in locations such as Brooklyn Bridge Park, Hudson River Park, Fresh Kills Park, the Times Square plazas, or the High Line. In a dense city like New York City, land is scarce and highly valuable, so the repurposing of underappreciated territory created by monofunctional or obsolete infrastructure to serve multiple new functions represents the next frontier in urban design. These spaces and plazas can serve as marketplaces, cafés, workshops, or recreational space.

NYC's overarching vision *OneNYC*, formerly *PlaNYC*, has planned for one million more New Yorkers by 2030, outlining initiatives related to housing and neighborhoods, parks and public spaces, brownfields, waterways, water supply, transportation, energy, air quality, solid waste, and climate change.[1] This framework helps to organize and direct public agencies as well as facilitate communication between community and nonprofit groups to catalyze a common desire for "A Greener, Greater New York."[2] Our current administration's focus on equity and resilience has now expanded the city's investment throughout the five boroughs to community parks and affordable housing in underserved neighborhoods.

As we consider the new *DEMO:POLIS* of New York, commerce, culture, and politics continue to be primary drivers in shaping the city. However, environmental, social, and health factors have also become more prominent determinants. Environmental actions due to climate change include protection of real estate and productivity, as well as of human life and cultural assets. The Clean Water Act, which was introduced in 1972, and a recent consent decree are now motivating the citywide green infrastructure plan, enabling open space projects such as the Gowanus Canal Sponge Park. When Superstorm Sandy devastated the city in 2012, causing an estimated 19 billion dollars in property damage, it prompted not only the public sector, which traditionally governs the public realm, but also the private and nonprofit sectors to initiate the transformation and reuse of underperforming urban infrastructure systems and right-of-ways. For example, the NYC Department of Transportation is making publicly owned land available to Business Improvement Districts and community groups through their Plaza Program.[3] More recently, this has been expanded with the planning for an El-Space Program,[4] based on the Design Trust for Public Space's study, to activate nearly seven hundred miles and millions of square feet of space under elevated infrastructure in New York City.

Studio OLIN, Bryant Park with free WiFi

Tod Williams and Billie Tsien, David Rubinstein Atrium at Lincoln Center

dlandstudio, Gowanus Canal Sponge Park

dlandstudio, Gowanus Canal Sponge Park, approach

Social and health factors also influence the importance of the public realm for wellbeing, connections between communities, and active lifestyles. From the early history of the city, public gathering space has also been an important component of NYC's *DEMO: POLIS*. Spaces for celebration and culture can also be places where citizens, on the one hand, come together to enjoy the nature of humanity, and on the other hand, express dissenting opinions enabled by a society that values free speech and democracy. Examples of the latter are Zuccotti Park or Union Square—places of public expression of a collective voice, the true *DEMO* of *DEMO:POLIS*.

NYC policy makers, planners, and design professionals are using public space, streetscapes, and large open spaces to promote more active lifestyles for commuting, livelihood, or recreation through walking, cycling, sports, and community gardening.

There are over nine hundred urban farms and gardens providing opportunities for communal activity and exercise as well as the production of fresh food in the city on vacant land and rooftops.[5] Moreover, community planning, stakeholder engagement, and activities beyond community board meetings and public hearings have played a critical role in revitalizing many neighborhoods across the five boroughs. Many of the changes were seeded by local communities well before the administration pushed them forward, codifying the overall vision. These factors have all contributed to forming new attitudes about the creation of and expectations for NYC's public open space in the twenty-first century. Neighborhoods that developed within this framework reflect incredible cultural diversity in a place where assimilation to unified cultural norms is sublimated to the common understanding of humanity in its many forms and expressions. New York is less of a melting pot than a complex salad.

Our public space is the end game in NYC. We are now making use of spaces that were underused or seen as unsuitable for development, creating networks to reknit the urban fabric. Public space provides a new identity for our city, comes to symbolize our city, or gives purpose to our city as a place for civic action and connection.

—SUSAN CHIN AND SUSANNAH DRAKE

1 City of New York, *OneNYC: The Plan for a Strong and Just City*, April 22, 2015, www1.nyc.gov/html/onenyc/index.html.

2 City of New York, *PlaNYC: A Greener Greater New York*, updated April 2011, www.nyc.gov/html/planyc/downloads/pdf/publications/planyc_2011_planyc_full_report.pdf.

3 NYC Department of Transportation, NYC Plaza Program, www.nyc.gov/html/dot/html/pedestrians/nyc-plaza-program.shtml (accessed February 9, 2016).

4 Design Trust for Public Space, *Under the Elevated: Reclaiming Space, Connecting Communities*, New York: Design Trust for Public Space, 2015, p. 101.

5 Design Trust for Public Space, *Five Borough Farm: Seeding the Future of Urban Agriculture in New York City*, New York: Design Trust for Public Space, 2012.

Public Space in São Paulo

What most impresses a visitor coming to Berlin is the superposition of stories in this place that is so clearly steeped in history. It is important not to erase them—even if that is a painstaking task—and to recognize them as a constituent of the urban space.

Public spaces reveal the underlying cultural construction that forms the public dimension of society. These relationships are constantly changing and must be permeable, open—like the spaces themselves.

In times of intolerance and xenophobia, the public space takes on a vital role, being designed to support the coexistence of different cultures and to help us understand the great opportunity that lies in welcoming others.

The best places we have for collective activities in São Paulo are the "unnamed spaces," as professor Flávio Motta once defined them. By rejecting a limitation to one single purpose, these spaces can be used in many different ways.

Hence, we have a need for the creation of empty, undefined spaces in the city—not wastelands, but opportunities for alternatives, for a utopia, a promising future. This goes back to the idea by Ignasi de Solà-Morales Rubió to design a continuity of time rather than fill up empty space.

Public spaces of large dimensions require a clear articulation of local, urban, and symbolic scale. A great benefit of living in a city is our right as citizens to move in and enjoy the public space. It should not be a privilege for those who live nearby, but should be available to everyone. —CRISTIANE MUNIZ AND FERNANDO VIÉGAS

Car-free Sunday, São Paulo

Anhangabaú, São Paulo

For us, coming from south of the equator, Berlin is impressive in its abundance of green spaces and the potential of urban voids giving rise to the expansion of a remarkable type of public space.

The total urban area of São Paulo amounts to approximately 1000 km^2. Around eleven million people are considered citizens of the city alone, which equals 110 inhabitants per hectare—a rather low density.

São Paulo has around eight million cars on its roads. If we assume that every vehicle needs an area of 20 m^2 on average, that means that 160 km^2 of urban space are assigned to cars. Adding to this number the 200 km^2 of roads and streets, we can conclude that more than one third of the total urban space is assigned to traffic. At the same time, we have only 30 km^2 of green areas and parks in the metropolitan area, which amounts to about 3 percent.

Insightful data on our city like the above presents us with a question: the concept of public space (where all activities are permitted and where we recognize ourselves as citizens) is directly related to the urban conditions we create. Just as the Inuit are able to see many different shades of white in their icy habitat (there are over one hundred words for snow in their native language), we can say that there are many different ways to perceive and understand the meaning of public space in our cities.

In São Paulo we are still sorely lagging behind: We need to define and consolidate these types of spaces. Perhaps in order to create open space, we need to begin by clearing the built-up area that sprawls far and wide over pristine land. We need to not only build, but also remove in order to gain the clearings that are necessary for the creation of open space for all citizens.

If, for example, we increased urban density to 220 inhabitants per hectare, we would only need half of the total urban area for housing. An even more desirable density of 440 inhabitants per hectare would result in occupation of only 25 percent of the total space.

Densification and simultaneous clearing of space is a necessity for our city.

If we accept what João Batista Vilanova Artigas said, that "the happiness of a people is measured by the beauty of its cities," we still have a long way to go in São Paulo. —ÁLVARO PUNTONI

Media Lab Berlin

Prof. Thomas Arslan, Prof. Nina Fischer,
Prof. Albert Lang, Prof. Jörg Stollmann

STUDENTS
Dovilė Aleksaitė, Eleanor Aylett-Jones, Viktor Dill, Karoline Fahl, Eszter Galambos, Sophie Goethe, Silvia Groeger, Martin Hofmann, Moritz Hossli, Elizabeth Kelly, Steffen Klotz, Lucas Maia, Shahed Naji, Judith Noack, Esteban Rivera, Tilmann Teske

DIE MITTE IST NICHT LEER [THE CENTER IS NOT EMPTY]
Prof. Jörg Stollmann (Professor); Anna Heilgemeir, Damar Pelger (Lehrbeauftragte); Katharina Hagg (wissenschaftliche Mitarbeiterin); Alice Geletey, Kathrin Krell, Lukas Pappert, Mathias Pudelko, Jens Schulze, Tilmann Teske, Anna Kristin Vinkeloe, Martha Wegenetz (Studierende); Stephan Becker, Robert Burghardt, Katrin Lompscher, Annette Maechtel, L.A. Müller, Verena Pfeiffer-Kloss, Sascha Schug, Silvia Schulz, Enrico Schönberg, Ruth Wolter, and many more (GesprächspartnerInnen); Beate Blau, Wohnungsgesellschaft Berlin Mitte (Kooperationspartner)

The Media Lab Berlin, a collaboration between degree programs from the Technical University of Berlin and the Berlin University of the Arts was founded in 2015 and is investigating urban public spaces for *DEMO:POLIS*. Between Alexanderplatz and the Kulturforum in Berlin, thirty students and instructors seek out public spheres and spaces. Contrary to what the singular term "public space" suggests, these spaces do not occur naturally. They are produced and contested by a multitude of social groups and associations. These perform everyday activities, establish conventions, enact policies, monitor compliance, or put up resistance. In democratic societies, this spatial controversy can be conducted openly, resulting in the thesis that each society receives the public spaces it deserves.

Media Lab advocates a radically transdisciplinary approach to research and teaching. At the Media Lab Berlin, students and instructors from all fields of study are free to initiate and realize their projects. Media Lab members participating in *DEMO:POLIS* include students and professors from the disciplines of Scenography, Film, Media Art, Urban Design, and Architecture. The Lab's projects are carried out utilizing both scientific and artistic methods and tools, striving towards the production of knowledge for a better society and a good life. To this end, the Media Lab Berlin also works on an equal footing with non-academic partners.

Three weeks prior to the workshop for *DEMO:POLIS*, the Media Lab Berlin team organized a walking tour from Alexanderplatz to the Kulturforum. Both students and instructors singled out locations in between the two landmark sites and presented their individual observations and questions on urban public spaces. Based on the group's common discussions, interdisciplinary teams were formed. During the project week in October, the Lab attended the presentations by international expert groups at the Akademie der Künste and participated in the debates. In the afternoons, positions and counterpositions regarding the experts' perspectives were developed. These discussions led to film and installation-based interventions that were presented and discussed in front of the plenary assembly at the end of the week.

In the months following the project week, the teams developed the projects for the *DEMO:POLIS* exhibition: *The Carpark* examines the former grounds of the "Führerbunker" in Berlin, which today serves as a parking area. This inconspicuous yet loaded public space is reconstructed in the exhibition through meticulous on-site data collection, reflecting upon its everyday use and historical significance. The project *Aufzeichnungen zur Tilgung* [Notes on Erasure] proclaims the *terrain vague* as a counter-model to deterministic urban planning. In *Rita Schäfer Won't Give Up*, the protagonist sets out on a quest to understand public space throughout pedestrian zones, archives and discussion panels and hits upon all kinds of discrepancies.

—THOMAS ARSLAN, NINA FISCHER, ALBERT LANG, JÖRG STOLLMANN

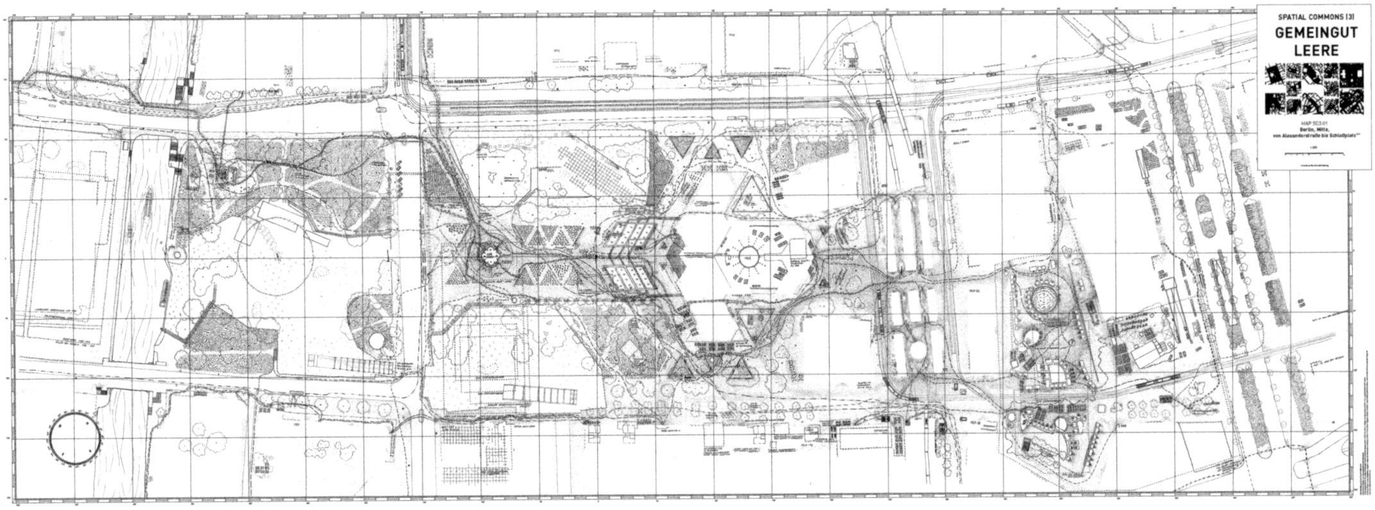

Die Mitte ist nicht leer [The Center Is Not Empty], hand drawing, 2015
Alice Geletey, Kathrin Krell, Lukas Pappert, Mathias Pudelko, Jens Schulze, Tilmann Teske, Anna Kristin Vinkeloe, Martha Wegewitz

Die Mitte ist nicht leer [The Center Is Not Empty] is a critical take on an inventory. In July 2015, eight students carried out a six-day mapping of Berlin's Mitte neighborhood. Observations, interviews, informal conversations, studies of sources as well as provocative 1:1-scale installations provided the foundation for an engagement with the site and its residents. Actions, memories, movements, narratives, activities, appropriations, and occupations shaping the area between the Marx-Engels-Forum and Alexanderplatz were laid down as layers of a map of the territory.

The Carpark

STUDENTS
Dovilė Aleksaitė, Eleanor Aylett-Jones,
Martin Hofmann, Esteban Rivera, Tilmann Teske

History is the subject of a construction whose site is not homogenous empty time, but time filled full with now-time [Jetztzeit].
—Walter Benjamin, 1940[1]

The Carpark is an experimental collaboration between five students of architecture, media, and art. The group members examined the premises of the former Führerbunker in Berlin-Mitte between Wilhelmstraße and Gertrud-Kolmar-Straße—now being used as a parking lot. The group measured and mapped the terrain and collected quantitative data between 3 and 4 PM on October 7, 2015. People, animals, plants, and inanimate objects were recorded, as well as small scenes and incidents. The collective findings were assembled as a text and served as the basis for the group's collaborative work.

The Carpark borrows its artistic strategy of quantitative observation from Georges Perec's *An Attempt at Exhausting a Place in Paris* (1975). Recontextualising scientific practices of data collection and protocols, the group develops its own poetic language.

1 Walter Benjamin, *Selected Writings, Volume Four: 1938–1940*, ed. Howard Eiland and Michael W. Jennings, trans. Edmund Jephcott et al., Cambridge, MA: The Belknap Press of Harvard University Press, 2003, p. 308.

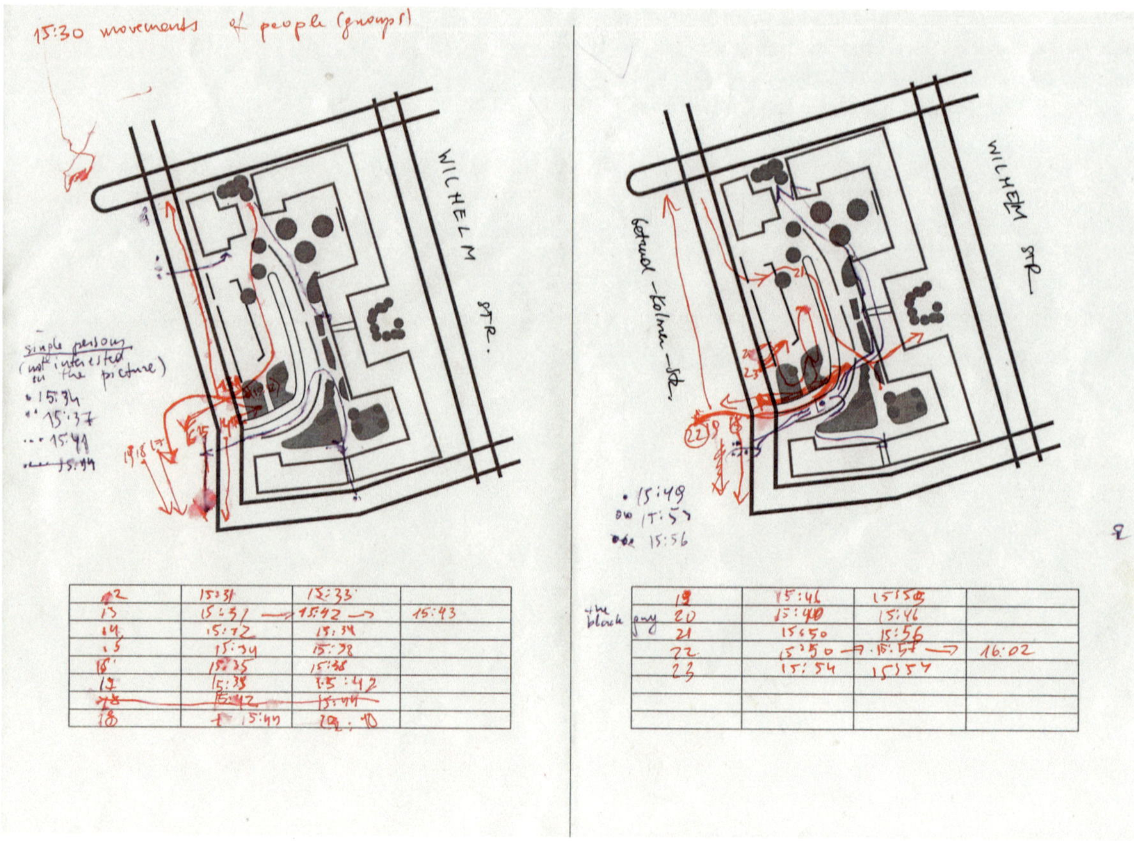

Map: movements

Date: October 7, 2015
Time: 15:00–16:00
Place: Berlin-Mitte, Gertrud-Kolmar-Straße, the carpark
Weather: cloudy, drizzly

The carpark is surrounded by a building.
It is 5 minutes from Potsdamer Platz.

In total there are 66 trees.

21 of them are located in the northern part of the space and 16 of them are located in the southern part.
In the center of the carpark stand two trees.
Next to the information board there are 3 Maple trees. [...]

[...] in total there are 85 parked vehicles.

45 of them are parked cars.
4 of them are bikes.
1 of the 4 is locked to a pillar.
1 is a scooter and one is a carrier.
3 of the cars are parked strangely on the pathway.

There are 5 fence-lines defining the carpark.
They are made of 270 wooden poles [...]

[...] It is 15:03.
A group of tourists arrives at the entrance of the carpark on the right-hand side.
Three men and two women take photos of the information board which stands in front of the parking space.
Another group takes six photos while walking further to the back, in a semicircle, until walking to the exit.
It is 15:10.
A car arrives in Gertrud-Kolmar-Straße and a man starts taking photographs from the inside. The car leaves towards the north.
Two birds fly from one smaller tree to a larger tree.
A dog walks by on the path behind the bushes.
A group walks in front of the carpark, six people take photos.
Three birds fly in circular motions around the trees and bushes.
A dog walks by on the left-hand side of the carpark just in front of the building.
It is 15:27.
A DHL delivery truck arrives.
The departure time is unknown. [...]

Detailed minutes (excerpt)

Rita Schäfer Won't Give Up

STUDENTS
Viktor Dill, Silvia Groeger,
Moritz Hossli, Elizabeth Kelly

Rita Schäfer works as an intern in an urban planning office in Berlin. Since the firm has no current projects in progress, Rita is sent out to search the city's public spaces for problems that the office can then "resolve."

Rita quickly realizes that the object of most agitated debates is "public space." She wonders what characteristics of a location make it public and, most of all, what "public" means in our society. Rita sets out on a search that takes her through the public spaces and sites in Berlin, trying to answer these and many other questions that arise along the way.

Over the course of her inquiry into theories, archives and panel discussions, the term "public" reveals itself to be full of inconsistencies and contradictions, and Rita's original plan to approach the subject is losing ground.

1 Alexander Kluge and Oskar Negt, "Introduction," in Kluge and Negt, *Public Sphere and Experience: Toward an Analysis of the Bourgeois and Proletarian Public Sphere*, trans. Peter Labanyi, Jamie Owen Daniel, and Assenka Oksiloff, Minneapolis: University of Minnesota Press, 1993, xlvi.

Interview with Martin Rein-Cano on October 6, 2015 at the architecture symposium during the International Workshop *DEMO:POLIS*

[...] the public sphere derives its substance from an intermediate realm that does not specifically express any particular life context [Lebenszusammenhang], even though this public sphere allegedly represents the totality of society.
—Alexander Kluge and Oskar Negt, 1972[1]

Interview with citizens at Washington Square, Berlin

Interview with citizens in front of the Reichstag, Berlin

Film Stills, © Viktor Dill, Silvia Groeger, Moritz Hossli, Elisabeth Kelly

Aufzeichnungen zur Tilgung

STUDENTS
Karoline Fahl, Eszter Galambos, Sophie Goethe, Steffen Klotz, Lucas Maia, Shahed Naji, Judith Noack

[...] architecture is forever on the side of forms, of the distant, of the optical and the figurative, while the divided individual of the contemporary city looks for forces instead of forms, for the incorporated instead of the distant, for the haptic instead of the optic, the rhizomatic instead of the figurative.
—de Solà-Morales Rubío, 1995[1]

Terrain vague is an openness in the urban fabric—unplanned, uncertain, uncapitalized, and parafunctional. It defies the logic of a deterministic urban system and the obsessive programming of public space. *Terrain vague* is a form of absence in the contemporary metropolis. It is formed by semantic emptiness. In an open choreography, uncoded space allows for a maximum of publicness—breaks, conflicts, fragments, confrontations, negotiations.

The installation *Aufzeichnungen zur Tilgung* [Notes on Erasure] shows the findings of a process of forensic research: instant on-site observations, filmic studies, props, and reflections on spatial models. The collected and extracted fragments are brought together as a spatial installation in an attempt to understand the multitude of *terrain vague* in its singularity.

1 Ignasi de Solà-Morales Rubió, "Terrain Vague," in Cynthia Davidson (ed.), *Anyplace*, Cambridge, MA: MIT Press, 1995, p. 123.

Archipelago Kulturforum Berlin

Prof. Heike Hanada

STUDENTS
Ka-Shing Chui, Assia Cirillo,
Giuseppe D'Angelo, Christian Hennemann,
Isabella Pullmann, Florian Wiegand

Heterotopias turn places into mutable spaces. There are certain rules in force, but only as long as these are observed by members of a society. As long as this happens, heterotopias are operative and can affect what happens at a place. The observance of rules and their infringement, the latter of which can lead to the disappearance of a heterotopia at a certain place, suggests a fundamental characteristic: in a society, every heterotopia can be arbitrarily given a new interpretation. It can, therefore, only be beheld for a finite stretch of time—one moment later, and it may have already lost its function.
—Michel Foucault[1]

The Kulturforum in Berlin is marked by indeterminacy. Its imperatives defy a legible order. It is uncomfortable, open, and difficult to control. It defiantly receives its visitors. The Kulturforum is an artificial assertion of the modern, an alien archipelago, a collection of stray islands.

What utopia can counter it, grow out of it—what idea of the public arises from it?

This workshop reflected on the entropy of public space in images, visual fragments; collages were composed out of readymade parts and transformed into a new reality.

Our observation of the Kulturforum's peculiar aloofness is accompanied by images by the architectural photographer Andrew Alberts. His photographic views and perspectives communicate a seemingly insurmountable emptiness between the buildings. Without clear hierarchies or representative structures, the paths lose themselves in mere juxtaposition. The great hall of the New National Gallery seems to hover above the profane indeterminacy of our time.

Foucault's notion of heterotopia implies the simultaneous existence of different forms of use for the same geographic site: It describes competing spaces, which would not exist without *place*, but which at the same time cannot be clearly defined by it.

This conceptualization can be readily applied to the interior worlds of the Kulturforum. With regards to the exterior spaces, there are no signs of public appropriation whatsoever. Public space in the Kulturforum remains fragmented—indeed it even seems expendable.

Andrew Alberts, Kulturforum, 2015

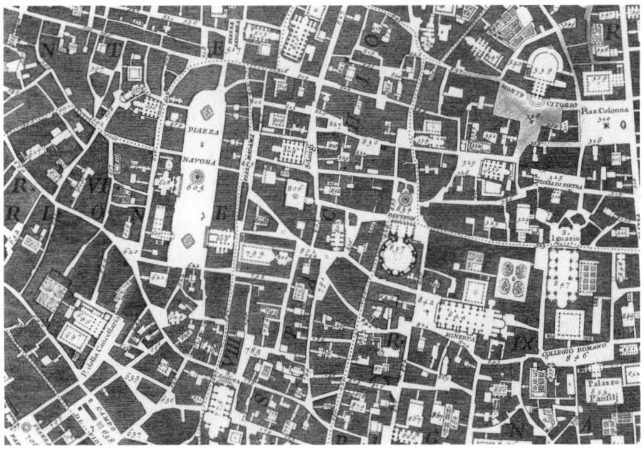

Detail of the Nolli Map, Rome, 1748

[The Generic City] is nothing but a reflection of present need and present ability. It is the city without history. [...It] is what is left after large sections of urban life crossed over to cyberspace.
—Rem Koolhaas[2]

The structure of the famous map of Rome created by Giambattista Nolli in 1748 provides a further point of departure for our analysis. In contrast to a classical figure-ground diagram, the Nolli Map clarifies, for the first time in the history of architecture, the relationship between a square and the publicaly accessible sacred spaces that border it. The map records the interweaving of public outdoor space with Rome's massive built substance. The interior of the Pantheon, for example, is here read as part of the urban structure. Over the course of centuries, Rome developed a direct dialogue between the city and its architecture. What emerged was a carefully staged, complex fabric of differentiated spaces that are linked together. The exterior space thereby corresponds to the respective interior spaces of the city's monuments.

Within Berlin, the Museum Island and the Kulturforum act as mutual counterparts with regards to their content. Both places bring together museums and cultural institutions of global import, placing them in a direct relationship with one another. The public exterior spaces of the Museum Island are strictly demarcated by the Spree. The entrance areas are clearly structured and create distinct framing situations in front of the respective building portals. While the Museum Island is, on the whole, much smaller than the Kulturforum—the former could readily fit inside the intermediary spaces of the latter—it comes across as monumental and leaves an emphatic, massive impression in the city. Architectural elements like steps, stairs, columns, pilasters, plinths, and attics serve to link the individual monuments to one another. The deliberate design of the exterior spaces reinforces spatial hierarchies and leads to the clear arrangement of and identity for the interior and intermediary spaces.

In Rem Koolhaas's view, the deficit of modernist urban design lies less in the quality of its isolated buildings than in the neglect of the spaces in between—a problem not of the monuments themselves, but of the relationship between them. Generic exterior space and its lacking interaction is reinforced in the twenty-first century by a boredom that is rich in variation, a limitless diversity without qualities. This generic urban space seems to be the most recent attack on the identity of the European city.
—HEIKE HANADA

1 Translated from Fred Truniger and Sabine Wolf, "Heterotopien," p. 3, http://www.christiaanse.arch.ethz.ch/upload/RC14.pdf.
2 Rem Koolhaas, "The Generic City," in Rem Koolhaas and Bruce Mau, *S,M,X,XL*, 2nd ed., ed. Jennifer Sigler, New York: The Monacelli Press, 1998, p. 1250.

Paris, Centre Pompidou

Berlin, Museum Island

Berlin, Kulturforum

Archipelago Propaganda!

STUDENT
Giuseppe D'Angelo

The life and death of a society are determined by the speed at which it can adapt, both politically and culturally, to the strong and inevitable pressures that interfere with its normal course.

Change is a normal stage of society because, especially in the twenty-first century, every area is constantly subject to a continuous reformulation of ideas, beliefs and theories; a continuous reaffirmation or rejection of rules; and, above all, a reformulation of relations between individuals, thus occupying the field of social action.

But if it is true that the condition of "ever-changing" is the very nature of society, it is also true that beyond a certain limit, society's collapse is not impossible. This limit is public space.

Public space defines a number of places with a liquid spatiality and meanings, but it only becomes concrete when contrasted with its reverse—private space. The distinction between the two spaces is the origin of their existence and reciprocity. The interaction between people within them is equally mutual and fluid.

Their simultaneous existence has slowly changed the use of public space, which has transformed from a place of democracy to one of shopping, of the marketing of individual experiences that are turning it into a caricature of public space, a Space of White Propaganda.

With this proposal, I tried to create a place that has the appearance of a public space—that is, a space that allows the sharing of personal experiences—but has the aim of a Space of White Propaganda, which merely allows people to share precise and preordained personal experiences. In doing so, I attempted to make visible the (invisible) processes that have already transformed public space.

A dystopian Luna Park such as the one shown here is in this sense a temporary experience, a new spatial reference, an event that increases the space's entropy and disorder—in complete opposition to the massive philosophy behind the architecture of the Kulturforum. A public space as constant propaganda.
—GIUSEPPE D'ANGELO

The Scharoun roller coaster

Loss of references

Apple National Gallery

Archipelago Massive Void

STUDENT
Assia Cirillo

The Kulturforum is actually an archipelago of beautiful architectures that voluntarily do not speak to each other. This aspect is so strong that we could fill the space in between buildings with water and they would keep on working perfectly.

These beautiful public cathedrals find it hard to relate to the spaces between them, turning them into wasted, unattractive areas.

In something that is between a utopian and a dystopian vision, a concrete basement platform suffocates all the buildings in a white blank, with the intention of underlining different aspects of that space.

When turned into this pure, untouched element, architecture itself appears as a clear reference. The act of isolation is reinforced, but this unique homogenizing measure underlines the character of the architectural objects.

This concrete platform, elevated from the ground, forces people to detach from the city and see everything from a different point of view. People are forced to separate from the rest of the city, landing on a detached island.

Underneath this platform, a wide, homogeneous space between the buildings is produced. The space is filled with functions and for this reason is crowded with people.

The platform does not touch existing buildings, leaving small voids around them. These voids provide the opportunity for visual interaction between people above and below the platform, thus creating public space.

But, what do these white platforms mean for public space?

In a modern society where all public events and spaces are often sponsored, guided and forced by private entities, filled with subtle or strong references, this utopian view is a calling for an untouched space in which people can easily relate or take time to remain alone without being continually stimulated.

—ASSIA CIRILLO

Below the platform

Dystopian future

Above the platform: reappropriation of references

Archipelago City-Scapes

STUDENT
Ka-Shing Chui

This project engages with the Kulturforum in Berlin. At its center is the concept of the urban landscape, as it was redefined after 1945: an aesthetic protest against the monumentality and heaviness of Nazi architecture. Axial organization and parallelism were eschewed in favor of a free, rhythmic order like that of a landscape formation. Landscape, the antithesis of geometric order, was seen as a metaphor for freedom. Hans Scharoun's goal with the Kulturforum was to artfully arrange its constituent parts to create a natural order for them in space. Today, due to the wide spatial barriers that separate the buildings, the arrangement of its parts seems merely diffuse and exhibits hardly any urban qualities. This project is about the question of how the Kulturforum could, with the help of densification, transform into a more urban space.

The superposition of the Kulturforum onto the urban grids of two reference cities—New York and Rome—allows for a collage-like investigation of the urban features that seem to accidentally emerge through the intervention. The typologies seen in the two reference cities are the result of historical processes of differing lengths, both of which produced high building densities. The two examples are interesting for their contrasting urban structures: New York with its strictly orthogonal block grid, and Rome with its organically developed urban layers and subtle meshing of alleys and squares. The method of the typological transfer allows the development of a counter-interpretation to the Kulturforum's current diffuse structure. The various "monuments" of the Kulturforum (the Philharmonie, the New National Gallery, the State Library, and the Matthaïkirche) are put into a new context, within which they—thanks to their arrangement and scale—stand out from the structure of the city around them. Instead of a mere collection of monuments, an urban and lasting piece of city comes into being.
—KA-SHING CHUI

New National Gallery/Manhattan

Matthaïkirche/Manhattan

Philharmonie / Manhattan

New York

The intervention using New York shows how a clearly ordered structure can counteract the Kulturforum and, at the same time, pacify it. The New York block structure was scaled down by 50 percent and adapted to the Kulturforum, so as to differentiate between the urban structure and the isolated cultural institutions. The buildings rise out of the rigorous grid like sculptures. The grain of the high-rise blocks distinguishes them clearly from the typical "Berliner Block." Squares are strategically cut out and adapted. Despite the high density, the buildings hardly seem cramped, as they create their own spaces around them. The New National Gallery floats within the compact density of Manhattan and becomes a part of Union Square. The Philharmonie crowds itself into the skyline and is promptly towered over by skyscrapers. Manhattan frames these monuments of Berlin Modernism and isolates them from one another, so that each building retains its own weight. The landscape-like Kulturforum is thereby transformed into a vertical cityscape.

State Library / Rome

Rome

Still more radical and, with regards to the identity of a modern metropolis, ostensibly strange at first is the superposition of the Kulturforum onto Rome's historic center. Wide, empty borderlands are filled with fragmented spaces and squares. Rome's seemingly arbitrary urban plan playfully embraces the Kulturforum. The modernist monuments replace the famous, wide piazzas of Rome. The interior spaces designed by Scharoun continue the city's public space. The National Gallery raises itself, like an Acropolis, above the city.

Philharmonie / Rome

Platz der Republik, Berlin

Prof. Bernd Albers
Christopher Richter

STUDENTS
Fabian Abel, Michelle Bähr, Anne Kozian, Sarah Vellmete, Nicole Wegner

Design Otto Kohtz, 1920

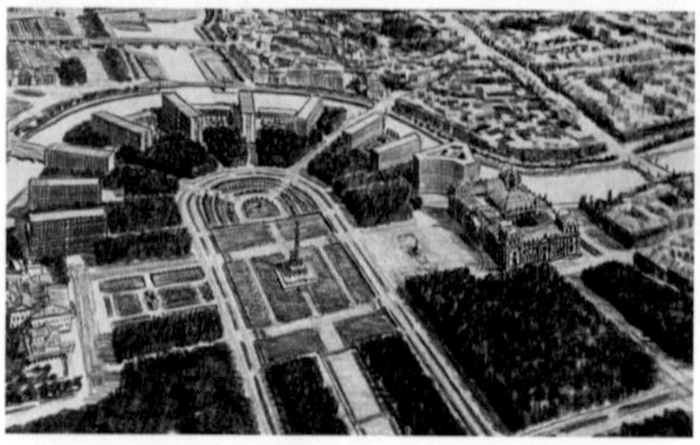

Design Hans Poelzig, 1929

Design Albert Speer, 1939

Berlin features both a surplus of free spaces for the public and a deficit in high-quality plazas and urban spaces. The conflict between "urban landscape" and "urban space" has clearly left enduring traces on the overall cityscape.

This dilemma manifests itself in a most exemplary manner in the government district around the Spreebogen in Berlin. Known originally as the "Alsenviertel," this area was initially developed from 1850 onwards as a bourgeois residential area with compact housing development. The construction of the Reichstag building in 1894 raised the neighborhood to a site of national significance and symbolic function. Since then, the Reichstag building and the Königsplatz—the plaza laid out in front of the parliament building—have shaped the area: from the 1920s onwards, various urban planning concepts were proposed for the area, which were intended to develop the parliament complex to compete with the surrounding housing development. None of those plans, however, were to leave the drawing board. But in the late 1930s, the National Socialists created precedents for further development in the area through their plans for a monumental north–south axis ending in a Halle des Volkes [Hall of the People]. These precedents would lead to the partial razing of the residential blocks, the relocation of the Siegessäule (a victory column that had previously stood on Königsplatz), and construction work to reroute the Spree. Thus, even before the neighborhood was flattened during wartime bombing, the fate of the Alsenviertel had already been sealed.

After 1945, the Reichstag building and its surrounding neighborhood fell into a period of hibernation—only in the first half of the 1980s did West Berlin begin to regain interest in the area. After 1990, the reunification of Germany and the decision to move the capital to Berlin elevated the Spreebogen to the central site of politics in the new German Federal Republic. With their "Band des Bundes" [Federal Belt] project, Axel Schultes and Charlotte Frank were able to propose a symbolic urban plan for the new government district in Berlin. The integral parts of this plan were realized in the subsequent years with the construction of the Chancellery and the administrative building for parliament members (Paul-Löbe-Haus); since 1999, the Reichstag building has been seat of the German parliament (Bundestag).

Looking at this urban space—or rather green space—with its mix of new and old monuments today, we are faced with the question of the quality and adequacy of the urban spaces to be found there. Considering the history of the site, it makes sense to superimpose the lost spatial organization and built form of the former Alsenviertel onto the Band des Bundes: in this way, a space both urban and political, a *res publica*, can be attained for both Berlin and Germany as a whole. —BERND ALBERS

Design Bernd Albers, 2014

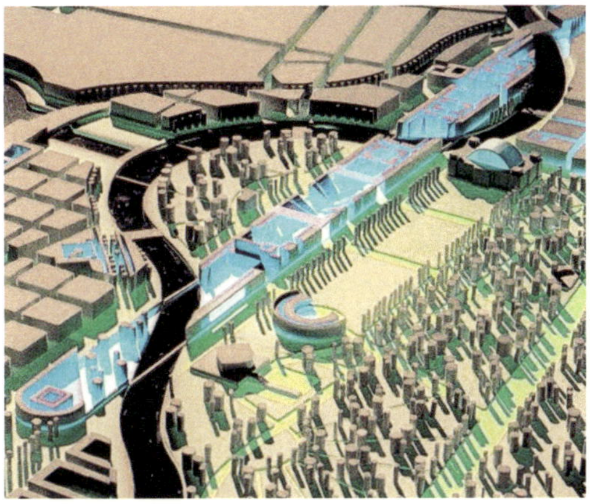

Design Axel Schultes and Charlotte Frank, 1993

Band des Bundes, realized 2005

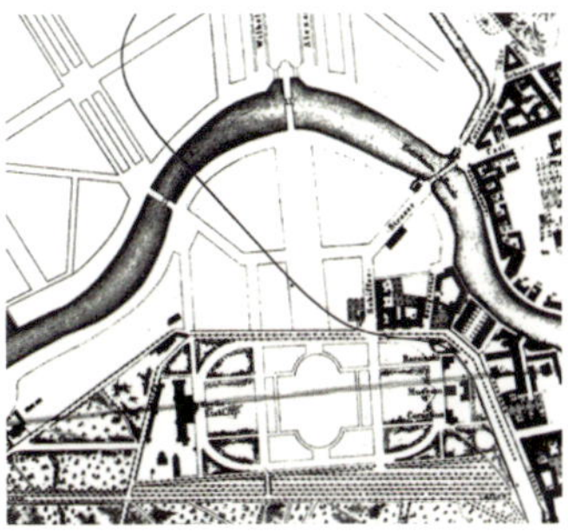

Map of Berlin, 1856

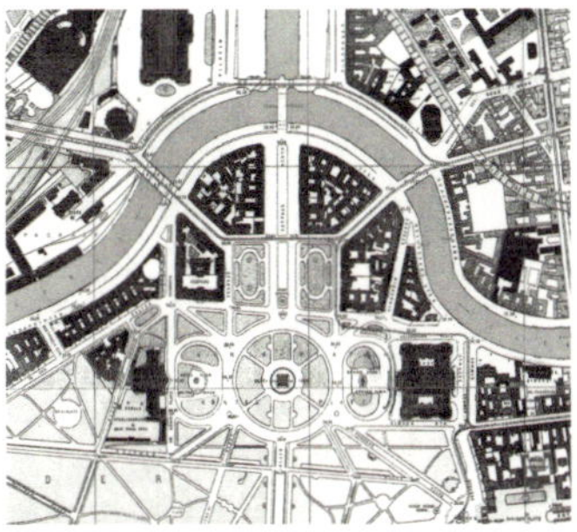

Map of Berlin, 1910

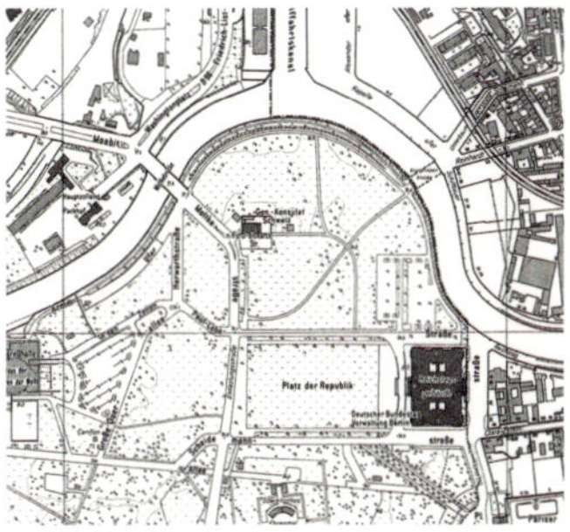

Map of Berlin, 1986

Map of Berlin, 2014

res publica

STUDENTS
Fabian Abel, Michelle Bähr, Anne Kozian, Sarah Vellmete, Nicole Wegner

In the best case scenario, public space is generated at those locations where it can achieve prominence within the urban context. By raising the question of the importance of a citizens' forum in the Band des Bundes, Bernd Albers formulated a thesis that allows a nuanced investigation of the site's urban history that goes beyond the status quo.

We took this as a starting point for further discussion, with the goal of not just designing a plaza, but also creating a highly urban space between the Reichstag and the main train station.

The Alsenviertel, decimated by both National Socialism and war, constitutes the spiritual background for this new urban center. By parceling and distributing public as well as private spaces, we can allow a piece of urban structure to come into being again—and with it, a high-quality spectrum of urban life.

Going back to the original idea behind "mixed-use quarters," the development of a new civic neighborhood next to government institutions can lead to a sustainable revitalization of the entire area. A series of new, publically accessible buildings is meant to complement the ensemble of Reichstag, Chancellery, and the administrative building for Members of Parliament (Paul-Löbe-Haus). Where the planned (but never built) civic forum was to stand, a large canvas canopy completes the vision of the Band des Bundes.

Farther south, a distinctive visitors' center inspired by the ancient Greek typology of the stoa serves to spatially define the square in front of the Reichstag building. A clearly defined spatial edge is exactly what is needed here, at the border with the Tiergarten.

On the site of the former Kroll Opera, an architectural concept similar to Berlin's Waldbühne amphitheater will provide a counterpoint to the Reichstag building. The idea of a civic forum, first proposed by Schultes and Frank, will thus be further developed, providing new reasons to visit the Platz der Republik.

At this politically and socially critical site, corresponding public spaces must be brought into being that will be able to live up to the importance of their location. These new streets and squares will integrate the outstanding but still isolated buildings into a continuous urban texture that will allow citizens to see this place as an integral part of their city once again.

—BERND ALBERS AND CHRISTOPHER RICHTER

Reichstag building with forecourt, around 1900

Alsenviertel with the Reichstag building in the background, around 1900

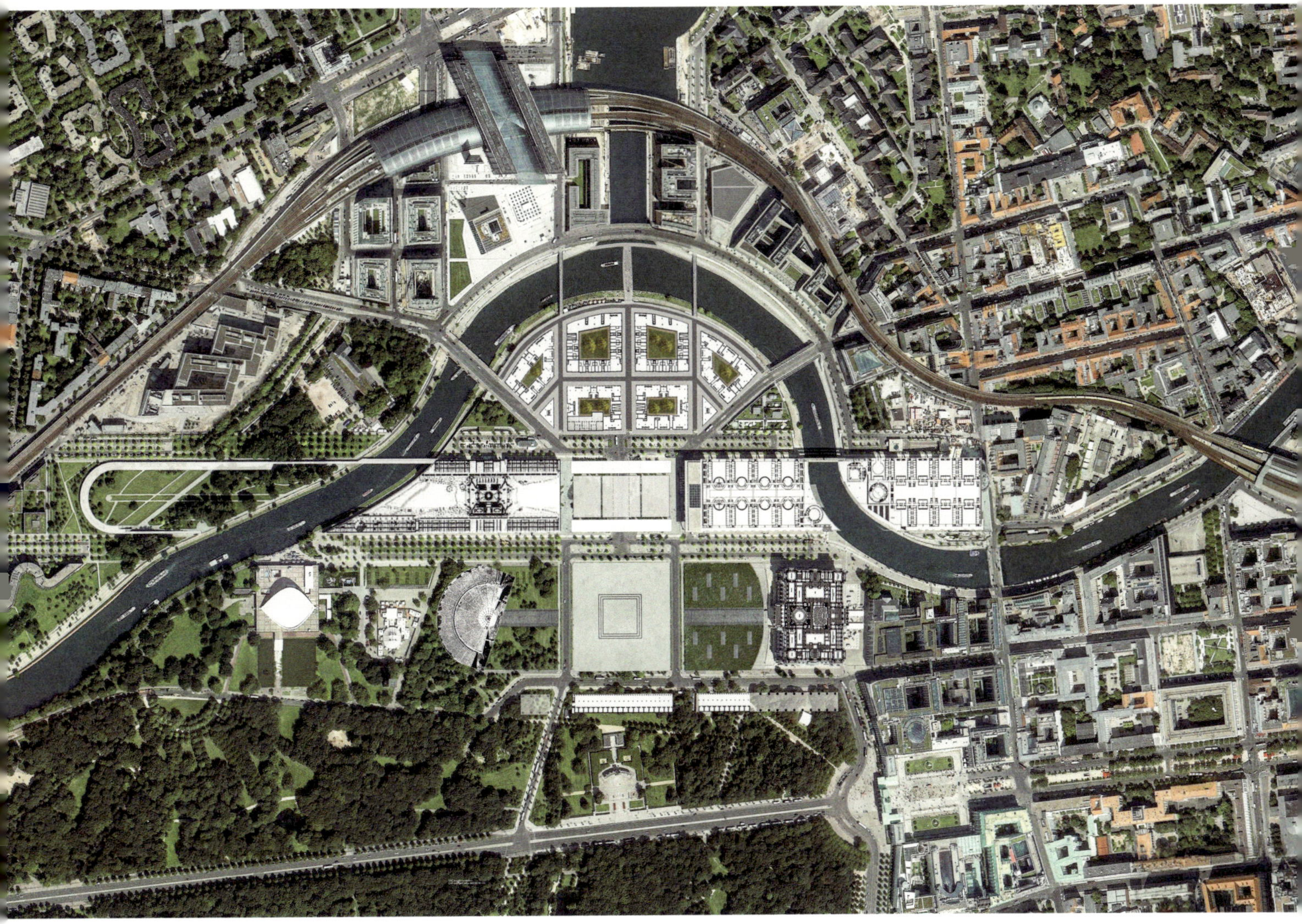

Workshop results, 2015

Álvaro Siza, Lisbon Expo 1998

Stoa of Attalos, Athens

Waldbühne, Berlin

Notes on Anklam

Prof. Hannes Brunner

STUDENTS
Veneta Androva, Lena Marie Emrich, Maria Turik

When first observing a place that is not yet familiar, we may be inclined, out of desire and curiosity, to observe impartially; this attitude is the best approach for registering each impression directly, without distortion.

Anklam appears to be a typical small German town—a place in the middle of a sparsely populated countryside, a setting that lends itself to sociological observations regarding the built environment of Central Europe.

Yet these initial observations of the site are, in fact, not as unmediated as one would like. For with the rise of social media and online forums, through contact with modern archives and instantly accessible travel guides, a plethora of information is made available to us even before we first set foot in the place. We are thus able to equip ourselves with plenty of prior knowledge, but even this act has already burdened us: an "innocent" experience of this city is hardly possible. In addition, innumerable reflections regarding the ruins of the built, destroyed, rebuilt, and dismantled city of Anklam impose themselves, and stand at our disposal like a palimpsest.

For this reason, we sought an independent method for observing and subsequently communicating our findings: here, the algorithmization of public space through a medial perspective is expanded through the practical incorporation of different levels of communication. Implicit in the approach is not only the inclusion of preconceived information, prejudices, and wishful thinking in the act of artistic research, but also their further development into hypotheses forming the basis of intentions, of sculpted figures, or even of historically based appropriations. In doing so, artistic practice is woven together with the actual, experienced atmospheres of cultural, social, and built space, and used to approach the subject of public space in Anklam. Through their projects, the students home in on the social contact points that serve to reinforce our stereotypes regarding the city's economic and political conditions.

Veneta Androva sheds light on—among others—a family business that has transformed itself into an important supermarket chain in northwest Germany, analyzing its role as a social hub in the city. Maria Turik's project experiments with a visual language that refuses to refer back to any recognizable, pre-established form. She installs a giant inflatable object on Anklam's market square. A crawling drop-like sculpture there provides a spatial framework for monitoring official and unofficial forms of communication. The third project ventures to identify with a historical figure: Lena Marie Emrich follows the trail of Otto Lilienthal, who investigated the fundamentals of flight in the 1860s. From that point on, man's view of his environment and his place within it has changed radically. Anklam was perhaps the first city in the world that was seen through human eyes in flight.

—HANNES BRUNNER

Nothing could be more appropriate for our observations of the city than a "self-dramatization" performed by locals on a stage designed just for that purpose: *Die Peene brennt!* [The Peene Is Burning!] Amateur performers adapt historical and contemporary aspects of Anklam into a brilliant open-air spectacle along the Peene River. Our first day of research in Anklam ended with a visit to the theater.
—HB

An Unabsorbed Drop Is Resting on the Market Square

STUDENT
Maria Turik

The voluminous pneumatic sculpture was initially made to linger on an unused plot of land in the Berlin district of Weißensee, just outside our art academy.

Its form suggests that the drop is on the go. It just paused for a moment while rolling down the earth's surface. As the earth presumably has its "ups" and "downs" everywhere, the drop goes wherever it wants.

The sculpture allows people to stick their heads through the slits in its sides. Still, they cannot slip inside with their entire bodies. That allows them to be inside and outside at the same time, to dwell in a state of transition.

When several people insert their heads into the object simultaneously, a special situation arises: they form a temporary unity that is held together and apart at the same time. It is similar to a conversation: people coming together, connected by the issue they are discussing, but also maintaining some distance, often unable to overcome it.

I decided to bring the drop to Anklam for the *DEMO:POLIS* project, since democracy is about searching for a consensus, about talking to each other. There are spaces made for sharing opinions and making communal decisions. At the same time, conversations create and change spaces by simply happening.

Another aspect I wanted to observe with the help of the drop was how the community encounters the unusual.

The roundish object—soft, transparent, and obviously useless—is an alien on Anklam's market square. The reaction and interaction of people with the strange is a way to see how society is doing. The video in the exhibition is a record of this process.

—MARIA TURIK

Puchacz 65

STUDENT
Lena Marie Emrich

To invent an aircraft is nothing. To build it, a beginning. To fly—is everything.
—Otto Lilienthal

I will be presenting a video installation on three channels. In one part of the installation, I engage with a figure closely connected with the city of Anklam: Otto Lilienthal, once known as the "King of Gliding," a pioneer of human flight, who was active in the late nineteenth century. He grew up in Anklam, which was also where he constructed his flying machines and, with them, undertook his first attempts at human-powered flight.

Another aspect of the installation shows as I take to the skies to observe the city and the landscape from above—an attempt to directly understand the human desire to fly and the feeling of gliding weightless in the air. This desire is central to our cultural history, a driving factor in many technological achievements. The engagement with the figure of Lilienthal will be interwoven with site-specific conditions and combined to create extraordinary film events. During the flight, one sees aerial images of the landscape around Anklam; instead of narrating these views, however, I begin to utter the names of ancient wind deities under my breath—as if I were engaging in a magic ritual. With this, those invisible, physical streams of air come into view; they flow into the contemplative and scientific approaches of the inventor and pave the way for a new achievement, one that manages to change an entire society while remaining eternally bound to its local cultural context.
—LENA MARIE EMRICH

famila ANK

STUDENT
Veneta Androva

The short film *famila ANK* investigates three sites (or, alternatively, non-sites) in the German city of Anklam, which inhabit the liminal space between public and private. The focus is on the hypermarket chain famila. The famila department store belongs to the family enterprise Bartels-Langness, founded in 1892, and its branches are predominantly to be found in the north of Germany. The famila store in Anklam is located in the center of the city, on the site of a former port facility that was just recently bought by the chain. Thus the business serves and affects social interactions not only at the urban periphery, but now also at points nearer to the center. The complex includes a variety of different businesses, such as a hair salon, café and bakery, a movie theater, a beverage store, a drug store, and even a specialty shop for pet food. In a very direct manner, this consortium of businesses serves to form local communication networks (similarly to shopping malls, which have provided comprehensive spaces for entertainment and consumption at the peripheries of motorized agglomerations since the 1980s). A central aspect of the filmic investigation was how famila positions itself within the city and what role it plays in the everyday lives of the locals.

The work counteracts images of this hypermarket with a look into local subcultures, which among others support another local business as a shelter for extremist views and activities. Once seen in person, this business seems rather insignificant, but medial distribution channels have given it a larger-than-life reputation that goes beyond the city itself. The clothing store "New Dawn: Streetwear/ Music & More" is likewise located in the center of the city, on the Marienkirchplatz. The business also runs an online store that offers various goods to a right-wing clientele.

Right across from this store is a fitness center and tanning salon. Both the members of this fitness center and shoppers at New Dawn are customers of the famila department store. To enter these spaces is to engage in a sort of social event; these sites therefore possess a connective function within the community while simultaneously allowing one to be present within a ritualized framework, in which interactions between inhabitants serve to create identity itself.
—VENETA ANDROVA

We Build for You

Prof. Günter Nest

STUDENTS
Marta Setúbal, Laura Engelhardt

Our first visit to Anklam, on a sunny September Sunday in 2015 between 10 AM and 5 PM: We decide to explore the city without any prior knowledge and with as neutral a perspective as possible. Getting around is difficult, for both the infrastructure and large parts of the inner city are under construction. We stumble across construction sites, construction signs, empty streets, empty playgrounds—and a lonely town square with an ice cream parlor, which seems to have set out tables and chairs for an apparently invisible clientele. The opposite end of the square features a large bakery with a café and a row of stores. Scattered groups of people on their Sunday walks sidestep the construction sites and comment on the renovation work. Our search for a public sphere finds itself at a dead end.

Standing on the town hall square, a giant construction site sign catches our attention. It reads: "We build for you." But who is "we," and who is "you"? Why not, for example, "we build for ourselves"?! Who is building for whom here? To what extent do the citizens of Anklam have a say in the shaping of their city? Do they have a say to begin with? We thus set off into the city to find answers to our questions.

During our tour, we come across four girls from the Anklam Carnival Club (ACC), who are rehearsing for an upcoming dance competition on the dirt lot of a construction site. A site in process, reappropriated during the short window of time offered by reconstruction. The new master plan for the city calls for a perimeter block development with green courtyards and underground garages. We wonder: will the girls be dancing there, too?

We have a conversation with the director of the Historical Museum, who is pleased with the mayor's plans to reconstruct the inner city and, with it, Anklam's historical urban structure. Afterwards, we meet with the staff of the DemokratieLaden [Democracy Store], an information center and event space for the promotion of democracy. They are critical of how little the local population was allowed to participate in the decision-making process and name a few local citizens who had been actively involved. We will meet with them on our next visit to Anklam.

Citizen meets citizen: a discussion in and around the Stadtpark

"Wir bauen für Sie" [We build for you]

Anklam Center: a new emptiness?

Second visit, two months later: We go for a walk with an activist who unsuccessfully argued against the new landscaping of the municipal park. The next day, we meet high-school students in the Demokratiebahnhof [Democracy Station], an autonomous youth center housed in a defunct railway station building. They are planning a demonstration against the right-wing scene in Anklam and describe their problems with the owner of the tourist agency that is also housed in the station—he is apparently a friend of the right-wingers. A more cheerful atmosphere can be found in the Mühlentreff youth center. The ZDF (a public-service television broadcaster in Germany) is planning to come; people are cooking, and the music group led by Patrice from Ghana is hard at work with rehearsals.

Where and how does the mental space of visions, of spatial representations, and of planning imagination diverge from social space, the space of direct social activity? How can these dissonances be detected and visualized through critical artistic practice? Following Henri Lefebvre, we interpret space as a product of the dialectic interaction between processes in physical, mental, and social spheres. In analyzing these processes, it becomes possible to draw conclusions about society as well as the conditions of its production. For this video composition, we investigated Anklam's "spaces in process"—that is, spaces in which the emergence of a public sphere still seems possible—considering their physical, mental, and social aspects, and reconstructed them using video, photo, and audio material. —GÜNTER NEST

Building Structure and Public Space— The Fischerinsel in Berlin

Prof. Regine Leibinger
Guest Prof. Dr. Matthias Graf von Ballestrem
Kai Nikolaus Grüne

STUDENTS
Stefana Dilova, Romina Falk,
Cornelius Giacalone, Max Rudolph,
Daniela Schaffarczyk, Maximilian Treiber

As part of the *DEMO:POLIS* project, students from the Chair for Architectural Design and Construction at the TU Berlin studied the relationship between building structure and public space in Berlin's Fischerinsel district. Classic tools of analysis such as the figure-ground diagram and the massing model do not seem to be suitable for this purpose, as they provide only limited information regarding the partitions and transitions between public and private spaces. Just relying on these tools, it is particularly difficult to interpret threshold situations, the transitions and continuation of public spaces into buildings, and the gradations and connections between various spaces with different levels of accessibility—and therefore also the public potential inherent in buildings. It was thus important to develop a special method for representing interior building structures in conjunction with exterior public spaces.

Along the axis from Schinkel's Altes Museum, through the public passage of the Humboldforum, then again along Breite Straße over the Fischerinsel until one reaches Wallstraße, nearing Kreuzberg: this stretch of central Berlin pits a plethora of different urban models and imaginations against each other in a starkly contrasting manner. In the north, the reconstruction of the City Palace, the accompanying upgrading of Breite Straße, the conception of the prayer house (House of One) on Petriplatz as a public forum, and the densification of the area surrounding Gertraudenstraße will change the immediate urban context in a way that will also influence the situation on the Fischerinsel. The development along Gertraudenstraße, which was begun in 2000 with a redensification program emphasizing perimeter block development, is now moving forward with a competition for new mixed-use residential buildings hosted by the Wohnungsbaugesellschaft Berlin-Mitte, a state-owned housing association. The area surrounding Wallstraße, which borders on the southern end of the Fischerinsel, has also been undergoing a process of densification in the last few years: here, the historic city blocks are to be restored and gaps filled. The modernist Fischerinsel is thus being closed in by traditionalist development on both sides. Its vast and park-like urban landscape, characterized by freestanding, twenty-one-story tower blocks, is becoming increasingly crowded in by perimeter blocks and their clearly demarcated urban spaces. Here, two different theories of public space confront each other.

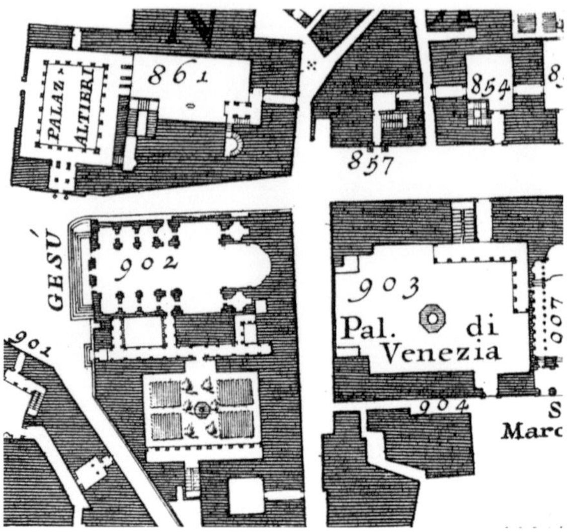

Detail, Nolli Plan, Giambattista Nolli, Rome, 1748

Detail, "The Bazaar of Isfahan, Twentieth Century," in Nader Ardalan and Laleh Bakhtiar, *The Sense of Unity: The Sufi Tradition in Persian Architecture*, Chicago: University of Chicago Press, 1973, pp. 98–99.

Detail, "City Plan of Pienza," in Fausto Formichi, Giancarlo Cataldi, et al., *Rilievi di Pienza*, Florence: Uniedit, 1977.

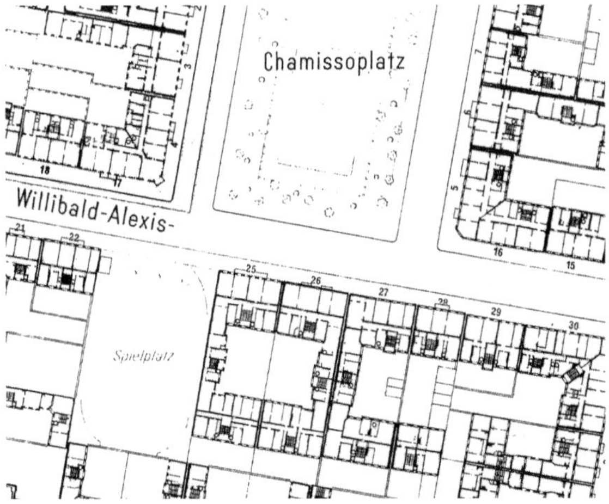

Detail, "Plan von der Gegend um den Chamissoplatz, Senator für Bau- u. Wohnungswesen Berlin (West)" ["Plan of the area around Chamissoplatz, Senator for Building and Housing, Berlin (West)"] in Johann Friedrich Geist and Klaus Kürvers, *Das Berliner Mietshaus 1862–1945*, Munich: Prestel, 1984, p. 275.

To make this development tangible on an architectural scale, the students used the *DEMO:POLIS* workshop to develop a comprehensive ground floor plan that encompasses all of the structures in the area under investigation. The most famous reference point for such an understanding of the city as a continuous network of public spaces is the so-called Nolli Map of Rome. While Giambattista Nolli only presented interiors that were fully accessible to the public, it was our goal to record all of the interior spaces in a manner that is faithful to structural reality. In doing so, we also wanted to investigate how architecture modulates thresholds and transitions between spaces with different levels of public accessibility. For this, other urban plans representing ground floor interiors in relationship to the surrounding exterior spaces provided a more suitable model, such as the Rilievi di Pienza from 1977 or the plan of the Isfahan Bazaar from 1969. Although a similar representational mode can be seen deployed in Johann Friedrich Geist's study *Das Berliner Mietshaus 1862–1945* for the area around Chamissoplatz, application of this format in Berlin on this scale and with this focus is new.

In the design seminar during the 2015/16 winter semester, the analytical medium developed in the workshop will become a medium for design. The seminar will allow students to investigate opportunities for redensification on the southern bank of the Fischerinsel. Hybrid developments with a large proportion of public uses are to be inserted between the monofunctional residential blocks. At the very beginning of the design process, students will use the structural ground floor plan to weave their proposed designs into the surrounding context at a scale of 1:500. In this way, the designs are to be conceptualized as a continuation and reinvention of an existing urban network of architecturally modulated spatial relationships.
—MATTHIAS BALLESTREM AND KAI NIKOLAUS GRÜNE

Structural ground floor plan (scaled, originally 1:500, 2.4 × 2.4 m)

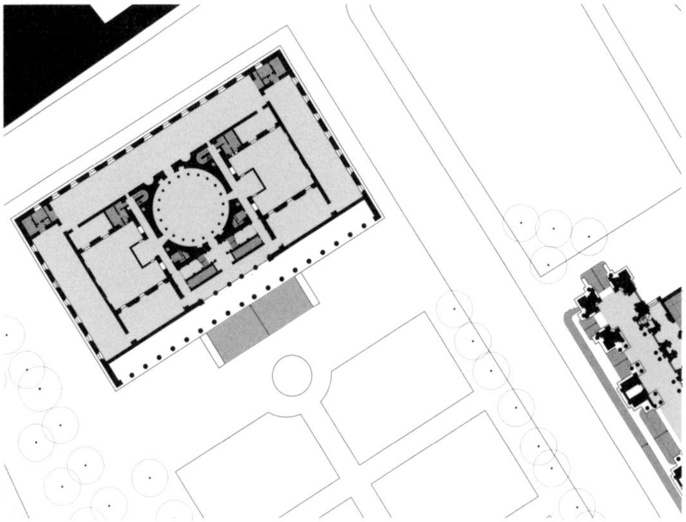

Lustgarten, detail (1:2000)
The Altes Museum and cathedral, which are public buildings dating from the nineteenth century, display a high level of porosity in their respective entrance areas. Public space permeates into the building tand is modified by massive, space-defining elements.

Breite Straße, detail (1:2000)
With the Berlin City Library, which was built into the historic royal stable complex in 1966, the border between interior and exterior is reduced to a thin line: the inner room of the library is only separated from the street by a glass façade.

Fischerinsel/Neue Roßstraße, detail (1:2000)
Inherent within the crosswall construction of the twenty-one-story tower blocks (completed in 1973) is the structural potential to open up the interior into public space. Yet today, the towers still stand isolated in an urban landscape envisioned by postwar modernity.

24/7 public

Semi-public

Private

Young Academy

Akademie der Künste at Hanseatenweg Campus, Werner Düttmann

JUNGE AKADEMIE [Young Academy]

Public space can be understood either objectively—in terms of generally accessible, pre-existing structures or deliberations regarding urban and green space planning measures that are yet to be realized—or subjectively—from the perspective of individuals, the users of those spaces themselves.

In defining public space, one naturally proceeds from the premise of individual and collective appropriations, of concretely manifested modes of behavior, which shape this space through public use together with, occasionally, digital communication (e.g., flashmobs, "smart cities").[1] People produce public space by defining it situationally or through real or medial practices. This can happen, for example, through repeatedly applying certain usage patterns—as one might develop habitual routes on daily walks—or through collective rituals such as markets, festivals, parades, demonstrations, and so on.[2] Both approaches—concrete-physical as well as medial-virtual—are connected in their actual implementation through a spectrum of constantly changing needs, interests, and functions. In the end, the central issue is design.

The quality of design in public spaces can be measured using two parameters: an enduring, identity-building orientation as well as the potential for facilitating and developing heterogeneous impulses that are able to weave together diverse individual gifts—often underappreciated talents—into a (co)productive community.

DEMO:POLIS stands for a "culture of with-one-another,"[3] a many-faceted cooperation that, depending on the topographic, climatic, or socio-historical context, gives expression to specific modes of self-organization—and not just the results of prevalent authorities with varying degrees of democratic participation and room for collective decision-making.

The phrase "Wir sind das Volk" ["We are the people"], popularized by the protest movement against the East German government in the period before the fall of the Berlin Wall, goes beyond its specific historic context to demonstrate a social awareness of the base, the *ur*-impulse of every so-called grassroots movement. This applies to any necessary societal transformation process and manifests itself in voluntary and spontaneous commitment to a cause—as is the case in Germany today, since neither the state nor the slow workings of administrative institutions are able to live up to acute challenges like the rapidly growing number of incoming refugees.

The motto of the *JUNGE AKADEMIE* [Young Academy] of the Akademie der Künste, "Vielfalt JA! – über Grenzen hinweg" [Diversity, Yes!—Beyond Borders],[4] underlines an attitude that has become unexpectedly topical against this backdrop. A new public format allows the artistic diversity to become visible: *AGORA ARTES*.[5] Under this title, we envision both a place for regenerative retreat, creative contemplation, and self-critical reflection and an opportunity for dynamically developing, experimentally operating, and artistically engaged research.[6] Above all, however, the name refers to the eponymous central, communal festivity, the public gathering of works and their creators, the complex experience of an interplay of the arts, their subjects, and their objects. The event is prepared in workshops, where artists get to know one another, then communally developed, and presented to the public in the form of a *res publica*, as an issue of public interest.[7] These program nights as well as longer-running installations during the "Month of the Fellows" serve to further the Akademie's goal of investigating relevant aspects of our present time from an artistic and social perspective. The *JUNGE AKADEMIE* stands for unconventional approaches and the viewpoints of another, younger generation that puts forth its own thought processes, perspectives, and methods for discussion through transdisciplinary and transculturally developed projects, searching for direct interaction with an interested audience. As part of *DEMO:POLIS*, *AGORA ARTES* will be integrated into the opening festivities, the event program, as well as a large, long-term Akademie exhibition on an equal footing with the members of all sections. Every year, talented artists from all over the world representing six different fields of the arts are chosen by a jury consisting of Akademie members; these are awarded a fellowship that allows them to stay in Berlin and work in one of the studio spaces in the Akademie's Hanseatenweg campus for a maximum of three months. They are considered fellows of the Akademie der Künste for a full year.

Our motto is derived from the primarily dialogically oriented concept of the *genius loci* as well as the aesthetics of the Akademie's campus in Hanseatenweg, designed in 1960 by the architect and later Akademie president Werner Düttman as an answer to the question: "What is an academy today?"[8] The *JUNGE AKADEMIE* therefore relates, on a fundamental level, to this spatial and temporal "manifesto," which forms the basis of the program's efforts to reinvigorate the spirit of synergetic and active diversity—materialized in a building with three distinct characters that together comprise a powerful unity, an InstantCultureCity.[9] Innovative approaches by young artistic talents from many different nations and cultures can add new and surprising qualities to this site. This wonderful place unites contradictions within itself and brings together extremes that also contend with one another in public space: inside and outside, public and private, subjective and objective, dominant opinion and marginal or excluded points of view. It is for this reason that a number of the transdisciplinary projects of the fellows engage directly with rather overlooked and neglected qualities of Düttman's architecture as well as the neighborhood surrounding it, the Hansaviertel (built as part of the building exhibition *Interbau 57*). These works not only deal with individual buildings and ensembles, but also the so-called "flowing green": the spaces in between—transitions between the different living concepts of the "city of tomorrow."

Present People, an interdisciplinary artistic intervention (performance dates: September 18 and 19, 2015; directed by Felix Lüdicke and Theresa Schütz) taking place on the so-called "Plaza of the Dawn" next to the Hansa Library (also by Düttmann), involved all of the fellows participating in the *DEMO:POLIS* exhibition. As an interactive performance, the artists went from door to door through the various buildings of the Hansaviertel—from high-rise towers and slabs to the low-rise bungalow settlements—and asked residents for tap water to fill a series of buckets. The filled buckets were then used to fill an empty, long-neglected pool in front of the library with water, meaning, and attention for the duration of two days, thus reviving the space as a social hub through communicative means. As a "village well, to which water is added instead of drawn from," this center, now brought back to life, managed to once again establish itself in the consciousness of the neighborhood. The performance was intended to facilitate sustainable, integrative processes within the neighborhood on various levels: self-initiated interactions, community-led projects, and other spontaneous actions that serve to make the local body politic visible.

The other contributions by *JUNGE AKADEMIE* fellows, of which Wilfried Wang, curator of the exhibition *DEMO:POLIS—The Right to Public Space*, chose to include three works (*Post | Opticon*, *Relax Now!*, and *Piedras apiladas*) in the central exhibition concept (Hall 2), serve to substantiate the *JUNGE AKADEMIE*'s credo of "diversity beyond borders." Using different aesthetic languages, these projects unite within themselves a multitude of artistic sensibilities and objectives. The broad spectrum of these communally developed concepts includes interactive installations, participative sculptures, film screenings, texts/manifestos, music compositions, booths for storytelling and listening, readings, conversations, architecture-related dance, theater in public spaces as well as both exterior and interior spaces, both as part of the exhibition and interventions in unexpected places in remote areas, nearby the Akademie as well as further afield in Berlin. The ten contributions come from young, internationally active artists from all fields. It is particularly worth noting that only two of them are solo projects; eight *DEMO:POLIS* projects demonstrate—corresponding to the mission of the Akademie—the transdisciplinary artistic *polis* of Akademie fellows from all over the world! All of the contributions could be realized thanks to the generous support of the Society of Friends of the Akademie der Künste. This has led to the consolidation and further development of a long-term relationship of trust between the *JUNGE AKADEMIE* and the Akademie itself, nurtured through close collaboration with its members (not just of the Architecture Section). The *JUNGE AKADEMIE* can thus participate in a new thematic focus of the Akademie as a whole, all the while continuously learning and developing in a way that would not have been possible based only on its own resources.

The fellows engage in part with aspects of *DEMO:POLIS* that have yet to be thematized in other artworks, such as references to unfamiliar, alternative public spaces. These include air space, made tangible through sound sample collages of radio waves (the performance *Puzzled Waves* by Sebastian Gräfe, part of the program evening *AGORA ARTES*); cairns, which are presented as archaic forms of "social sculptures" located on the coast of Galicia (*Piedras apiladas* by Sebastian Gräfe and Felix Lüdicke); or a river, which—right before it flows into the sea—is sent off with appropriate decorum by *Water Music Suite No. 2*, performed by a brass band both above and under water in a particularly Dadaesque act (performance and installation by Sebastian Gräfe and Matthias Kranebitter, part of the program evening and the project presentation *AGORA ARTES*).

Other projects by the *JUNGE AKADEMIE* pick up on topics relating to public space such as advertisement (*Relax Now!* by Liat Elkayam and Matthias Kranebitter), violence, protest, suspicion, criminalization, exclusion, subversion, surveillance, and conspiracy (*Post | Opticon* by Theresa Schütz and Aslı Özarslan), the encounter with the unfamiliar (*Du, Fremder*, a performance and short film set on Berlin's Alexanderplatz by Caitlin van der Maas, Sebastian Gräfe, and Matthias Kranebitter), the continuous flow of movement as a symbol for life, constant change, and the ongoing democratic process of negotiating diverse, contradictory interests (the dance performance *Morph Us*, performed in the atrium and on the roof of Hall 3, by Caitlin van der Maas, Otavio Schipper, and Amir Teymuri), or the loss of lively traditions of direct social events and spontaneous cultural communication, as seen in the expression of acrobats, storytellers, jugglers, and others, who together constitute a colorful, exuberant collection of activities in open-air public space in the documentary project *Al Halqa* by Thomas Ladenburger. The latter presents the origins of public space as defined by humans, archaic forms of education, and an expression of the public sphere that has existed long before its ossified and in many cases disproportionate manifestation as city and institution. It is an appeal for a "movement" based on (self-)critical perception through art and culture, guided responsibly by the collective.

---

1 Christian Schneegass, "Urban Media Cultures: Public Space through Urban Screens and Media Architecture," in Susa Pop, Gernot Tscherteu, and Ursula Stalder (eds), *Urban Media Cultures*, Stuttgart: avedition, 2012, pp. 18–20.

2 For more, see the following project, initiated and led by the author on May 14–15, 2010 as a twenty-four-hour performance together with a complex creative collective: "Übergänge: Leben in der Stadt?" as part of FFF_K/FeldForschungsFestival_Kultur.2010 in central Berlin, a collaboration between the Akademie der Künste (Pariser Platz), Junges Deutsches Theater, Medizinhistorisches Museum der Charité, Naturkundemuseum, and various other partners in the form of universities and free initiatives. The event was documented on video and can be found online: https://vimeo.com/120690008 and https://vimeo.com/121010593 (last accessed January 25, 2016).

3 Christian Schneegass, Introduction to the transdisciplinary "future workshop" *Culture Is It!* (May 5–6, 2006) at the Akademie der Künste, in collaboration with und.Institut für Kunst, Kultur und Zukunftsfähigkeit e.V., id22: Institut für kreative Nachhaltigkeit, and other partners.

4 JUNGE AKADEMIE, Akademie der Künste, Berlin (www.adk.de/jungeakademie/de); see also: Christian Schneegass, "Vielfalt JA!—über Grenzen hinweg," "Genius Loci/DialogPotentiale/Führung mit Hausgeist," "Monat der Stipendiaten," "Akademie-Themenschwerpunkt 'Schwindel der Wirklichkeit,'" "Villa Serpentara-Stipendiaten," and "Ellen-Auerbach-Stipendium für Fotografie," in Akademie der Künste (ed.), *JUNGE AKADEMIE 2014*, Berlin: Akademie der Künste, 2014, pp. 8–73.

5 Christian Schneegass, "Agora Artes. Die Junge Akademie: 'Drehscheibe' für transdisziplinär forschende Bewegung reflektiert (be)zeugenden Zeigens und diverser Diskurse," in Hermann Parzinger, Stefan Aue, and Günter Stock (eds), *ArteFakte: Wissen ist Kunst. Kunst ist Wissen. Reflexionen und Praktiken wissenschaftlich-künstlerischer Begegnungen*, Bielefeld: transcript-Verlag, 2014, pp. 357–368.

6 See the following contribution by the author, written as the initiator of the "experimental studio" of the section for Visual Arts at the Akademie der Künste (founded March 6, 1992 on the impulse of the board of the Akademie der Künste): "Ästhetische Ökonomie: Situative Kreativität mit begrenzten Möglichkeiten," in Christian Schneegass (ed.), *minimal—concept: Zeichenhafte Sprachen im Raum*. Akademie der Künste. Amsterdam/Dresden: Verlag der Kunst, 2001, pp. 272–307; see also the author's text on art, sustainability, ethics, and aesthetics in *experimentcity—berlin: selbstorganisiert! Kulturen der nachhaltigen Stadtentwicklung: Wohnprojekte + Kreativzentren, Wirtschaft + Freiraum*, Experimentdays 2006. Berlin: id22. Institut für Nachhaltigkeit und Senatsverwaltung für Stadtentwicklung Berlin, 2006, p. 7.

7 Christian Schneegass, "Res publica: Wie konkret ist der öffentliche Raum als Begegnungs- und Erfahrungsraum?," in Silvia Breitwieser, *Res Publica: Arbeiten im öffentlichen Raum*, Berlin: Metro Verlag, 1995, p. 45.

8 Schneegass, "Agora Artes," pp. 18–33.

9 Christian Schneegass, "Junge Akademie: Interdisciplinary and International Fellowship Program," in Wilfried Wang (ed.) *Culture:City* Berlin/Zürich: Akademie der Künste Berlin and Lars Müller Publishers, 2013, p.67; Matthias Sauerbruch, "*Culture: City*: Content and Form," in *Culture:City*, p. 19.

The Pastoralist's Neurotic Nature Manifesto

Our world is, so to speak, dissociated like a neurotic.
—Carl Gustav Jung

While we have gained some skill sets, other skills have suffered: the art of conversation, the art of looking at people, the art of being seen, the art of being present.
—Christy Wampole

One of the symptoms of an approaching nervous breakdown is the belief that one's work is terribly important.
—Bertrand Russell

1 / Pompous declaration of this new thingie:
We are this and that group. We think that art now is so and so. We are going to do such and such, because those who did it before us got it all wrong. We need this and that for art's future and for our sake. So, we are now going to do this and that. Now. Right now. We would go into specific details—but—we're very low on serotonin and the Ritalin we just took hasn't kicked in yet.

2 / Mandatory built-in paradoxical clarification:
This momentous manifesto was not conceived and assembled in order to declare a new art movement. Oh no, this manifesto's motivations run deeper. We, the Pastoralists, ideally aim to serve as catalysts, leading humanity through a new path. Some might consider this a paradox, since the text is titled "Manifesto" and the Pastoralists are artists by nature, profession, and dwindling bank account. We wish to comply with these nitpicking individuals talking in our heads: the revolutionary changes we strive for will indeed lead to a different set of artistic standards and results, but only as a byproduct. We don't want to nestle up to art. We want to fuck it.

3 / Manifestos are emotional creatures.
We have read some manifestos, and they are mostly angry. Do not let this movement's name fool you. The Pastoralists are (ironically enough) an irritated bunch. And what is our main cause of anger and agitation? Precisely that: irony. We are the children of irony, irony is the ethos of our postmodern cynical generation. Manifestos declare authentic wishes for change and the liberation of the human spirit. But could those be legitimate/possible goals in our day and age?

Once we, as representatives/members of our generation, write a manifesto, it cannot be one, even if its title says it is. Manifestos are officially and terminally over for us. They're history, relics that belong to a different time, when people actually took pride in ideals and believed in change. We can be nostalgic about those days and write a homage to/parody of a manifesto, making fun of the format, attempting to lure the reader into laughing at and with it. The result is surely spoiled and lacking in comparison to the original deal.

Let's face it, criticizing us will only serve as a diluted form of our own affliction. Irony is the most self-defensive mode, as it allows a person to dodge responsibility for his or her choices, aesthetic and otherwise.

For many of us born in the 1970s and 1980s—members of Generation X or Y—and particularly middle-class Caucasians, irony is the primary mode of dealing with daily life. One need only dwell in public space, virtual or concrete, to see how encompassing this phenomenon has become. It is inherent in almost every category of contemporary reality, including art, advertising, politics, fashion, and television.

Most of our daily existence is spent on our cellphones/the Internet, places that serve as a magnifying glass of this phenomenon. We are absorbed in the virtual public space, where one can only quote ideology/cite meaning because sincerity and directness might cause ridicule and shame. Quick gratification, short texts, the virtual over the actual. Granted, the digital revolution has many advantages, but one of its disadvantages is that we can always hide our true selves in a public space, virtual or real, behind our cells or irony.

And furthermore, we must ask: could it be that irony itself is the cause of our existential neurosis? The price of irony is steep: never being shaken or admitting true passion even to oneself. Even though we deploy irony, feel almost compelled to do so, it is our firm conviction that it is a slippery slope—personally, morally and socially dangerous. Being a function of fear, a form of surrender, irony leads to cultural numbness and defeat.

We, the Pastoralists, claim to be merely a symptom/manifestation of irony. We pledge to address the problem instead of the symptom, subvert our own perspective, dare to hope. In order to do that we turn to a cure that is purest in its non-ironic form: nature. Animals, plants, and landscapes are never ironic. Only humans are.

It might be naïve to believe that nature is even out there. After having read Theodor W. Adorno, we believe that humans can only try to cultivate nature—that ever since language was created, humans lost all other connection to nature.

Here we go again, surrendering before the fight even starts, claiming all has been said and done. We won't go gently into that bad night. We will step away from irony, and so should you. The world is round, but it ain't hollow. Don't take our word for it—just go out there and see for yourself.

Naturally, you should make sure you get a Wi-Fi signal and ask for the password.

—LIAT ELKAYAM AND SEBASTIAN GRÄFE

Things to do in public space (at least) once in a lifetime

Climb a tree.

Sit on a mountaintop.

Stop for a minute and smell the jasmine. Roses are so overrated.

Take a shower in the rain.

Spend a night in the woods or the desert—alone.

What's that sound? Something touched my ear! Oh, it's really dark out here!

Eat a wild mushroom.

Take a walk until you get lost.

Fall down a rabbit's hole.

Watch death.

Fuck in the rain, in a lake, on a pile of leaves, until there is sand all over you.

Fail to get that itchy sand out of your butt.

Draw a circle in the sand.

Dance in circles holding hands.

Make a wish upon a shooting star.

Count the stars (at nighttime).

Count the birds (at daytime).

Stop counting things for a while—it's such a European habit—and find a seagull gliding through the sky. Take a mental ride with it as it soars higher and higher on warm air.

Shout out loud, or even better: Scream, or even better: Scream naked.

Lean against the wind.

Scream against the wind.

Swim against the current.

Float on your back in a lake and look for shapes in the clouds.

Realize that if gravity wasn't holding you back, you could fall into the sky forever.

Kiss a tree, they've been hugged enough.

Look at your own reflection in the pond.

See the stars reflecting in the pond?

Now jump into and through this portal to the other side of the world.

Handle the abyss.

Burn your sorrows.

Squash grapes with your feet.

Wait a year, then get wasted on your own wine.

Let the sun melt away your butter, your brain, your wings.

Follow a bee to its hive.

Follow a river to the sea.

But why would you follow a river to the sea?

Hey, you don't have to, but it could be nice.

Notice the vectors around you: the river moving to the left, the wind blowing from the north, the hare passing you at a 30° angle, changing direction, then changing again. There is always input—noise and sound, shapes and colors.

Linger long enough to discover: what gets on your nerves first, your surroundings or yourself?

Find a friend who can tell the temperature by the different chirping of the crickets.

Resist the urge to take something out of nature and back home with you.

Stay in the city for half a year, walk the grey pavement, join the rat race.

Race the turtle, but don't let the turtle get a head start.

Ask yourself whether you really miss the whales.

Whistle through a leaf. Rattle a dry pod.

Sit under an apple tree and wait for an apple to fall on your head.

Fall asleep.

Ouuuch.

Throw a beach ball to a big black dog. It's a ball!

Avoid wet dogs, unless you wish to be wet.

Chase away the raccoons, before they chase you away. Yes they can.

Cross the same lake twice. Yes you can.

Swim with a swan.

Walk from cool water to hot sand and vice versa. Wave Sebastian Kneipp hello.

Wish it could always be like this.

Accept that mere wishing makes it impossible.

Do not contemplate what might be better.

Do not dwell on what might be over soon.

Vibrate.

Do not mention Buddha to me again, I am into animism now.

Kill your own food.

Serve as a mosquito's lunch.

Pick a basket full of berries.

Pick a fight against the elements.

Visit a coal mine, a sewage plant, a clearing in the forest quarry.

Demonstrate, see that nothing happens, go into the woods again.

Avoid a hurricane. If you can.

Pick up a big stone and count the life forms under it.

Find out that one side of the rock doesn't know the other side exists (and even if it did it wouldn't give a fuck).

Smoke a tree, taste the breeze, feed the sun.

Look at the horizon—there is a dark dot there that becomes a tiny black silhouette that grows into a human-shaped figure of someone you love.

Kiss with tongues.

Be a little grateful for this, you selfish fuck.

Do nothing. I dare you.

Consider: if you were the last person on the planet the whole world would be a public space.

Bask in the sunlight. It's supposed to be the best of disinfectants.

Get your vitamin D while you can. In 4.5 billion years, the sun will expand and finish us off anyway, so we must build a ship and find a way to get to the final space, *the* public space—space.

FELIX LÜDICKE, THERESA SCHÜTZ,
ASLI ÖZARSLAN, AMIR TEYMURI

Present People

COLLABORATORS
Dominique Autschbach
Sebastian Bührig
Sebastian Gräfe
Matthias Kranebitter
Thomas Ladenburger
Korbinian Lechner
Caitlin van der Maas
Aslı Özarslan
Iver Ohm

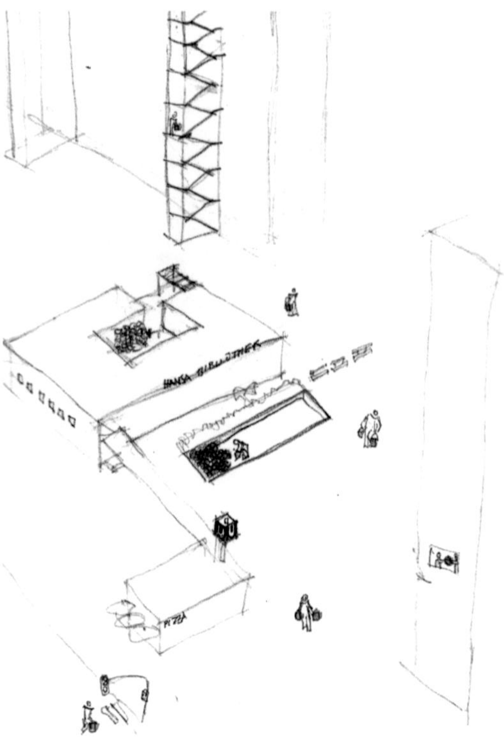

Sketch for the logistics of the intervention

The social sculpture *Present People* considers the moment when society intervenes in public space—for a space only becomes public when it is being used. The intervention site is the decorative pool in front of the library in Berlin's Hansaviertel. The building and its pool stand for the ideals of the *Interbau 57*, out of which the Hansaviertel, with its postwar modernist housing blocks, was developed. The library and its pool were attempts to make education and water, both luxury goods at the time, easily accessible. Today, the pool stands empty. This public space is in search of a new context, use, and meaning.

Present People imparts temporary purpose and form to the site. The decorative pool is transformed into a village well, but in reverse: water is not taken from it, but rather added to it. Ten artists go from door to door in the Hansaviertel carrying 600 buckets. The buckets are collected and lined up one by one in the pool—some of them full, some of them empty—filling the space with transparent bodies. The ostensible order of the installation process aims to encapsulate the ambivalence of public spaces that are designed according to high standards, but are neglected later on. A performance on the next day serves to interrupt this order. Felix Lüdicke calls for the buckets to be refilled. Theresa Schütz climbs into the pool, uses blue dye to make the different levels of water in each bucket visible, and transfers water from full buckets to others that are less so. While the positions and relations of the buckets remain unchanged, the water levels and their colors equalize. Schütz's performative act interprets the political dimension of public space as a mélange of diverse, coinciding practices that cause, enable, and exclude one another simultaneously. Despite stemming from a desire to create enduring equality, these practices seem only to further articulate unequal relationships.

In the *DEMO:POLIS* exhibition, *Present People* will be documented through sculptural, acoustic, photographic, and filmic material, approaching the subject matter from a variety of perspectives. Buckets will be placed at select locations as "narrative sculptures," appearing in conjunction with sound collages by Amir Teymuri that work with comments on the art intervention made by ten Hansaviertel residents. A life-sized photo collage in the atrium, superimposing images of the intervention taken at various intervals from the same perspective, will concentrate action and extend the atrium of the exhibition hall into public space. A film by Aslı Özarslan will take the perspective of water and dive into a sea of buckets. Thomas Ladenburger will create a floor projection that enables visitors to directly experience the imagery and activity of the water basin. —FELIX LÜDICKE AND THERESA SCHÜTZ

Installation in basin at Hansaplatz

Performance "Collecting Water" during the intervention *Present People*

Performance "Balancing Water" during the intervention *Present People*

ASLI ÖZARSLAN, THERESA SCHÜTZ

Post | Opticon

In many democratic societies today, consumers are emancipating themselves through online and interactive means to become producers of public discourse themselves. With the wish to open up new latitudes for self-determination, the need for attention and visibility converges with the possibilities of a modern knowledge and network society in which borders are (in)voluntarily shifted and formerly distinct spheres come together. A vague terrain thus forms itself.

This walk-in installation, which derives its effect from transparencies and is composed of two complementary, inverted chambers, marks a transition and threshold area in the exhibition space. It invites visitors to engage with their own sense of perception: reflections of the self and of others overlap, and the act of observation is transformed into a self-observation of the observed.

This leads to a confrontation and raises questions about the boundaries of the individual in an age of mass surveillance—and how, in the hybrid condition of interdependency created between porous private spheres, digital interfaces, online networks, and normalized surveillance practices, public space can be thought of as a site for social emancipation to begin with. When do I become part of public space—when I am inside, or when I am outside? Is it all a question of perspective? What will happen with and within us, when all aspects of our lives have ultimately become public? What role does the media play in this? Or the permanent release of data, videos, and images? And what if one does not want this information to be released? What role is played by the hidden or the act of hiding? Will such an act raise suspicion?

A narrow corridor separates the two chambers, which stand open towards one another. A web of technologies comes together in the intermediate space between the two chambers. A camera records people in front of and within the installation, bringing them into view simultaneously. Upon entering the installation, the visitor is confronted by a vision of the fragmented self. Here, within an open communication process with the multitudes inherent in the "I," the "we," and the "other," the image shown on a monitor weaves together fragments of various self-representations into a new whole. —ASLI ÖZARSLAN AND THERESA SCHÜTZ

Sketches of the installation

Photomontage of perceptual effects through mirroring and transparency

Relax Now!

Relax Now! is an artwork in the form of a commercial catalog selling a set of instant relaxation experiences.

Relax Now! deals with observations in the area of conflict between cultural hegemony and autonomy in public spaces, reflecting on the subject through a specific form: the catalog. The catalog itself represents a contemporary, printed version of public space: it feeds capitalist society with wishes, role models, and instructions for living, and is handed out freely, without charge, to all.

For this project, we invented an imaginary international corporation titled Relax Now! This corporation will launch its catalog in Berlin due to the city's success in branding itself as relaxing in the past.

The tourist industry in Berlin is experiencing higher growth rates than any of the city's other business sectors. The city's "looseness" is part of the attraction. This can be seen in the built environment of the city itself: after the Second World War, many parts of Berlin were rebuilt and designed to be less crowded and greener. Berlin has labeled itself "multikulti": it has a loose marijuana policy, a gay-friendly atmosphere, and a booming art/club/music scene that takes place in public spaces around the city. These are all meant to make tourists forget the dark past lurking around every corner.

The Relax Now! catalog offers our viewer/consumer a set of relaxation products—products that are contradictory and therefore highly revealing. The first of these products is music, used mostly manipulatively in public spaces. The constant background texture created by so-called "easy listening music" stands in stark contrast to the desired experience of peace and quiet. Most public spaces are so-called "flat spaces." They are one-dimensional since they are not free spaces at all, but rather culturally occupied, bound in a system, and subordinated to an authority that allows only limited uses and behaviors.

Relax Now! stands for hysteric meditation, roisterous quietness, and efficiency-enhanced calmness, to be realized as soon as possible, at the highest level possible—a hyperbole that mirrors our grotesque, stressful times.

—LIAT ELKAYAM AND MATTHIAS KRANEBITTER

Relaxing along the water, Berlin

SEBASTIAN GRÄFE, FELIX LÜDICKE

Piedras apiladas

Stacked stones [*piedras apiladas*] on a milestone

Sign at a milestone noting the borrowed stone sculpture

Who isn't familiar with cairns, those piles of stones that one finds along hiking paths? They originated as an archaic form of signposts and are still in use throughout the world today. Most of them take the shape of a small tower, or conical stacks of large rocks with at least three layers, since it's unlikely that such a form could accidentally be produced naturally. Cairns are particularly intended to aid orientation in inaccessible and confusing terrains, such as mountains or deserts. Besides their function as trail markers, cairns are often endowed with spiritual or cultural meaning as well. Even in modern societies with good signage and ubiquitous navigation devices, people still continue to create cairns. One adds another stone to the pile, as if to say: "I, too, have taken this path. You are in the right place." Cairns, therefore, are also a form of communication, upon which the scenic and cultural characteristics of a region accumulate. They are at once social sculptures, collective definitions of space, and a participatory form of architecture that is in constant renewal.

For the project *Piedras apiladas* [Mounted Stones], Sebastian Gräfe and Felix Lüdicke traveled to the Galician coast in northwest Spain in search of these collective stone sculptures. Here, in the area around Finisterre, one finds the endpoint of various branches of the Way of St. James [*Camino de Santiago*], along which pilgrims from around Europe make their way to Galicia. Time and again, these pilgrims create cairns on top of the stone markers along the pilgrimage path.

On site, the artists measured, mapped, and carefully dismantled a number of these works, the product of many hands. In their place, the artists—just like in a museum—left a sign explaining that the cairn is temporarily on loan to the Akademie der Künste in Berlin. Presented on pedestals as self-sufficient works of art in the exhibition hall, the *Piedras apiladas* are able to fully articulate their sculptural qualities. At the end of the exhibition, the stones will be brought back to their original sites and reassembled—from a trail marker to an autonomous work of art and back again.

—SEBASTIAN GRÄFE AND FELIX LÜDICKE

Al Halqa—Story Box

The circus performers of the Djemaa El Fna Square in Marrakesh, Morocco

"Al-Halqa" is a concept in the Arabic language that means "circle" or "ring." In this particular context, it points to the group of people centered around the circus artists who perform on the Djemaa El Fna, a public space in Marrakesh, Morocco. In 2001, UNESCO recognized the performances by these so-called "Hlaiqi" as an Intangible Cultural Heritage. These immaterial forms of expression—dance, music, song, storytelling, ritual healing, mythological readings of weather patterns, and geomancy—are passed down and continuously reinterpreted by the performers. These performers acquire this knowledge solely through oral and gestural transmission from the previous generation, only to pass it on again, having adapted it to contemporary conditions.

The Story Box

The Story Box is part of the larger *Al Halqa* project, which engages with the Djemaa El Fna in a variety of different ways. The project began with a documentary feature film that concentrates on the transmission of the art of storytelling between a father and son. A second part of the project was the kinetic/cinematographic sculpture *Al Halqa Kinetics* (alhalqa-kinetics.com), which was shown at the Haus der Kulturen der Welt (Berlin) in 2011. The virtual Djemaa El Fna Museum (www.jemaaelfna.com) gives the project a constant presence, even when there are no individual events taking place.

Seen from the outside, the Story Box resembles a photo booth. Once inside, visitors are invited to take a seat on a swivel chair and turn themselves into storytellers in front of a rolling camera. A second Story Box will be installed in Marrakesh at the same time as it is shown in Berlin. The stories from the visitors in Berlin will thus mingle with stories from visitors in Marrakesh in a virtual public space, that of the virtual Djemaa El Fna Museum.

—THOMAS LADENBURGER

CAITLIN VAN DER MAAS,
OTAVIO SCHIPPER, AMIR TEYMURI

Morph Us

DIRECTOR AND CONCEPT Caitlin van der Maas
COMPOSITION Amir Teymuri
INSTALLATION Otavio Schipper
PERFORMER Jiseon Kwon

The moment you open this door, you step into a completely different space: the outside world. This world has a lot of space. This space is divided into all kinds of places. These places are accessible to all. We meet there.

Something in the space changes when we meet. We change because you are in my space or I am in yours; we are in our space, in a mutual place. We look at each other and move on. We think about something. We mirror ourselves. We project. We quickly glimpse at our reflections in a window. We don't talk. We never stop. Nothing can get in our way, because the places are open. Even when they are supposed to be closed, they are open, because they open themselves to me. The space changes me, I change the space, and you change the space and me. *It looks totally different with you in it.*

A research project on the metamorphosis of the body in public space. The public body moves differently from the private body. On the threshold between acting and dance; a dancer searches for the public body and the way it is transforming.

In an interplay between music composed by Amir Teymuri and set design by Otavio Schipper, the dancer finds her way through public space on the way to ever-higher spheres.

—CAITLIN VAN DER MAAS

CAITLIN VAN DER MAAS,
MATTHIAS KRANEBITTER, SEBASTIAN GRÄFE

You, Stranger

DIRECTION AND LIBRETTO Caitlin van der Maas
COMPOSITION Matthias Kranebitter
STAGE DESIGN Sebastian Gräfe
ACTOR 1
ACTOR 2
SOPRANO María José Rodriguez
ELECTRIC GUITAR Nicola Hein

What is strange for you, when you live in a big city? In Berlin, you'll find the entire world. Every culture in one spot. *We know already. Seen it before. Smells funny, but it's alright.* Is there still something strange to you in the city, something that'll have you looking up?

What would happen if a stranger were to come to Berlin right now? He arrives, goes to Alexanderplatz. Franz is waiting for a stranger. He lost his job, because the father of this stranger had died. The only son had sacrificed his father in order to save humanity. This had not worked out, since humanity did not believe him—and that is why Franz is calling this stranger to account. Because the stranger could not save the world and because he, the Devil, is now out of work, since no one else wants to be saved anymore.

The three temptations is a ritual taken from an old magazine, found in the bathroom of an obscure hotel. Three questions by Franz for Jesus, which Jesus denies.

Du, Fremder is a quarrel between the fatherless and the jobless, between Jesus and the Devil, in winter on Alexanderplatz—a place where nothing and nobody is strange.

A musical theater performance and short film shot on Alexanderplatz on the question of who this stranger is and whether we are still able to recognize him—or even be aware of him. For how are we to recognize this retuned man, this man-who-has-become-strange, when nobody remembers anymore?

— CAITLIN VAN DER MAAS

Jesus Come
It's cold, let's make it quick

Franz Jesus, are you depressed?
You don't give a damn
And they, they don't know who you are anyway

Jesus I know
Come
He's dead
That was your last regular job

Franz Shit

Through the megaphone:
So, kneel down for me. Then you'll get all
the riches you'll want in the world

Jesus kneels down

Franz What do you want

Jesus Nothing

Silence. Franz is irritated

Jesus Come
Onwards

Franz You know what's going to come next

Jesus Number two: turn stone into bread

Franz I think we've mixed up the sequence

Jesus Whatever
Come

Lady Magdalena sings
Scream
Jesus scream
Let us see your dyed hands
Let us lick your cried eyes
Laugh at the benevolent
Laugh at the little man
We look at you like a pop star from the Seventies
Long gone, long raved out
Sometime it made sense to believe
But time is gone by and so should you

During the chanting and raving of the blind singer a little girl appears
She looks hungry
And begs for a little money
She wants to give him a stone in return
Jesus takes the stone, looks at it and throws it into the empty well
The girl looks up

Jesus What'd you expect? A miracle?

He searches his pockets and digs out a plastic bag with a sandwich in it and gives it to her

The little girl Give me your money, not your sympathy bread, sucker

Franz What do you want, then?

Jesus Nothing

Franz You can have that

The Devil runs up to Magdalena and takes her by the hair
He starts hitting her

Jesus looks on and wants to go towards the Kaufhof mall
The girl takes his hand

Magdalena screams:
Ow, Jesus

A woman runs across the street
A man comes and forces her to stand still
The man hits her
Then another man comes
Without a word
He takes her place
The first man hits him
He hits ***him*** *again, and hits* ***him*** *once more*
More and more people flock to the scene and look on
A musician, a loser, a student
A circle forms itself
The man being hit
Turns his face
One cheek
And then the other
One hit after another
And so on
Then, once the other had had enough
And calms himself down a bit,
The man being hit looks at him
And asks if he is doing okay
The man stands there bewildered
He cries
Quietly
The man who has been hit walks away
The crowd follows him though
They look at him
With eyes that beseech him to speak
About truth
About goals
About justice
And above all:
Salvation

Water Music Suite No. 2

A composition for the honorable reception of a river into the sea: Version for the Warnow with five trombones

The collaboration between the visual artist Sebastian Gräfe and the composer Matthias Kranebitter began with the idea of bestowing particular honor to a river as it arrives at the sea. At its mouth, the river goes through a transformation process. It achieves its maximum width, and yet simultaneously ends, dissolves, crosses over into something else.

To mark this occasion, a brass band plays a piece that was especially composed for the river. Due to its use in everything from funerals and processions all the way to parades and state receptions, the brass band is a symbol of western ceremonial traditions. Here, the band plays *for* the river, anthropomorphizes it, and therefore makes it more tangible. This humorous gesture allows us to relate easier and more playfully to the river, to nature. In doing so, theatrics and gravity are playfully avoided.

The musical composition does not try to represent the river, nor is it simply a homage; rather, the work is translated into the logic of the river itself. For one, the musical qualities of flowing water—which depend on factors such as temperature, flow rate, salt content, etc.—are incorporated into the composition. Furthermore, the sounds produced by some of the instruments are conducted into the water using hoses: the composition thus speaks directly with the voice of the river.

—SEBASTIAN GRÄFE AND MATTHIAS KRANEBITTER

Underwater recording at the mouth of the river

Temp. t	Salt-content S ‰	0	10	20	31	37
	σ	-0,13	8,01	16,06	24,91	29,74
0°	ρ	0,99987	1,00801	1,01606	1,02491	1,02974
	10^8K	5119	4971	4842	4705	4634
	v	1397,8	1412,7	1425,7	1440,1	1447,7
	v_1	1399,8	1413,8	1425,8	1440,2	1447,9
	v_2	1410,2	1421,6	1432,9	1445,4	1452,3
6°	ρ	0,99997	1,00789	1,01580	1,02442	1,02915
	10^8K	4912	4788	4672	4549	4485
	v	1426,9	1439,5	1451,6	1464,9	1471,9
	v_1	1427,4	1439,5	1451,6	1464,9	1472,1
	v_2	1434,1	1445,5	1456,9	1469,4	1476,2
12°	ρ	0,99952	1,00704	1,01505	1,02346	1,02813
	10^8K	4755	4644	4539	4429	4370
	v	1450,5	1462,2	1473,2	1485,3	1491,9
	v_1	1450,5	1461,7	1472,9	1485,3	1492,0
	v_2	1455,4	1466,8	1478,1	1490,6	1497,5
18°	ρ	0,99862	1,00651	1,01387	1,02220	1,02680
	10^8K	4643	4538	4441	4339	4285
	v	1468,4	1479,7	1490,3	1501,6	1507,6
	v_1	1469,3	1479,6	1489,9	1501,2	1507,4
	v_2	1474,0	1485,4	1496,8	1509,3	1516,1

Acoustic analysis of water relating to temperature and salinity

Excerpt from the composition

Mouth of the Warnow River with lighthouses

A2 ARCHITECTS was established by Peter Carroll and Caomhán Murphy in 2005. Based in Dublin, the practice is founded on a shared interest in both the continuing development of architectural practice and the unchanging, essential nature of architecture. From its origins in educational building and residential work, the practice has grown to encompass urban realm projects, curation, and exhibition design. A2 was nominated for the European Union Prize for Contemporary Architecture / Mies van der Rohe Award (2015) for Pulp Press, Kistefos, Norway, and has won national and international awards, including multiple Royal Institute of Architects of Ireland and Architectural Association of Ireland Awards. www.a2.ie

FABIAN ABEL Student in the master's program in Architecture and Urban Design at Potsdam University of Applied Sciences. He has been living in Berlin since 2011.

JULIA ALBANI Lisbon- and Berlin-based curator and co-director of the cultural communications agency BUREAU N. Since 2003 she has supervised exhibitions, conferences, and publication projects in the fields of architecture, design, and urbanism, first at urban drift in Berlin, then at the Swiss Architecture Museum in Basel, before joining the curatorial team of the Architecture Triennial in Lisbon in 2009. In 2010, she curated the Portuguese Pavilion at the Venice Architecture Biennale.

BERND ALBERS Professor for Design and Building Construction at Potsdam University of Applied Sciences. Architect and urban planner based in Berlin. After architectural studies in Berlin, work in research and design in Zurich and Berlin. Since 2001, director of Bernd Albers—Gesellschaft von Architekten.

ANDREW ALBERTS Born 1959 in Vancouver, raised in Cologne. Architectural studies at the Technical University of Berlin. Teaching positions at the Berlin University of the Arts, the Technical University of Berlin, and the Beuth University for Applied Sciences Berlin. 1989–2008 associate partner of the architecture offices AHS and HEIDE | VON BECKERATH | ALBERTS. Member of the board of trustees of the BDA Galerie Berlin. Lives and works as an independent architect and photographer in Berlin.

DOVILĖ ALEKSAITĖ is a student in the master's program in Art and Media at the Berlin University of the Arts. She comes from Lithuania, where she completed a BA in Sociology.

VENETA ANDROVA Born 1985 in Sofia, Bulgaria. Studies Visual Arts at the Berlin Weißensee School of Art.

THOMAS ARSLAN Chair of the subject area "Narration with and in Technical Visual Media" within the program Art and Media (KuM) at the Berlin University of the Arts. Director and screenwriter based in Berlin. Films include *Gold* (2013), *Im Schatten* (2010), *Dealer* (1999). http://medienhaus.udk-berlin.de/pages/Thomas_Arslan.

ELEANOR AYLETT-JONES is from Great Britain. Her background is in fine art and philosophy. Currently she is in the class for Experimental Film and Media Arts at the Berlin University of the Arts.

MICHELLE BÄHR Student in the master's program in Architecture and Urban Design at the Potsdam University of Applied Sciences. She has been living in Berlin since 2010.

MATTHIAS GRAF VON BALLESTREM Architecture studies in Berlin and Los Angeles. In 2010, he taught as a guest professor at Cornell University. In 2011, he was a scholar at the German Academy Villa Massimo in Rome. In 2013, Ballestrem earned a PhD in implicit space perception. Since 2013, he is guest professor in Architectural Design and Construction at the Technical University of Berlin.

BARKOW LEIBINGER German-American architectural firm, based in Berlin and New York and founded by Regine Leibinger (born in 1963 in Stuttgart, Germany) and Frank Barkow (born in 1957 in Kansas City, USA). Among their designs are the Biosphere in Potsdam, Germany; the Customer and Administration Building, the Gate House, and the Campus Restaurant in Ditzingen, Germany; the Trutec Building in Seoul, and the Tour Total in Berlin. Winners of the third place for the Hines Tower competition on Alexanderplatz. www.barkowleibinger.com

MANUEL BOROBIO SANCHIZ holds a master's degree in architecture from the School of Architecture of Navarra (1998) along with a master's in urban planning from the Instituto Nacional de Administración Pública (INAP, 2005). 1998–2009, independent consultant for territorial and urban planning, working with different regional governments. Among his most important projects from this period is the study of the historical territory of the Way of Saint James, with the aim of planning and managing their heritage and landscape (2007). 2009–2015, director and chief executive responsible for managing the territory and landscape of Galicia, developing and directing the Spatial Planning Guidelines, the Coastal Management Plan, the Landscape Strategy, (both recognized by awards from UN-Habitat), or the ongoing Aquaculture Management Coastal Plan for the region. Associate professor at the Universidad de Santiago de Compostela.

HANNES BRUNNER Born 1956 in Lucerne, Switzerland, lives in Zurich and Berlin. Currently professor at the Berlin Weißensee School of Art. Until 2008, chairman of the Fine Arts Motion Graphic program at NYIT (New York Institute of Technology) in Abu Dhabi, UAE; and professor at Muthesius Academy in Kiel, Germany. He has a degree in Architecture from ETH Zurich and an MFA in Photography from the Art Academy in Kassel, Germany. www.hannesbrunner.com.

RICKY BURDETT Professor of Urban Studies at the London School of Economics and Political Science and director of LSE Cities and the Urban Age program. Chief advisor on architecture and urbanism for the London 2012 Olympics and architectural advisor to the Mayor of London from 2001 to 2006. Director of the 2006 Architecture Biennale in Venice.

FRAUKE BURGDORFF Born in 1970, is a member of the board of Montag Stiftung Urbane Räume, a private foundation that initiates projects opening opportunities for neighborhoods with socioeconomic issues. She studied spatial planning in Kaiserslautern and Dortmund, working subsequently as an urban planner and urban researcher in Antwerp, Aachen, and Gelsenkirchen. She was head of StadtBauKultur NRW from 2002 to 2005 and has written extensively on themes relating to neighborhood and urban development as well as edited various books.

EL CAMPO DE CEBADA is an ongoing project started in 2010. Organized by local residents, the project aims to encourage the temporary occupation of a vacant lot at Cebada Square in central Madrid with the help of several collectives such as Zuloark and TPX.

CLAUS-CHRISTIAN CARBON holds the Chair for General Psychology and Methodology at the University of Bamberg since October 2008. In 2010, he founded EPÆG, an international research group dealing with the themes of ergonomics, psychological aesthetics, and design. He teaches and conducts research in the fields of aesthetics, design, ergonomics, perception, and the measurability of affective and cognitive variables. Carbon is a co-editor and member of the editorial board for a number of scientific journals (*Perception, i-Perception, Art & Perception, Musicae Scientiae, Advances in Cognitive Psychology*). In 2013, he founded the Bamberg Graduate School of Affective and Cognitive Sciences (BaGrACS), which aims to conduct scientific research in cognitive and affective processes.

NUNO CERA Born in 1972 in Beja, Portugal. Lives and works in Lisbon. Photographer and video artist. Recipient of various international stipends and awards, including the João Hogan Scholarship of the Calouste Gulbenkian Foundation (2001), a residency at the International Studios and Curatorial Program in New York (2006), the Fondación Botin Grant (2012), and the International Artist Residency of the Centre International des Récollets (2013).

SUSAN CHIN is executive director of the Design Trust for Public Space, a nationally recognized incubator that transforms and evolves the city's landscape with public agencies and community collaborators since 1995. Prior to joining the Design Trust, she served as Assistant Commissioner for Capital Projects at NYC Department of Cultural Affairs for over twenty years, supporting more than $3 billion in new construction, revitalization, and public art projects citywide. Vice president on the American Institute of Architects board, numerous awards, including AIA New York State's 2013 Kideney Gold Medal and 2011 Del Gaudio Award, Loeb Fellowship at Harvard and distinguished alumna from Ohio State University. Member FAIA, honorary member ASLA.

KA-SHING CHUI is a student in the bachelor's program in Architecture and Urban Design at the Potsdam University of Applied Sciences.

ASSIA CIRILLO is a student in the bachelor's program in Architecture and Urban Design at the Potsdam University of Applied Sciences. She is an exchange student from Naples, Italy, and has been living in Berlin since 2014.

ELIAS CONSTANTOPOULOS Professor, Department of Architecture, University of Patras and the Postgraduate Program, National Technical University of Athens. He studied at the Bartlett School of Architecture, UCL. President, Hellenic Institute of Architecture, Vice president, Hellenic Society for Aesthetics, and Docomomo member. Co-founder of 9H Gallery and SigmaDesign, co-editor of *9H* and *Ntizain* journals, consultant editor, *Architecture in Greece* and *Design + Art in Greece*. Has published monographs on Valsamakis, Antonakakis and Krokos as well as over 100 articles. Curator of exhibitions and conferences.

RUTH DALTON Professor of Building Usability and Visualisation at the University of Northumbria at Newcastle, England. An alumnus of University College London, she has worked as a licensed architect for Foster + Partners and Sheppard Robson Corgan Architects; key projects include the Carré d'Art de Nîmes, Palaçio de Congresos in Valencia, and Kings Cross International Terminal, London (unbuilt). She has taught at the Architectural Association, Georgia Institute of Technology, and the Bartlett, UCL.

GIUSEPPE D'ANGELO is a student in the bachelor's program in Architecture and Urban Design at the Potsdam University of Applied Sciences. He is an exchange student from Naples, Italy, and has been living in Berlin since 2014.

VIKTOR DILL studies Arts and Media at the Berlin University of the Arts, focusing on experimental film.

STEFANA DILOVA is a student in the bachelor's program in Architecture at the Technical University of Berlin. She was born in Sofia, Bulgaria, and spent her childhood there and in Sendai, Japan. Since 2013, she has been working as a student assistant in the office of the Chair for Architecture Theory Prof. Jörg Gleiter (TU Berlin).

SUSANNAH DRAKE Principal, DLANDstudio Architecture + Landscape Architecture, a multidisciplinary design firm that has received national and international urban design awards from the AIA, ASLA, and Chicago Athenaeum among others. Recipient of grants from the Graham Foundation, the New England Interstate Water Pollution Control Commission, the James Marston Fitch Foundation, the New York State Council on the Arts, and the Center for Architecture for research on campus landscapes and large-scale urban infrastructure projects. Former president and trustee of the New York ASLA and former trustee of the Van Alen Institute.

LIAT ELKAYAM is an Israeli writer, culture critic, and journalist. She was editor for the Israeli daily newspaper *Haaretz*, writes a weekly column for *Haaretz* magazine and teaches creative writing at Sapir College. Her short stories have appeared in various anthologies including *Maaboret* and *Wir vergessen nicht, wir gehen tanzen* (S. Fischer, 2015). Berlinale Talent Campus Scholarship. Elkayam's first novel *The Mammal Machine* will be published in 2016. Berlin Fellow at the Akademie der Künste, 2015.

LENA MARIE EMRICH born 1991, is an artist working and living in Berlin. She is in her diploma year at the Berlin Weißensee School of Art, where she studies with Albrecht Schäfer and Vlado Velkov. This spring, she received a PROMOS Grant to go to New York to assist Alfredo Jaar in his studio in Chelsea.

LAURA ENGELHARDT is a student in the master's program Raumstrategien at the Berlin Weißensee School of Art. Previously, she studied Architecture and Art in London and Stuttgart.

KAROLINE FAHL is a master's student in the Architecture program at the Technical University of Berlin. She received her bachelor's degree in anthropology and history from the Free University of Berlin and the Université de la Réunion.

ROMINA FALK is a student in the master's program in Architecture at the Technical University of Berlin. She has been living in Berlin since 2009.

NINA FISCHER is chair of the subject area Experimental Film/Media Arts within the program Art and Media (KuM) at the Berlin University of the Arts. Nina Fischer & Maroan El Sani are artists based in Berlin. Their work is exhibited internationally and was awarded—among others—a scholarship from the German Academy Villa Massimo in Rome. From 2007 until 2010 they were appointed associate professors for Film and Media Art at Sapporo City University, Japan. www.fischerelsani.net; http://medienhaus.udk-berlin.de/pages/Experimenteller_Film

JULIA FÖRSTER For over ten years, Julia Förster has worked as a curator, consultant, and project manager in various cities around Europe. Ever since she wrote a treatise on the question "Creative City Berlin—What Happens When Berlin Wants to Stay Sexy, but No Longer Poor?" the trained cultural theorist has preferred to work with formats that bridge the gap between art, sociology, and urbanism, thereby bringing diverse actors to the table. Most recently, she coordinated and co-curated the exhibition "We-Traders: Swapping Crisis for City," which was commissioned by the Goethe-Institut and shown all over Europe. For the *DEMO:POLIS* exhibition, she is working with Zuloark to curate a program centered around the Universal Declaration of Urban Rights that will take place within the exhibition's Urban Parliament. www.juliafoerster.net

NORMAN FOSTER Born in 1935 in Reddish, Stockport, United Kingdom. Winner of the Pritzker Prize in 1999. Member of the Akademie der Künste Berlin. www.fosterandpartners.com

ESZTER GALAMBOS is a master's student in Visual Communication at the Berlin University of the Arts. She received her bachelor's degree from the Moholy-Nagy University of Art and Design in Budapest.

MIRIAM GARCÍA GARCÍA Architect, urban landscape planner, and researcher, dealing with a wide spectrum of aspects associated with landscape, urban development, and regeneration processes. General director of Urban and Territorial Planning in Cantabria (2003–2007) and currently principal of the landscape architecture office Landlab, whose projects have been recognized both nationally and internationally with awards. Together with Manuel Borobio Sanchiz, she was director of the Galician Coastal Management Plan (2008–2011). She has been invited to speak at several schools for urban planning and landscape architecture and teaches at the School of Design of the University of Pennsylvania, the Universidad de Zaragoza, and in the master's program in Landscape Architecture at the Universitat Politècnica de Catalunya.

ALICE GELETEY is a student in the master's program in Architecture at the Technical University of Berlin. She previously studied in the bachelor's program in Architecture and Urban Design in Potsdam and in Milan.

CORNELIUS GIACALONE is a student in the master's program in Architecture at the Technical University of Berlin. He originally hails from Munich, completed his bachelor's degree at the University of Hannover, and has been living in Berlin since 2013.

SOPHIE GOETHE is a master's student in Architecture at the Technical University of Berlin. She did her undergraduate studies in Hamburg and Valencia. Study trips have brought her beyond European borders many times.

SEBASTIAN GRÄFE Born in 1976 in Grimma, Germany, visual artist. He studied Fine Arts at the HBK Brunswick. Gräfe lives and works in Berlin and Reitwein/Oder. Berlin Fellow at the Akademie der Künste, 2015. www.imperimental.org

SILVIA GROEGER studies Urban Design at the TU Berlin. She has a degree in Landscape Architecture.

KAI NIKOLAUS GRÜNE Architect based in Berlin. He previously taught at the Brandenburg University of Technology in Cottbus and has been teaching at the Technical University of Berlin since 2013. In 2012, he was a scholar at the German Academy Villa Massimo in Rome and in 2013 an architect-in-residence at the Goethe Institut Rotterdam.

HANS HAACKE Born in 1936 in Cologne. Studies at the State Art Academy Kassel (today the Art University Kassel), 1956–1960. Based in New York since 1965. Taught at the Cooper Union, New York, 1967–2002. Participation in the *documenta* (four times) and in Biennials in Venice, São Paulo, Sydney, Tokyo, Johannesburg, New York, Gwangju, and Sharjah. *DER BEVÖLKERUNG* (2000–), permanent installation in the Reichstag Building, and *Denkzeichen Rosa Luxeumburg* (2006), Rosa-Luxemburg-Platz, Berlin. *Gift Horse* (2015), Fourth Plinth, Trafalgar Square, London. Golden Lion for the German Pavilion at the Venice Biennale, 1993 (with Nam June Paik). *Libre Échange*, a conversation with Pierre Bourdieu (English: *Free Exchange*, Stanford: Stanford University Press, 1995).

GUIDO HAGER Trained as gardener and landscape architect, joint proprietor of eponymous landscape architecture office with locations in Zurich and Berlin. For over thirty years and together with over thirty-five employees, he has worked on squares, streets, and parks that invite their users to linger and provide nature with more space for diversity. His most significant renovations of landmark gardens include the late-baroque Rechberggarten and the Arboretum in Zurich, the terraced baroque garden of the Béatrice-von-Wattenwyl-Haus, and the landscape garden Elfenau in Bern as well as the flower garden in Berlin's Treptower Park. His most important new designs are the "Undine" promenade along the Rhine in Basel, the Rudolf-Bednar-Park in Vienna, and the Schlosspark Harburg in Hamburg. Member of the Akademie der Künste Berlin.

HEIKE HANADA Professor for Building Design at the Potsdam University of Applied Sciences. Architect and urban planner based in Berlin. After architectural studies and research positions in Berlin and Tokyo, she founded Heike Hanada—Laboratory of Art and Architecture in 2007. Major designs include the expansion of the Asplund library in Stockholm (2007) and the New Bauhaus Museum, Weimar (2012).

SEÁN HARRINGTON ARCHITECTS is an award-winning Irish architecture practice, renowned for its inclusive approach to designing public spaces for people, including the Rosie Hackett Bridge, Dublin Millennium Bridge, and the Granby pop-up Community Park. Sustainable and energy-efficient designs include the award-winning York Street social housing development in Dublin's city center. Recent projects also include the giant opening umbrellas in Dublin, awarded the 2014 ICONIC Design Award for Architecture from the German Design Council. Seán Harrington has taught and lectured about architecture widely, including in Germany, Spain, Switzerland, UK, Poland, France, Russia, and Ukraine. Seán grew up in West Berlin in the early 1970s.

ANNA HEILGEMEIR is a lecturer at the Chair for Urban Design and Urbanization at the Technical University of Berlin. She lives and works as an architect in Berlin.

BIRGIT HEIN Born in 1942 in Berlin. 1966–88 experimental films, performances, and installations with Wilhelm Hein. Co-founded XSCREEN in Cologne in 1968. Own films since 1991. Since 1971, numerous publications on experimental film, among them *Film im Underground* (Berlin, 1971) and *Film als Film* (Stuttgart 1977). Films in various international collections, among them at the Musée d'Art Moderne Paris (Centre Pompidou), Cinemathèque Royale de Belgique in Brussels, and the Sprengel Museum in Hanover. From 1990 to 2008 professor for Film and Video at the Hochschule für Bildende Künste Brunswick. Member of the Akademie der Künste Berlin and vice-director of the Section for Visual Arts.

WILHELM HEIN Born in 1940 in Duisburg, Germany. Filmmaker and performance artist. In 1968, he co-founded XSCREEN in Cologne, the first space for subcultural events in Germany. From 1966 to 1988, he worked with Birgit Hein, shooting films and organizing events. Together with Birgit Hein, he participated in *documenta 5* (1972) and *documenta 6* (1977). Between fall 1981 and summer 1982, he spent time in New York at MOMA-PS1 on a fellowship funded by the City of Cologne.

LUTZ HENKE is a cultural scientist (MA) and curator focusing on art in the public domain. He has been awarded a grant from Ólafur Elíasson's Institute for Spatial Experiments at the University of the Arts Berlin and taught in the master's program Raumstrategien at the Berlin Weißensee School of Art. Henke realizes artworks in close collaboration with artists such as Santiago Sierra or Wermke/Leinkauf, and works with a variety of institutions and museums. Until 2014, he directed the independent art space Senatsreservenspeicher in Berlin-Kreuzberg.

CHRISTOPH HÖLSCHER has been professor of cognitive science at ETH Zurich since 2013. He holds a PhD in Psychology from the University of Freiburg, senior research fellow at the Bartlett School of Architecture, UCL, and is a visiting professor at Northumbria University in Newcastle, England. He aims to understand the interaction of humans and their physical, technical and social environment, working with architects on orientation and navigation in buildings and urban environments.

REINHILD HOFFMANN Born in 1943 in Sorau, Silesia. Studies in Dance at the Folkwang Hochschule Essen, class of Kurt Jooss. 1970–1973 dancer at Theater Bremen. 1975–1978 director of the Folkwang Tanzstudio together with Susanne Linke. 1978–1986 director of the Bremer Tanztheater (until 1981 with Gerhard Bohner). Move to the Schauspielhaus Bochum together with her company in 1986 (until 1995). Guest performances in Germany and internationally. Since 1995, freelance work as choreographer and director for opera and music theater. Recognized, among others, by invitations to the Berliner Theatertreffen 1982, 1983, 1984,1986, Order of Merit of the Federal Republic of Germany, First Class. Member of the Akademie der Künste since 1997; 2007–2015 deputy director of the section for performing arts.

MARTIN HOFMANN Born in Berlin, studies Art and Media (since 2013), and previously Architecture at the Berlin University of the Arts.

BARBARA HOIDN Born in Karlsruhe, studied architecture at the University Karlsruhe, Germany. In 2001, she founded Hoidn Wang Partner together with Wilfried Wang in Berlin. Associate professor at the O'Neil Ford Chair at The University of Texas at Austin. 1999 Loeb Fellow at the Harvard GSD, Cambridge. She has taught at the ETH Zurich; the RISD, Providence, RI; and the Harvard GSD, Cambridge. 1994–2000, she was head of the office of the Senate Building Director in Berlin. She has curated many exhibitions, symposia, and conferences on architectural and urban design topics, and is editor of numerous books and exhibition catalogs.

MORITZ HOSSLI studies Art and Media at the Berlin University of the Arts. He has a bachelor's degree in Art and Communications from the College for Art and Design, Lucerne, Switzerland.

NORBERT HUSCHNER is director of the Department for World Heritage, Tourism, and Culture of the Hanseatic City of Wismar.

ANDREW KEEN Born in 1960 in Hampstead (UK), studied History and Political Science in London, Sarajevo, and Berkeley. He has taught at various universities in the United States and founded a successful Internet company in Silicon Valley in 1995. The British-American author, speaker, and entrepreneur is among the world's most influential critics of the Internet. Andrew Keen lives with his family in Berkeley and is the author of a popular blog. www.ajkeen.com/

ELIZABETH KELLY has a BFA in Film and Television from New York University. She is currently working on her master's degree in Theater Stage Design and Scenography at the TU Berlin.

JAN KLEIHUES The Berlin architect Jan Kleihues cut his teeth working with Peter Eisenman, Daniel Libeskind, John Hejduk, and Rafael Moneo. In 1992, he founded the architectural office Jan Kleihues in Berlin and, in 1996, the office Kleihues + Kleihues together with Josef Paul Kleihues and Norbert Hensel. The office is active both domestically and internationally. Its projects range from educational, administrative, retail, and residential buildings all the way to the planning and realization of museums. The office has locations in Berlin, near Münster (Germany), and Oslo. Jan Kleihues is dedicated to a holistic understanding of architecture, designing everything from urban master plans to door handles. He has taught as a guest professor at the Berlin University of Applied Sciences, the Università di Bologna—Facolta di Architettura "Aldo Rossi" in Cesena (Italy), and the Beuth University of Applied Sciences in Berlin. Since 2011, he has been professor at the Potsdam School of Architecture, a division of the Potsdam University of Applied Sciences.

STEFFEN KLOTZ is a master's student in Urban Design at the Technical University of Berlin. He holds a bachelor's degree in landscape architecture and has been working in this field since 2011.

ANNE KOZIAN Student in the fifth semester of the bachelor's program in Architecture and Urban Design at the Potsdam University of Applied Sciences. She has been living in Berlin since 2011.

MATTHIAS KRANEBITTER studied composition in Vienna, Amsterdam, and Graz (Austria). His work has been recognized by, among others, the 2013 Publicity Award of the Austro-Mechana licencing agency and a support grant from the City of Vienna in 2014. He is a co-founder of the Unsafe+Sounds Festival and the BlackPageOrchestra. Berlin Fellow at the Akademie der Künste, 2015.

CAMERON KRAUS Born 1987 in Texas. Holds a bachelor's degree in Graphic Design from Harding University and master's degree in Architecture from The University of Texas at Austin School of Architecture (UTSOA). Worked as an intern architect at the office of Gigon/Guyer in Zürich and an architectural designer at Gensler Austin. He has been involved in the design of various publications through the Center for American Architecture and Design (CAAD) at UTSOA and is currently working in Berlin as a freelance designer.

KATHRIN KRELL is a student in the master's program in Urban Design at the Technical University of Berlin and has a bachelor's degree in landscape architecture. She was born in Zurich and has been living in Berlin since 2013.

ANNE LACATON Born in 1955 in Saint-Pardoux-la Rivière, France. Architectural practice together with Jean-Philippe Vassal in Paris since 1989. 2006 Erich Schelling Architecture Prize. www.lacatonvassal.com

THOMAS LADENBURGER Born 1975 in Ellwangen/Jagst (Germany), artist and filmmaker. Lives in Berlin. 1997–1998 studied Interdisciplinary Media at the San Francisco Art Institute, 1998–1999 studied at the Kunsthochschule Kassel, 1999–2005 graduate studies in experimental media design at the University of the Arts Berlin. Berlin Fellow at the Akademie der Künste, 2015.

ALBERT LANG Director of the interdisciplinary Raumlabor within the program Bühnenbild und Szenischer Raum (Stage Design and Scenic Space) at the Technical University Berlin. Theater and opera director based in Berlin. Worked for Bayerisches Staatsschauspiel, Semperoper in Dresden, Schauspielhaus Hamburg, and the Burgtheater in Vienna, among others. www.tu-buehnenbild.de/person/prof-albert-lang/

REGINE LEIBINGER Born in 1963 in Stuttgart, Germany. Studied Architecture in Berlin and at Harvard University, and was visiting professor at the Architectural Association in London and Harvard University. Since 2006, professor for Architectural Design and Construction at the Technical University of Berlin. Founded the architectural practice Barkow Leibinger together with partner Frank Barkow in 1993.

CAROLINA LEITE Born 1988 in Porto, Portugal. Master's degree in architecture from the Faculdade de Arquitectura da Universidade do Porto (FAUP) and Università di Roma Tre. In Porto, she worked with cccb Arquitectos and Álvaro Siza. She is currently working in Berlin with Hoidn Wang Partner.

FELIX LÜDICKE Born in 1977 in Munich, trained as a landscape gardener and studied landscape architecture. Research associate at the Chair of Landscape Architecture, and Public Space at the University of Technology in Munich, focusing on intervention and participation.Berlin Fellow at the Akademie der Künste, 2015.

REGULA LÜSCHER Born 1961 in Basel, Switzerland. Since 2007,Senate Building Director/Secretary of State in the Senate Department for Urban Development and the Environment, Berlin. Studied Architecture at the ETH Zurich. From 1987 to 1989, work in architectural firms in Zurich and Vienna. 1989–1998, own architectural office in Zurich in partnership with Patrick Gmür. 1998 appointed Head of Department at the City of Zurich Office of Urban Planning, also member of the management. In 2000 promotion as Head of Urban Planning (regional and land-use planning, urban development of the City of Zurich, member of management). 2001, appointed Deputy Director of the Zurich Office of Urban Planning. From 1989 to 2007 various teaching positions at ETH Zurich and other colleges in Switzerland. Since 2012, honorary professor for Urban Renewal at Berlin University of the Arts. Holds supervisory board mandates with WBM Wohnungsbaugesellschaft Berlin-Mitte mbH and BIM Berliner Immobilienmanagement GmbH; member of the board of trustees of Nationale Stadtentwicklungspolitik; member of the foundation councils of Stiftung Preußischer Kulturbesitz, Stiftung Berliner Schloss—Humboldtforum, and Stiftung Preußische Schlösser und Gärten Berlin-Brandenburg; member of the Baukollegium.

CAITLIN VAN DER MAAS is a theater director. 2012–2015 assistant director at the Münchner Kammerspiele, where she directed *Doktor Faustus Lichterloh* (musical theater, 2014), *Train of Thought* (reading, 2014), and *Ein guter Krimi* (short film, 2015). Other pieces she has directed include: *Face Me* (with Sandra Hüller, 2015) and *PLAYGROUND #1, #2, #3*, and *#4* (youth theater). Berlin Fellow at the Akademie der Künste, 2015. www.caitlinvandermaas.com.

LUCAS MAIA Born in São Paulo in 1984, Lucas Maia studies Art und Media at the Berlin University of the Arts. He graduated in Economics at the Universidade Federal de Santa Catarina, studied Cinematography at the Escuela Cinematografica Argentina and afterwards Visual Arts at the Berlin University of the Arts.

FLORIAN MATZNER Born in 1961. Art historian and exhibition curator, living in Munich and Rosignano Marittimo, Italy. 1991–1998 exhibition curator at the Landesmuseum in Münster, since 1998 Professor for Art History and Art Theory at the Academy of Fine Arts in Munich. Numerous publications and exhibitions about contemporary art.

JEANINE MEERAPFEL Since 2015 president of the Akademie der Künste, film director, screenwriter, and producer. Born in 1943 in Buenos Aires, Argentina, where she attended the city's School of Journalism before going on to work as an editor and freelance journalist in Argentina. 1964–1968, studies at the Film Institute, Hochschule für Gestaltung, Ulm, Germany, classes of Alexander Kluge and Edgar Reitz. She filmed her first motion picture, *Malou*, in 1980. Numerous award-winning documentary and feature films such as *Melek Leaves* (1985) and *La Amiga* (1988). 1990–2008, professor at the Academy of Media Arts in Cologne, Film Department. A collection of her films was released on DVD by Neue Visionen Medien in 2008. In 2012, her latest film, *My German Friend*, an Argentine-German co-production, was released in cinemas. Since 1998, member of the Film and Media Arts Section of the Akademie der Künste. She was the Deputy Director of this Section from 2012 to 2015. Prizes and awards (a selection); 1981: International Federation of Film Critics (fipresci) Award in Cannes for *Malou*; 1985: German Film Critics' Award (Preis der deutschen Filmkritik) for *Melek Leaves*; 1989: German Film Award and Argentine Oscar nomination for *La Amiga*; 2000: Female Artists' Award of the German Federal State of North Rhine-Westphalia (Künstlerinnenpreis des Landes Nordrhein-Westfalen); 2001: special award at the Argentine festival Mar del Plata for *Anna's Summer*; 2012: Prize of Honor for her complete works at the International Film Festival Innsbruck. www.meerapfel.de

ANDRÉS MIGNUCCI Born in 1957. Puerto Rican architect, urbanist, and teacher. Mignucci studied architecture at the MIT (1982) and worked as an urban designer with Stephen Carr and Kevin Lynch. He is the recipient of the National Architecture Prize in 2001 and 2002 and the Henry Klumb Award in 2012. In 2005, Andrés Mignucci was elected to the College of Fellows of the American Institute of Architects. Mignucci teaches Design, History, and Theory of Architecture at the School of Architecture, University of Puerto Rico and is Villum Fonden Visiting Professor at the School of Architecture in Aarhus, Denmark.

ELFI MIKESCH Born in 1940 in Judenburg, Austria. Trained as a photographer. In Berlin since 1964. Active as photographer, camerawoman, director, and educator. Since 1976, creator of feature and documentary films. Camerawoman for, among others, Werner Schroeter, Rosa von Praunheim, Theresa Villaverde, Lilly Grote, Harald Bergmann, and Monika Treut. In 1984, she founded the independent production company Hyena Films together with Monika Treut. Since 1991, member of the Akademie der Künste, Section for Film and Media Arts. Since 2011, member of the department Cinestyria Film Art, a part of the cultural department of Styria, Austria.

ROZANA MONTIEL is the founder of the Mexico-based architectural firm ROZANA MONTIEL | ESTUDIO DE ARQUITECTURA. The studio works with a wide variety of projects in different scales and layers that range from the city to micro-objects, artifacts, and books. Montiel has won several national and international prestigious awards, and her interdisciplinary work has been published in renowned architectural digests, as well as exhibited in Mexico, Spain, France, Germany, the United States, England, and China and presented in the Venice, São Paulo, Rotterdam, and Lima biennials. She has just been selected as one of the 2016 Emerging Voices award from the Architectural League of New York.

STEFAN MÜLLER ARISONA is professor of Computer Science at the University of Applied Sciences and Arts Northwestern Switzerland (FHNW) and senior research fellow at ETH Zurich, Switzerland. His main interests are the application of computer graphics, digital media, and human-computer interaction principles to a variety of fields, such as architectural and urban modeling, digital art and entertainment, or digital media authoring. He graduated in Electrical Engineering at ETH Zurich, received his PhD from the University of Zurich, and was Swiss NSF fellow at the University of California, Santa Barbara. As a founding principal investigator of ETH Zurich's Future Cities Laboratory, he resided in Singapore from 2010 to 2014. robotized.arisona.ch

CRISTIANE MUNIZ Born in 1970 in São Paulo, Brazil. Master's degree at the Faculty of Architecture and Urbanism, University of São Paulo (FAU-USP). Professor of Project and Practice at Escola da Cidade's undergraduate program. Coordinator of the postgraduate *sensu lato* program Architecture, Education, and Society at Escola da Cidade. Visiting professor and lecturer. Partner of Una Arquitetos, based in São Paulo, since it was established in 1996.

MICHAEL MUSCHNER Filmmaker and director, composer. Together with Reinhild Hoffman: *Vor Ort* (theater piece and film, 1997); *Die kleine Zeit (vor der Antwort)* (film, 2000); *Huit à 8* (film, 2003); *Viele Männer sind in einem Mann* (film, 2015).

SHAHED NAJI Born in 1980 in Tripoli, Lebanon, Shahed Naji studied painting at the Institute of Fine Art of the Lebanese University and has worked throughout the Middle East on art-based social projects and teaching. He is currently a student in the master's program in Theater Stage Design and Scenography at the Technical University of Berlin.

MICHAEL NAJJAR Born in 1966 in Landau, West Germany. German artist. He has been living and working in Berlin since 1988. His work is shown in museums, galleries, and at biennials around the world. www.michaelnajjar.com

GÜNTER NEST earned a PhD in urban and regional planning with a study on the role of voluntary organizations in coastal Andhra Pradesh, India, after studying Architecture, History of Art, and Dramatics, as well as Urban and Regional Planning. Consultant, photographer, and curator for urban planning and design, with emphasis on local strategies for urban development in varying cultural contexts. He teaches at the Berlin Weißensee School of Art and holds an honorary professorship at the Institute for Architecture of the Technical University of Berlin. Since 2004, visiting professor at the University School of Design in Mysore, India.

JUDITH NOACK is a current student at the Technical University of Berlin, working on her master's degree in Theater Stage Design and Scenography. She previously worked as a set decorator for film and television in Cologne and Quito.

ASLI ÖZARSLAN Born in 1986 in Berlin. 2007–2011 studied Theater and Media at the Universität Bayreuth (Germany), as well as Philosophy and Sociology at the Université Sorbonne IV in Paris. She has participated in film workshops in Turkey and in Israel. Her films have been shown at international festivals and have won several prizes. Besides her work on artistic projects such as films or video installations, Özarslan works as a freelance journalist. She has been studying documentary filmmaking at the Filmakademie Baden-Württemberg since 2012. Berlin Fellow at the Akademie der Künste, 2015.

MARIA MANUEL OLIVEIRA Architect (School of Fine Arts of Porto, 1985) and, since 1997, associate professor at the School of Architecture at the University of Minho. She is the director of the school's Center for Studies, where she conducts work on architectural and urban design. She is member of the Lab2PT. Her latest research has focused on modern architecture in Lusophone countries, particularly in Mozambique and Brasilia. She has lectured at the Faculty of Architecture at the University of Porto and at the University of Angola. 1988–2002, she was a partner in an architecture studio, and between 1983 and 1986 she collaborated with the Guimarães Department of Urban Planning.

LUKAS PAPPERT Student in the master's program in Urban Design at the Technical University of Berlin. He received his bachelor's degree in Urban and Regional Planning from the University of Kassel.

DAGMAR PELGER is a lecturer at the Chair for Urban Design and Urbanization at the Technical University of Berlin. She is an architect and research associate at the Karlsruhe Institute of Technology.

JULIO CÉSAR PÉREZ HERNÁNDEZ Practicing architect and urban planner, professor and author of "A Master Plan for 21st Century Havana" as well as the books *Inside Cuba* (2006) and *Inside Havana* (2011). President of the Council for European Urbanism (CEU) and International Network for Traditional Building, Architecture, and Urbanism (intbau) Cuba Chapters. Harvard Loeb Fellow. www.caesar-studio.net/wordpress.

DIMITRIS PIKIONIS (1887–1968 in Athens) Greek architect and professor at the National Technical University of Athens (NTUA). He studied Civil Engineering at the NTUA and became friends with Giorgio de Chirico. He then studied Painting in Munich and Paris, and trained as an architect at the studio of Chifflot. Between 1935 and 1937 he published the *Trito Mati* [Third Eye] journal of art and architectural theory. His most important works are the Primary School in Pefkakia (Lycabettus, 1932), the Filothei Playground (1961–1964), and the landscaping of the area surrounding the Acropolis of Athens (1951–1957).

JOŽE PLEČNIK (1872–1957 in Ljubljana) Slovenian architect and disciple of Otto Wagner. Founding member of the Faculty of Architecture, Ljubljana in 1919. Responsible for giving Ljubljana its modern-day identity through designs such as the Triple Bridge, the city's Market Hall, and the Promenade on the Ljubljanica River. Important works also include the refurbishment of the castle in Prague.

CORDELIA POLINNA Born in 1975, studied Town Planning and Urban Design in Berlin and Edinburgh. Cordelia Polinna established the practice Polinna Hauck Landscape + Urbanism in 2008. 2011–2013 she was a visiting professor of Sociology of Architecture and Planning at TU Berlin. Since 2015, she is director at Urban Catalyststudio. 2012–2014 member of the academic steering committee for Berlin's spatial development strategy BerlinStrategie 2030. Member of the Scientific Committee of the Housing Company Degewo and Deutsche Akademie für Städtebau und Landesplanung (DASL).

DAMJAN PRELOVŠEK Born in 1945, studied Art History in Ljubljana, where he received his diploma in 1969 with a thesis on the Zacherl House in Vienna. Herder Fellow at the Institute for Art History at the University of Vienna. From 1971, he was active as a researcher—and later, dean—at the Institute for Art History of the Slovenian Academy of Sciences and Arts. Guest professor at the University of Salzburg. Since 1992, member of the European Academy of Sciences and Arts in Salzburg. 1998–2002, Slovenian ambassador to the Czech Republic.

MATHIAS PUDELKO Architecture student in the master's program at the Technical University of Berlin. After studying in Weimar and the USA, he worked at the architectural office Kuehn Malvezzi, among others.

ÁLVARO PUNTONI Born in 1965 in São Paulo, Brazil. Architect (1987), master (1999) and PhD (2005) degrees at the Faculty of Architecture and Urbanism, University of São Paulo (FAU-USP). Project professor since 1990, currently teaches at FAU-USP (since 2001) and at the Escola da Cidade (since 2002), where he is a founding partner and coordinator of the Graduate Council and specialization course "America: a look through its architecture." Guest Professor in the program "Taller Sudamerica" at FADU, Buenos Aires. Currently leads the GrupoSP office in São Paulo.

CHRISTOPHER RICHTER has been working in the architectural office of Bernd Albers since 2014. He received his master's degree from the program in Architecture and Urban Design at the Potsdam University of Applied Sciences.

ESTEBAN RIVERA is a master's student in Art and Media at the Berlin University of Arts. He is Colombian and has been living in Berlin since 2013.

MAX RUDOLPH is a master's student in Architecture at the Technical University of Berlin and works for Sauerbruch Hutton. He received his bachelor's degree from the Münster School of Architecture.

MICHAEL RUETZ Photographer and Berliner, born in Lietzensee. For thirty years, he served as professor for Communication Design at the Brunswick University of Art (Hochschule für Bildende Künste Brunswick). His work has been recognized by the Otto Steinert Prize and the Villa Massimo Prize, as well as its associated fellowship in Rome. He is an Officier de l'Ordre des Arts et des Lettres of the Republic of France and a member of the Akademie der Künste. Sole inheritor and executor of the estate of the photographic artist Heinz Hajek-Halke.

SADAR+VUGA was founded by Jurij Sadar and Boštjan Vuga in Ljubljana in 1996. The office's best-known built works are the Chamber of Commerce and Industry of Slovenia, the Entrance Hall of the National Gallery of Slovenia, the Sports Park Stožice, the Air Traffic Control Center in Ljubljana, and the Cultural Center of EU Space Technologies in Vitanje. The office has been awarded numerous prizes for its projects, including the Bauwelt Prize, Iconic Award, Archmarathon Award, Piranesi Award and has been nominated for the Mies van der Rohe Award eight times. SADAR+VUGA's work is featured as part of the permanent collection at the Architekturmuseum of TU München and the MAO Ljubljana and published in the monographs *SADAR+VUGA: A Review, Formula New Ljubljana, DD17: Tendencies*, and *3D-2D: Adventures In and Out of Architecture.*

DANIELA SCHAFFARCZYK is a student in the master's program in Architecture at the Technical University of Berlin. The Berlin native received her bachelor's degree from the Beuth University for Applied Sciences.

OTAVIO SCHIPPER Born in 1979 in Rio de Janeiro, Brazil. Artist. Berlin Fellow at the Akademie der Künste, 2015.

CHRISTIAN SCHNEEGASS Since 2012 head of the Junge Akademie [Young Academy] at the Akademie der Künste Berlin, where he was also the section leader of Kunst+ Gesellschaft from 2007 to 2012, 1985–2007 secretary of the section for Visual Arts. Initiator of various interdisciplinary projects, exhibitions and symposia. He has also served on various juries and committees. 2008–2013 board member of the Neuer Berliner Kunstverein (nbk), 1994–1997 member of the advisory board and again 2002–2006. Participation in various expert workshops. www.adk.de/jungeakademie/de

BERNHARD SCHNEIDER Born in 1941; architect, planner, consultant. Member, advisory board of the Architekturpreis Berlin e.V.; activities with various initiatives of the Zukunft Berlin Foundation; among others in charge of the foundation's Kulturforum initiative; 1981–89 staff officer under Berlin's Senator for Urban and Environmental Development and the Senator for Cultural Affairs, respectively. 1991–95 steering committee member for the Stadtforum Berlin. Publications: *Stadtentwicklungsplan Öffentlicher Raum,* (Berlin Senate, 1995; co-author). *Daniel Libeskind, Jewish Museum Berlin* (Prestel, 1999, 2001). *BerlinStudy* (European Commission/Berlin Senate, 2001; co-author).

FRIEDER SCHNOCK is a Berlin-based conceptual artist, photographer, curator, and cultural theorist (field of research: land art, conceptual art), as well as a Rockefeller Alumnus. Working in multiple media, he investigates how memory and social surroundings relate to geographic and cultural conditions. Together with Renata Stih (Stih & Schnock), he has developed projects such as *Bus Stop*, a proposal for the Berlin Holocaust Memorial; *Places of Remembrance*, a decentralized monument in Berlin-Schöneberg; *Einladung/ Berlin-Alexanderplatz*, NGBK; and *Signs from Berlin*, Jewish Museum New York. Dr. Schnock teaches Visual Studies at the Beuth University of Applied Sciences, Artefacts in Transition at the Leuphana University, Lüneburg, and a spectrum of topics relating to "Art and Memory" at American institutions such as RISD, MICA, Brown, and Princeton.

THERESA SCHÜTZ Born in 1983 in Vienna, Austria. She studied architecture in Vienna, worked as an assistant in the Institute of Local Planning (TU Wien) and conducted research at the Interdisciplinary Center for Urban Culture and Public Space (TU Wien) on the topic of the emancipation and politics of public space. Researcher at the Hidden-Institute in Berlin. Since 2015, she also directs, together with Rainer Steuer, the "T/Labor" for multiple art and transdisciplinary collaboration at the Viennese artists' collective UNOs | umding+ortsam. Berlin Fellow at the Akademie der Künste, 2015.

JENS SCHULZE is a student in the master's program in Urban Design at the Technical University of Berlin. Since 2015, he has worked as a tutor in the postgraduate master's program in Urban Management at the same university.

MARTA SETÚBAL Born in 1985 in Portugal. Architect's degree in 2009, Lisbon. Living in Berlin since 2010. Currently studying in the master's program Raumstrategien at the Berlin Weißensee School of Art.

YUMA SHINOHARA Curatorial assistant for the *DEMO:POLIS* exhibition at the Akademie der Künste. Berlin-based editor and translator of texts in architecture and design. Holds a degree in Architectural History and Comparative Literature from Columbia University, New York. Prior to joining Hoidn Wang Partner, he worked for Ruby Press, Berlin, and Storefront for Art and Architecture, New York.

RENATA STIH is a Berlin-based concept artist, dealing with social sculptures, strategies in public space, and museums as sites of collective and politico-cultural memory. To this end, she develops interdisciplinary art projects that go beyond the conventional artistic mode of the exhibition. Her collaboration with Frieder Schnock (Stih & Schnock) has produced not only the monument projects shown here, but also exhibitions such as *Raft with Stranded Objects*, Saint Louis Art Museum; *Rosie Won the War*, Boca Raton Museum of Art; *Lacan Doesn't Live Here Anymore*, LES Gallery, New York; and *Was brauchen wir Kunst, wir brauchen Kartoffeln*, Staatsgalerie Stuttgart. She teaches Art, Technology, Film, and Media at the Beuth University of Applied Arts as well as Art Strategies at the Leuphana University in

Lüneburg. She has also taught at institutions such as RISD, the School of the Art Institute of Chicago, and ZHDK Zurich. She is a Rockefeller Alumna, laureate of the Obermayer German-Jewish Awards, and currently the chairwoman of the Art Advisory Committee of the Senate Chancellery Office for Cultural Affairs, Berlin. In addition, she works as a curator and essayist with a focus on art, film, and gender.

JÖRG STOLLMANN Director of the Chair for Urban Design and Urbanization at the Institute for Architecture, TU Berlin. Architect and urban researcher based in Zurich and Berlin. His exhibitions have been shown at Storefront for Art and Architecture in New York, MoMA New York, Malmö Konsthall, and the German Academy in Rome. www.cud.tu-berlin.de

FERNANDO TÁVORA (1923–2005 in Matosinhos, Portugal) Graduated in Architecture from the Porto School of Fine Arts (which became FAUP in 1952) and was later invited to become a professor there. In the late 1950, he took part in the "Survey on Portuguese Architecture" as well as several CIAM and Team 10 meetings. Besides his academic career, Távora worked as a practicing architect; He also worked as a consultant for several municipal governments across Portugal, as was the case in Guimarães. He is known today as an influential architect and teacher, as well as a key person in the modernization of the Porto School of Architecture.

100% TEMPELHOFER FELD is a citizen's action group from Berlin that campaigns against official plans of the Berlin Senate to build on the Tempelhofer Feld (the former grounds of Tempelhof Airport) since 2011. Their declared objective is the complete preservation of the grounds as an "open landscape in the middle of the city." In 2012, the group initiated a process to write a prohibition on further building on the field into law; in 2014, this motion was successfully adopted by a vast majority of voters in a referendum.

TILMANN TESKE studied Urban Studies at the Bauhaus University Weimar and the UNAM in Mexico City. Since 2013 he has been a student in the master's program for Urban Design at the Technical University Berlin.

AMIR TEYMURI Born in 1984 in Kermanshah, Iran. 2004–2010, student of Music at the Faculty of Fine Arts of the University of Tehran. 2010–2014, he studied composition at the University of Music Freiburg with Prof. Cornelius Schwehr. Currently studies composition with Orm Finnendahl at the University of Music in Frankfurt am Main. Berlin Fellow at the Akademie der Künste, 2015.

TODO POR LA PRAXIS (TPX) takes the form of a laboratory for aesthetic and alternative cultural projects. The collective is made up of a multidisciplinary team that devotes part of its work to the construction of collaborative micro-architectural or micro-urban devices focusing on the reconquering of public space for collective use.

MAXIMILIAN TREIBER born in Starnberg, is a master's student at the Technical University of Berlin. He received his bachelor's degree from the Münster School of Architecture and has been living in Berlin since 2014.

MANOS TSANGARIS Born in 1956. Composer, drummer, and installation artist. His compositions are internationally acclaimed and have been performed at several renowned festivals. Since 2009, professor of Composition at the Hochschule für Musik Carl Maria von Weber in Dresden, since 2009, member of the Akademie der Künste Berlin. Since 2010, member of the Sächsische Akademie der Künste. 2012–2013, artist-in-residence at the Zurich University of the Arts (ZHdK); starting in 2016, he will be the artistic director for the Munich Biennale for New Music Theater (together with Daniel Ott). He founded the Internationale Institut für Kunstermittlung in 2009 (www.iike.de) and has done research in the field of scenic anthropology. www.tsangaris.de

MARIA TURIK Born in 1982, grew up and studied Linguistics in East Siberia. 2012–2015, student of Sculpture at Burg Giebichenstein in Halle under Andrea Zaumseil. Since 2014, studies at the sculpture department of Berlin Weißensee School of Art.

REINALDO DE LA C. URIARTE MOSQUERA Born in 1957 in Pinar del Río, Cuba. Graduate (1981) in Architecture from the Instituto Superior Politécnico José Antonio Echeverría (CUJAE), Havana. PhD in 2003 Geographic Sciences, Universidad de Alicante, Spain. Titular professor at CUJAE, Havana. Member of the National Union of Writers and Artists of Cuba (UNEAC), National Union of Architects and Engineers of Cuba (UNAICC), and the Cuban Association of Social Communicators (ACCS). Works in architecture, landscape architecture, interior and accessibility design, visual as well as digital art. www.uriarte.pinarte.cult.cu.

MICHAEL VAN VALKENBURGH is an American landscape architect. After studies in Landscape Architecture at Cornell University and the University of Illinois at Urbana-Champaign, he founded Michael Van Valkenburgh Associates in 1982. He is the recipient of various prizes, including the National Design Award in Environmental Design from the Cooper-Hewitt National Design Museum (2003) and the Arnold W. Brunner Memorial Prize in Architecture from the American Academy of Arts and Letters (2010). 2010 Brendan Gill Prize from the Municipal Art Society of New York for the Brooklyn Bridge Park. Charles Eliot Professor in Practice of Landscape Design at Harvard University's Graduate School of Design.

JEAN-PHILIPPE VASSAL Born in 1954 in Casablanca, Morocco. Architectural practice together with Anne Lacaton in Paris since 1989. 2006 Erich Schelling Architecture Prize. www.lacatonvassal.com

SARAH VELLMETE is a student in the seventh semester of the bachelor's program in Architecture and Urban Design at the Potsdam University of Applied Sciences. She was born in Berlin.

FERNANDO VIÉGAS Born in 1971 in São Paulo, Brazil. Architecture and master's degree at the Faculty of Architecture and Urbanism, University of São Paulo (FAU-USP). Board member, project professor, and coordinator of the postgraduate *sensu lato* program "Civilization America: Geography, City, and Architecture" at Escola da Cidade. Visiting professor and lecturer. Partner of Una Arquitetos, based in São Paulo, since it was established in 1996.

ANNA KRISTIN VINKELOE is a student in the master's program in Architecture at the Technical University of Berlin. She received her bachelor's degree in business administration from the RWTH Aachen.

JÖRN WALTER Born 1957 in Bremen. Since 1999, chief building director of the Free and Hanseatic City of Hamburg. 1976–1982, studies in City and Regional Planning at the University of Dortmund. 1982–1984, professional teaching period in Düsseldorf. 1985–1990, head of the Department of City Planning und Environment, Maintal. 1991–1999, head of the City Planning Office, Dresden. 1997, visiting professor for Urban Design at the Technical University Vienna. 1998, lecturer for Urban Design at the Technical University Dresden. 2001, professor at the University of Fine Arts Hamburg (HfbK), 2014, professor at HafenCity University Hamburg. Member of the German Academy for City and Country Planning (DASL), the Academy of Fine Arts Berlin-Brandenburg, and the Saxon Academy of Fine Arts. Since 2000, member of the Architecture Section of the Akademie der Künste Berlin.

WILFRIED WANG Born in Hamburg, studied architecture in London; partner with John Southall in SW Architects (1989–1995). In 2001, with Barbara Hoidn, founder of Hoidn Wang Partner in Berlin. Since 2002, O'Neil Ford Centennial Professor in Architecture at The University of Texas at Austin. Founding co-editor of *9H* Magazine (1979); co-director of the 9H Gallery (1985–1990). Director of the German Architecture Museum (1995–2000). Taught at the Polytechnic of North London, University College London, ETH Zürich, Städelschule, Harvard University, and the University of Navarra. Author and editor of various architectural mono- and topographs. Co-editor of the O'Neil Ford Mono- and Duograph Series. Chairman of the Erich Schelling Architecture Foundation; foreign member of the Royal Swedish Academy of Fine Arts, Stockholm; member and deputy director of the architecture section of the Akademie der Künste, Berlin; honorary member of the Portuguese Chamber of Architects.

MARTHA INGUND WEGEWITZ is a student in the master's program in Urban Design at the Technical University of Berlin. She has been working as a landscape architect at relais Landschaftsarchitekten since 2011.

NICOLE WEGNER is a student in the master's program in Architecture and Urban Design at the Potsdam University of Applied Sciences. She has been living in Berlin since 2010.

WERMKE/LEINKAUF Matthias Wermke and Mischa Leinkauf are visual artists. Their works have been shown in countless international exhibitions, discussed in a variety of publications, and awarded with numerous prizes and grants. In 2014, the duo swapped out the two American flags on top of the Brooklyn Bridge for two *White American Flags*, thus drawing international attention.

ZULOARK is a group of architects, designers, builders and thinkers operating within the fields of architecture, urbanism, design, pedagogies, research, and development.

BLANCA ZÚÑIGA ALEGRÍA Born in Chile. After studies in Architecture at the University of Chile, postgraduate studies in Housing and Urbanism at the Architectural Association School in London. Founder and principal of SpreAAd Arquitectos in Talca, Chile. Assistant professor in architecture at the University of Talca, Chile.

Author abbreviations: (BH) Barbara Hoidn, (CL) Carolina Leite, (YS) Yuma Shinohara, (WW) Wilfried Wang

IMAGE CREDITS

(T) Top, (M) Middle, (B) Bottom, (L) Left, (R) Right

9 Bernard Capelle
10 Latz + Partner
12 Pere Vivas / Triangle Postals
13 Barbara Hoidn
15 Ian Langsdon / picture alliance
17 Carolina Leite
21–24 Cordelia Polinna
27 Iwan Baan
30 Tobias Ross-Southall
31 Snøhetta
33 (T) Iwan Baan; (M),Greg Jarem; (B) William Michael Fredericks / Design Trust
34 (T) Dana Wall / Design Trust; (M) David Schalliol (B) Nic Lehoux
35 Marten van Wijk / Design Trust archive
36 Wang Weijen Arch / Design Trust archive
39 (T, B) Michael Van Valkenburgh Associates, Inc.; (M) Alex MacLean
40 Paul Warchol
41 (TL) Alex MacLean; (TR) Lexi Van Valkenburgh
43 Elizabeth Felicella
45–47 Roman Mensing
49–50 VG Bild-Kunst, Bonn, 2016/ Renata Stih & Frieder Schnock
55 Mussklprozz / Wikimedia Commons CC BY-SA 3.0
56 raumlaborberlin
59 SenStadtUm Berlin
61 Axel Viola / Montag Stiftung Urbane Räume
62 Alexander Jahn / Montag Stiftung Urbane Räume; Eberhard Weible / Montag Stiftung Urbane Räume
65 Tom Bonaventure / Saphire / F1 online
66 (T) ullstein bild; (M) Jost /ullstein bild
67 Bernhard Schneider
69 Jaime Latorre Soto
70 Felipe Saravia Arias
71 Carolina Guzmán
73 Claus-Christian Carbon
75 Future Cities Laboratory
77 Stefan Müller Arisona
82–83 Gerhard Kiesling / bpk
84 J. C. Selter / Wikimedia Commons
85 (T) Wikimedia Commons; (BL) SenStadtUm Berlin; (BR) Landesarchiv Berlin
86 (L) SenStadtUm Berlin; (TR) Eveline Schmidt / Landesarchiv Berlin; (BR) Thomas Platow / Landesarchiv Berlin
87 Elkawe / Wikimedia Commons
88 Kleihues + Kleihues
89 (T, BR) Stefen Lotz / Kleihues + Kleihues (BL) Kleihues + Kleihues
90–91 Barkow Leibinger
92–93 Zentral- u. Landesbibliothek Berlin
94 Yuma Shinohara
95 (TR) Neudin / ullstein bild; (TL) ullstein bild; (B) Histomap Berlin / Landesarchiv Berlin
96 (T) Danigel / ullstein bild; (B) Histomap Berlin / Landesarchiv Berlin
97 (T) Yuma Shinohara; (B) SenStadtUm Berlin
98–99 Michael Najjar
100–101 Michael Ruetz
102–103 Michael Najjar
104–105 Nuno Cera
108–109 Roberto Rodriguez
110 Lucas Dolega / picture alliance / dpa
111 Thiago Benicchio
112 Burcu Tüm
113 Jakob Huber
114 Roberto Rodriguez
115 Nicolas Cruchon
116–119 VG Bild-Kunst, Bonn, 2016/ Birgit and Wilhelm Hein
120 Reid Joslin
121 VG Bild-Kunst, Bonn, 2016/ Renata Stih & Frieder Schnock
122–123 Elfi Mikesch
124–125 VG Bild-Kunst, Bonn, 2016/ Wermke/Leinkauf
126–127 Michael Muschner / TIGERFILM
128 Tom Simpson, Mayor of London's Fourth Plinth Commission
129 (T) VG Bild-Kunst, Bonn, 2016 / Hans Haacke. Courtesy the artist and Paula Cooper Gallery, New York; (B) VG Bild-Kunst, Bonn, 2016 / Hans Haacke. Courtesy the artist and Paula Cooper Gallery, New York. Photo/Bild: Steven Probert.
130–131 Max Schwarzlose
132–133 Etienne Frossard
134 Jože Plecnik/ Museum and Galleries of Ljubljana
135 Damjan Prelovšek
136 (T) Jože Plecnik / Museum and Galleries of Ljubljana; (B) Damjan Prelovšek
137 Damjan Prelovšek
138 (T) Jože Plecnik / Museum and Galleries of Ljubljana; (B) Damjan Prelovšek
139 Damjan Prelovšek
140 Hélène Binet
141 (T) Hélène Binet; (B) Dimitris Pikionis / Benaki Museum Athens
142 Tobias Ross-Southall
143 (T) Dimitris Pikionis / Benaki Museum Athens; (B) Elias Constantopoulos
144 Dimitris Pikionis / Benaki Museum Athens
145 (T) Hélène Binet; (B) Dimitris Pikionis / Benaki Museum Athens
146–148 Carolina Leite
148 (B) Luís Ferreira Alves / CMG
149 Carolina Leite; (BR) Luís Ferreira Alves / CMG
150 Fernando Távora / Marques da Silva Foundation; (T) A Muralha; (M) José Luís Braga / Museu Alberto Sampaio
151 (T) Ana Pereira; (B) Fernando Távora / Marques da Silva Foundation
152 (T) CMG; (B) António Amaro das Neves
153 Rita Burmester
154 CE.EAUM; (BR) Rita Burmester
155 CE.EAUM
156–159 Lacaton & Vassal Architectes
160 Foster + Partners
161 Nigel Young / Foster + Partners
162 Foster + Partners; (BL) Nigel Young / Foster + Partners
163 Foster + Partners
164 Foster + Partners; (B) Nigel Young / Foster + Partners
165 (T) Nigel Young / Foster + Partners; (B) Foster + Partners
166 Hansestadt Wismar
167 Ulrich Jahr / Wismar – von – oben
168 Stadtarchiv Wismar
169 (T) Ulrich Jahr / Wismar – von – oben; (B) Oswaldo Díaz Medina
170–174 Xunta de Galicia
175 Tobias Ross-Southall
176 Matt Urbanski
177 Alex Maclean
178 (T) Elizabeth Felicella; (B) Alex Maclean
179 Michael Van Valkenburgh Associates, Inc. (BL), Susannah Drake; (BR) Elizabeth Felicella
180 Elizabeth Felicella; (BL) Michael Van Valkenburgh Associates, Inc.
181 Elizabeth Felicella
182–183 Miran Kambič
184 Andrés Mignucci Arquitectos
185 Andrés Mignucci Arquitectos; (B) Pedro Hiriart / Andrés Mignucci Arquitectos
186 Andrés Mignucci Arquitectos; (B) Max Toro / Andrés Mignucci Arquitectos
187 (T) Andrés Mignucci; (B) Andrés Mignucci Arquitectos
188 Sadar + Vuga
189 (T) Miran Kambič for Sadar + Vuga; (BL) Studio AKKA; (BR) Sadar + Vuga
190 (T) Sadar + Vuga; (B) Miran Kambič for Sadar + Vuga
191 Sadar + Vuga
192 (T) Sadar + Vuga; (B) Jan Bockholt, Ronja Engelhardt
193 (T) Martin T. Schulte, Stefan Pips; (M) Karolina Jagła, Tomasz Madej, Maciej Oczkowski; (B) Katharina Balke, Lea Keil
194 Biblioteca Nacional de España
195–199 Campo de Cebada and Zuloark, CC BY-SA
200–201 Blanca Zúñiga
202–203 Campo de Cebada and Zuloark, CC BY-SA
204 Seán Harrington Architects
205 (T) Alice Clancy /A2 Architects; (B) Seán Harrington Architects
206 (T) Alice Clancy / A2 Architects; (B) Luke Giblin / A2 Architects
207 (T) A2 Architects; (BL) Alice Clancy / Seán Harrington Architects; (BR) Seán Harrington Architects
208 (T) Alice Clancy / Seán Harrington Architects (B) Seán Harrington Architects
209 (T) Alice Clancy / A2 Architects; (B) Sam Bishop / A2 Architects
210 100% Tempelhofer Feld
211 (T) Carolina Leite; (B) Reinhard von Wegerer
212–213 Carolina Leite
215 (T) Wilfried Wang; (B) Christian Riis Ruggaber
216 (T) Hager Partner AG; (B) Thomas Oberender
217 (T) Hager Partner AG; (B) Thomas Oberender
218 Rozana Montiel Estudio de Arquitectura
219 Sandra Pereznieto
220 Rozana Montiel Estudio de Arquitectura
221 (T) Sandra Pereznieto; (M) Rozana Montiel Estudio de Arquitectura
223–225 Tobias Ross-Southall; Oswaldo Díaz Medina; Michael Van Valkenburgh Associates, Inc.
228–229 Karin Lelonek
230 (T) Dan Heller; (B) Caesar Studio Architects & Planners
231 Reinaldo de la C. Uriarte Mosquera
232 (T) OLIN / Sahar Coston-Hardy; (B) Barbara Hoidn
233 dlandstudio
234 Barbara Hoidn
235 Nelson Kon
237 Schulze, T. Teske, A. Kristin Vinkeloe, M. Wegewitz
238 Martin Hofmann, Esteban Rivera, Tilmann Teske
240 V. Dill, S. Groeger, M. Hossli, E. Kelly
241 E. Galambos, S. Goethe, K. Fahl, S. Kotz, L. Maia, S. Naji, J. Noack
242 Andrew Alberts
243 From private collection
244 Giuseppe D'Angelo
245 Assia Cirillo
246–247 Ka-Shing Chui
248 (T) Architekturmuseum der TU Berlin; (M) Wilhelm Ernst & Sohn, Berlin; (B) Verlag Rizzoli Milan
249 (T) Bernd Albers; (ML) A. Schultes und C. Frank; (MR) Vincent Mosch; (BL) Bezirksamt Charlottenburg-Wilmersdorf von Berlin Stadtentwicklungsamt Fachbereich Vermessung; (BML) Edition Gauglitz (Verlag); (BMR) SenStadtUm Berlin; (BR) 2015 GeoBasis-DE/BKG, 2015 Digital Globe (Google Earth)
250 (T) Library of Congress Prints and Photographs Division Washington D.C.; (B) Globus Verlag, Berlin
251 (T) Bernd Albers; (BL) Jeff Jerome Galinsky; (BR) SUNY / State University NY Oneonta; (BR) Bezirksamt Charlottenburg-Wilmersdorf
252 Hannes Brunner
253 Maria Turik
254 Lena Marie Emrich
255 Veneta Androva
256 (T) Laura Engelhardt; (B) Günter Nest
257 Günter Nest
258 From private collection
259 (T) Nader Ardalan, Laleh Bakhtiar; (M) Fausto Formichi, Giancarlo Cataldi et. al.; (B) Johann Friedrich Geist, Klaus Kürvers
260–261 FG Leibinger / Ballestrem
262–263 Christian Schneegass
268 Felix Lüdicke
269 (T, BL) Felix Lüdicke & Theresa Schütz; (BR) Thomas Ladenburger, Felix Lüdicke & Theresa Schütz
270–271 Theresa Schütz & Rainer Steurer
272 Matthias Kranebitter
273 VG Bild-Kunst, Bonn, 2016 / Sebastian Gräfe, Sebastian Gräfe & Felix Lüdicke
274 Thomas Ladenburger
275–276 Caitlin van der Maas
278–279 VG Bild-Kunst, Bonn, 2016/ Sebastian Gräfe, Sebastian Gräfe & Matthias Kranebitter

The editors have endeavored to identify all copyright holders and photographers. If despite our intensive research any person entitled to rights should have been overlooked, legitimate claims shall be compensated within the usual provisions.

ACKNOWLEDGMENTS

The following supporters and lenders have contributed greatly to the success of the catalog by providing us with material and information: A2 Architects, Fabian Abel, Paula Abrunhosa, Bernd Albers, Andrew Alberts, Dovilė Aleksaitė, Luís Ferreira Alves, Veneta Androva, Giuseppe D'Angelo, Hillary Archer, Felipe Saravia Arias, Thomas Arslan, Eleanor Aylett-Jones, Víctor Azevedo, Michelle Bähr, Matthias Graf von Ballestrem, Otto-Friedrich-Universität Bamberg, Barkow Leibinger, Benaki Museum, Thiago Benicchio, Architekturmuseum TU Berlin, Landesarchiv Berlin, Kunsthochschule Berlin-Weißensee, Technische Universität Berlin, Universität der Künste Berlin, Vítor Bilhete, Hélène Binet, Joseph Bivona, Nuno Borges, Polina Borisova, José Luís Braga, Hannes Brunner, Rita Burmester, Béatrice Busjan, Camões-Instituto da Cooperaçaõ e da Lingua, El Campo de Cebada, Peter Carroll, Matevž Čelik, CE:EAUM Centro de Estudos da Escola de Arquitectura da Universidade do Minho, Nuno Cera, Juan Chacón, Susan Chin, Ka-Shing Chui, Assia Cirillo, Elias Constantopoulos, Paula Cooper Gallery, Rui Costa, Petra Dehniger, Viktor Dill, Stefana Dilova, Manuel Domínguez, Susannah Drake, Jasmin Dulic, Kirsten Dunne, Liat Elkayam, Lena Marie Emrich, Laura Engelhardt, Biblioteca Nacional de España, Acción Cultural Española, Karoline Fahl, Romina Falk, Nina Fischer, Fliegerclub „Otto Lilienthal" Anklam e.V., Julia Förster, Foster + Partners, Miguel Frazão, Annett Freier, Jaime Freitas, Esther Galambos, Ute Gallmeister, Jon Garbizu, Miriam García García, Cornelius Giacalone, Sophie Goethe, GRADIS skupina G d.d., Sebastian Gräfe, Silvia Groeg, Kai Nikolaus Grüne, Câmara Municipal de Guimarães, Hans Haacke, Guido Hager, Heike Hanada, Seán Harrington, Katy Harris, Birgit & Wilhelm Hein, Margarete Heitmüller, Lutz Henke, Christian Hennemann, Nicola Höschle, Reinhild Hoffmann, Martin Hofmann, Dr. Wilfried Hornburg, Moritz Hossli, Jakob Huber, Laura Hunt, Norbert Huschner, Dagmar Jacobsen, Dieter Jaufmann, Nils Jörn, Alexis Johnson, Miran Kambic, Joanna Kamm, Betty Kelly, Kleihues + Kleihues, Steffen Klotz, Gabriele Knopf, Astrid Köppe, Nelson Kon, Maja Kovač, Anne Kozian, Matthias Kranebitter, Leti Arvaniti Krokou, Lacaton & Vassal, Thomas Ladenburger, Albert Lang, Regine Leibinger, Mestni muzej Ljubljana, Muzej za arhitekturo in oblikovanje Ljubljana/Museum of Architecture and Design Ljubljana, London City Authority, Blaž Lozej, Felix Lüdicke, Dr. Bernd Lukasch, Caitlin van der Maas, AC/E Madrid, Lucas Maia, Gayle Mault, Oswaldo Medina, Kerstin Meyer, Andrés Mignucci, Elfi Mikesch, Carolina Molina, Rozana Montiel, Cristiane Muniz, A Muralha Associação de Guimarães para a defesa do Património, Michael Muschner, Shahed Naji, Studio Michael Najjar, NC_Studio, Günter Nest, Judith Noack, Institut für 4D Technologien der Hochschule für Technik der Fachhochschule Nordwestschweiz FHNW, University of Northumbria, Aslı Özarslan, Maria Manuel Oliveira, Paulo Pacheco, Ana Pereira, Julio César Pérez Hernández, Diego Peris, Doreen Piper, Ana Porok, Botschaft von Portugal, Fachhochschule Potsdam, Conceição Pratas, Damjan Prelovšek, Catarina Providência, Isabella Pullmann, Álvaro Puntoni, Christopher Richter, Jan Riley, Esteban Rivera, Roberto Rodriguez, Patricia Röder, Paul Rohlfs, Joachim Roncin, Tobias Ross-Southall, Arquivo RTP, Max Rudolph, Michael Ruetz, SADAR + VUGA, Museu Alberto Sampaio, Manuel Borobio Sanchiz, Matteo Sanguinetti, Daniela Schaffarczyk, Otavio Schipper, Petra Schramm, Theresa Schütz, Simone Schulz, Max Schwarzlose, Paul Seck, Marta Setúbal, Ana Patrícia Severino, Fundação Instituto Arquitecto José Marques da Silva, João Pereira Silva, Simone Snedic, Jaime Latorre Soto, Špela Štern, Stih & Schnock, Jörg Stollmann, Bernardo Távora, 100% Tempelhofer Feld, Tilmann Teske, Amir Teymuri, Ana Tostões, Michela Tota, Alessandra Trainiti, Maximilian Treiber, Manos Tsangaris, Burcu Tüm, Maria Turik, Matt Urbanski, Reinaldo de la C. Uriarte Mosquera, Michael Van Valkenburgh, Sarah Vellmete, Fernando Viégas, Georg Vrachliotis, Lisa Wagner, Nicole Wegner, Wermke/Leinkauf, Florian Wiegand, Archiv der Hansestadt Wismar—Amt für Welterbe, Tourismus und Kultur, Stadtgeschichtliches Museum der Hansestadt Wismar, Maruša Zorec, Future Cities Laboratory ETH Zürich, Zuloark, Blanca Zúñiga, Bogo Zupančič

We would like to thank the many participants who, with their great personal commitment and in parts "pro bono" efforts, have significantly helped in the realization of this ambitious undertaking. First and foremost our thanks go to Carolina Leite, our office collaborator, for the comprehensive design and curatorial work, as well as Yuma Shinohara for the research and curatorial assistance. With the design of the catalog and the typographic design of the exhibition Cameron Kraus has achieved an impressive feat. We thank Thomas Kramer, head of the publisher Park Books, for his knowledgeable and smooth preparation and realization of a complex manuscript, and the editors, at their head Lisa Schons, as well as the translators for their meticulous work on the texts. Thanks also to Birgit Landgraf from the printers DZA, Druckerei zu Altenburg GmbH for the excellent prepress advice and guidance.

We are grateful to the participants of the International Workshop especially for the inspiring discussions ahead of the exhibition, including the experts Lutz Braun and Mayor Michael Galander, and Beatrix Wittmann-Stifft from Anklam; Birgit Wend and Stefan Rommelfanger from Gelsenkirchen; as well as Maria Berning, Annalie Schoen, and Martin Rein-Cano from Berlin, who have all provided facts and data for the workshop participants during the two-day symposium.

Our thanks go to all the artists, architects, archives, and the many private lenders of exhibition and catalog material (all of whom are mentioned in the list on this page), and of course all the institutions whose logos are reproduced here: altogether a fascinating look behind the scenes of a multi-layered and many-headed preparatory effort.

We are grateful to the Akademie der Künste for having commissioned us to curate this exhibition. We would like to thank all sections and all departments for their participation in this project. For their constant support we would like to thank Klaus Staeck and Jeanine Meerapfel, as well as Johannes Odenthal. Our special thanks go to Michael Bräuer, Carolin Schönemann, Jacqueline Saliba, and Karin Lelonek from the architecture section, as well as the Gesellschaft der Freunde der Akademie der Künste that has proven to be a congenial partner of the curatorial team. We thank the founding donors of the O'Neil Ford Centennial Chair in Architecture at The University of Texas at Austin for having provided the possibility of funding the catalog design from the endowed professorship. We thank Stefan Müller Arisona and his team for their generosity in making the 3-D urban modeling program available to the exhibition visitors. Our thanks are also due to Claus-Christian Carbon and his team for their preparation of the visitors' questionnaire.

CATALOG

This catalog is published in connection with the exhibition
DEMO:POLIS—The Right to Public Space
at the Akademie der Künste, Berlin
March 12–May 29, 2016

EDITOR
Barbara Hoidn

EDITORIAL BOARD
Barbara Hoidn, Wilfried Wang

EDITORIAL ASSISTANCE
Cameron Kraus, Carolina Leite, Yuma Shinohara

DESIGN AND TYPOGRAPHY
Cameron Kraus

TRANSLATIONS
Lisa Rosenblatt, Yuma Shinohara, Wilfried Wang

COPY EDITING
Benjamin Liebelt, Lisa Schons

PROOFREADING
Charlotte Eckler

TYPEFACES Plantin, Vinkel
PAPER FLY Extraweiß
LITHOGRAPHS, PRINTING, AND BINDING
DZA Druckerei zu Altenburg GmbH, Thuringia

Park Books
Niederdorfstrasse 54
8001 Zurich
Switzerland

www.park-books.com

English edition: ISBN 978-3-03860-005-3
German edition: ISBN 978-3-03860-004-6

EXHIBITION

CURATOR UND EXHIBITION DESIGN OF HALLS 1 AND 2
Wilfried Wang

DIRECTOR OF THE INTERNATIONAL WORKSHOP AND EXHIBITION DESIGN OF HALL 3
Barbara Hoidn

EXHIBITION TEAM Hoidn Wang Partner: Barbara Hoidn, Carolina Leite, Emilia Knabe, Victoria Knabe, Cameron Kraus, Yuma Shinohara, Wilfried Wang, as well as the team of the Junge Akademie (Young Academy): Christian Schneegass, Miriam Papastefanou, Daniela Obkircher, and the cooperating universities: Stefan Müller Arisona, Fachhochschule Nordwestschweiz FHNW; Ruth Dalton, University of Northumbria; Christoph Hölscher, ETH Zürich; Claus-Christian Carbon, Forschungsgruppe der Universität Bamberg; and the teams of the participating universities of the International Workshop: Regine Leibinger, Kai Nikolaus Grüne, Matthias Graf von Ballestrem, Technische Universität Berlin; Albert Lang, Nina Fischer, Thomas Arslan, Jörg Stollmann, Media Lab, Universität der Künste Berlin und Technische Universität Berlin; Hannes Brunner, Günter Nest, Kunsthochschule Berlin-Weißensee; Bernd Albers, Heike Hanada, Fachhochschule Potsdam; the Initiators of the Urban Parliament Zuloark Berlin: Julia Förster, Juan Chacón; Marion Neumann, Martina Krafczyk, Education Program Kunstwelten, Akademie der Künste

TYPOGRAPHY AND GRAPHIC DESIGN
Cameron Kraus

EXHIBITION INSTALLATION
m.o.l.i.t.o.r GmbH, Berlin: Martin Müller, Marco Unterhaslberger, Michael Zeyfang, Stephan Rändel

HANGING
Mount Berlin

MEDIA TECHNOLOGY
BeamAround GbR, Berlin, Christian Sonntag; visionB Kunstservice UG; Frank Kwiatkowksi (Light)

AKADEMIE DER KÜNSTE, BERLIN Johannes Odenthal, Program Director; Michael Bräuer, Director of the Architecture Section; Carolin Schönemann, Secretary of the Architecture Section; Nicola Beißner, Karin Lelonek, Jacqueline Saliba; Stefan Kaltenbach, Registrar; and Wolfgang Hinze, János Kachelmann, Kathy Lieber, Antje Mollenhauer, Reinhard Pusch, Simone Schmaus, Jörg Scheil, Isabel Schlenther of the Technical Department

PRESS AND PUBLIC RELATIONS Brigitte Heilmann, Marianne König, Anette Schmitt, Martin Steinmetz, Mareike Wenzlau with BUREAU N: Julia Albani, Gudrun Landl, Joanne Pouzenc

Akademie der Künste, Hanseatenweg 10, D-10557 Berlin
www.adk.de

The Akademie der Künste is funded by the Federal Government for Culture and the Media

AKADEMIE DER KÜNSTE

The exhibition and catalog are co-sponsored by the O'Neil Ford Centennial Chair, School of Architecture, The University of Texas at Austin

The University of Texas at Austin
School of Architecture

and supported by the Gesellschaft der Freunde der Akademie der Künste

Gesellschaft der Freunde der
AKADEMIE DER KÜNSTE